P9-DVE-177

PERSPECTIVES

ON MASS COMMUNICATION

HISTORY

COMMUNICATION TEXTBOOK SERIES

Jennings Bryant — Editor

General Communication Theory and Methodology

Jennings Bryant — Advisor

STARTT/SLOAN • Historical Methods
in Mass Communication

PILOTTA/MICKUNAS • Science
of Communication: Its
Phenomenological Foundation

SLOAN • Perspectives on
Mass Communication History

PERSPECTIVES

ON MASS COMMUNICATION

HISTORY

~

Wm. David Sloan

1991

LAWRENCE ERLBAUM ASSOCIATES, PUBLISHERS
Hillsdale, New Jersey   Hove and London

Copyright © 1991, by Lawrence Erlbaum Associates, Inc.
All rights reserved. No part of the book may be reproduced in
any form, by photostat, microform, retrieval system, or any other
means, without the prior written permission of the publisher.

Lawrence Erlbaum Associates, Inc., Publishers
365 Broadway
Hillsdale, New Jersey 07642

Library of Congress Cataloging-in-Publication Data

Sloan, W. David (William David), 1947-
    Perspectives on mass communication history / Wm. David Sloan.
        p. cm. -- (Communication textbook series)
    Inlcludes index.
    ISBN 0-8058-0835-3 (c). -- ISBN 0-8058-0863-9 (p)
    1. Mass media--United States--History. I. Title. II. Series.
    P92. U5S56 1991
    302.23'0973--dc20   91-14957
                                                    CIP

Printed in the United States of America
10 9 8 7 6 5 4 3 2 1

CONTENTS

Preface

A Note on Teaching

This book is based on the philosophy that the teaching of communication history should emphasize critical thinking. Teaching should, that is, try to involve the student intellectually rather than simply provide facts. It is but noting a truism to state that for generations thousands upon thousands, indeed, millions of people have taken an intense interest in history. Why, we may ask as we attempt to discover how to create student interest in history, have substantial numbers of people in every generation maintained an intense interest? Is it not because they found—and continue to find—a special fascination in the study of history? And from whence does that fascination originate?

If history teachers can answer the question, they will have discovered the means by which to encourage student interest today. Frequently over the last few decades one has heard teachers lament that communication students have no interest in history and that something special, something unique must be done to keep their attention. As often as not, the recommended solution has been a resort to games and entertainment. Dress up like Ben Franklin, suggests a teacher, and perform antics in front of a class of collegians. Fill every lecture with slide shows, declares another. Is that, one is tempted to ask in response, what teachers should be doing to encourage students to recognize the value of history or to sustain a fascination with history through this present generation? Did the study of history survive with great vitality through previous generations simply because of its entertainment value? Is today's generation different? Has television—one of the main culprits entertainer teachers cite for the necessity of performing before students—destroyed history? If television can be blamed for declining student interest, can it not also do a better job of entertaining than a classroom teacher can; and if it can, is not history dead as a topic of commanding interest if the best that teachers can do is provide a poor form of entertainment through classroom performances?

The fascination with which millions have viewed history did not result from entertainment, but from something much deeper and much more stimulating. Of a certainty, one of the appeals that history has for many people is artistic. Many get a kind of aesthetic pleasure from reading history. For those people who have been most intensely interested in history, however, its appeal has been not only aesthetic but, more importantly, intellectual. By that description, we do not mean to imply stuffy cerebralism. We allude to the vibrancy that occurs when the mind is challenged and it robustly encounters intriguing ideas. We mean, simply, the type of fascination that can come only from the stimulating life of the mind.

How can the teacher foster student fascination with history? We believe teachers should use an approach that challenges the student to think. Although there are various means by which a teacher may issue the challenge, we have found in our own teaching that one effective way is to approach history not as a cut-and-dried recitation of a collection of facts but as a multifaceted past of which historians have given many explanations. Furthermore, many of the explanations have directly contradicted one another.

Why are there such contradictions, one might ask, in explanations of a real past that existed objectively and in only one way? One of the answers to the question is that historians have approached history with different *perspectives* or, to use another term, from different *schools of interpretation.* As the student begins to probe that question and to assess the various explanations and interpretations, a fascination with history begins to form. Varying perspectives impart a vitality to history that the student might not gain from a study of mere chronology of facts.

But interpretations hold more value that just being pedagogical tools. A knowledge of interpretations is indispensable if the student is to understand history as told by historians. Take a simple example. Consider that Historian A states that a muckraker sincerely attempted to bring about liberal social reform, while Historian B states that the same muckraker was motivated mainly by concern for maintaining his or her social status amid changing social conditions. How can the student reconcile the contradictory explanations? Without an awareness of the presence of interpretation in the writing of history, the student may assume that both explanations are accurate. But how, the student may ask, can both be accurate if they are contradictory? The end result for the student may very well be mere confusion. The resolution to the contradiction is quite simply that the two historians gave the differing explanations because they held different interpretive perspectives. An understanding of interpretations—as opposed to a mere familiarity with facts—will aid the student in arriving at a more comprehensive and satisfying knowledge of history.

Each essay in this book discusses the major interpretations of an important topic in mass communication history. Each is divided into four parts. At the beginning, the essay provides a brief narrative history of the topic. The intent is to provide students some familiarity with the factual features of the topic so that they will be better prepared to understand and assess the work that historians have done. Following the narrative, each essay provides a detailed discussion of the major schools of interpretation on the topic, including summaries of important historical studies from each school. For the most part, the individual studies were either the first or the most substantial ones that historians wrote on the topic, or they were studies that presented an intepretation cogently or forcefully. The body of each essay concludes with a discussion of significant questions that historians have raised about the topic and of questions that remain unanswered. They are supplemented with additional questions about the quality of the historical work itself. Appended at the end of each essay is a list of suggested readings divided according to schools of interpretation. The specific readings were selected because of their importance or because they are good examples of particular interpretive approaches. When books have been included, individual chapters have been indicated in an effort to keep the volume of reading to a minimum.

In the interest of space, the number of readings has been kept to a minimum. For the teacher wishing to have more, a number of sources are available. Some of the essays refer to several works that are not included in the list of readings. Those works are directly pertinent to the issues under consideration and make for excellent reading. References to scores of articles and books on each topic may be found in *American Journalism History: An Annotated Bibliography*, Wm. David Sloan, comp. (Westport, CT: Greenwood Press, 1989). The fullest bibliography on the subject, it includes more than 2,500 works. Many teachers also will have their own lists of works they consider important and from which they may wish to assign student readings.

Although teachers may use the essays in a variety of ways, they may wish to have students read the essays and then read a selection of works from the list of readings. Selections from a variety of schools normally will be more instructive than from only one school. Teachers may wish to have students answer specific questions about each reading. Typical questions could include some such as these:

1. What is the central thesis of the work?
2. How does the work demonstrate the perspective of a particular school of interpretation?
3. How adequate is the research used for the work? How could it be improved?
4. What questions for additional significant historical study does the work raise?

The essays, readings, and questions at the end of each essay may be used as a basis for fruitful classroom discussion of either the topic or the historical work that has been done on it.

Along with serving as a pedagogical resource, this book will prove useful also to researchers in communication history. Historians will find that it can serve as a reference source and review of the literature that catalogues the major questions and issues that other historians have confronted. Today's researcher may wish to select some of those questions for his or her own study. Likewise, students hunting for history topics to research may use the book to identify the most important questions and those still pressing for answers.

Indeed, the most important questions always are in need of better answers. This book discusses the questions historians have raised. The variety of answers they have given will, we hope, encourage students to strive to find the best answers.

1

Perspectives on Mass Communication History

Two pasts exist side by side. One is the real past, the past as it truly occurred. The other is the past as explained by historians.

Let's compare the two. The real past existed as reality and therefore was comprised of concrete, objective facts, dates, people, events, and other hard details. It existed not only in reality but in a specific time. That is, it took place in definite years, days, and hours. The historian's past, on the other hand, is comprised of efforts to present the real past in a comprehensible form. Although it may draw on real facts from the real past and may bear some resemblance to the real past, it exists in the historian's mind rather than in the objective world and occurs in the historian's present rather than in the real time of the real past. It also is molded by the effort of the historian to organize selected details from the past into a coherent and cohesive structure.

For most of us, historians serve as mediators between us and the real past. Because most of us acquire most of our knowledge of the past from historians' accounts, how they tell history is of utmost importance. What we know of the real past comes mainly from historians' explanations. It is therefore important to us as students of history to understand the approaches that historians take to telling their accounts of history.

The purpose behind serious historical study should be to provide an account that closely resembles the real past. Historical study is foremost a search for truth about the past. To help assure that a historical account provides a reasonably accurate depiction of the past, the field of historical study has developed certain standard practices. These practices are discussed further in Chapter 2. Despite the standards, however, some historians' accounts of the past provide a better resemblance to the past than other historians' accounts do. One reason for the difference is the differing ability or rigor with which historians employ the practices. Some historians, quite honestly, are better at doing the job than others are.

Even among historians of equal ability, however, contrasting accounts of the past arise. One of the prime reasons is that historians

1

write from particular points of view. These points of view are called "perspectives," and historians' explanatory frameworks that result from these perspectives can be referred to as "interpretations."

It is clear enough to most students of history that historians do indeed provide differing interpretations. But why, one may ask, do interpretations and reinterpretations occur? There are a number of reasons that one may give in answer to that question. The most obvious is that historians are human beings; and, like other human beings, each one has his or her own, distinctive interests, attitudes, values, and outlooks. So, just as today there are both Republicans and Democrats among voters, there are historians with differing ideas and views. To expect human beings to divest themselves of their distinctive characteristics upon becoming historians would be to ask the magical. Historians, being human and though perhaps trained in the rigorous methods of historical research, bring to their study of the past their own views. It is natural, then, that they sometimes should provide different interpretations of the same subject matter. Although critics are tempted to claim that interpretations are merely artificial devices that distort the past, most historians earnestly think of an interpretation as the most legitimate way of providing a valid explanation of history.

Beyond the personal reasons for interpretations, however, there are others. One of the most important reasons is that new perspectives arise with new generations. Each generation, although it may be influenced by the views of its parents' time, has its own attitudes and outlooks. Each holds to the views distinctive of its own age, the climate of opinion that holds sway in any generation. Those views influence the historians of that generation to look at the past from a particular perspective. Furthermore, each generation thinks it is more knowledgeable or advanced or sophisticated than the previous generation. That sense of superiority results in historians believing that they can provide a better explanation or interpretation of history than their predecessors did.

Other reasons for reinterpretations include the emergence of new research methods and the appearance of new sources of research material. As an example of the former, one may point to the use of statistical devices such as content analysis in media history. Such methods provide new ways to examine the past. As to the second reason, it is a common occurrence for new information to be unearthed that sheds new insight on an old subject. Newly opened private correspondence, for example, may add new details to an editor's views or motivations and thus suggest a reassessment.

Changing interpretations of media history also have resulted periodically from changes within the history profession. The backgrounds and outlooks of historians have varied during different stages, and certain perspectives have been dominant at different times. Generally speaking, historians have written from three broad categories of perspectives: ideological ones, professional ones, and cultural ones.[1] Within each category, one may identify distinctive schools of interpretation. These schools will be discussed in detail in subsequent chapters, but at this point a brief overview of the most prevalent schools will be useful.[2]

Ideological Perspectives

A number of schools of interpretation have given preeminence to political and social issues and attitudes in explaining mass communication history. Because of journalists' tendency to take an adversarial view of the relationship between the media and government, most ideological historians have been prone to adopt the conflict approach of the Progressive school. At various times, however, other ideological interpretations have been employed.

Nationalist School—The earliest histories of America's mass media were written by Nationalist historians in the 18th century. Deeply patriotic, these historians displayed a strong pride in the accomplishments of the nation and the progress of its free institutions. They believed that the overarching theme in the history of civilization was the advance in human liberty. Contrasting the corrupt political system of Great Britain with that of their own country, they

---

[1]This discussion of schools does not include the "Whig" interpretation; but since students may occasionally come across that term, a brief discussion of it is in order. The first to recognize the existence of the Whig approach was the British historian Herbert Butterfield in *The Whig Interpretation of History* (London: Bell and Sons, 1931). He pointed out that most British historians traditionally had written with an implicit preference for classical liberalism and democracy, favoring Whig politics rather than its Tory opposition. They conceived of history as a natural progression toward such modern concepts. The term "Whig" was first applied to American communication history by James Carey in 1974 in his article "The Problem of Journalism History" (*Journalism History* 1 [1974]: 3-5, 27). He used it, however, not in Butterfield's political terms, but more generally to denote journalism historians' assumption that progress was the underlying principle of history. The Whig interpretation, he concluded, provided the basis for most works on American journalism history. Despite Carey's misconstruction of the term—and even though the only interpretation of American communication that came close to a true Whig interpretation was the Nationalist approach of the early 1800s—a number of communication historians adopted Carey's Whig terminology. Despite the fact that such a reference to the diverse interpretations of communication history clearly is erroneous, some historians still occasionally use it when describing the field.

[2]The following discussion borrows heavily from the description of historiographical schools contained in James D. Startt and Wm. David Sloan, *Historical Methods in Mass Communication*, Chap. 2, "Interpretation in History" (Hillsdale, NJ: Lawrence Erlbaum Associates, 1989), 19-39.

sensed that America, the cradle of liberty, was destined to lead the world to greater and greater freedom. They believed that the American press and its editors were influential and patriotic figures who contributed to the progress of the nation and its ideals of liberty. Influenced by the ideas of the Enlightenment, with its emphasis on natural rights and the people's preeminent role in government, they nevertheless were generally conservative. Typically gentlemen from prominent New England families, they tended to side with established order and with Federalist and Whig politics against the Republican and Jacksonian opposition.

Romantic School—The primary characteristic of Romantic historians in the last half of the 18th century was not ideology. Nevertheless, they held views that were virtually identical to those of the Nationalist historians. Believing history to be the story of the unfolding advance of human liberty and the key player to be the United States, Romantic historians also held to the conservative ideology of their Nationalist predecessors. The distinguishing features of Romantic histories were their narrative style and their emphasis on the role of great men. Under the influence of the Romantic movement in the arts, historians such as James Parton wrote with a literary flair about the lives of individuals; and under their pens, history came to be viewed as a branch of literature.

Progressive School—Reacting to the Nationalist and Romantic view of America as a land of liberty for everyone, Progressive historians began in the early 20th century to substitute a concept of ideological conflict. The change in interpretation resulted in part from a change in the history profession. Replacing the gentlemen historians and amateurs were college-trained educators in the emerging departments of journalism at various universities. Because America's public universities opened their doors to everyone, these new professional historians came from various levels of society. Representing various geographic regions, they began to shift some of the emphasis away from journalism in New York and New England to that in other sections of the country. Influenced by the Progressive reform movement and by Progressive historians from outside mass communication, these educators and many quasi-historians from the ranks of working journalists began to view the past as a struggle in which the liberal press was pitted on the side of freedom, liberty, democracy, and equality against the powerful forces of wealth and class. They argued that the history of America could be found in the conflict between the rich and the poor, the aristocratic and the democratic. The press, sometimes manipulated by America's powerful self-interested conservative forces, was a key instrument in their ability to maintain control. Likewise, Progressive historians claimed, the press had been central to the successful efforts of liberals to bring about reform and progress. They believed the primary purpose of the media was to crusade for liberal social and economic causes—to fight on the side of the masses of common, working people against the entrenched interests in American business and government. The fulfillment of the American ideal required a struggle against those individuals and groups that had blocked the achievement of a fully democratic system. Progressive historians often placed the conflict in economic terms, with the wealthy class attempting to control the media for its own use. The picture they presented was clearly black-versus-white, good (that is, liberalism) against evil (conservatism). Despite its transparent ideological bent, the Progressive school has provided the premise for more works on mass communication history than has any school other than the Developmental, which is discussed later.

Consensus School—The Consensus interpretation originated just prior to World War II as a direct reaction to the Progressive interpretation. Whereas Progressives emphasized conflict as the key ingredient in American history, Consensus historians argued that history was marked not primarily by conflict but instead by broad agreement among Americans on fundamental principles. Although disagreements existed, they took place within a larger framework of agreement on such essentials as a belief in democracy, freedom, and constitutional law. Within the context of communication history, the Consensus interpretation attempted to refute the Progressive view that a natural animosity should exist between a liberal press and established institutions such as government and religion. Consensus historians argued instead that the media served best when they worked with the other institutions in American society in an effort to solve problems and improve conditions. Because journalists have tended toward liberal ideology and because they have held a conflict view of the media and government, the Consensus interpretation has not been employed as widely in mass communication history as in the broader study of American history. Nevertheless, it has lent itself to numerous studies on particular topics, especially those involving periods of great crises such as wartime.

Along with these major ideological schools, a number of others have provided substantial scholarship on particular topics. Among those worthy of mention are Feminist, Black Militant, Neo-Conservative, Marxist, and Business schools. Each has offered its distinctive assessment of various episodes and issues in mass communication history.

Professional Perspectives

Because most historians of mass communication have come out of a background in the media professions, they have tended to bring professional perspectives to their historical work. These perspectives have ranged over a wide spectrum, including, for example, libertarian views on freedom of the press, liberal views on political and social issues, and critical assessments of media performance. By far, however, most historical studies written from a professional perspective have employed certain central tenets associated with what are considered "proper" professional practices and outlooks. This perspective has accounted for approximately one-half of all works written about mass communication history and is therefore identifiable as a school to itself. It is the Developmental school, its name deriving from the concept that the key feature of mass communication history has been the origin, performance, and development of those "proper" practices.

Developmental School—The Developmental interpretation originated with Frederic Hudson's 1873 work, *Journalism in the United States, From 1690 to 1872*. The interpretation grew out of changes that had taken place in the newspaper industry. In 1833 Benjamin Day founded the New York *Sun*, America's first successful general-interest penny newspaper. It created a revolution in journalism, in attitudes about what the nature of newspapers should be, and in historians' views about communication history. Following Hudson's reasoning, historians began to think that proper journalism was that type associated with the *Sun* and other penny newspapers. They then reasoned that the history of journalism was essentially the story of how journalism had progressed to reach the point of development embodied in the penny press. Since Hudson's time, the Developmental interpretation has provided the underlying assumptions of the majority of studies of American mass media history. Developmental historians' primary concern was how the press became a journalistic instrument. Like other historians, they tended to view the past in terms of the present; but in contrast to historians from other schools who considered the media in relationship to issues and situations outside the mass communication environment, they attempted to explain and evaluate history by its contributions to present professional standards.

Hudson's *Journalism in the United States* was greatly influenced by the practices of the penny press. Hudson had been managing editor of the New York *Herald*, the newspaper that more than any other of the time emphasized news over opinion as the proper function of newspapers and that had been the most successful mass newspaper in American history. Coming from a news-oriented background and assuming that the *Herald's* characteristics were the appropriate ones for newspapers, he tended to explain earlier journalism in terms of how it performed in accordance with the successful practices of the *Herald* and how those practices had developed in the past.

As mass communication began to professionalize in the late

1800s, interest in its history began to grow. As a result, historical studies increased in number. Although differing on a few particulars, they largely echoed Hudson's themes. Most later historians came out of the mass communication professions, and many in the 20th century taught in professionally oriented college programs in journalism, broadcasting, and advertising. They believed the professional standards that had developed over time to be the appropriate and proper ones, and they began to apply even more universally the concept of professional progress in the history of communication.

The Developmental interpretation had a pervasive impact on historical assumptions because most textbooks for college courses in communication history were cast in terms of the professional framework. With textbooks such as Frank Luther Mott's *American Journalism* (1941), the Developmental interpretation became entrenched in historical thinking. Studied by generations of students and future historians, the textbooks tended to reinforce the explanation that the history of American mass communication was the story of how the media evolved in their professional characteristics. Being generally positive about the professions in mass communication, Developmental textbooks also exercised a major importance by providing a favorable view of the American media and reinforcing a pro-media outlook among communication students and professionals.

After World War II, several events contributed to the expansion of the professional concept of the news media as entities that ideally should be autonomous from outside authority and independent of other parts of society. Influenced much by the media's role in such episodes as the civil rights movement of the 1950s and 1960s, the Vietnam War, and the Watergate political scandal, Developmental historians—though retaining the concept of professional progress— sometimes viewed history as a clash between the media and established institutions such as government, religion, the military, big business, and the White racial majority. Thus, whereas Progressive historians, for example, had emphasized the media as a means of working within society to achieve social and political change, Developmental historians tended to emphasize such historical trends as press freedom and media-government relations in which the media confronted other units of society.

Cultural Perspectives
In the early 1900s, a handful of historians began to react to the approaches of the Romantic and Developmental schools that emphasized the role of individuals as key factors in advances in the media. Influenced greatly by the thinking from the University of Chicago's prestigious School of Sociology, these historians argued

that attention should be focused not on individuals but on impersonal social forces. Within the last 20 years, historians operating
from such concepts have come to constitute the largest group among
communication historians. Their fundamental premise is that the
media operated in a close interrelationship with their environment.
The forces that acted on the media included such as the geographic
environment and political ideology, to which historians devoted a
number of studies. Of most interest to historians, however, were
three specific factors: sociological forces, economics, and technology. Those three received such an amount of attention that each
could constitute a school by itself. Because, however, of their adherence to the basic principle of environment-media interrelationship,
historians taking such an approach are considered to comprise one
large school, that of Cultural history.

Cultural School—The impetus for the Cultural interpretation
may be traced to a work on urban sociology by Robert E. Park of the
University of Chicago. In "The Natural History of the Newspaper,"
published in 1925, Park argued that the evolution of American journalism resulted from its interaction with the surrounding culture.
The press, he said, was "the outcome of a historic process in which
many individuals participated without foreseeing what the ultimate
product of their labors was to be. The newspaper, like the modern
city, is not wholly a rational product. No one sought to make it just
what it is. In spite of all the efforts of individual men and generations of men to control it and make it something after their own
heart, it has continued to grow and change in its own incalculable
ways."[3] The primary factors in determining the nature of the
newspaper, Park stated, were the conditions of the society and the
system in which the press operated.

Although some historians in other schools had attempted to explain the media as institutions somewhat separate from society,
Cultural historians considered the media as a part of society and
therefore influenced by various factors outside the media themselves. Whereas most historians had assumed the media had a major influence on society, Cultural historians were interested in the
reverse effect: the impact of society on the media.

This perspective accounted for a major change in historical outlook. Until the 1950s media influence was so widely accepted that
historians often based their studies on the concept of influence. With
behavioral research studies in the 1950s beginning to suggest that
the persuasive power of the mass media was limited, historians
largely downplayed the idea of direct persuasive media influence

---

[3]Robert Park, "The Natural History of the Newspaper," in Robert Park,
Ernest W. Burgess, and Robert D. McKenzie, *The City* (Chicago: University of
Chicago Press, 1925), 88.

on society and substituted for it the concept that the media themselves were a product of social influences.

The changed perspective on influence had other effects. One result was a virtual disappearance of the "great man" explanation of communication history. Rarely did Cultural historians frame their studies around the role that an individual had played in affecting the media. More and more studies also shifted their focus from the media giants in the northeast to journalists on the frontier and in other sections of the nation. Although some of the shift in interest was caused by the emergence in the Midwest of the major doctoral programs in journalism education, followed by other programs in the South and West, the frontier studies placed an emphasis on the environmental conditions in which the media operated and their effect on the media.

Symbolic-Meaning School—A notable impetus in encouraging studies from a particular kind of cultural perspective was provided in 1974 by publication of James Carey's article "The Problem of Journalism History" in the inaugural issue of the journal *Journalism History*. Carey limited his definition of "cultural" history to the relationship between the media and human "consciousness" and stated that historians studying journalism should be concerned principally with the "way in which men in the past have grasped reality." The role the press played historically in that process of grasping reality, he said, is the key to journalism history.[4] Historians who have tried to apply Carey's approach frequently have used the term *symbolic meaning* to describe it.

The strongest arguments for using Carey's approach have been made by his former students at the universities of Iowa and Illinois. Trained in philosophical and sociological approaches to studying mass communication, rather than in historical research, they have tended to rely on theory more than on historical documentation as the basis for their argument. As a result, they have provided little historical evidence to substantiate the media-reality theory. Still, Carey's proposal has exercised considerable influence in encouraging theory-oriented historians to look at the media from that perspective.

The Value of Interpretation

The proper purpose of historical study is to determine the truth about the past. Interpretation, one could argue, actually distorts that purpose because it imposes the historian's view on the past. Even, however, if one grants for the sake of argument the validity of that objection, interpretation still holds considerable value in the study of

---

[4]James Carey, "The Problem of Journalism History," *Journalism History* 1 (1974): 3-5, 27.

history. Its benefits are, indeed, multifaceted.

First, interpretation serves as an organizing principle. The entire past is made up of innumerable items ranging from dates to names to episodes and to anything else one may think of. We could say that the past is simply a massive hodgepodge of details that may or may not have been related to one another. The human mind, however, seeks organization. It looks for relationships. In studying and explaining the past, historians serve this human characteristic by attempting to bring a structure to the details of the past. An interpretive framework is one of the most useful devices they employ. It serves to provide a core concept around which details can be arranged.

Interpretation also is useful as a technique for attempting to explain the fundamental factors that operated during particular historical times. Along with describing the past, the key task of the historian is to explain why the past was as it was. Without such explanation, the telling of history would tend to be a bare recitation of data. Interpretation acts as a primary explanatory principle. As mentioned earlier in this chapter, most historians do not simplistically consider their interpretive perspective an artificial device but earnestly think of it as the most legitimate way of providing a valid explanation of history. The reason most historians adhere to a particular interpretation is that they honestly believe it is the most valid way to make sense of the past. Without an interpretive framework, a historian would have little means by which to provide an underlying explanation or an organizational perspective. Interpretation helps the historian to make sense of a vast array of details and complicated relationships.

A final value of interpretation is that it provides a means by which historians can reveal the relevance of the past to their own generation. If we did not see any pertinence that the past holds for us today, most of us probably would have little interest in history's old, distant details. History gains much of its meaning and interest for us when the historian can explain its relevance to today. Since one of the reasons that new interpretations arise is the climate of opinion in the historian's own time, new interpretations help assure a continuing freshness and relevance to history. They make it possible for us to look at history from the perspective of today.[5]

The Problems of Interpretation

Despite the obvious value of interpretation, it nevertheless can give

---

[5]Contemporary perspective should not be confused with the historical error of present-mindedness. The latter is the tendency of historians to examine the past with the concepts unique to the present and judge it by today's standards rather than on its own terms.

rise to problems. Generally, the problems arise when a historian gives interpretation preeminence over the factual substance of the past. There are, to be sure, some "historians" who are so confident that their theories and philosophies are correct that they have no need of historical evidence to support them. One must be suspicious anytime a writer makes or implies such a statement. Furthermore, the student should be extremely cautious about accepting an interpretation—or, for that matter, even an explanation—unless the historian provides adequate evidence to justify it.

Even though principles regarding the necessity of evidence have been practiced in historical study for generations, and even though the dangers in the simplistic application of theory and interpretation to history are well known, one still finds occasional historians disregarding the principles and repeating the errors. Their most common misuses of interpretation have been the following:

*Giving interpretation, or theory, preeminence over fact. Interpretation should not be predetermined. Good historians do not set out with a theory and marshal facts to fit it. Interpretation should arise implicitly from discovered facts.

*Ignoring evidence. This error is similar to the previous one. However, whereas the first error is involved primarily in the conceptual approach to history, this second one is involved in the actual practice of researching history. Some historians have been so ardently committed to their particular interpretation that they failed to use evidence adequately. There have been several types of failure. One has been to make broad assumptions from scanty evidence. Another has been the questionable explanation of the meaning of particular evidence. Another has been the use of inadequate types of sources, that is, mainly, secondary rather than primary sources. All of those errors can be found in numerous works written by historians more strongly committed to their perspective than to evidence. In communication, the errors have been especially noticeable among historians writing from the Progressive and symbolic-meaning perspectives. The fact that such errors have occurred so frequently among those historians should alert the student to be especially aware of the possibility of their showing up in any historical work.

*Over-simplifying the past so that actions are explained by single, monolithic causes. This error may be referred to as both reductionism and determinism. Reductionism is the practice of reducing a number of possibly subtle and complex causes to a single cause. Determinism is its handmaiden. It assumes that a force or combination of forces mechanistically determines attitude, human behavior, or any of various types of actions. Most historians are unconvinced of single causes and by deterministic explanations. Determinism, as a form of reductionism, forces historians to be too selective, even manipulative, in choosing supporting evidence in a manner that fails to correspond to the great diversity of human reality. Historians are skeptical about the determinist's assumption that the key to human experience lies in a mechanistic force that lies beyond human control. The determinist, they believe, imposes an inevitability on history that never existed.[6]

Discussion

Although serious potential problems exist in the application of interpretation to history, it still occupies an important and valuable place in historical study. We noted previously its value to the historian. It also should be noted that a knowledge of interpretation is of critical value to the student as well. It is essential to gaining a proper understanding of historical work and, thus, ultimately an understanding of history. The following chapters will introduce the student to the most important interpretations that historians have employed to explain the major topics in American communication history. Before embarking on a study of the various interpretations, however, in Chapter 2 we will examine the relationship of interpretation to truth in history.

As you study the various interpretations, ask yourself several questions about them.

1. To what extent does a particular interpretation offer what appears to be a reasonable explanation of a topic?

2. Does the use of interpretation help or hinder the historian's ability to offer a reasonable explanation?

3. Does the historian offer satisfactory evidence to justify the interpretation?

4. What types of evidence could a historian use to make a stronger case?

5. Does a historian seem more interested in arguing for an interpretation or in presenting a truthful account of the past?

6. What appear to you to be the major strengths and weaknesses of each interpretation?

7. To what extent are interpretations based on "present-mindedness," that is, the error of applying present-day values and ideas to the past?

8. Would the telling of history be done better without the use of interpretations?

9. Is it possible for history to be told without the use of interpretation?

---

[6]For more detailed discussion of this issue, see Startt and Sloan, Chap. 7, "Explanation in History," 141-155.

Readings

Carey, James, "The Problem of Journalism History," *Journalism History* 1 (1974): 3-5, 27.

Eason, David L., "The New Social History of the Newspaper," *Communication Review* 11 (January 1984): 141-151.

Grob, Gerald N., and George Athan Billias, eds., Ch. 1, "Introduction," pp. 1-17, *Interpretations of American History*, Vol. 1. New York: Free Press, 1967.

Higham, John, Ch. 1, "The Construction of American History," pp. 9-24, *The Reconstruction of American History*. London: Hutchinson University Library, 1962.

Kobre, Sidney, "The Sociological Approach in Research in Newspaper History," *Journalism Quarterly* 22 (1945): 12-22.

Nevins, Allan, "American Journalism and Its Historical Treatment," *Journalism Quarterly* 36 (1959): 411-422.

Nevins, Allan, "New Lamps for Old in History," *American Archivist* 17 (January 1954): 4-12.

Park, Robert E., Ch. 4, "The Natural History of the Newspaper," pp. 80-98, Park, Ernest W. Burgess and Robert D. McKenzie, *The City*. Chicago: University of Chicago Press, 1925.

Sloan, Wm. David, "Introduction," pp. 1-9, *American Journalism History: An Annotated Bibliography*. Westport, CT.: Greenwood Press, 1989.

Startt, James D., and Wm. David Sloan, Ch. 2, "Interpretation in History," pp. 19-39, *Historical Methods in Mass Communication*. Hillsdale, NJ: Lawrence Erlbaum Associates, 1989.

2

The Study of History:
Interpretation or Truth?

Let us begin with a statement of fact: The study of history is one of the most important dimensions of modern thought. It provides the framework for so much else and is the best guarantee available for the integrity of knowledge about the past. Naturally, it can be proven easily that history has been abused at times. Personal and national interests, popular whim and emotionalism, and the fogs of romantic misperception have distorted it. Propagandists and the entertainment industry have exploited it. Sometimes it has been employed for purposes harmful to society. It is worth remembering, however, that the scholarship associated with it is among the best and most vigorous of any field of learning and that it contributes to the well-being of contemporary life.

The purpose motivating that scholarship is varied. Curiosity moves some people to undertake it; the sharpening of identity encourages others. In the case of the former the simple but timeless desire to know about significant past events and personalities or how things of the present came to be provides sufficient reason for serious study. The latter serves as a type of collective memory for understanding self and society, or some group or institution within society. Others embrace the study for the broad background it provides for comprehending the present and engaging the future. Some turn to it seeking knowledge of change; others, of continuity, tradition, and human nature. In the opinion of some people, there is an ethical value in history. They might claim that history fosters a sense of humility, stimulates an awareness of other people and cultures, encourages consideration of humanistic (if not eternal) values, and increases appreciation of certain social responsibilities that concern all humankind. In this essay we shall assume that the study has abundant and worthy purpose and proceed to the central concern of the study itself—the search for historical truth. The search for

By James D. Startt
Valparaiso University

truth in its metaphysical or absolute sense is the task of theologians and philosophers. When historians refer to truth in history, they mean the state of a proposition being in accord with the facts upon which it rests. They mean that the expressed proposition is as accurate a representation of an appropriate past reality as it is possible to achieve.[1] It would appear to be a simple task to articulate the truth in this manner, but that which appears easy is, in fact, deceptive and complicated. The end sought can never be achieved in full. In their reconstruction of some part of the past, historians can only approach complete truth. Because it is imperative that this approach be made for the sake of civilization and culture, we shall examine first a sampling of the problems that impair the effort and then basic guidelines that can make it as viable as possible.

Obstacles to Truth in History

Common sense leads us to recognize the vastness and complexity of history. Curiosity about the past, David Hume once said, "excites a regret that the history of remote ages should always be so much involved in obscurity, uncertainty, and contradiction."[2] His reflection can apply to the near as well as the distant past, for everything that has happened soon becomes unknowable to some degree. All past events occur in relationship to various personal and impersonal forces. Who can know, much less express, them all in their endless variety? Everyone who inquires into history, moreover, is part of the present and is in some way bound by its social and cultural standards. Complete detachment is impossible and probably would be undesirable at any rate. The record of a past event is never perfect, nor is the vision of the beholder of that record. Indeed, obstacles of many sorts abound to fetter the cause of truth in history. Imperfect records or poorly understood records can impair knowledge of the people and events of the past. The same can be said of personal prejudice and racial, class, national, and occupational biases. For the purpose of discussion we shall consider some obstacles to truth created by poor construction and then some related to faulty generalization.

The burden of proof in history is the responsibility of historians. They must locate and study the evidence, and the quality of the evidence directly relates to the quality of interpretation. "The first test by which any historical work must be judged," one authority on historical methodology observes, "is how far its interpretation of the

---

[1]See, for example, Oscar Handlin, *Truth in History* (Cambridge: Harvard University Press, Belknap Press, 1979), 118, and Lester D. Stephens, *Probing the Past: A Guide to the Study and Teaching of History* (Boston: Allyn and Bacon, 1974), 52.

[2]David Hume, *The History of England*, 6 vols. (1754-1762; new ed., Philadelphia: Porter and Coates, 1776), Vol. 1: 25.

past is consistent with all the available evidence."[3] One of the basic rules of research is that interpretation must be based on an examination of the full record. Yet, publications continue to appear based on inadequate sources. Despite the many excellent studies by historians in our time, there appears to have been a lowering of standards regarding sources and documentation of sources. Too often media historians have failed to resist this tendency. Sound history, however, rests on an imaginative and comprehensive search for all available evidence pertaining to the inquiry. In most cases, that search should go back to primary sources. Also, since the time of Leopold von Ranke, historians have recognized the rule that all interpretation is supposed to stand on fact. This has not always been the case.

At times some historians have elevated interpretation over fact. A case in point is the work of certain of the revisionist historians who concerned themselves with the origins of the Cold War. In a probing evaluation of their work in 1973, Robert J. Maddox drew attention to the fact that their work contained numerous rudimentary errors. He demonstrated that their work stood on "practices such as splicing together diverse statements to produce fictitious speeches and conversations, altering the meaning of sentences through the use of ellipses, and wrenching phrases out of time sequences and contexts, among other things."[4] Other historians soon confirmed his findings. Yet the revisionists continued in their work and even found scholarly support for it. It would appear that only interpretation counted, not documentation. Consequently, such history little serves the cause of truth, and it gives bite to the statement of the British historian D. C. Watt when he remarked that "American historiography of the Cold War tells us very little of the Cold War, much of the American intellectual history in the 1960s and 1970s."[5] History of this sort is only pseudo-history because it contains flawed craftsmanship.

Some fallacies that mar history are less intentional than the preceding case of faulty interpretation. Again consider the records of history. They are of many sorts, but a general rule of research is this: Trace a point to its best source. In many cases this is a primary source, and in some cases a primary source is an original source.[6]

---

[3]John Tosh, *The Pursuit of History: Aims, Methods and New Directions in the Study of Modern History* (London: Longman, 1986), 29.

[4]Robert J. Maddox, "The Rise and Fall of Cold War Revisionism," *History* 73 (May 1984): 423. For the complete version of his critique, see his *The New Left and the Origins of the Cold War* (Princeton: Princeton University Press, 1973).

[5]Quoted in Maddox, "The Rise and Fall of Cold War Revisionism," p. 416.

[6]For a discussion of the distinction between primary, original, and secondary sources see James D. Startt and Wm. David Sloan, *Historical Methods*

Too often writers use secondary sources for the raw material of their works, and thus rely on information gathered by other people for other purposes.

Too frequently also writers violate another rule of research regarding sources. Historians are supposed to have mastered the art of distinguishing between the types and authoritativeness of sources used. The newspaper as an historical source can serve as an example in this instance. Do historians make adequate allowance for the variation found among newspapers? In many cases they do, but too often they fail to make the proper differentiation. There was, for instance, a great difference in the early 20th-century British press between "popular" and "quality" papers in terms of size, purpose, and readership. Nevertheless, historical accounts involving the British press at that time often fail to make the distinction. There are, of course, also many differences among newspapers published in the United States. They vary not only in terms of type and tone but also in terms of character, which, in the case of an individual paper, might change in the course of time. The New York *Times*, for instance, did not always possess the prestige it enjoys in the 20th century. In her classic study of newspapers as historical sources, Lucy Salmon wrote many years ago: "The historian cannot evade responsibility of at least attempting to understand the personality of the newspaper if he is to make use of it as historical material, for upon the personality of the newspaper as a whole depends its power for good or for evil."[7] Historians who wish to avoid indiscriminate references to sources that weaken the validity of text will find her advice as relevant today as when those lines were written.

Regarding the authoritativeness of sources, the New York *Times* is again illustrative. It is frequently cited as a newspaper of record and a publication known for its trustworthy news. In many respects, it deserves that reputation. Years ago, however, Walter Lippmann and Charles Merz proved that the *Times'* reporting of the Russian Revolution and its aftermath was full of inaccuracies.[8] If the *Times'* reports of such a great event were flawed, it stands to reason that those of other papers probably were too. How often must a newspaper as an historical record be questioned? In fact, there are many reasons why newspaper accounts of events might be flawed, and the time factor in making those reports is only the most obvious one. The newspaper is typical of other historical records. Conditions of creation and preserving of record must be considered in any use

---

in *Mass Communication* (Hillsdale, NJ: Lawrence Erlbaum Associates, 1989), 114-117.

[7]Lucy Maynard Salmon, *The Newspaper and the Historian* (New York: Oxford University Press, 1923), 74.

[8]Walter Lippmann and Charles Merz, "A Test of the News," *New Republic* (4 August 1920), 1-42.

of these materials. Historians must, therefore, always examine these records with another rule of research in mind: "When looking at this document, what else can be seen?" Truth demands such attention.

Another rule of research deserves consideration in order to avoid faulty construction of argument. Simply stated, it is that context must inform text, but in practice it receives too little attention. The word *race* can serve as a case in point. It must be understood in the context in which it is used. References to *race* appear frequently in the 19th-century press; and on into the 20th, public figures used the word proudly in speeches. But what did it mean? Theodore Roosevelt and Henry Cabot Lodge used it interchangeably with *nation*. In other cases at that time it may have had an anthropological, cultural, or even biological meaning. Distinctions must be made. The same can be said for many other terms (e.g., propaganda, public opinion, etc.) that find their way into the records of history. This need to decipher past terminology reminds us that interpretation of the human past requires the ability to interpret its record. Failure to develop the necessary skills to accomplish that task can impair truth in history.

If the cause of truth can be hindered by the failure to locate, employ, and interpret the record in a proper manner, it can also be hampered by certain tendencies of projecting the present back into the past. These present-minded fallacies can take many forms, some more popular than others. In a sense it can be said that any unexamined popular historical generalization blurs the search for truth about the past. Too often such a popular generalization fails to reflect the true past and becomes an expression of a fixed idea. Consider, for instance, how present definitions are projected back into the past with popular usage of terms such as *imperialism, the people,* and *the state.* Such terms have experienced dramatic change over time. David Hackett Fischer provides the following example of how the static idea of a democratic society had influenced popular perceptions of three centuries of American history:

> The result is a historiographical equivalent of the Dance of the Seven Veils, featuring the damsel Democracy herself, and a half dozen willing helpers. First, Roger Williams helps her out of a sombre shroud of Puritan black. Then Benjamin Franklin rends a red coat with his lightning rod, and Thomas Jefferson tugs off a covering of Hamiltonian buff and blue, to expose an earthy homespun of Old Hickory brown. The rude garment falls to pieces, revealing a cloak of Confederate gray, which Lincoln removes with magnanimous gestures. Next there is a gilded robe, embroidered with Black Fridays and costly touches of Tweed, which miraculously yields to a checkered cloth of Pop-

ulist red and Progressive lily white, with a free-silver lining. The last veil finally falls away, and beauteous Columbia stands revealed, with a blue eagle tattooed on her belly.[9]

At least that projects the idea through the 1930s. Beyond that we shall have to imagine what garment would suit "damsel Democracy" in World War II and the Cold War, or during the 1950s, 1960s, and 1990s.

G. Kitson Clark labeled a particular type of the fixed idea fallacy "generic statements."[10] He used that term in reference to popular, present generalizations about groups of people that can find their way into history. The groups may be based on race, creed, class, nationality, political preferences, and so on. Thus in history, as in mass communication, many tidy references to "the Germans," "the protestants," "the lower class," and "the media" can be found when in fact the group delineated was far more complex than the image conveyed by the word. The same can be said of many other generic groupings. Think of almost any social, political, or economic grouping. Are proper distinctions made between "conservatives" and "reactionaries," between "liberals" and "radicals," or even between "Fascists" and "Nazis"? Can we refer to the South and Southerners? Or, are there really many Souths and, consequently, many Southerners? Do not terms like *medieval* or *Victorian* lose much of their meaning when measured against the great variety of life they cover? When we read that a nation wanted this or that, what are we reading? Germany wanted an empire in the 1880s, wanted war in 1914, and wanted revenge after the Versailles Settlement of 1919. Who actually wanted these things, and why did they want them? These popular, unexamined generic references lack the necessary precision to be convincing. On the other hand, any generalization about such large entities might be uncertain due to its very nature. Readers, however, can expect two things of historians in these matters: (a) that they themselves have a clear idea of what they mean by collective references, and (b) that their generic descriptions rest on evidence.[11] Present generalizations will always exist and penetrate back into the past. It is the job of historians to make them as truthful as possible.

Historians are also expected to recognize national myths for what they are and to explain them accordingly. They are intuitive by nature and come out of a shared or imagined historical experience. Historians and journalists help to perpetuate them. Although

---

[9]David Hackett Fischer, *Historians' Fallacies: Toward a Logic of Historical Thought* (New York: Harper and Row, Harper Torchbooks, 1970), 153.

[10]G. Kitson Clark, *The Critical Historian* (New York: Basic Books, 1967), Chap. 11.

[11]Ibid., p. 160.

they may serve a national purpose (e.g., they explain confusion, inspire a people, and rationalize policies), they also can outdistance truth. The Puritan Myth, the New (American) World Myth, the Manifest Destiny Myth, and others have at times been a powerful force working on national sentiment. They should be presented in that manner and submitted to the same scrutiny that historians are supposed to give to all large ideas. It should be remembered too that national myths can become self-fulfilling prophesies, and at the very least they tend to encourage reductionist thinking. The latter can lead to an unreal conversion of complex into simple issues. It can produce "good vs. bad," "saints vs. sinners," and "heroes vs. villains" thinking. Such emotional reductionism represents a serious impediment to truth in history.

But all reductionism is not of the emotional variety. Some is based on reason. Consider the problems of causation in history. The effort to isolate causes, locate "the cause," or measure causes can distort reality. "Every attempt in historical writing," Jacques Barzun and Henry F. Graff explain, "to formalize causal description or make a show of exactitude by assigning one 'paramount' cause and several 'contributory' causes ends in self-stultification."[12] This often neglected advice should be a basic rule of historical methodology. What caused the spread of Christianity or the passing of Rome in the West? Did capitalism cause Protestantism, or was the reverse true? What or who caused the brutalization of the freed Black people after the Civil War? Or, in the case of mass communication, why did the patriot press denounce King George III in the years before the American Revolution? Why did the penny press appear when and as it did? Who or what was responsible for yellow journalism or for the performance of network television coverage of recent presidential elections? Problems of causation do not yield simple quantifiable answers. They deal with conditions in time and should be a matter of explanation rather than artificial delineation.

Or, consider the case of determinism and related instances of the use of theory to explain history. Without entering into a lengthy discussion of history and theory, it can be said that historians in general have hesitations about using theory to explain the past and insist that it be used with care. Art, politics, race, religion, industry, and war are some of the variables of the mainstream of human history just as government control, technology, commerce, conviction, and passion are some of the variables of mass communication history. All the variables associated with any past act must be taken into account, and it is a precariously formed generalization that al-

---

[12]Jacques Barzun and Henry F. Graff, *The Modern Researcher*, 4th ed. (New York: Harcourt Brace Jovanovich, 1985), 189.

lows either a single variable or an outside speculation to determine the nature of an object under investigation. Sometimes, for instance, the economic factor is considered the most important in explaining human institutions. That thesis cannot be supported beyond doubt. Human activity is never free of religious, cultural, and psychological influences. Does the "great-man" theory explain the workings of the 19th-century penny press as is sometimes suggested? Theories both grand and specific are valuable. They contain insights that can help to unlock past mysteries. They must not be allowed, however, to negate the basic rule that history is multidimensional. It occurs in time and space, and it occurs in relation to many human conditions.

As the foregoing examples indicate, there are many obstacles to truth in history. The first step to take in avoiding them is to recognize their existence. There exists, moreover, a canon of criticism to guide historians in their pursuit of the truth about past realities. This large body of criticism varies somewhat according to the subject of an inquiry, but certain of its general features need to be comprehended regardless of the particularities of a given study. We now turn to a discussion of these general features.

The Critical Method

When the renowned Dutch historian Pieter Geyl returned to the lecture hall in 1945, five years after his arrest by the Germans who occupied his country, the first thing he addressed for his students was the value of criticism. He said it was the "first duty of independent scholarship" and claimed that it was a bulwark of Western Civilization.[13] Accordingly, he reminds us that careful evaluation lies at the core of the study of history. If it is true, as Carl Becker once said, that everyone is his or her own historian, it is also true that people involved in history must be their own critics. The canon of criticism they recognize begins with an appreciation of self in history.

The past may be infinite and immutable, but historians are fallible and live in a changing present. In recapturing a part of the past, they can never be free of the present. Consequently, there is a subjective side to all history. The word *subjectivity*, as Trygve Tholfsen reminds us, "no longer holds the same terror for us that it did for the theorists of scientific history. For them, 'subjectivity' was a demon to be exorcised, in order to produce knowledge of pristine 'objectivity.'"[14] Today historians still value the ideal of objectivity

---

[13]Pieter Geyl, *Use and Abuse of History* (1955; reprint ed., Hamden, CT: Archon Books, 1970), 72.

[14]Trygve R. Tholfsen, *Historical Thinking: An Introduction* (New York: Harper and Row, 1967), 225.

and desire to discover how things really were, and no one wants history to be shaped by unguarded subjectivity or unrestricted relativity. How do they deal with the subjective factor? They try to see themselves in the longer perspective they apply to the object of their study and to recognize their own presuppositions and values and to place them in a critical framework. Barzun and Graff cite this ability to "see around themselves" or "self-awareness" as one of the qualities historians most need to develop.[15] Construed in this way, "subjectivity" is far removed from "bias." It should be considered as part of historians' judgment, much in the manner that honesty and accuracy are part of that judgment. "An objective judgment," Barzun and Graff observe, "is one made by testing in all ways possible one's subjective impressions, so as to arrive at a knowledge of objects."[16]

"Made by testing" is the key idea. It runs all through historical methodology. Historians begin by submitting the materials of the past to testing. No type of evidence is more important to historians than primary materials. They provide not only information but also a feel for that information. They can offer an intimate appreciation of the formation of policy and opinion, of how events occurred, and of how institutions operated. The primary record is vast, and the subject of inquiry determines its type (e.g., written, visual, oral, or physical). The most common source is the written record, which may also be called a document, and the critical method associated with it is also applicable for many other types of records. In this case, historians first determine the exact type of document they are examining. Was it a statement of background information or one of command? Was it a public document like a newspaper or a speech? If it were, it must be understood as a public record and judged accordingly. Many documents like the various journalistic publications have numerous parts. Each must be understood on its own grounds. A given newspaper, for instance, may have had a limited news coverage or editorials that attracted little notice, but it may have had excellent drama reviews or business reports. Once historians establish a document's type, they then submit it to tests of external (when necessary) and internal textual criticism. The former, which applies mainly to original records, establishes authenticity; the latter, credibility. Such testing becomes automatic and is part of the continuous effort to discover the truth about the human past.

A body of secondary literature also exists to aid historians in that effort. It too must be scrutinized. No present historical inquiry should be drawn from the work of other historians, yet old and

---

[15]Barzun and Graff, *Modern Researcher*, 58.
[16]Ibid., p. 184.

newer authorities must be studied.[17] Therein current researchers may find chronological data and contextual information. In some cases they may acquire a keen appreciation of ideas and forces active in the past. Some secondary literature contains suggestive descriptions, interpretations, and even theories that could be useful. It can provide a means for testing conclusions reached in a present inquiry. This literature represents a valuable resource for contemporary historians, but it can only be used when weighed against the content of the appropriate primary records. "Every historian," wrote Oscar Handlin, "must. . . be his own reviewer and assimilate into his own fund of knowledge the old works of enduring value as well as the new. That demands the application of rigorous standards of critical evaluation and assessment."[18]

The critical process continues when historians proceed to interpret information drawn from historical sources. Interpretation of materials, in this sense, occurs at several levels. First it takes place at the level of finding the meaning of specific objects and then at the broader level of explaining larger and sometimes cumulative objects. Both of these types of objects can be called "facts" of history. A third level of interpretation exists, that of grand conceptualization of all human experience such as Arnold Toynbee, Karl Marx, and others attempted. It can be suggestive, particularly in terms of theoretical explanation, and it should be studied both in its cyclical and progressive versions. But it really represents a type of metahistorical speculation. We shall concentrate on the first two levels, for they represent the realm in which most historians operate.

Consider first the interpretation of a specific object of limited historical presence. Facts of this sort may be an item, an event, a person, or even an idea, but they should not be confused with data, which might be defined as uncontested routine information. Facts do not stand alone; they have images attached to them. Historians interpret them. To state that Ida Tarbell died in 1944 tells us little. It is data. But to discuss her career and work as a muckraker requires interpretation and provides a historical fact. Understanding a historical fact is one of the most difficult tasks historians face. All such facts are, as we have already seen, multidimensional. In an effort to understand them, historians employ a variety of analyses when appropriate (e.g., content analysis, quantitative analysis, psychoanalysis, etc.). They use the tools of chronology, comparison, and corroboration. They design questions to provide answers about the what, how, and why of a fact. Finally, in reaching conclusions about this fact, they ask several master questions about it and of

---

[17]G. R. Elton, *Political History: Principles and Practice* (New York: Basic Books, 1970), 74.

[18]Handlin, *Truth in History*, 115.

themselves: Do I understand the nature of this fact? Do I understand its vital relations to associated human, cultural, institutional, and physical factors? Do I understand all of the forces that acted upon it? Have I made allowance for the constraints to human thought and action that affected it? What authority do I have for making this statement about it? Some of the facts encountered at this level are larger and more complicated than others, and as a study proceeds so grows the need to deal with ones of yet larger scope.

At this point a "fact" can become an object of immense scope. It might be the American Revolution, or the Cold War, or, in terms of mass communication history, the New Journalism. These facts are cumulative because they include, like the pieces of a puzzle, many facts of lesser scope. How do they fit together? In answering that question, the preceding criteria for evaluating specific facts still apply. But now the relationship between the specific facts and overall perception of the larger puzzle calls for additional judgment. A fact's purpose, nature, meaning, and sometimes matters of its causation deserve attention at this point. Gaps have to be closed, inferences made. That being the case, it is necessary to recall that all historical generalization must derive from evidence and reflect context. Interpretations at this level should convey indications of the spirit of the times of the object studied. Inferences must be reasonable and based on probability, and because of the inferential element in these interpretations, the inferences should be properly loose and qualified. They should not, however, contain questionable or easily refutable conclusions. Beware also of "too-perfect" explanations.[19] They probably are imposed on the materials of history from the outside and are apt to be suspect. At this point, more than at any other in implementing methodology, historians need to take their audiences into their confidence. They need to explain how they resolved particular problems of explanation and how their conclusions reflect representative evidence. They must persuade audiences that knowledge of what real people did in the past is not only knowable but also worth knowing. That calls for careful and reflective interaction between historians and their materials.

The use of critical methodology, however, in gathering, deciphering, and explaining historical material cannot guarantee truth in history. The perils of faulty composition remain. Proper composition requires disciplined attention as much as any other element of history. It has its own critical apparatus. Vocabulary needs to be examined and reexamined. Does the language employed have the controls needed to avoid rhetorical excess and misrepresentation? Does it sharpen the outlines of reality? Ordinary events should not become "amazing," and qualities of greatness should not be at-

---

[19]Ibid., p. 125.

tributed to ordinary people, or even to most major historical figures. When the exceptional figure who deserves to be discussed in terms of possible greatness does appear, the discussion should be a balance of reasons why such a claim can be advanced for that individual and of his or her mortal flaws. Believability and accuracy should be the hallmarks of the vocabulary of historical compositions. The exact noun must be found to convey the connotation intended; the exact verb, to describe its movement.

Moreover, because people should expect both clarity and freshness in the history they read, it must be free of jargon, clichés, and slang. There are yet other hallmarks of writing to acknowledge. A logical and natural sense of order should shape the composition and a reasonable tone permeate it. It must have the necessary evidences of documentation (e.g., quotations, footnotes, etc.), and they must be well-crafted. To make matters more difficult, a historical composition is supposed to have style enough to save it from dullness and to invite the contemplation of others. It has often been said that historians are in part artists, and any historical narrative that overcomes the perils of composition while remaining committed to the real past proves the point.

Discussion

Validity can still be found in the old saying that truth is the beginning of wisdom. That idea applies to history, which is committed to finding the truth in the past, and to the idea that present wisdom can benefit from knowledge of it. The objective is not an overarching truth to explain all things, but an aggregate of many truths. About these truths historians will continue to speculate and interpretation will follow interpretation. That obstacles to truth in history should be avoided whenever possible, and critical methodology employed is the least that people can expect of historians. Interpretations of the deeds of men and women in the past that fail in these respects will receive the little attention they deserve. The consideration of the relationship between interpretation and truth raises a number of questions.

1. Which interpretations deserve continued attention?

2. What makes one interpretation better than another?

3. The answer to Question 2 involves the commitment to the search for truthfulness that makes good history reliable and gives it integrity of character. Yet despite the need for truth in history, can it be argued that more than truthfulness is involved in the study of history?

4. On the other hand, does a study of history without truthfulness deserve the name "history"?

Readings

Barzun, Jacques, and Henry F. Graff, Ch. 8, "Pattern, Bias, and the Great System," pp. 193-216, *The Modern Researcher*, 4th ed. New York: Harcourt Brace Jovanovich, 1985.

Boorstin, Daniel J., Ch. 1, "From News Gathering to News Making: A Flood of Pseudo-Events," pp. 7-44, *The Image: A Guide to Pseudo-Events in America*. New York: Atheneum, 1961; repr. 1987.

Clark, G. Kitson, Ch. 2, "The Dangers of History and Their Cure," pp. 4-12, *The Critical Historian*. New York: Basic Books, 1967.

Conkin, Paul K., and Roland N. Stromberg, Ch. 10, "Causation," pp. 174-196, *The Heritage and Challenge of History*. New York: Dodd, Mead, 1971.

Davidson, James West, and Mark Hamilton Lytle, Ch. 13, "From Rosie to Lucy: The Mass Media and Images of Women in the 1950s," pp. 364-394, *After the Fact: The Art of Historical Detection,* 2nd ed. New York: Knopf, 1986.

Elton, G.R., Ch. 4, "Explanation and Cause," pp. 112-155, *Political History: Principles and Practice*. New York: Basic Books, 1970.

Fischer, David Hackett, Ch. 6, "Fallacies and Causation," pp. 187-215, *Historians' Fallacies: Toward a Logic of Historical Thought*. New York: Harper and Row, Harper Torchbooks, 1970.

Gottschalk, Louis, Ch. 1, "The Evaluation of Historical Writing," pp. 3-25, *Understanding History: A Primer of Historical Method*. New York: Knopf, 1950; repr. 1966.

Gustavson, Carl B., Part 4, "Basic Historical Processes," pp. 97-176, *The Mansion of History*. New York: McGraw-Hill, 1976.

Handlin, Oscar, Ch. 5, "Historical Criticism," pp. 111-144, *Truth in History*. Cambridge: Harvard University Press, Belknap Press, 1979.

Himmelfarb, Gertrude, Ch. 9, "History and the Idea of Progress," pp. 155-170, *The New History and the Old*. Cambridge: Harvard University Press, Belknap Press, 1987.

Isenberg, Michael T., Ch. 8, "History and the Individual," pp. 125-141, *Puzzles of the Past: An Introduction to Thinking About History*. College Station: Texas A & M University Press, 1985.

Nevins, Allan, Ch. 9, "Ideas in History," pp. 261-300, *The Gateway to History*, rev. ed. Garden City, NY: Doubleday, Anchor Books, 1962.

Robinson, James Oliver, Part 4, Ch. 3, "We Are All Progressives," pp. 295-307, *American Myth, American Reality*. New York: Hill and Wang, 1980.

Salmon, Lucy Maynard, Ch. 17, "How Far Can the Past Be Reconstructed from the Press?" pp. 468-492, *The Newspaper and the Historian*. New York: Oxford University Press, 1923.

Startt, James D., and Wm. David Sloan, Ch. 6, "Historical Sources and Their Evaluation," pp. 113-140, *Historical Methods in Mass Communication*. Hillsdale, NJ: Lawrence Erlbaum Associates, 1989.

Stephens, Lester D., Ch. 4, "Explanation and History," pp. 61-77, *Probing the Past: A Guide to the Study and Teaching of History*. Boston: Allyn and Bacon, 1974.

Stone, Gerald, Ch. 1, "What Has Been Written and Why," pp. 13-19, *Examining Newspapers: What Research Reveals About America's Newspapers*. SAGE Comm Text Series, Vol. 20. Newbury Park, CA: 1987.

Taft, William H., Ch. 6, "Merger of the Historian and the Journalist," pp. 67-78, *Newspapers as Tools for Historians*. Columbia, MO: Lucas Brothers, 1970.

Tholfsen, Trygve R., Ch. 9, "The Historical Approach," pp. 241-260, *Historical Thinking: An Introduction*. New York: Harper and Row, 1967.

Tosh, John, Ch. 8, "History and Theory," pp. 127-151, *The Pursuit of History: Aims, Methods and New Directions in the Study of Modern History*. London: Longman, 1986.

3

The Colonial Press, 1690-1765:
Mirror of Society or Origin of Journalism?

The first mass media in the American colonies were pamphlets and broadsides (one-page sheets printed on one side) that addressed single issues. In accounts of media history, however, historians normally emphasize the beginnings of the newspaper. Although debate exists, they usually give credit to Boston's *Publick Occurrences, Both Foreign and Domestick* as the colonies' first such publication. Founded by Puritan publicist Benjamin Harris in 1690, the paper lasted only one issue, suppressed by governing authorities because Harris had not obtained their approval prior to publication.

It was 14 years later before the colonies saw the second effort. Boston again was the location, with the local postmaster, John Campbell, securing official sanction before launching the *News-Letter* in 1704. Campbell's successor as postmaster, William Brooker, brought competition to the newspaper field when he began the Boston *Gazette* in 1719, followed in 1721 by the *New-England Courant*. Founded on opposition to the Puritan clergy and their advocacy of smallpox inoculation, the *Courant* was started by the most strident members of Boston's lone Anglican church and was printed by Benjamin Franklin's older brother James. Their goal was to use the issue of inoculation to destroy the popularity of the Puritan clergy as part of their larger effort to establish Anglicanism as the official religion in Massachusetts.

These first colonial newspapers, like the others that followed them, usually contained four pages about the size of today's typewriting paper. In appearance they were gray, with headlines set in type that was little larger than body type and with few or no illustrations. The content consisted of essays, with religious ones especially popular, and short items of news. Much of the news was foreign, especially English. Two reasons accounted for the attention to foreign news: Cultural and transportation ties were to England, and intracolonial transportation was difficult. Furthermore, the papers frequently downplayed local news because the proprietors assumed that local readers already knew about the events. News accounts were brief, often only one sentence; and printers showed no great concern for timeliness. News reports often piled up until earlier reports could be printed. The operators of newspapers typically were printers, rather than "editors" as we think of them today, who produced the papers as only one part of their printing businesses.

Printers made little systematic attempts at news gathering, employing, for example, no reporters or correspondents. Instead, Atlantic commerce served as the main source of news, bringing information to colonial newspaper offices by way of English newspapers and letters. For colonial news, printers depended on letters and newspapers from other towns.

The most notable name among colonial printers was that of Benjamin Franklin. Apprenticed to his rash brother to learn the trade of printing, Benjamin in 1722 seized his opportunity to escape. In Philadelphia in 1729 he was able to buy a newspaper, the *Pennsylvania Gazette*, that was filling its pages with the contents of an encyclopedia. He did away with the encyclopedic aspect and made the paper livelier and newsier, improved its appearance, and upgraded its advertising. Pragmatic in his approach, he kept an eye on the money-making potential of newspapers and began what could be considered America's first newspaper "chain." He retired from newspaper work at the age of 42 and moved into the other endeavors from which he gained most of his fame.

Steady growth in the number of newspapers marked the colonial period. From one newspaper in 1704, the number grew to 18 in 1760 and to 38 on the eve of the American Revolution in 1775. A total of 78 papers had been in existence at one time or another during those years.

The interest of communication historians has been attracted to the colonial press for the obvious reason that the colonial period provided the beginnings of American journalism. It was during the colonial period that the country had its first newspapers and its earliest attempts at various journalistic practices. The press was in its infancy, and virtually everything it tried for the first time has drawn the attention of historians. Probably no other period in American communication history has had such a large percentage of its journalists singled out for historical study. In looking at the journalists and the colonial press in general, historians have directed most of their work at the large contexts of the nature of the press and the role newspapers played in American colonial life and in the development of American journalism. The questions they have tried to answer have dealt for the most part with the influence of the press in the early life of America, the influence colonial society had on the press, and the origins of journalistic practices.

In studying the colonial press, historians have been influenced greatly by their own times and the conditions of journalism and so-

ciety at the time of their writing. In general, the Romantic historians of the 19th century, writing during an era in which pride in
American progress and achievements was popular, took a nationalistic approach and explained the press as influential or important in
the early development of the nation. Cultural historians, writing for
the most part in the first half of the 20th century (a period during
which cultural, social, and environmental changes had greatly affected the style of life in America), attempted to explain the press in
terms of its interaction with society. Their underlying theme, influenced by the concepts propounded in the growing discipline of sociology in American universities, was that the characteristics of the
press were the result of social influences, although the press at the
same time played an important role in colonial society. Developmental historians, whose studies of the colonial press proliferated
after 1930 and were written at a time during which journalism was
gaining sophistication as a profession, attempted to explain the
colonial press as the origin of later practices in journalism. Their
work often was concerned with chronicling early developments,
and their historical view incorporated directly the journalistic
standards of their own time.

Despite such differences in outlook, historians of all three
schools tended to agree about the nature and importance of the press.
Journalism, they believed, was in its crude beginnings, but its raw-
ness and inexperience were not serious faults because they were the
natural characteristics at such an early stage. On the other hand,
historians thought of the infant newspapers as influential and significant factors in both the national life and the day-to-day affairs
of their own localities. Thus, with few exceptions historians concluded that the colonial press performed in a way that merits little
criticism.

The Romantic School

In number of volumes, the works of the Romantic historians comprise the smallest contribution to the study of the early press. Most
Romantic works were biographical, often considering their subjects
as important patriotic figures who contributed to the progress of
America and her institutions. Usually from respectable, conservative families from the Northeast, Romantic historians especially
favored journalists who were from that region and who were patriotic but not disrespectful toward established values and traditions.

Romantic historians also found considerable interest in the
printing trade of the colonial period and in the nature of the contents
of newspapers. Like later historians, they believed that printing was
a major aspect of colonial life and public affairs and recognized the
essential nature of the relationship between printing and newspaper
publishing. Much of their work, however, consisted of little more

than cataloging contents and compiling bibliography.

James Parton's *Life and Times of Benjamin Franklin* (1864), one of the earliest biographies of a colonial journalist, typified Romantic studies of the colonial press. As its subject, it took the member of the colonial press who has been by far the most popular one with historians. In general, historians of all schools have attempted to emphasize the fact that until the middle of his life Franklin was a printer and journalist, that journalism was his first love, and that much of his later success, especially in his writing, was rooted in his earlier journalistic training. Parton, sometimes called the father of American biography, especially praised Franklin's competence as a businessman, editor, and owner of the *Pennsylvania Gazette*. Through his talent and his respectability, Franklin was able to make the *Gazette* "incomparably the best newspaper published in the colonies."

For Franklin's older brother James, however, Parton's enthusiasm showed more reserve. Whereas Parton's treatment of Benjamin demonstrated the Romantic approach of favorable biography, his evaluation of James revealed the Romantic historians' critical view of radical change. Parton was censorious of radical democratic movements in American history and thus was not inclined to agree with James' attitudes and practices. Although Boston readers were accustomed to dullness in their newspapers, Parton wrote, James' *New-England Courant* was the "most spirited, witty, and daring" colonial newspaper and was America's "first sensation newspaper." Still, its success was not altogether praiseworthy, for sarcasm and ridicule of the established religious authorities characterized the paper, and its printer and writers offered nothing of value as a substitute. "The brethren at whom [James Franklin] aimed his ridicule," wrote Parton, "were seriously striving, with the best light they had, to become good and better men. To that end, they were making weekly and daily efforts. . . . This was the advantage they had over their witty adversaries; and this was the reason why they at length prevailed. The brethren may have been going toward Jerusalem in a painful, roundabout, and irrational manner, but they were *going*. The young Couranters had not made up their minds whether or not there was a Jerusalem. To use Franklin's own simile, they were knocking out the bung of the beer-barrel, *before* providing the cask of wine. This was the course pursued by all the wits of that scoffing century, from Voltaire, downward; and that was the reason why, with all their genius and knowledge, they produced a merely transitory effect. The poor peasants who went to mass in Voltaire's village were doing their best to be good men. Voltaire was chiefly striving to show Europe what a witty man Voltaire was; and hence, the poor peasants were wiser in their generation than the children of light."[1]

The later Romantic historian S. G. W. Benjamin provided a similar evaluation of colonial printers. Writing in the 1880s about the colonial press as it ushered in the American revolutionary period, Benjamin told history in the framework of narrative biographies of a number of prominent colonial journalists. Although he criticized the weak character, abusiveness, and "sensationalism" of James Franklin, he praised colonial journalists overall as "men of character and ability." His portrait of the Boston printer Thomas Fleet typified his approach. Fleet, Benjamin said, "was evidently a genuine Yankee in enterprise and versatility. . . . He was possessed of a vein of keen, coarse wit that was suited to the times and aided the popularity of the [Boston *Evening*] *Post*. The squibs, lampoons and advertisements in its columns bear internal evidence of being the productions of the indefatigable Fleet." Colonial printers, Benjamin concluded, wielded considerable influence and played a positive role in helping to bring about the Revolution. They "understood their opportunity," he wrote, "and made the quill and the printing-press scarcely less potential in asserting and securing the liberties than the forum and the field." Although some of the writings that appeared in newspapers might have been "acrimonious and severe," Benjamin excused their style because the times were critical and "the life of a nation was at stake."[2]

The Cultural School
Cultural historians, who produced most of their works in the 1930s and 1940s, were especially concerned about the interrelationship between journalism and colonial society. Their works normally dealt with the nature and cultural role of the press, and they found that journalism usually mirrored society and that social, political, cultural, and political factors greatly influenced its character. At the same time, they considered the press the primary medium through which society voiced its opinions and an important factor in influencing public views, a focus of colonial opinion and a forum of discussion, as the historian Lyon F. Richardson put it.[3]

Elizabeth Cook provided the first major Cultural study of the colonial press. In *Literary Influences in Colonial Newspapers, 1704-1750* (1912), a survey of material that appeared in newspapers, she argued that the weekly newspaper was the most important source

---

[1]James Parton, *Life and Times of Benjamin Franklin* (New York: 1864), 218, 78, 95.

[2]S. G. W. Benjamin, "A Group of Pre-Revolutionary Editors. Beginnings of Journalism in America," *Magazine of American History* 17 (January 1887): 9, 28.

[3]Lyon F. Richardson, *A History of Early American Magazines, 1741-1789* (New York: Thomas Nelson and Sons, 1931).

in the dissemination of non-sectarian literature and that newspapers were to a large extent non-news literary journals that emphasized such material as essays, prose, and poetry. Circumstances conspired to create that characteristic. Cut off from news because of the crude transportation system and from politics because of government sensitivity, the editor had to look for other types of content. The model the editor imitated was the English literature of the period. "He might write homilies," Cook noted, "and he sometimes did. But he knew that his readers were not suffering from any lack of religious and ethical instruction. His subscription list could hardly be kept up if he made his newspaper a mere auxiliary to the pulpit. The people must have something new and entertaining that they would pay for. Thus at length the first bold experiment of writing essays and verse on English models was tried. The result was a definite type of literary weekly which flourished in the colonies."[4]

Although Cook's study was a pioneering effort, an extensive delineation of the Cultural interpretation was left to Sidney Kobre, who in a number of works attempted to explain colonial journalism as "a product of environment." The leading exponent of the Cultural interpretation, Kobre believed the nature of the press at any time in American history could be explained in large measure by the sociological influences acting on it. In *The Development of the Colonial Newspaper* (1944), a study of the years 1690-1783, he attempted to show how "the changing character of the American people and their dynamic social situation produced and conditioned the colonial newspaper." The first American newspapers as typified by Benjamin Harris' *Publick Occurrences* and John Campbell's *News-Letter*, were in effect products of economic, social, and cultural conditions, including city growth, the public's desire for political and commercial news, and the need of business for an advertising medium. The public's and printers' ideas about political self-determination, a new American philosophy then taking shape, greatly affected the character of the colonial newspaper. Colonial publishers, Kobre argued, "altered the character of their products to conform to. . . transformations in society. . . . Expensive machinery, large personnel and extensive office buildings and plants were not necessary. Given these economic and technological conditions, a free press was easily secured for the people. It would automatically result, the colonists thought, as long as publishers were freed from political control."

The Cultural school's third major work on the colonial press was Clarence Brigham's *Journals and Journeymen: A Contribution to the History of Early American Newspapers* (1950). The study

---

[4]Elizabeth C. Cook, *Literary Influences in Colonial Newspapers, 1704-1750* (New York: Columbia University Press, 1912), 4.

generally was a survey of miscellaneous characteristics of newspapers from 1690 to 1830, with an emphasis on how their operations worked in the context of social and economic conditions. One of several of Brigham's observations was that even though the approach of the Revolution helped increase circulation, one of the chief worries of early newspaper publishers was attempting to collect subscription payments. Another characteristic was the lack of sophistication in technology, resulting among other things in the limited use of only crude illustrations. Outside factors also affected news coverage, for the slowness of travel and communication made it inevitable that printing of news usually was delayed until several days or weeks after an event had occurred.

In a number of studies on more limited topics, Cultural historians analyzed the relationship between society and specific newspapers, individual journalists, and various journalistic practices. In a 1930 study of the *Connecticut Courant*, E. Wilder Spaulding concluded that although colonial newspapers were still the "drab, unpretentious by-product of the tiny print-shop" they were an integral and important part of American life. In the period just prior to the American Revolution, Hartford's *Courant* was a "remarkably accurate mirror of the city's ways of thinking" and served "as a medium for agitation" for political changes. America, Spaulding said, "wanted only opportunity for putting her ideas on paper," and the "prosaic little American newspaper" became the outlet because it was "the most effective mirror of the life and thought of its community" and reflected "accurately the ideals, the heart-throbs, and the disappointments of its neighborhood."[5]

Although such colonial papers served as media for the expression of opinion, Cultural historians considered them important also for their function of providing news to their readers. The emphasis on news was especially strong in Anna Janney DeArmond's 1949 biography *Andrew Bradford: Colonial Journalist.* Bradford published Philadelphia's *American Mercury* from 1719 to 1742. For the *Mercury*, a representative colonial paper, according to DeArmond, timeliness was both the key and the obstacle in journalism. News, printed on a schedule that was as up-to-date as possible, was the primary purpose of the newspaper, but Bradford in his quest for timely news had to contend with limitations that contemporary circumstances presented. He took most news from other papers, both foreign and domestic; and, although the *Mercury* carried colonial news, foreign news, especially that from England, predominated. Despite Bradford's concern for timeliness, however, his plan for publishing recent and thorough information often was thwarted by

---

[5]E. Wilder Spaulding, "The *Connecticut Courant*, A Representative Newspaper in the Eighteenth Century," *New England Quarterly* 3 (1930): 443, 445.

breakdowns or delays in the colonial communication and transportation systems that were caused by such factors as bad weather and tardy arrival of ships.

Cultural historians agreed that social factors were critical to the nature of the colonial press, and most assumed that the press in turn was important to the life of colonial society. A handful of historians, however, questioned whether the press was really an integral factor in the vitality of America or of individual communities. The most forceful critique of the limited role of newspapers was provided by Ronald Hoffman in a 1969 article, "The Press in Mercantile Maryland: A Question of Utility."[6] After examining the growth of the economy of the upper Chesapeake region from 1760 to 1785 and the press' role in that development, Hoffman concluded that even though newspapers were helpful, convenient, and useful, they were not essential or vital to the prospering of Maryland's merchant community or its economy.

The Developmental School
Although Developmental historians, who provided the largest number of studies of colonial journalism, often considered the press important to colonial society, they were more concerned with the colonial press as the genesis of journalism in America. They viewed the history of journalism as the story of its progress from a crude beginning to its advanced nature during the time of their own studies. It was in colonial journalism that they searched for and often believed they found the origin of many later aspects of the American press. Thus, in general, Developmental historians explained colonial journalism primarily as the beginning of the progress that was to be seen in journalism in the eras that followed. Many of their studies therefore were concerned with documenting journalistic "firsts" and the origins of press practices. Such topics, for example, as English influences on American journalism, pamphlets as predecessors of newspapers, America's first newspaper, its first newspaper chain, its first Sunday paper, the question of what is America's oldest continuously published newspaper, early episodes in the development of freedom of the press, and the origin of advertising abounded in Developmental studies.

The foremost practitioner of the Developmental interpretation was Frank Luther Mott. Although he acknowledged that the press had to be considered in the context of its environment, he was more concerned with documenting the progress of journalism and its practices. His most important work was his history of American journalism published in 1941. *American Journalism; A History of*

---

[6]Ronald Hoffman, "The Press in Mercantile Maryland: A Question of Utility," *Journalism Quarterly* 46 (1969): 536-544.

Newspapers in the United States Through 150 Years: 1690 to 1940
viewed the past primarily as the story of how journalism had
reached its modern state; and Mott entitled his narrative of the colonial press "The Beginners, 1690-1765." He detailed such topics as the
earlier European patterns upon which American publications were
based, pamphlets and other forerunners of the newspaper, and early
episodes involving freedom of the press. Among the journalistic
"firsts" he chronicled were the first American newspaper, Harris'
Publick Occurrences; "the first continuous American newspaper,"
Campbell's *News-Letter*; and the appearance of entertainment and
the first American newspaper crusade, both in James Franklin's
Courant. To these were added narratives of such items as the "first
American newspaper consolidation" (the Boston *Journal* and
Gazette in 1741), the "first serial story in an American newspaper"
(Daniel Defoe's *Religious Courtship* in Samuel Keimer's *Pennsyl-
vania Gazette*), the "first titled essay series in an American paper"
("Plain Dealer" in the *Maryland Gazette*), the first illustration (a
sea-ensign in the Boston *News-Letter* in 1707), and so on.

Although Mott appreciated the fact that colonial newspapers were
operating under journalistically unsophisticated conditions, he
tended to explain the early press in terms of later standards. Thus,
for example, he observed that the Boston *News-Letter*, because of its
content and writing style, "seems very unexciting to a modern
reader" and that Campbell's "theory of the presentation of foreign
news [emphasizing an organized historical record over recency]
gave little consideration to timeliness." Other aspects of the colonial
press such as methods of newsgathering, page appearance, the job of
the editor, and the absence of editorial pages also were explained
with an implicit comparison to later practices. In general, Mott's
evaluation of the colonial press was that it was relatively crude by
20th-century standards but that it had provided a solid foundation
for journalistic practices and achievements that were to come in
later periods. Although he found much lacking in the attitudes and
performance of many early editors, Mott believed that there were
others—such as James Franklin with his attempt to free the press
from control by authorities, Benjamin Franklin with his several
innovations, and the Bradford family of Pennsylvania with their
high standards for printing and their sense of the role of the press—
who had recognized what journalism was supposed to be and do and
had made worthy contributions to the quality and development of the
American press.[7]

Although the numerous Developmental historians normally
shared Mott's viewpoints, they did not agree on one major point:

---

[7]Frank Luther Mott, *American Journalism* (New York: Macmillan, 1941), 3-
70.

whether the colonial newspaper was primarily a journal of news or
an organ of opinion. The contrasting views were apparent as early
as the mid-1930s with publication of Matthias Shaaber's article
"Forerunners of the Newspaper in America" in 1934 and of Edwin
H. Ford's "Colonial Pamphleteers" two years later. Shaaber considered colonial journalism to be based on a tradition of news, whereas
Ford explained the tradition as one of opinion. Before the first
American newspapers were published, according to Shaaber, printers who were interested in serving their own causes or making
money published pamphlets and broadsides containing news. Before 1665, because there were no private commercial presses, most of
the material that was published in the colonies came in official
statements from the government informing the public of government policies and actions. The private, occasional pamphlets and
broadsides which were issued later usually were published on the
occasion of some event such as the death in 1685 of Charles II of England. Thus, journalism, which Shaaber defined as "the printing
and sale of news for the information of the public or for the profit of
the publisher or for both reasons,"[8] had been established almost 40
years before the advent of newspapers and essentially was news oriented. In other studies of colonial journalism, Developmental historians concluded that news was the most important content of newspapers; that essays, statements of opinion, and literary material
were only fillers; and that the press' emphasis on news and sensationalism began not with the penny press in the 1830s as had generally been assumed but with colonial newspapers in the 1700s.

In contrast, Edwin Ford concluded that the most important colonial pamphlets were those by "editorial writers" who helped develop
and lead public opinion on contemporary issues and who laid the
foundation for the later practice of editorial writing. In a descriptive, anecdotal narrative of pamphleteering, Ford explained that the
colonial pamphlet "played no small part in the American pre-news-
paper era by establishing the precedent of sound, intelligent comment on public affairs by men who were leaders in national and
civic life." The pamphlets "may reasonably be considered the colonial progenitors of the modern American editorial," according to
Ford, and the "tradition of independent and fearless expression of
opinion" which the pamphleteer "had handed down was to set the pattern for generations of future American editors."[9]

Developmental historians who shared Ford's view generally
agreed also that colonial journalists were libertarians who opposed

---

[8]Matthias A. Shaaber, "Forerunners of the Newspaper in America," *Journalism Quarterly* 11 (1934): 346-347.

[9]Edwin H. Ford, "Colonial Pamphleteers," *Journalism Quarterly* 13 (1936):
24, 25, 36.

the control that civil and religious authorities had in colonial thought and society. Thus, they considered one of the primary aspects of colonial press history to have been journalists' struggle for liberty and equality against authorities, whom historians usually viewed negatively as oppressors of civil liberty and free thinking. Some Developmental historians reasoned that one of the earliest major victories of colonial journalism had been in freeing itself from the influence of religious authorities. They argued that the press, in a struggle against the theocracy that controlled colonial society, won its freedom from interference by religious authorities in a gradual process as a byproduct of the larger issue of freedom of expression. With such an outlook, Developmental historians credited even Samuel Keimer, whom most historians had considered an eccentric publisher at best because of his encyclopedic approach to publishing information, with redeeming merit because he helped free the colonial newspaper from religious influence. Chester Jorgenson wrote that Keimer's *Pennsylvania Gazette*, which Jorgenson concluded had as its underlying characteristic an emphasis on science and rationalism, provided the "dawn of the emergence of a liberal spirit suggestive of English deism" and as such helped destroy the control that religious orthodoxy traditionally had held over the press.[10] Various other historians pictured the colonial journalists in such roles as heroes of freedom of the press who had the temerity to oppose authority, guardians of the liberties of the public, and opponents of racism. The picture of colonial journalists that emerged from Developmental historians generally was one of stalwart fighters for the rights of the press and the welfare of the public.

Discussion

The key concern of historians of the colonial press has centered on the question of how the press can best be understood: as the projection of the personality and character of the individuals who ran the newspapers, as an institution whose development and character were the result of the general forces in colonial society, or as the origin of American journalism. Grouped around this central question are a number of others that historians have asked or that are in need of being answered. Several of the questions focus on the nature of historical study itself.

1. If individuals were, as the Romantic historians believed, the key factors in colonial newspaper history, what was the character of those individuals? Did the Romantic historians paint an unrealistically favorable picture of the newspaper operators?

---

[10]Chester E. Jorgenson, "A Brand Flung at Colonial Orthodoxy: Samuel Keimer's 'Universal Instructor in All Arts and Sciences,'" *Journalism Quarterly* 12 (1935): 272-277.

2. Did Romantic historians place too much importance on the role of the individual, as the Cultural historians claimed? Or did the Cultural historians themselves, by emphasizing outside forces, inaccurately downplay the role of the individual?

3. In attempting to demonstrate that cultural forces influenced the press, what evidence is necessary? Is it adequate to produce, as Cultural historians have tended to do, evidence of general trends in society, or must the historian demonstrate a direct relationship between such forces and individual newspapers?

4. What role did ideas about the practice of "journalism" play in the colonial press?

5. How appropriate is it in historical study to read back into history, as Developmental historians have been prone to do, the principles of "proper" journalism as practiced in the historians' own time?

6. What seems to have been the essential nature of the colonial press?

7. What factors accounted for that character?

Readings

Romantic School

Benjamin, S. G. W., "A Group of Pre-Revolutionary Editors. Beginnings of Journalism in America," *Magazine of American History* 17 (January 1887): 1-28.

Parton, James, Ch. 7, "The First Sensation Paper," pp. 72-96, *Life and Times of Benjamin Franklin.* New York: 1864.

Cultural School

Brigham, Clarence, "Advertisements," pp. 27-36, *Journals and Journeymen.* Philadelphia: University of Pennsylvania Press, 1950.

Cook, Elizabeth C., Ch. 2, "The New England Weekly Journal," pp. 31-56, *Literary Influences in Colonial Newspapers, 1704-1750.* New York: Columbia University Press, 1912.

Eberhard, Wallace B., "Press and Post Office in Eighteenth-Century America: Origins of a Public Policy," pp. 145-154, Donovan H. Bond and W. Reynolds McLeod, eds., *Newsletters to Newspapers: Eighteenth-Century Journalism.* Morgantown, WV: School of Journalism, West Virginia University, 1977.

Hoffman, Ronald, "The Press in Mercantile Maryland: A Question of Utility," *Journalism Quarterly* 46 (1969): 536-544.

Kobre, Sidney, "The First American Newspaper: A Product of Environment," *Journalism Quarterly* 17 (1940): 335-345.

Spaulding, E. Wilder, "The *Connecticut Courant*, A Representative Newspaper in the Eighteenth Century," *New England Quarterly* 3 (1930): 443-463.

Wroth, Lawrence C., "The First Press in Providence," American Antiquarian Society, *Proceedings* 51 (October 1941): 351-383.

Developmental School

Aldridge, A. Owen, "Benjamin Franklin and the *Pennsylvania Gazette*," *Proceedings of the American Philosophical Society* 106 (1962): 77-81.

Ford, Edwin H., "Colonial Pamphleteers," *Journalism Quarterly* 13 (1936): 24-36.

McMurtrie, Douglas C., "The Beginnings of the American Newspaper," pp. 7-28, *The Beginnings of the American Newspaper*. Chicago: Black Cat Press, 1935),

Mott, Frank Luther, Ch. 1, "First Newspapers in 'The New England,'" pp. 3-23, *American Journalism*. New York: Macmillan, 1941.

Nelson, William, "Some New Jersey Printers and Printing in the Eighteenth Century," American Antiquarian Society, *Proceedings* 21, n.s. (1911): 15-56.

Nordin, Kenneth, "The Entertaining Press: Sensationalism in Eighteenth-Century Boston Newspapers," *Communication Research* 6 (1979): 295-320.

Shaaber, Matthias A., "Forerunners of the Newspaper in America," *Journalism Quarterly* 11 (1934): 339-347.

4

American Revolutionary Printers, 1765-1783: Powerful Radicals or Ineffective Conservatives?

In the 1760s newspapers began to give a growing amount of attention to issues involved in the relationship between the American colonies and Great Britain. With Parliament's passage of the Stamp Act of 1765, the issues became more sharply focused. The act provided that various items, including newspapers, be printed on stamped paper that carried a special tax. Newspapers responded in various ways, but by some fashion or another all avoided printing on the stamped paper. The Stamp Act and the newspaper reaction to it served as catalysts for the beginning of what is considered the Revolutionary period in media history.

As issues intensified during the following years, newspapers adopted a variety of responses. Some became leading voices for trenchant Patriot calls for independence, whereas some urged continued loyalty to England. A few attempted to take a neutral ground. As radical Patriots grew more vocal, however, the Loyalist newspapers and neutral ones alike found that their positions were increasingly unpopular and at times dangerous. Eventually, most Loyalist papers were silenced or found safety only under the protection of the British military, and neutral ones adopted the Patriot stance.

With the onset of hostilities in 1775, conditions for newspapers quickly grew difficult. Their fortunes depended on which army controlled the local town. One of their biggest problems was the shortage of supplies, especially newsprint. Paper prices increased sharply, and newspapers frequently found themselves with no paper on which to print. The war also added difficulties to a news-gathering system that was in peacetime crude at best. Newspapers relied on the chance arrival of private papers, official messages, and other newspapers. Each paper printed some local information, which other papers picked up. The war also increased the tardiness of news. Military campaigns, poor financing, and bad roads hampered the postal service; and English newspapers, always a prime source of news, were received irregularly. Newspaper mortality also was great, with only half of the 70 journals that printed at one time or another during the war still in operation at its end.

The role the press played in the events of the period, and likewise the effect the period had on the press, have intrigued historians. Were printers the advocates of revolutionary thought, or were they traditional in attitudes and moderate in actions? Did they influence a move in American public opinion toward acceptance of independence, or did they have little effect on American thinking and on the conduct of the Revolution itself? Historians, reflecting the views of their times on both the American Revolution and the nature of journalism and mass communication, have given vastly different answers to these questions.

How the press performed under the circumstances that the Revolution imposed is the thread that ties together most historical works on the Revolutionary press. Some historians—primarily those interested in detailing the development of the modern profession of journalism—studied the press of the Revolutionary period with less regard for the relationship between the war and newspapers than for evolutions and changes in journalistic practices. These historians were attracted particularly to such details as the content of newspapers, procedures of news coverage, and economic aspects of running a printing shop. They thought of Revolutionary printers more as early practitioners of journalistic ideals than as partisans in political conflict. This view gained strength beginning in the 1930s as journalism developed stronger and stronger characteristics as a profession and as journalism educators began to write about history. Most historians, however, were more interested in the press as it related specifically to the independence movement and the Revolution. Among such historians there were sharply divergent views.

In general, two broad topics provided the sources of disagreement. One was the political attitudes that printers held; the other was the amount of influence printers exercised in the initiation and the outcome of the Revolution. In analyzing Revolutionary printers' attitudes, most historians argued that printers truly were ideological revolutionaries in their views on liberty and political democracy. A more recent group of historians, however, was not nearly so favorable in its evaluation of the printers' attitudes. These historians, who had viewed the growth of journalism as a business in the 20th century and who believed that economics could explain the primary motivation of people's actions, concluded that printers had taken particular stands on Revolutionary issues because such stands would benefit their printing businesses.

On the question of the influence writers and printers had on the Revolution, historians split into two clearly opposing schools. The traditional and predominant school accepted with little doubt the conclusion that the press had exercised pervasive impact in both bringing about the Revolution and effecting the American victory.

The other school—which gained adherents beginning in the 1950s, when research into persuasive theory of mass communication began to question the media's influence on public opinion—challenged the traditional acceptance of the effectiveness of the Revolutionary press. It argued instead that real events were more important than propaganda and writers' arguments in molding public opinion.

The Nationalist School

The ideological interpretation of Revolutionary printers as revolutionary in their attitudes has been an enduring one. It was propounded in the first history of American newspapers, Isaiah Thomas' *History of Printing in America* (1810), and has its advocates even today. Yet the underlying concepts of historians who argued that the printers were radical differed considerably, and historians who came to the same conclusion about printers' ideology disagreed on their motivations. Historians of the 19th century, who basically were nationalistic in outlook, took pride in America's dedication to liberty and pictured Patriot printers and writers as staunch advocates of democracy while portraying Great Britain in the role of tyrant.

In the mid-1800s historical works especially tended toward biography, and historians singled out a number of prominent printers and writers for treatment. William Wells' biography *The Life and Public Services of Samuel Adams* (1865) typified the Nationalist approach. Adams, Wells wrote, was the leading advocate of American independence, the "Father of the Revolution." British "royal vengeance," therefore, would have made him "the first victim of the scaffold" had the Revolutionary effort failed. Because "the righteous principle of the Revolution is admitted, and posterity has reaped the benefits resulting from its successful achievement," Wells explained as his reason for writing Adams' biography, "it is but justice that his part in the great drama should be ascertained." His subject, Wells observed, "toiled. . . long and arduously to secure. . . the goodly heritage of freedom" for other Americans and possessed a deep "desire for the advancement of his country, . . . incorruptible integrity and republican simplicity of character." A frequent contributor of essays to newspapers, Adams "warned his countrymen against the growing usurpations of power by the mother country, and endeavored to keep the principles of Colonial rights before the public." His writings provided evidence of "his amazing industry, his courage, ceaseless vigilance, and wise statesmanship, and his cheerfulness and fortitude amid disasters. They display his early championship of Colonial rights. . . ; his positive principles at the dawning of the Revolution; his far seeing, yet prudent measures for effecting a separation from the mother country, when redress of grievances was evidently hopeless; his ingenious and gradual direction of public opinion into an habitual contemplation of Independence. . . ."[1]

In his classic work *Journalism in the United States from 1690 to 1872* (1873), Frederic Hudson, although a Developmental historian, combined the Nationalist approach with an emphasis on printers as the leaders of the Revolutionary movement. He viewed the period of the Revolutionary press, which he defined as 1748 (when Samuel Adams founded the *Independent Advertiser*) to 1783, as "an important era in journalism and liberalism everywhere." America's news centers, Hudson wrote, became its revolutionary centers also, much because of the repressive and capricious actions of Britain. "The arbitrary acts of the agents of the home government," he argued, "the Stamp Act, the persecutions of the Franklins and the Zengers, began to react upon the people." Patriot printers, exhibiting their tolerance for opposing viewpoints, attempted to keep their papers impartial, even though in sentiment they favored the American Patriot movement. However, the retaliatory actions of Tories—including, for example, the withdrawal of advertising—finally forced printers to give up impartiality, and the press became one of the leaders in the vigorous growth of a spirit of independence. "Men of brains," Hudson declared, "became constant and fearless contributors to the Press. . . [and all] the leading minds had become editors, pamphleteers, and agitators. All others were readers and believers." Samuel Adams' *Independent Advertiser*, for one, "was assisted by a club of ardent young rebels. . . [and] was full of free thought and free speech." Edes and Gill's Boston *Gazette* very early "was the resort of the leading spirits of that day," a decade before the Boston Massacre and 15 years before the signing of the Declaration of Independence.[2]

The Progressive School

A similar conclusion about printers' ideology emerged from a later group of historians, but these historians took issue with the positive view of mainstream American ideals that the 19th-century Nationalist school had propounded. Instead, they argued that the American Revolution was as much a revolt against the control America's wealthy class had on the country as against English authority. These Progressive historians, most of whom believed that conservatives were motivated primarily by economic self-interest, reasoned that those Revolutionary printers served best who had advocated the

---

[1]William V. Wells, *The Life and Public Services of Samuel Adams* (Boston: Little, Brown, 1865), vi, viii, 30, ix.

[2]Frederic Hudson, *Journalism in the United States from 1690 to 1872* (New York: Harper and Row, 1873), 102, 105, 127.

cause of the common man against the economic and political domination by the elite.

This view was most apparent in a number of studies of Tom Paine. Although early historians often had condemned Paine as an atheist and radical who opposed responsible government, biographies of Paine by Moncure Conway and Eric Foner, both critics of elitism in America's social, economic, and political structure, painted him as an advocate of freedom, truth, and democracy. Conway's *The Life of Thomas Paine*, published in 1892, was the first book-length biography of Paine and was intended to rescue his reputation from the opprobrium of a conservative America that detested his radical religious and political views. Conway, like Paine, opposed traditional social values. Born into an aristocratic family in the antebellum South, he later was influenced by the philosophy of Ralph Waldo Emerson and entered the Unitarian ministry. For the remainder of his life Conway was a critic of America's smug Victorian society and used the pulpit to prick the conscience of America's conservative, wealthy class. With these views, he found much to admire about Paine.

Likewise, Foner supported the working class and opposed the special favor and position that America's wealthy held. In his 1976 biography *Tom Paine and Revolutionary America*, he described Paine as an opponent of hereditary authority and a proponent of representative government. From an impoverished background himself, Paine wished to help the downtrodden, advocated the rights of the common man, and proposed separation from England as the means of achieving those goals. Although he believed in the importance of property and wealth, he was opposed to hereditary privilege and advocated egalitarianism instead. Thus, he became a leading advocate of a liberal, democratic philosophy; and his primary goal was to replace the inequalities and abuses of colonial society with a democracy of equality.

Likewise, Progressive historians condemned Revolutionary printers who failed to support social justice and class equality. They believed printers' business interests frequently provided the motivation for their social attitudes. Influenced by concerns over American racial attitudes and the civil rights of America's Black citizens in modern society, these historians focused their attention on racial views in early America. In studying the Revolutionary press, they concluded that later prejudice had its origin in colonial times and that even those printers who supported Patriot liberty in the Revolution had little concern for the welfare of Negroes. In general, they concluded that Revolutionary printers were a prejudiced group with repressive views.

In "The Image of the Negro in the *Maryland Gazette*, 1745-75" (1969), Donald Wax attempted to discover the journalistic origins of present-day attitudes about race. The *Gazette*, he said, presented the colonial "image of the Negro as property and hence subject to further exchange." Stories in the *Gazette* offered readers "a Negro whose total image was many-sided and complex, an image which saw the Negro as property but which also revealed his human qualities." Those qualities that portrayed the slave in derogatory terms, however, received most attention. Thus, the *Gazette* gave the overall picture of Blacks as potentially violent, criminally inclined, infantile, comic, and possessing other similar traits. Because such a portrayal indicated White attitudes toward Blacks, today's "pattern of race prejudice and discrimination," Wax concluded, "are deeply set in the nation's past."[3]

In a similar study of Philadelphia journalism during the Revolutionary period, William Steirer Jr. argued that printers were anything but radical in their views of Blacks. Steirer's 1976 article "A Study in Prudence: Philadelphia's 'Revolutionary' Journalists" examined the issues of the role Blacks were to play in the colony and state of Pennsylvania as discussed in the press. He found that Philadelphia's printers had only a few moments when they spoke out boldly for reform of the racial and slave systems in America. Steirer explained the editors' reluctance to champion liberalized practices in terms of their financial interests. The editors, he said, were small businessmen who wished to protect their investments and who feared that advocating reform would have been flirting "with financial troubles that no small printer/businessman needed." Thus, he argued, the editors who supported independence from Britain were not dedicated to reforming society. Instead, "prudence and caution, not bravery and idealism," dominated their attitudes and behavior.[4]

The Economic School

Steirer's views on the motivations of Revolutionary printers closely resembled those held by a group of recent historians who began to give more attention to the economic motivations of printers. Many of these historians, however, concluded that printers' attitudes had little to do with political or social ideology but were determined by their business interests solely. Although resembling Progressive historians in their emphasis on economic causes in history, these historians—unlike the Progressives—placed little emphasis on class conflict. They were writing at a time when 20th-century news media had come to be run to a large extent by corporations and pub-

---

[3]Donald Wax, "The Image of the Negro in the *Maryland Gazette*, 1745-1775," *Journalism Quarterly* 46 (Spring 1969): 73-80, 86.

[4]William F. Steirer Jr., "A Study in Prudence: Philadelphia's 'Revolutionary' Journalists," *Journalism History* 3 (1976): 16-19.

lishers who devoted more attention to business operations than to journalistic aspects of the media. Economic historians argued that the same such interest in newspapers as business properties could be found among publishers in all eras of American history. Thus, these historians reasoned, in determining Revolutionary printers' attitudes, financial factors were of prime importance. In general, they concluded that one of two situations normally existed: that printers would have preferred to be neutral and objective but wound up supporting those groups that provided the income to printers, or that printers set out to make money and cared little about what stands they had to take or journalistic practices they had to use to make their operations profitable.

O. M. Dickerson, for example, argued that the primary reason the British were able to keep the loyalty of colonial editors such as James Rivington and John Mein was the government's awarding of printing contracts. In "British Control of American Newspapers on the Eve of the Revolution"[5] (1951) Dickerson concluded that because printing was a business, printers normally ran material that was favorable to authorities who controlled the purse strings and that printers who wished to receive government business had to act as government advocates. Editors on the Patriot side of the conflict found themselves in a similar situation.

In "David Hall and the Stamp Act"[6] (1967) Robert Harlan analyzed the *Pennsylvania Gazette* printer's ideological journey to the Patriot viewpoint. Hall, realizing that his newspaper was the most important financial aspect of his printing business, allowed the *Gazette's* editorial policies to conform more and more to those of the Patriots as opinions polarized following the Stamp Act crisis. It was apparent to him that his policy of nonalignment had been the chief cause of a substantial decline in subscriptions and that he was in danger of losing his paper if he did not reverse his policy. Although Harlan thus emphasized the financial motivations behind Hall's ideology, he concluded that even though the printer's conversion to the Patriot cause was occasioned by financial considerations, the change in ideology was not insincere and that by 1766 Hall's new beliefs were firmly fixed, thus changing a former loyal subject of the British government into an enemy.

Of a similar tone was Alfred Lorenz's 1972 biography *Hugh Gaine: A Colonial Printer-Editor's Odyssey to Loyalism*, with a subject whose change in ideology was exactly opposite that of Hall. Gaine, according to Lorenz, was primarily oriented toward busi-

---

[5]O. M. Dickerson, "British Control of American Newspapers on the Eve of the Revolution," *New England Quarterly* 24 (1951): 455-468.

[6]Robert Harlan, "David Hall and the Stamp Act," *The Papers of the Bibliographical Society of America* 61 (1967): 13-37.

ness and did whatever was necessary to prosper. During a period in which partisanship was expected of editors, Gaine successfully straddled the fence to gain financially. To some extent, however, his stand was a result of his belief that a newspaper should be fair and impartial. Because of his nonpartisanship and emphasis on the financial operation of his newspaper, he contributed substantially, Lorenz argued, to the development of modern business-oriented, objective journalism.

Although historians such as Harlan and Lorenz were not entirely critical of Revolutionary printers' profit motivation, Dwight Teeter argued that the sole purpose of some editors was to make money and that ideology and journalistic principles were irrelevant. Teeter's 1975 article "John Dunlap: The Political Economy of a Printer's Success" traced the *Pennsylvania Packet* printer's career as he maneuvered through the Revolutionary war in a quest to better his business position. Although the war was disastrous for some of his competitors, Dunlap conducted his paper to gain favor with politically powerful men. In his attempt he was successful and, Teeter claimed, typical of printers of his time. In the *Packet's* operation and in his other business ventures, Teeter concluded, Dunlap was "the quintessence of the successful eighteenth-century printer-businessman who used his ties to government to assist in building a fortune. . . . He was doubtless what many enterprising printers of the eighteenth century hoped to become: rich."[7]

The Consensus School

Such emphasis on class and social differences and economic motivations was severely challenged by Consensus historians. Reacting against the Progressive explanation of the Revolutionary press as an agent in a conflict between groups over the social and economic structures, these historians argued that even though Americans may have disagreed on isolated issues, their differences took place within a broader realm of agreement on underlying principles. The Revolution and the press' role in it, Consensus historians argued, were primarily democratic rather than economic or social.

The foremost advocate of this interpretation was Bernard Bailyn. He expounded the argument first in his 1965 work *Pamphlets of the American Revolution, 1750-1776* and then elaborated it in *The Ideological Origins of the American Revolution*, the 1967 winner of both the Pulitzer Prize and the Bancroft Prize for history. Pamphlets were perhaps the most important forum for the expression of opinion during the Revolutionary period, according to Bailyn. They revealed that "the American Revolution was above all else an ideolog-

---

[7]Dwight L. Teeter Jr., "John Dunlap: The Political Economy of a Printer's Success," *Journalism Quarterly* 52 (1975): 3-8, 56.

ical, constitutional, political struggle. . . [and] that intellectual developments in the decade before Independence led to a radical ideal-
ization and conceptualization" of American attitudes. The ideas of
England's "Commonwealthmen" such as John Trenchard and
Thomas Gordon, who had advocated radicalism on behalf of religious dissenters, social radicals, and politicians opposing the government, were transmitted directly to the colonists. American leaders feared that a sinister conspiracy had developed in England to
deprive citizens of the British empire of their long-established liberties. It was this fear that lay at the base of the views expressed in the
pamphlets. The ideas in the pamphlets then became the determi-
nants in the history of the period by causing colonists to change their
beliefs and attitudes. These ideas challenged traditional authority
and argued that "a better world than had ever been known could be
built where authority was distrusted and held in constant scrutiny;
where the status of men flowed from their achievements and from
their personal qualities, not from distinctions ascribed to them at
birth; and where the use of power over the lives of men was jealously
guarded and severely restricted."[8]

In studies that analyzed the newspaper press but was much more
limited in scope, Maurice Cullen Jr. reached the same conclusion
as did Bailyn. In a 1969 article entitled "Middle-Class Democracy
and the Press in Colonial America," Cullen examined the public's
economic opportunity, the extent of political democracy, and the
colonies' literacy rate and concluded that the Revolution was not a
class struggle, as Progressive historians had argued. Instead, he
suggested, in its most basic form it was a fight for democracy, with
the press itself seeking political separation from England.[9]

The Developmental School
Developmental historians argued, however, that printers were not
essentially partisan, political, or oriented toward profit. Primarily
concerned with the development of journalistic practices including
objectivity and impartiality, these historians generally viewed with
favor printers' attempts to avoid taking sides in the Revolutionary
dispute. The predominant view of the Developmental school of interpretation was that those printers who became partisan did so only
after they found that impartiality was difficult in practice. "The
very nature of the printer's business," wrote Charles Thomas in
1932, "made neutrality in a civil struggle impossible for him. The
ordinary inhabitant, even though he favored one side and had no

---

[8]Bernard Bailyn, ed., *Pamphlets of the American Revolution, 1750-1776*
(Cambridge, MA: Belknap Press, 1965), "Introduction."

[9]Maurice R. Cullen Jr., "Middle-Class Democracy and the Press in Colonial
America," *Journalism Quarterly* 46 (1969): 531-535.

desire to be neutral, could remain in a city and conduct his business regardless of the fortunes of war if he was willing to remain quiet; but the editor of a newspaper could not remain quiet. The few who tried to remain neutral soon discovered such a course to be impossible."[10]

These Developmental historians considered journalism history to be, in effect, the unfolding of the story of the evolution of modern press practices. Their view of the past was molded by journalism standards of their own times, and they normally evaluated journalism of the past by those standards. They were especially concerned about the challenge the partisan political conditions of the Revolutionary period presented to the journalistic ideals of nonpartisanship, impartiality, press independence, and freedom of expression.

One of the earliest studies to enunciate this view was S. I. Pomerantz's "The Patriot Newspaper and the American Revolution"[11] (1939). Pomerantz was less concerned with the Revolutionary press as an instrument of the Patriots than as an early institution of acceptable journalistic practices. He directed his attention to newspapers of New York and New Jersey and argued that they deserved praise for their journalism principles and high standards. Editors, he observed, did commendable jobs in news reporting, avoidance of personal abuse in their arguments, accuracy of information, moderation of tone, open-mindedness toward the conflicting sides in the Revolution, and adherence to principle.

A number of Developmental historians in lengthier studies of individual printers added detail to Pomerantz's evaluation. In *William Goddard, Newspaperman* (1962) Ward L. Miner gave particular attention to the printer of the *Maryland Journal* as a fearless advocate and defender of freedom of the press. Goddard, although pro-Patriot in sentiment, insisted on freedom to print material from both sides of the conflict and would not withhold news critical of the colonial viewpoint even though Patriot mobs attempted to intimidate him. In a similar vein, Richard Hixson explained Isaac Collins, founder and editor of the *New-Jersey Gazette*, as an individualist who sympathized with the Patriot cause but who defended his right to print whatever material he wished. He would not "willingly compromise," Hixson wrote, "on matters of truth or principle or the high professional standards he set himself."[12]

The nonpartisan view of Developmental historians was perhaps

---

[10]Charles Thomas, "The Publication of Newspapers during the American Revolution," *Journalism Quarterly* 9 (1932): 358.

[11]S. I. Pomerantz, "The Patriot Newspaper and the American Revolution," 305-331, in R. B. Morris, ed., *The Era of the American Revolution* (New York: Columbia University Press, 1939).

[12]Richard Hixon, *Isaac Collins: A Quaker Printer in 18th Century America* (New Brunswick, NJ: Rutgers University Press, 1968).

most evident in a work by Robert Ours on the Tory printer James Rivington. Whereas Rivington's contemporaries and most non-Developmental historians had considered Rivington to be an aristocratic enemy of the colonial cause, Ours viewed him as a praiseworthy advocate of press objectivity and truthfulness. In "James Rivington: Another Viewpoint" (1977) Ours described the New York printer—who was the "best hated of all Tory editors" because Patriots thought he distorted and slanted facts—as an individual who stood up for his beliefs in impartiality and neutrality. Freedom of the press, argued Ours, "dictated that he, as a printer, open his columns to all viewpoints. That he attempted to do this seems clear upon a close inspection of his newspaper." Because of this journalistic philosophy, Ours credited Rivington with a major contribution to American journalism, for he "had an excellent pattern to offer journalists in his policies regarding impartiality and freedom of the press." However, Rivington's "direct legacy to American journalism virtually was nil—largely because of his reputation as a Tory liar," an unfortunate outcome because "his newspaper was one of the better ones in the colonies."[13]

This Developmental view of press impartiality received an elaborated interpretation with the publication of Kenneth Stewart and John Tebbel's *Makers of Modern Journalism* in 1952. Stewart and Tebbel agreed that the press should be impartial toward sides in political conflict, but they reasoned that the press itself should be in conflict with authority. Thus, whereas non-Developmental historians had considered the press to be an arm of the Revolutionary movement because of partisan motives, Stewart and Tebbel argued that the press should oppose authority, no matter what the nature of that authority, because the primary purpose of the press is to guard against power-seeking officials. They viewed the entire history of American journalism as a struggle of the press against such individuals and saw the Revolutionary press as the genesis of journalists' recognition that their proper role was an anti-government one. American newspapers, they wrote, "began as the voice of revolution"; and, although in the 20th century they swung "from radical revolt to solid conservatism," throughout history they have been distinguished by "a freedom of thought and action unsurpassed anywhere else in the world." During the colonial period the press remained "the tool of government" because officials feared to set it free; but in the period just preceding the Revolution, printers demonstrated that the press "could be used as a powerful instrument of revolt, and thereby realized the worst fears of tyrants and dicta-

---

[13]Robert M. Ours, "James Rivington: Another Viewpoint," in Donovan Bond and W. Reynolds McLeod, eds., *Newsletters to Newspapers: Eighteenth-Century Journalism* (Morgantown: West Virginia University, 1977), 219, 230.

tors." The Revolutionary printers thus laid a foundation for American journalism, whose practitioners "have been considered dangerous men by those who crave absolute power and authority." Such authorities, Stewart and Tebbel declared, have "for centuries. . . recognized clearly. . . that a printing press in the hands of a man who is bound in its use only by the voice of his own conscience is a threat to total government."[14]

The Communication-Effects School

Despite such diverse interpretations, the historical view of printers as advocates of revolution and liberty dominated, and a number of historians proceeded to an analysis of a related subject. The question they attempted to answer was this: Assuming that printers and writers favored independence, what influence did they have on bringing about the American Revolution and on its execution?

Most historians agreed with the assessment of David Ramsey in his 1789 work, *History of the American Revolution*. He asserted that writers had been indispensable. "[T]he pen and the press," he wrote, "had merit equal to that of the sword."[15] Ramsey accepted without question the view that typified his era: that the press was of enormous importance in molding public opinion. Such a belief has underlain most historical studies of the role of the press in the Revolution. With that belief as a starting point, most historians' works were attempts primarily to document how the press exercised its potential for persuasion. Typical of this viewpoint was S. G. W. Benjamin's 1887 article "A Group of Pre-Revolutionary Editors. Beginnings of Journalism in America." Placing his study in the framework of biographies of printers, as most Nationalist historians did, Benjamin provided brief narratives of a number of individuals from Benjamin Harris in 1690 through the Revolution and based his history on the thesis that the early American press had served as a great power in influencing public attitudes and events. Favorably viewing the positive role of the press in helping bring about the Revolution, Benjamin declared that colonial printers "understood their opportunity, and made the quill and the printing-press scarcely less potential [sic] in asserting and securing the liberties than the forum and the field."[16]

The first historian to provide an extensive documentation of the influence thesis, however, was Arthur M. Schlesinger. In a number

---

[14]Kenneth Stewart and John Tebbel, "The Editors of Revolt," *Makers of Modern Journalism* (New York: Prentice Hall, 1952), 3-23.

[15]David Ramsey, *History of the American Revolution* (Philadelphia, 1789), Vol. II, 319.

[16]S. G. W. Benjamin, "A Group of Pre-Revolutionary Editors. Beginnings of Journalism in America," *Magazine of American History* 17 (January 1887): 1-28.

of articles and finally a book-length study, he argued that the most important factor in bringing about the Revolution was public opinion and that in changing public opinion the newspaper was the primary agent. In a 1935 article, "The Colonial Newspapers and the Stamp Act," Schlesinger stated his thesis in a preliminary form. When American colonists "began to feel the tightening grip of imperial control after 1767," he said, "they naturally resorted to the printing press to disseminate their views and consolidate a favorable public support."[17] In this and several articles on newspapers in various towns, Schlesinger concluded that the papers were an important medium for propaganda and played a significant role in transforming the public's attitudes. This interpretation then was expounded most completely in Schlesinger's 1958 book, *Prelude to Independence: The Newspaper War on Great Britain, 1764-1776.* The book was intended as a study of the role of the press in bringing about the "real American revolution": the "radical change in the principles, opinions sentiments, and affections of the people" that preceded the Revolution. It detailed the press' part in the reaction to each of the successive events that eventually culminated in the war for independence. Unlike most colonists, who saw events from the limited perspective of their own colony, printer-editors often had moved around among several colonies, Schlesinger wrote, and thus were more continental in their outlook. They therefore held the view that what affected one colony affected all, and they advocated unity among the colonies. The repeal of the Stamp Act, whose passage was unwise because it struck so directly at printers, was a tremendous victory for the press and encouraged printers to more intense opposition to British authority. In many events afterward, such as the Tea Act of 1773 and the public uproar against it, it was the press, according to Schlesinger, that played a leading role. Eventually, the press' agitation resulted in the colonists declaring war. Although Schlesinger pointed out that a number of factors other than newspapers had helped instigate the war, he argued that the independence movement could hardly have succeeded "without an ever alert and dedicated press."

Within a decade after Schlesinger's first article appeared, a number of other historians authored works varying in subject matter but arriving at the same conclusion. Among the most significant studies were John C. Miller's 1936 biography *Sam Adams, Pioneer Propagandist*; a series of articles by R. A. Brown on various northeastern newspapers;[18] and Philip Davidson's detailed 1941 work,

---

[17]Arthur M. Schlesinger, "The Colonial Newspapers and the Stamp Act," *New England Quarterly* 8 (1935): 63-83.

[18]R. A. Brown, "New Hampshire Editors Win the War: A Study in Revolutionary Propaganda," *New England Quarterly* 12 (1939): 35-51; "The Newport Gazette, Tory Newssheet," *Rhode Island History* 13 (1954): 97-108, and

Propaganda in the American Revolution, 1763-1783. At least a score
of later articles and books on various printers and newspapers detailed the influence they had on the Revolution.

Such studies confronted few dissenters while it was generally
accepted that the mass media exercised influence on public opinion.
Beginning in the 1950s, however, more and more research into the
effects of mass communication in modern America started casting
doubts about the media's persuasiveness. In light of such research, a
number of historians started to exhibit a more dubious attitude toward contentions that the press of the past had exercised a strong,
pervasive influence on American society. Borrowing on recent
communication theory, several historians of the Revolutionary
press began to examine it without being predisposed to conclude that
it had influenced colonists' attitudes toward independence. Generally, these historians reasoned that colonists' predisposition and
events of the real world had a greater impact on shaping public opinion than the press had.

This reinterpretation of press influence was presented most cogently in Carl Berger's *Broadsides and Bayonets: The Propaganda
War of the American Revolution* (1961). A study of both American
and British propaganda efforts in various media during the war
years of the Revolution, the book argued that propagandists' schemes
were less meaningful in affecting opinions and beliefs than were
events such as military victories. Words were less important than
facts. By 1777 at the latest, Berger argued, most minds were made
up, and there was little that propaganda efforts could do to change
them. British and American supporters and officials made a number of attempts to convert, persuade, or intimidate people who seemed
vulnerable, but most were futile. Both sides failed in their efforts
aimed at achieving such goals as subverting the Hessian allies of
Britain, winning support of American Indians, and fomenting a
slave insurrection in the American South. Because hard facts and
people's beliefs about what was really occurring held more weight
than what propagandists told people to believe, Hessians remained
loyal to their military agreements with Britain, Indians stayed
neutral or took sides as they were impelled by solid economic or political motives, and Britain's provocation of slave insurrection
merely embittered and fortified slaveholders. The greatest impact
on public opinion, according to Berger, came not from the work of
propagandists, such as Benjamin Franklin's diplomacy in Europe,
but from the news of the war, such as the American victory at
Saratoga. As a rule, Berger concluded, neither persuasive appeal,
nor threats, nor tricks could compare in influence with military

14 (1955): 11-20; and "The Pennsylvania Ledger: The Tory News Sheet,"
Pennsylvania History 9 (1942): 161-175.

victories or political and economic facts.

Discussion

Because of the critical importance of the Revolutionary period to American history, the subject of the Revolutionary press continues to be a topic of lively debate, and a number of questions confront historians.

1. The most provocative question remains the nature of the motivation and ideology of printers. Were these early newspaper operators dedicated to the ideals of liberty and democracy, as the early Nationalist and later Consensus historians believed? Or did printers betray their true reactionary motives by their failure to advocate liberal social reform, as Progressive critics argued?

2. As with other periods in media history, the Progressive historians' warm attachment to liberal ideology raises questions about the balance of their perspective. In arguing their case that printers were motivated by financial self-interest and narrow social views, have Progressive historians made a convincing presentation?

3. Whether one accepts the Progressive or the Nationalist /Consensus view, the enticing question of press influence on the Revolution remains. Was the press important in affecting pubic opinion, or was it ineffectual?

4. What evidence is necessary to argue the case? In the absence of "scientific" evidence required by today's social and behavioral theorists among communication researchers, can the historian justifiably make claims about press influence on the Revolution? On the other hand, is it any more valid to make claims that the press was *not* influential?

5. The debate over press influence during the Revolutionary period raises the broader question for historical research, "How must the historian go about examining media influence?"

Readings

Nationalist School

Hudson, Frederic, Part 3, "The Revolutionary Press," pp. 102-140, *Journalism in the United States from 1690 to 1872*. New York: Harper and Row, 1873.

Wells, William V., Ch. 13, "Debates in Parliament. . . ," pp. 268-281, *The Life and Public Services of Samuel Adams*, Vol. I. Boston: Little, Brown, 1865.

Progressive School

Foner, Eric, Ch. 4, "Paine, the Philadelphia Radicals and the Political Revolution of 1776," pp. 107-144, *Tom Paine and Revolutionary America*. New York: Oxford University Press, 1976.

Steirer, William F., Jr., "A Study in Prudence: Philadelphia's 'Revolutionary' Journalists," *Journalism History* 3 (1976): 16-19.

Wax, Donald, "The Image of the Negro in the *Maryland Gazette*, 1745-1775," *Journalism Quarterly* 46 (1969): 73-80, 86.

Woodward, W. E., Ch. 4, "Paine Writes a Best Seller," pp. 66-84, *Tom Paine, America's Godfather*. New York: Dutton, 1945.

Economic School

Dickerson, O. M., "British Control of American Newspapers on the Eve of the Revolution," *New England Quarterly* 24 (1951): 455-468.

Harlan, Robert, "David Hall and the Stamp Act," *The Papers of the Bibliographical Society of America* 61 (1967): 13-37.

Lorenz, Alfred L., Ch. 7, "Fair Liberty's Call," pp. 50-64, *Hugh Gaine: A Colonial Printer-Editor's Odyssey to Loyalism*. Carbondale: Southern Illinois University Press, 1972.

Parker, Peter J., "The Philadelphia Printer: A Study of an 18th Century Businessman," *Business History Review* 40 (Spring 1966): 24-46.

Yodelis, Mary Ann, "Who Paid the Piper? Publishing Economics in Boston, 1763-1775," *Journalism Monographs* 38 (1975).

Consensus School

Bailyn, Bernard, Ch. 1, "The Literature of Revolution," pp. 1-21, *Ideological Origins of the American Revolution*. Cambridge, MA: Belknap Press of Harvard University Press, 1965.

Skaggs, David C., "The Editorial Policies of the *Maryland Gazette*, 1765-1783," *Maryland History Magazine* 59 (1964): 341-349.

Sloan, Wm. David, and Maurice R. Cullen Jr., Ch. 3, "The Revolutionary Press, 1765-1783," pp. 43-61, Wm. David Sloan, James G. Stovall, and James D. Startt, eds., *The Media in America*. Worthington, OH: Publishing Horizons, 1989.

Developmental School

Hixson, Richard F., Ch. 4, "Newspaper Editor," pp. 85-113, *Isaac Collins: A Quaker Printer in 18th Century America*. New Brunswick, N J: Rutgers University Press, 1968.

Mott, Frank Luther, "The Newspaper Coverage of Lexington and Concord," *New England Quarterly* 17 (1944): 489-505.

Ours, Robert M., "James Rivington: Another Viewpoint," pp. 219-234, Donovan Bond and W. Reynolds McLeod, eds., *Newsletters to Newspapers: Eighteenth-Century Journalism*. Morgantown: School of Journalism, West Virginia University, 1977.

Pomerantz, S. I., "The Patriot Newspaper and the American Revolution," pp. 305-331, R. B. Morris, ed., *The Era of the American Revolution*. New York: Columbia University Press, 1939.

Stewart, Kenneth, and John Tebbel, Ch. 1, "The Editors of Revolt," pp. 3-23, *Makers of Modern Journalism*. Englewood Cliffs, NJ: Prentice Hall, 1952.

Thomas, Charles, "The Publication of Newspapers during the American Revolution," *Journalism Quarterly* 9 (1932): 358-373.

5

The Party Press, 1783-1833:
Political Sycophant or Party Leader?

During the decade following the end of the Revolution, what had appeared to be a unity among Americans based on common values began to splinter. By the mid-1790s political differences had grown so sharp that the people of the new nation began forming factions. The earliest factions grew into the Federalist and Republican parties. With the demise of the first party system, factions coalesced into two new parties, the Whigs and the Jacksonian Democrats.

The ardent political feelings of the period had a profound effect on the press. Newspapers took on an increasingly political nature, and a distinguishing feature of the period was the press' intimate involvement with partisan politics. Newspapers such as the *Aurora* of Philadelphia, first under the management of Benjamin Franklin Bache and then of William Duane on the Republican side, and the *Gazette of the United States* on the Federalist, subverted all their operations to serving a political cause. Many of the newspapers became prominent in party operations from the local level all the way to the national capital.

Going hand-in-hand with the political nature of the press were practices that defied what today we consider the proper standards of newspaper practice. Party newspapers submerged news to political argument, for example, and worked closely with partisan cohorts rather than operating independently. Partisan fervor frequently gave vent to scurrilous attacks on opponents, violating today's ideal of moderate, objective writing.

Party newspapers predominated in America from the 1780s until the mid-1800s, finally giving way to the more popular penny newspapers. As a result of the partisan nature of the press, few periods in the history of the American media have been subject to as varied evaluation as that of the party press. For most of the 19th century, partisan journalists were treated as romantic personal figures who participated in a crucial epoch of political history. In the early part of the 20th century, many of them were considered heroes who had helped wage the fight for broader democracy against wealthy aristocrats dedicated to rule by the elite. For most of this century they have been denigrated as nothing better than publishers of scurrility and sycophants to politicians. Recently, however, their reputations have begun to be restored by a handful of historians who believe they performed as well as they could and often as political leaders in conditions that were difficult at best.

Historical evaluation of partisan journalism thus has tended to extremes. On one hand, the period of the party press has been described as the worst years of American journalism's history, indeed almost not worth studying. On the other, party editors have been interpreted as important figures in the development of the American political system.

The Romantic School

A majority of the 19th century Romantic historians, writing within a framework of narrative biographies of editors from the Northeast, explained the party press within the contexts of a Hamiltonian-Jeffersonian split of 1789-1816 and a Whig-Jacksonian split of 1824-1832. Although journalists often were chronicled as literary figures, most of the historical works were predominantly political in tone, with most attention devoted to the press against a panorama of national politics. Because historians typically were gentlemen from New England's socially and politically elite families, they tended to react negatively to the shift away from the aristocrats' participation in government that had occurred with Jefferson's and Jackson's elections. Most historians treated Federalist and Whig editors, who had been on the side of elitist rule, favorably. They sometimes blamed Republican and Democratic editors for the exclusion of men of higher principles from public office and for their replacement by men who pandered to the desires of the mass public. Although Romantic historians usually approached their subjects from a partisan point of view, most of them, regardless of their political leanings, were strongly nationalistic and considered the history of America as the advancing revelation of the nation's leadership role in mankind's improvement. They viewed the American press as highly influential and as one of the primary factors in the advance.

They interpreted party press editors as honorable men of high character and motives who fulfilled the American ideal of achievement that could be made in a society of opportunity and individualism. They had known many of their subjects as personal friends and therefore held them in high regard, as men who were, as one historian wrote, "universally respected and beloved by those who knew them." The editors seemed to these historians to be men of "good sense and probity of purpose, temperateness and moderation ... [who] amidst all the heats of faction... never fell into violence... [and enjoyed] both reputation and many friends.... By [their] constant merit. . . sober sense. . . moderation, and. . . integrity, [they] won and invariably maintained the confidence of all on that side of politics with which [they] concurred. . . and scarcely less concili- ated the respect of. . . opponents."[1]

The Romantic interpretation of the party press was readily ap- parent in the work of Joseph T. Buckingham. A journalist who, among other achievements, founded the Boston *Courier*, a pro-Whig paper, in 1824 and had worked with the journalists of the party press, he was, like most Romantic historians, intimately acquainted with many of the people and episodes about which he wrote. One of the ear- liest histories of American journalism, Buckingham's *Specimens of Newspaper Literature: With Personal Memoirs, Anecdotes, and Reminiscences* (1850) combined narrative history with autobiogra- phy. Composed primarily of pleasant and anecdotal descriptive bi- ographies, it emphasized journalists whom Buckingham had known and extracts from their papers, most of which were in New England. Favoring the Federalist and Whig causes, Buckingham spoke of the editors of those parties as high-minded men.

Most other Romantic historians provided similarly favorable biographies. They observed in party journalists a combination of characteristics comprised in part of nationalism, patriotism, love of the freedoms bestowed by America, strong character, and influence in national affairs. In his biography *Noah Webster* (1883), which emphasized the Federalist editor as a "man of letters," Horace Scudder described Webster as a man who "liked to think that he had a hand in pretty much every important measure in the political and literary history of the country in those early days."[2] Basing the bi- ography largely on Webster's own diary, Scudder explained him as a patriot who loved his nation and all the benefits it made possible for its citizens. The party journalist as a man of strong character provided the interpretive theme for George S. Merriam's *Life and Times of Samuel Bowles* (1885). Although the study dealt primarily with the journalistic career of Samuel Bowles II after 1844, it de- scribed him in the 1820s and 1830s as a young newspaperman who had ambition for great achievements and a character to effect them. Merriam interpreted Bowles, who took over the editorship of the Springfield (Mass.) *Republican* from his father, as an important figure in journalism and American society who exercised a wide influence on both. Merriam's work illustrated well the Romantic concept of the growth of a man and the betterment of mankind and its institutions. Bowles was sincere and bold in his beliefs and, as a result, developed to fulfill his individual potential for good. In the

---

[1]Charles Lanman, "The 'National Intelligencer' and Its Editors," *Atlantic Monthly* 6 (October 1860): 481, 471.

[2]Horace Scudder, *Noah Webster* (Boston: Houghton Mifflin, 1883), 6.

progress of journalism, according to Merriam, the "old partisan" style of journalism was replaced in the 1830s with a "new journalism," the penny press. Although Merriam considered the advance in journalism favorably, his concept of progress did not decry—as the 20th-century Developmental interpretation did—the party press. Merriam simply assumed that journalism, like mankind, was moving forward in that relentless stream of progress ordained by natural law.

The Progressive School

As the Progressive reform movement swept America after 1900, party press historians became more sympathetic to the liberal causes of the Jeffersonian and Jacksonian press, and a shift took place in its historical interpretation. Republican and Democratic editors replaced Federalists and Whigs as the more popular subjects. A majority of historians came to view the Jeffersonian and Jacksonian editors as advocates and protectors of the rights of the people. Some Progressive historians viewed the history of the press as a means of pointing out its contrasts with the press of the 20th century, which they believed was controlled by conservative financial forces and served the interests of the business class against the rights of the people. They considered the Jeffersonian and Jacksonian press especially important in the fights against aristocratic rule, to guarantee fuller participation of the public in the affairs of the nation, and to assure fuller civil liberties, especially freedom of the press. Progressive historians described the political split as one between the liberal and idealistic views of the Jeffersonian and Jacksonian editors and the conservative and materialistic views of the Federalists and Whigs. They looked especially favorably on the importance of the Republican press to a democratic society, while praising Jefferson's views on freedom of the press. They viewed the liberal political system that the Jacksonian press emphasized as the natural triumph of the democratic ideal. Progressive historians emphasized the importance of journalism to democracy and political advance throughout American history. They praised Republican and Democratic editors for their contributions to the growing rights of the people. Writing from a clearly pro-Jeffersonian/Jacksonian point of view, they reasoned that the Republican and Democratic newspapers had as their purpose representing "the people" in a political fight between the rich and the poor. They contended that Jefferson and Jackson wanted to use the press to establish the rule of public opinion and the Federalists wanted to use it to give perpetual political control to the aristocracy.

The Progressive ideological dichotomies were enunciated in Richard Hooker's *The Story of an Independent Newspaper: One Hundred Years of the Springfield Republican, 1824-1924* (1924).

Hooker identified the Springfield (Mass.) *Republican* with the fight against elitism and the ultimate triumph of democracy in America. The paper was born, he said, to be a partisan voice opposing aristocratic Federalism and advocating democracy. Its founder, Samuel Bowles I, "recognized the need of a determined direction for the new paper, which was to be 'a genuine democratic press' representing the Republicans." Despite the attempts of wealthy men to sway the course of the paper, Bowles rejected "the lure of greater financial returns, to be had for the paper through the practice of other ways."[3]

Similarly, William E. Smith wrote of the most prominent Jacksonian editor in the fight for democracy. In "Francis P. Blair, Pen-Executive of Andrew Jackson" (1931) Smith described the Washington *Globe's* editor as "the greatest partisan journalist and defender of Jacksonian democracy." Jackson, Smith reasoned, was the true representative of the people and depended on their support for his political triumphs, and he was able to obtain it through the "tremendous" influence of Blair and his paper. Blair, who "was of the people and had lasting faith in them," was instrumental in Jackson's democratic program because he "effectually convinced the multitudes of the good intents and purposes" of Jackson.[4]

The Progressive interpretation of the party press was presented in its most provocative form with the publication of Bernard Fäy's *The Two Franklins: Fathers of American Democracy* in 1933. In a laudatory account, Fäy described Benjamin Franklin Bache, editor of the Philadelphia *Aurora*, as the most important of the Republican leaders who brought about America's sweeping changes in political ideas and democratization between 1790 and 1800. Even more than such leaders as Thomas Jefferson and James Madison, Fäy suggested, Bache formulated Republican political strategy, directed its attack, "first gave. . . form to radical opinion in the United States and fashioned the Democratic Party."[5]

Although such a Progressive approach to interpreting the party press declined in the following years, a number of other works in the Progressive tradition appeared even until recently, most approaching Republican editors as liberal and progressive leaders. Later stages of historical interpretation also have reflected the conflict approach embodied in the Progressive school of historiography and generally have been inclined more to favor the Jeffersonian-Jacksonian editors than those on the Federalist-Whig side.

---

[3]Richard Hooker, *The Story of an Independent Newspaper* (New York: Macmillan, 1924), 7, ix.

[4]William E. Smith, "Francis P. Blair, Pen-Executive of Andrew Jackson," *Mississippi Valley Historical Review* 17 (March 1931): 543.

[5]Bernard Fäy, *The Two Franklins* (Boston: Little, Brown, 1933), 361.

The Developmental School

In its persistence and acceptance, the Developmental interpretation—which began in the mid-1800s and continued to gain strength for the next century—provided the most pervasive and enduring explanation of the party press. Developmental historians were especially interested in the outstanding newspapers and editors that had influenced the progress of the press. Within such a structure, the party press fared poorly. Historians concluded that not only was the political period of journalism a dead one but also that the character of the press was deplorable and that the most important advances in journalism were simply the establishment of more newspapers and an increase in publication frequency. The party period's partisanship and scurrility led Developmental historians to name it as among America's least meaningful and its newspapers as among the worst. They regarded the party press years as some of the bleakest and darkest of American journalism. The era of the partisan press, as a result, was attributed little importance and was neglected as relatively insignificant. Because newspapers were partisan, Developmental historians assumed that the political period was an unjournalistic one that offered little of importance to the historical development of the press. They usually derided editors for subservience to politicians and for the abusiveness of their attacks on opponents.

When historians attempted to show the value of the party press, they attributed it to nonpartisan areas such as enlargement of press freedom, development of editorials, and admission of reporters to sessions of the United States Congress. Positive studies were restricted to limited areas of journalistic techniques or to individual newspapers and journalists whom their biographers described as being atypical and better than contemporaries. These historians pictured the individual editors and newspapers as being caught in their partisan journalistic time but attempting to perform by higher professional standards. In the mainstream of the Developmental interpretation, however, the party period was considered at best a transitional period in the development of American journalism and at worst a fairly meaningless period devoid of journalistic progress but filled with irresponsible personal and political attacks.

Such an interpretation was founded on the historical assumption that journalism had been developing as a matter of natural progress to the condition in which historians viewed it in their own time. Tending to view the past from their own temporal perspective and to evaluate journalism of the past by standards of the historians' own age, the Developmental historians interpreted the press by standards including thorough, fast, accurate, objective news; enlightened and effective presentation of opinion; mass popularity; and a combination of press independence and responsibility. Because the party press' performance of and progress toward those standards were weak, partisan journalism fared poorly with Developmental historians. The party press met neither the standard of independence from politicians nor the standard of unbiased reporting and temperate editorial comment.

The attitude of Developmental historians was due to the professionalization of the occupation of journalism. The first Developmental history of American journalism, Frederic Hudson's *Journalism in the United States, from 1690 to 1872* (1873), was also the first survey history to deal with the party press period after penny newspapers had appeared. Many journalism historians since Hudson drew heavily on his interpretations and information. Hudson had been managing editor of the New York *Herald*, a paper that emphasized news over opinion more than did any other papers of the mid-1800s. With his news-oriented background, he thus evaluated earlier newspapers in terms of how they conformed to the concept of a newspaper as a news medium and a journal popular with the masses of readers and independent of party influence. He included narratives of various episodes involving newspapers and biographical character profiles of leading journalists and then concluded that the party press was primarily political in nature, that politicians controlled it, that it was important and influential in politics, that it was vituperative, and that the partisan period was a negative one from the standpoint of journalistic development.

The primary problem, he suggested, was that the press was under political control and therefore was prevented from developing professional standards. Newspapers were necessary to "place the nation on a solid foundation. . . . Journalism, however, had not yet become a profession. It was a power with the people, but it was managed by ambitious political chiefs, as armies are manoevered by their generals. It was, during these fifty years [1783-1833], a Party Press." During the party period, Hudson admitted, the press had progressed in some areas, but "its views and opinions on public affairs were the inspiration of politicians and statesmen. Editors. . . felt their power in all elections, and in all great questions that agitated the public mind, but they were bound to party. Independence of opinion and expression, outside of party, was political and financial ruin." Despite such problems in journalism, Hudson with the historian's hindsight could see that the penny press would soon emerge and thus could observe that "the world was moving, and its soul was marching on."[6]

As the field of journalism in the late 1800s began to professionalize, interest in the history of the profession began to grow. As a re-

---

[6]Frederic Hudson, *Journalism in the United States* (New York: Harper and Row, 1873), 142.

sult, historical studies of the press increased in number. Although differing on a few particulars, they largely echoed Hudson's themes. Benjamin Ellis Martin provided the first refined elaboration of the party press as an insignificant and scurrilous episode in the development of journalism in "Transition Period of the American Press—Leading Editors Early in This Century" (1887). Unifying the biographies of political editors from the 1790s to the 1820s was the theme that the partisan press was unique for "its coarseness and cruelty, its venomous vigor of invective, its contempt for all that should be sacred in political warfare and in private life."[7]

As journalism in the 20th century became more sophisticated as a profession, it developed more standards considered appropriate and proper for the press. Historians, many of whom had a background in the profession, began to apply even more universally the concept of professional development, so that, after Progressive history had crested, the Developmental interpretation pervaded most historical studies. Many works were devoted entirely to chronicling the development of particular aspects of journalism such as the editorial function and news gathering, whereas others were based implicitly on the assumption of development.

The Developmental interpretation of the party press as scurrilous, subservient to politicians, and insignificant in the professional evolution of journalism became entrenched with the publication of a number of survey history textbooks over the next half century. In *History of American Journalism* (1917), James Melvin Lee stated his criticism of the party press even more strongly than Hudson had done and provided a model of the party press that most later textbooks would use. Party newspapers, as Lee described them, excelled in libelous and scandalous attacks. "The darkest period in the history of American journalism," he declared, "was that which began at the close of the second war with England [War of 1812], a time truthfully characterized as the 'period of black journalism.'" As measured against proper standards, he concluded, the party press was degraded, filled as it was with vile and gross personal attacks and insults. In addition to failing in the area of temperateness, it also failed because, as the organ of parties, it did not perform its "legitimate" journalistic functions. The proper functions, Lee reasoned, were independence and concern for truth.[8]

By the time of Lee's book, the growth of journalism education was being felt as an influence on the study of history; and his work was followed by the publication of a number of other textbooks, in-

---

[7]Benjamin Ellis Martin, "Transition Period of the American Press— Leading Editors Early in This Century," *Magazine of American History* 17 (April 1887): 273.

[8]James Melvin Lee, *History of American Journalism* (Boston: Houghton Mifflin, 1917), 143.

cluding one by a prominent educator who was to have a major impact on the direction of historical interpretation. Although the party press seemed to have sunk as low as possible with Lee's history, it was with the publication of Frank Luther Mott's textbook that partisan journalism's reputation as a black mark on American journalism was most firmly stamped.

In *American Journalism: A History of Newspapers in the United States through 250 Years, 1690 to 1940* (1941) Mott interpreted press history within the Developmental paradigm, refined the critical explanation of the party press Lee had given, and coined a phrase that a number of other historians picked up as aptly characterizing journalism in the early 1800s. Mott, rewording Lee's description, termed the period 1801-1833 the "Dark Ages of American journalism." He found little good to say about the party press. "The most notable feature of the journalism of the years 1783-1801," he declared, ". . . was the ardent partisan political propaganda." During the years of 1801-1833, he said, few papers were ably edited, and they abounded with vituperation, abuse, and corruption.[9]

Such a view of the party press pervaded historiography for much of the 20th century. Individual editors—who had been popular topics of biographies by the Romantic and Progressive historians—rarely were selected for study, and those who were often received harsh treatment. Similarly, the party press was found wanting in contributions to the improvement of important techniques in American journalism. In a survey of the history of news, for example, Edith Merwin Bartow's *News and These United States* (1952) criticized party editors, "still notorious" for their "shrill and bitter" writing,[10] for failing to appreciate the significance of the news behind the major social and political currents of their time. The partisan nature of the party press limited its quality, Bartow explained, and honest reporting was not accepted, making the papers poorly, recklessly, and futilely conducted.

The Cultural School

In the fourth stage of interpretation—that of Cultural history which began in the 1920s—there emerged a generation of historians who began an attempt to reevaluate the character of the party press. Some historians in the school began to look at the party press in its own social and cultural milieu without reference to the professional evolution of journalism. Although Developmental historians attempted to explain the press as an institution somewhat separate from society,

---

[9]Frank Luther Mott, *American Journalism: A History of Newspapers in the United States through 250 Years, 1690 to 1940* (New York: Macmillan, 1941), 169, 113.

[10]Edith Merwin Bartow, *News and These United States* (New York: Funk and Wagnalls, 1952), 84, 85.

Cultural historians began to consider the party press as a part of society and therefore influenced by various features outside the press itself. How such forces as economics, politics, technology, and culture acted on or influenced the press became a prime concern of historians. Thus, such questions as what factors were responsible for the founding of newspapers and under what financial conditions newspapers operated began to involve the historians' interest. In effect, Cultural historians reversed the Romantic and Progressive approach to studying journalism. The working of society on the press—rather than vice versa—provided the starting point of much historical work.

Some early cultural studies—such as those by Donald H. Stewart and Jerry W. Knudson—continued to reflect the Developmental influence. Stewart's *The Opposition Press of the Federalist Period* (1969), a revision of his 1950 doctoral dissertation, provided primarily a collection of Republican newspaper comments on various political topics. Although Stewart suggested that newspapers were important in the first party system, he generally was critical of the tone and methods of the press, pointing up its many excesses. He did, however, attempt to justify the party press in part with the Developmental argument that some editors, contrary to prevailing practices, did try to operate "under standards of decency, reasonableness, and impartiality."

Like Stewart's book, Knudson's several articles on the Federalist-Republican press were based on a doctoral dissertation and largely reprinted newspaper quotes. Although his work indicated that the party press was important to the political system and functioned with great vitality, Knudson implied that the period of party journalism constituted, in Mott's terms, a "dark ages." His dissertation detailed the editorial reactions of four Republican and four Federalist papers to the administrations of Jefferson from 1801 to 1809 on seven major issues and secondarily attempted to describe the development of various journalistic techniques. In "Political Journalism in the Age of Jefferson" (1974), a distillation of the dissertation, Knudson pointed out that partisan journalism was operating strongly during the years of America's first party system and that Bache's and Duane's *Aurora*, not the more temperate *National Intelligencer* as other historians had contended, was the leading Republican paper. While pointing out the vitality and effectiveness of the party press, Knudson at the same time concluded that "partisan journalism was costly for the prestige of the institution of the press."[11]

Although Cultural historians for the most part worked within the

---

[11]Jerry Knudson, "Political Journalism in the Age of Jefferson," *Journalism History* 1 (1974): 23.

Developmental framework and continued to interpret the party press disparagingly, in the 1960s a second generation of Cultural historians began to design a counterargument to the "dark ages" evaluation of the party press. Most of their interpretation was based directly on studies of the newspaper role in the political system. In contrast to earlier scholars, these historians suggested that the party press should be evaluated less on its contributions to journalistic development and more on the part it played in American politics. They argued that the Developmental approach evaluated the party press without regard to the fact that no such standards as political independence and impartiality that Developmental historians applied were recognized in the early 1800s and that journalists envisioned their role as a political, not a neutral, one. Slighted, according to these historians, was the fact that the party press made invaluable contributions to the development of the American political system at the most critical time in its history. Although this argument resembled that of the Progressive historians, the recent Cultural historians did not base their interpretation primarily on a liberal-conservative ideological split as the Progressive historians did. The interpretation was based on journalistic/political rather than ideological considerations.

Most of these historians in effect dismissed the idea that the American press had been developing throughout its history to its present state. They suggested that the press of the past cannot be evaluated by standards of the present, but rather should be measured by how well it fulfilled its specific purpose. The purpose of the partisan press, they reasoned, was primarily political. The revolutionary egalitarian ideas about government that emerged during the period profoundly affected the nature of journalism. Editors found themselves in the middle of the political struggle that was going on, first a struggle between Republicans and Federalists and later between Jacksonian Democrats and Whigs. The purpose of editors, according to historians, was not to be impartial, but to fight however they could for the victory of one side or the other. Because the nature of the political system was based ultimately on the will of the people, appealing to public opinion became crucial. The primary tool for doing so was the newspaper. In such an environment, the press took on a political function. Its intent, these historians said, was not to be primarily a news medium. Nor was it even to be impartial, and editors became devoted advocates of causes and, in some instances, leaders within parties. Because the avowed purpose of the party press was to be partisan, historians argued that it can be understood only by a clear recognition of its political intent.

The first historian to attempt a major reevaluation of the party press was William E. Ames. In a series of studies on the political press of Washington, D.C., he argued directly that the party period did not constitute a "dark age" of journalism. Because of the limitation on acceptable campaigning methods during the second party system, he and Dean S. Olson suggested in "Washington's Political Press and the Election of 1824" (1963), the press was an important and probably influential factor in the election. Newspapers, they pointed out, were the "sole means of communication of the candidates to the voters." The party caucus in 1824 had broken down, the campaigning was waged on personality rather than on issues, and personal campaigning was frowned on, all being factors contributing to the importance of the role the press played. As a result, Ames and Olson concluded, "the campaign was waged largely through the newspapers. . . [which] responded to the need of the times and the candidates."[12] In two subsequent studies, Ames attempted to refute the historical cliché that political patronage had corrupted the party press. Instead, he argued, it freed newspapers from potential pressures that could be exerted by either advertisers or mass reader interests. The party press as a result often operated independently from outside financial influences.[13]

In his most detailed work on the party press, *A History of the National Intelligencer* (1972), Ames described his purpose as an attempt to confront the "dark ages" concept by showing that the Washington newspaper, even though founded as a partisan journal, performed by high journalistic standards. In effect, he thus used a quasi-Developmental approach while refuting the Developmental interpretation. Basing his observations of the party press as a whole on his study of the *National Intelligencer*, he generalized that "political journalism, rather than being the dark age of the American newspaper, offered a higher quality information and interpretation of American society than at any other time in American history."[14] Contrary to prevailing historical opinion, he argued, government patronage increased the number of papers with competing viewpoints, the coverage of government news, and the diversity of news interpretation.

In more broadly based studies, two other historians, Gerald J. Baldasty and Wm. David Sloan, attempted to revive the party press' historical standing through examining the roles newspapers played in the early party systems. Baldasty, a former student of Ames, not

---

[12]William Ames and Dean S. Olson, "Washington's Political Press and the Election of 1824," *Journalism Quarterly* 40 (1963): 344, 350.

[13]William E. Ames and Dwight L. Teeter, "Politics, Economics, and the Mass Media," in Ronald T. Farrar and John D. Stevens, eds., *Mass Media and the National Experience* (New York, 1971), 38-63; and William E. Ames, "Federal Patronage and the Washington D. C. Press," *Journalism Quarterly* 49 (1972): 22.

[14]William E. Ames, *A History of the National Intelligencer* (Chapel Hill: University of North Carolina Press, 1972), ix.

only attempted to refute the "dark ages" evaluation but also argued that Democratic editors were more than journalistic leaders. They were leaders in the political party. The press, he said, provided a "forum for public opinion. . . but its role in American political society was far more extensive. In particular, editors formed the nucleus of political organization in the 1820s and 1830s, and thus were central to the dramatic growth in partisan activity that characterized the age of Jackson."[15] Newspapers served as leaders on a national level, but they also occupied that role in localities throughout the nation. After examining newspapers in New York State, Boston, Charleston, and Washington, D.C., Baldasty concluded that newspapers in the national capital provided the leadership for partisan news and opinion, thus giving cohesiveness to party organization, and that contemporaries considered newspapers essential if victory were to be achieved at the election polls. "The political editor was much more than a scurrilous pen-for-hire," Baldasty suggested in reference to the traditional criticism of the party press. "Some editors. . . gained national recognition as political analysts, debaters and even as important advisors to politicians and statesmen." The role they played was in part journalistic, but it also was political. Party editors "were more than writers, for they served in elective office, as party spokesmen, and as campaign organizers." They were, in effect, "leaders of the new party system."[16]

Taking an approach similar to Baldasty's, Sloan also argued that partisan editors were integral to the party system. He directed his attention, however, to America's first party system—that of the Federalists and Republicans—and to the role of the press in national rather than local politics. In several articles published in the 1980s, he critiqued the Developmental interpretation of the party press and pointed out that party papers performed a number of functions that were central to the operation of national politics. Party editors, he suggested, believed that they were working during a time of important political questions and that "they would have failed in their devotion to truth and in their duty to serve the best interests of their country had they not stood up for their political convictions."[17]

---

[15]Gerald J. Baldasty, "The Press and Politics in the Age of Jackson," *Journalism Monographs* 89 (1984): 2.

[16]Gerald J. Baldasty, "The Boston Press and Politics in Jacksonian America," *Journalism History* 7 (1980): 104, 108. See also Baldasty, "The Charleston, South Carolina, Press and National News, 1808-47," *Journalism Quarterly* 55 (1978): 519-526; "The New York State Political Press and Antimasonry," *New York History* 64 (July 1983): 261-279; and "The Washington D.C. Political Press in the Age of Jackson," *Journalism History* 10 (1983): 3-4, 50-53, 68-71.

[17]Wm. David Sloan, "The Early Party Press: The Newspaper Role in American Politics, 1789-1812," *Journalism History* 9 (1982): 19. For a similar

Examining the party papers within the context of the political conditions of their own times, Sloan argued that historians had erred by judging them according to later standards. He found that scurrility, for example, the style of expression for which historians had condemned party editors, was natural for the times and politicians often encouraged it. Neither were editors motivated primarily by monetary reward, as some historians had claimed, but instead were sincerely committed to the ideological causes they supported. In the end, he argued, "the party press must be evaluated by its importance to the early political system. It cannot be explained or measured in terms of today's standards of a neutral or adversary relationship of the press to government. The party press was an integral part of the political system and was regarded as such by politicians and journalists."[18]

Discussion

The strong sentiments on politics that many journalists and historians hold have been both baneful and beneficial for the study of the party press. The strong interest in politics has attracted historians to that subject, but today's ideas about the independence of the press from politics have tended to influence historical views on party press practices. That raises the question of what role today's values and attitudes should play in historical study.

1. Can historians properly understand the party press by looking at it in the context of today's standards?

2. Which is more appropriate: to evaluate the press by the practices of the time or by standards considered proper for the press in the historian's time?

3. If the historian does not apply today's perspective, of what value is the study of history to people of today?

4. In terms of the party press, which approach offers more value: to examine the newspapers in the context of their role in the early political system, or by today's standards of the press' political independence?

5. Regardless of which approach is used, historical study has left a number of questions about the party press. The most significant deals with the essential nature of the press. Was the press a critical factor in the political system, or was it a journalistic failure?

---

view, see Sloan, "The Federalist-Republican Press: Newspaper Functions in America's First Party System, 1789-1816," *Studies in Journalism and Mass Communication* (Spring 1982): 13-22.

[18]Wm. David Sloan, "Examining the 'Dark Ages' Concept: The Federalist-Republican Press as a Model," *Journal of Communication Inquiry* 7 (Winter 1982): 114-115. See also Sloan "Scurrility and the Party Press, 1789-1816," *American Journalism* 5 (1988): 97-112; and "'Purse and Pen': Party-Press Relationships, 1789-1816," *American Journalism* 6 (1989): 103-127.

6. Were editors important figures in party politics, or were they the sycophants of politicians?

Readings

The Romantic School

Buckingham, Joseph T., Vol. 2, Ch. 2, "The Columbian Centinel," pp. 58-117, *Specimens of Newspaper Literature: With Personal Memoirs, Anecdotes, and Reminiscence*, 2 vols. Boston: Redding, 1850.

Lanman, Charles, "The 'National Intelligencer' and Its Editors," *Atlantic Monthly* 6 (October 1860): 470-481.

Scudder, Horace E., Ch. 4, "Political Writings," pp. 111-149, *Noah Webster*. Boston: Houghton Mifflin, 1881.

The Progressive School

Fäy, Bernard, Ch. 5, "The Dawn of the *Aurora*," pp. 196-207, *The Two Franklins: Fathers of American Democracy*. Boston: Little, Brown, 1933.

Payne, George Henry, Ch. 10, "After the Revolution," pp. 135-152, *History of Journalism in the United States*. New York: Appleton, 1920.

Smith, William E., "Francis P. Blair, Pen-Executive of Andrew Jackson," *Mississippi Valley Historical Review* 17 (March 1931): 543-556.

The Developmental School

Bartow, Edith Merwin, Ch. 7, "Cockades To Cocked Hats," pp. 83-99, *News and These United States*. New York: Funk and Wagnalls, 1952.

Hudson, Frederic, Ch. 10, "Organization of the Great Political Parties," pp. 141-157, *Journalism in the United States from 1690 to 1872*. New York: Harper and Row, 1873.

Lee, James Melvin, Ch. 10, "Party Press Period, 1812-1832," pp. 140-163, *History of American Journalism*. Boston: Houghton Mifflin, 1917.

Levermore, Charles H., "The Rise of Metropolitan Journalism, 1800-1840," *American Historical Review* 6 (April 1901): 446-465.

Martin, Benjamin Ellis, "Transition Period of the American Press—Leading Editors Early in This Century," *Magazine of American History* 17 (April 1887): 273-294.

Mott, Frank Luther, Ch. 9, "The Dark Ages of Partisan Journalism," pp. 167-

180, *American Journalism: A History of Newspapers in the United States through 250 Years, 1690 to 1940*. New York: Macmillan, 1941.

The Cultural School

Ames, William E., "Federal Patronage and the Washington D. C. Press," *Journalism Quarterly* 49 (1972): 22-30.

Baldasty, Gerald J., "The Press and Politics in the Age of Jackson," *Journalism Monographs* 89 (1984).

Knudson, Jerry, "Political Journalism in the Age of Jefferson," *Journalism History* 1 (1974): 20-23.

Sloan, Wm. David, "'Purse and Pen': Party-Press Relationships, 1789-1816," *American Journalism* 6 (1989): 103-127.

6

Freedom of the Press, 1690-1800:
Libertarian or Limited?

One of the most pervasive topics in American media history has been freedom of the press. Historians have viewed it as one of the cornerstones of America's political system, and practicing journalists correctly consider it as fundamental to America's system of news, information, and opinion. In the study of press freedom, historians have given special attention to the period from 1690 (when America's first newspaper was founded—and suppressed) to 1801 (when the Alien and Sedition Acts expired). It was that period, they suggest, that saw the genesis of freedom. The foundation of liberty was laid, they reason, during the first century or so of American journalism, for a number of episodes occurred that decided the fundamental concepts of press freedom. The paramount one was the adoption of the First Amendment, which serves as the basis for all American law regarding press freedom. Historians therefore have regarded that early period as critical in determining the nature of freedom of the press, indeed in deciding even whether there was to be freedom, and in serving as the groundwork for most later developments.

Three episodes stand out in the early history of American press freedom. The first was the trial of New York printer John Peter Zenger from 1734 to 1735. His supporters welcomed the jury verdict of "not guilty" as a monumental triumph for freedom against British tyranny. The second—and probably the most important in the entire history of American press freedom—was the adoption of the First Amendment to the U.S. Constitution in 1791, declaring that "Congress shall make no law respecting an establishment of religion, or prohibiting the free exercise thereof; or abridging the freedom of speech or of the press; or the right of the people peaceably to assemble and to petition the Government for a redress of grievances." Despite the wording, in 1798 the Federalist-controlled Congress

By Wm. David Sloan, *University of Alabama*
and Thomas A. Schwartz, *Ohio State University*

passed the repressive Alien and Sedition Acts, the third episode of critical importance. These episodes provided more than ample fodder for the attention of historians.

Historical interpretation of freedom of the press has centered primarily on the question of whether the early American concept was truly libertarian. Historians have differed sharply on whether Americans believed in complete freedom or simply supported it on a limited basis when freedom served their cause. Debate among historians began in earnest with the publication of Leonard Levy's *Freedom of Speech and Press in Early American History: Legacy of Suppression* in 1960. Levy argued that the concept of freedom of the press in early America included no more than freedom from prior restraint. His study, one of the most influential works ever published on journalism history, touched off a tempest.

Previous historiography had consistently assumed that the libertarian tradition was strongly rooted in America from the time the first newspaper appeared. Virtually all historians, no matter when they were writing or what their school of historiography, had written within a libertarian context, viewing journalists as advocates of free expression and the dominant American attitude as one of complete freedom of thought. In the 19th century, Nationalist historians considered the United States the cradle of liberty and the leader for the improvement of mankind. A libertarian acceptance of freedom of expression flowed naturally, they believed, from Americans' fundamental beliefs. The Progressive historians of the 20th century also believed that most Americans were libertarians but that wealthy and aristocratic classes had attempted to suppress freedom of the press. A central feature of American and journalism history, therefore, had been a conflict of social, political, and economic groups, in which the mass, democratic class fought to overcome the repression which the wealthier class had attempted to impose. Progressive historians assumed that elitist leaders had exploited "freedom of the press" for their own ends. Instead of a check on government, the press became a tool for preserving entrenched interests. A third group of Professional (mainly Developmental) historians, writing in the 20th century and composed primarily of professors in law and journalism schools, legitimized the modern approach to the ticklish issues of freedom of expression in favor of the press. The legists sought historical support for a libertarian ideology that offered the "marketplace of ideas" as a constitutional model. Journalism professor-historians sought historical support for the practices and ideals of the journalism profession and for the elevated status of the press.

Levy's work stood these traditional interpretations on their head. Most historians since 1960 have written about freedom of the press in reaction to Levy or have had his assessment clearly in mind. The legal and journalistic historians perceived Levy's research as a danger to their ideologies; and, joined by other historians who held the traditional view of America as a land of liberty, they mounted a vigorous defense of the libertarian position.

The Nationalist School

The Nationalist period provided the initial documentation and interpretation of the history of American press freedom, and its histories ranged from the contemporaneous to the beginning of the 20th century. The authors were men of leisure with the time to pursue history as an avocation, men of professional classes, and journalists with a bent toward history.

The Nationalist historians wrote of freedom of the press in terms of the fulfillment of the individual, incorporating the Enlightenment concept of natural rights into the romantic ideal of the perfection of mankind. Working within a framework of the unfolding advance of civilization, historians attempted to reveal the progress of freedom of the press within an overall story of the developing liberty of mankind and, in particular, of the American people. They viewed the nation itself as the cradle of libertarianism. Most of these historians wrote about freedom of the press in terms of the political splits of early America, between colonists and British authorities and between Patriots and Tories. Their attention centered on the colonial and revolutionary periods, when Americans were struggling to free themselves from oppressive British rule, and virtually ignored the early years of American independence. Fulfillment of human rights, they believed, had been accomplished with the separation from England.

They pictured the sides in the conflict as those who advocated the natural rights of liberty and those who supported authoritarian government. Isaiah Thomas, American journalism's first historian, expressed the Nationalist interpretation of the struggle in classic Enlightenment terms. "The rulers in the colonies of Virginia in the seventeenth century," he said, "judged it best not to permit public schools, nor to allow the use of the press and thus, by keeping the people in ignorance, they thought to render them more obedient to the laws, and to prevent them from libelling the government, and to impede the growth of heresy, &c."[1] Thomas' Enlightenment concept persisted in most histories that followed, even in those written as late as the early 20th century. Robert Livingston Schuyler, for example, in *The Liberty of the Press in the American Colonies Before the Revolutionary War* (1905) wrote that colonists' arguments for freedom were based on their contention that they had

---

[1] Isaiah Thomas, *The History of Printing in America* (Worcester, MA: 1810), 7.

"constitutional" rights as Englishmen and, according to Lockean theory, natural rights as individuals. Their intent, he reasoned, was to safeguard individual liberty from government infringement.

Nationalist historians interpreted specific episodes in the same context, considering, for example, the Zenger case as a landmark in the advance of liberty. In one of the first historical studies of press freedom, Benson J. Lossing in 1878 wrote that the case "was a notable struggle in the province of New York for the maintenance of the liberty of the press." Considered in all its social, political, and historical contexts, "the struggle constituted one of the most important events in the early annals of the state." The controversy, he said, revolved around two factions, one supporting "royalty and its prerogatives; the other . . . sovereignty of the people and freedom of thought and of speech." Placing the Zenger case in the long natural-rights tradition, Lossing reasoned that it involved "the great principles enunciated in the Magna Charta and the Bill of Rights. It raised the question of the right of the subject to criticize the conduct of the ruler, the liberty of speech, and the freedom of the press." Contemporaries viewed it as the beginning of American liberty, revealing the "philosophy of freedom both of thought and speech as an inborn human right."[2] In the standard biography of Zenger, *John Peter Zenger, His Press, His Trial and a Bibliography of Zenger Imprints* (1904), Livingston Rutherford concluded that the trial fulfilled the libertarian concept and made a significant impact on the practice of press freedom. For one thing, he said, it "first established in North America the principle that in prosecution for libel the jury were the judges of both the law and the facts." Second, "the liberty of the press" was made "secure from assault, and the people became equipped with the most powerful weapon for successfully combating arbitrary power, the right of freely criticizing the conduct of public men." Furthermore, the "result of the trial had imbued the people with a new spirit; henceforth they were united in the struggle against governmental suppression."[3]

Even though later historians added some particulars to their studies of early freedom of the press, the libertarian interpretation which the Nationalist historians employed continued as the basis for explaining journalistic freedom.

The Progressive School
The Progressive historians of the early 20th century added the his-

---

[2]Benjamin J. Lossing, "Freedom of the Press Vindicated," *Harper's New Monthly Magazine* 57 (July 1878): 293, 295.

[3]Livingston Rutherford, *John Peter Zenger: His Press, His Trial and a Bibliography of Zenger Imprints* (New York: Dodd, Mead, 1904), 131.

tory of the early independence period of the United States to their studies, assuming that total victory of human freedom from government oppression had not been achieved with independence. Instead, the Progressives viewed with apprehension the Federalist attempts to maintain the political power for the elite. They believed the Alien and Sedition Acts which the Federalists passed in 1798, and the struggle of the masses of common people against them, to be part of the continuing fight of the people to liberate themselves from the suppressive domination by an entrenched, conservative minority.

In one of the most substantial accounts focusing on the progress of American newspaper freedom, *The Development of Freedom of the Press in Massachusetts* (1906), Clyde A. Duniway detailed the slow evolution of liberty within an overall story of the attempt of the people to open government proceedings to public view. In colonial Massachusetts, the royal government tended to place restrictions on freedom of expression and arbitrarily to exercise control over the press. Until 1730 careful supervision of newspapers was specified by law; but editors struggled against restrictions, supervision gradually diminished, and more and more newspapers were published without license. After 1730 the colonial governor was no longer required to maintain censorship, but criminal prosecutions for seditious libel were relied on to check the press. After the Revolution and under the state constitution, unrestricted but undefined freedom became a part of the law. Despite such protection the press still was prosecuted under the Sedition Act, and it was not until the passage of a just and reasonable libel law in 1827 that the press finally gained its complete freedom.

In the struggle for freedom, Republican editors were portrayed favorably by Progressive historians as fighters for liberty, whereas advocates of government restrictions were pictured as tyrants attempting to repress the people. Federalist officials used highhanded methods to enforce restrictive laws, courts packed juries, and Federalist judges interpreted the laws favorably in accord with Federalist sentiment. In *The Public Life of Thomas Cooper, 1783-1839* (1926), Dumas Malone constructed the Progressive portrait of a Republican defender of press freedom. Cooper was convicted under the Sedition Act for a libel of President John Adams, sentenced to six months in jail, and fined $400. One of the earliest advocates of a libertarian doctrine of press freedom, he was fearless in defying the Alien and Sedition Acts, and his most firmly held belief was a person's right to freedom of expression. Malone characterized Cooper as idealistic, individualistic, even radical in his view on the rights of the individual, a philosopher who fit perfectly the pro-Jeffersonian Progressive view of Republicans as pure advocates of democracy.

The Professional/Developmental School

Although the Progressive interpretation of press freedom enjoyed a brief popularity, another approach originating in the early 1900s was more enduring. This approach embraced the dominant libertarian assessment of history and received contributions from three distinct groups of historians. The first was made up of legal scholars interested in the implementation of a libertarian First Amendment policy in the courts; the second, political historians interested in the libertarian approach for a cohesive theory to explain the formation of the republic, including the role of the First Amendment and the press; and the third, media historians interested in the libertarian ideology necessary for the advancement of the journalism profession.

Supreme Court Justices Oliver Wendell Holmes Jr. and Louis Brandeis had fashioned a libertarian interpretation of the First Amendment in court decisions beginning in 1919. Court opinions, however, though essential to contemporary law, did not explain history. The job of analyzing history for legal purposes was left to legal historians. Although the opinions of Holmes and Brandeis and other later libertarian justices contained quotations from the writings of Jefferson and Madison, the citations were highly selective to establish a seemingly irrevocable historical foundation for the modern libertarian perspective. Yet their historical research, such as it was, was of no small significance in the history of freedom of the press. It not only made a substantive contribution to the development of thought on the subject, but it also influenced the way in which historians methodologically approached the subject. Harvard Law Professor Zechariah Chaffee and other legal scholars trained in the adversarial spirit of law schools advocated similar views with thoroughly documented and articulate monographs, which won wide acceptance in intellectual communities.

Until 1960, the prevailing attitude of historians squared with these legalistic justifications for the Supreme Court's jurisprudence. In the 1940s and 1950s, political historians offered explanations of events and trends consistent with the libertarian interpretation. They argued that the thoughts and actions of political leaders and newspaper editors reinforced the position that the modern libertarian theory of freedom of the press was born before the First Amendment. Vincent Buranelli's *The Trial of Peter Zenger* (1957) embodied the libertarian evaluation of Zenger as a heroic advocate of freedom of the press against tyrannical laws and authorities in 1734. Buranelli painted the Zenger episode in black-and-white terms of good versus evil—liberty versus repression—and marked Zenger's trial for seditious libel as a milestone in the American concept of press freedom. Zenger and his supporters, Buranelli wrote, became "something to be referred to whenever the liberties of the subject were endangered."

The two best books on the Alien and Sedition Acts were John C. Miller's *Crisis in Freedom* (1951) and James Morton Smith's *Freedom's Fetters* (1956). Both historians argued that the laws did not express the prevailing sentiment among the American people, but were instead politically motivated attempts by Federalists to silence their opposition, the Republicans. Miller explained that the laws were enacted during a time of perceived national crisis, when a war with France seemed imminent. Federalists used the period of hysteria brought on by the excesses of the French Revolution to their advantage to enact legislation intended to protect themselves from criticism by opponents. Like Miller, Smith concluded that the laws were a logical development of the Federalists' authoritarian views on government and were not in accord with the dominant American attitude toward freedom and democracy. He did argue, however, that the laws had a positive influence in that they played a prominent role in shaping the development of the American tradition of civil liberties, with its emphasis on majority rule and individual rights.

Despite such temporary setbacks as the Alien and Sedition Acts, the libertarian school maintained, the American concept of press freedom has been traditionally libertarian, taking the First Amendment as its guarantee, and has continually expanded. In *The Birth of the Bill of Rights* (1955), Robert Rutland declared that the rights guaranteed in the first 10 amendments were, in the minds of the people of the time, extremely important and inviolable by the government. Even the opponents of the Bill of Rights were advocates of democracy and supporters of the rights themselves, basing their opposition on the argument that having the rights specified in written form might lead to their being interpreted too narrowly.

Media studies concentrated on three subjects: aspects of early philosophies of freedom of the press that resembled modern interpretations, individuals whose journalistic or political behavior seemed to make them heroes in the advancement of enlightened thought, and particular events as landmarks in the hard-fought battle for freedom. Media historians placed all of them in the longer story of the evolution of the press from outside influence and regulation. Individuals who in some way had made contributions to freedom were treated favorably as libertarians, and their service was detailed for how it enlarged the concept and practice of press freedom. When apparent inconsistencies existed in stands the individuals had taken on freedom, historians frequently attempted to rationalize the inconsistencies as fitting into an overall libertarian philosophy. The most popular biographical subjects have been William Bradford, William Goddard, Benjamin Harris, James Franklin, Benjamin Franklin, Philip Freneau, Thomas Jefferson, and John Peter

Zenger. Their actions in defiance of authority were considered advances in freedom, as it is enjoyed today. Media historians viewed such events as the government's suppression in 1690 of America's first newspaper, Harris' *Publick Occurrences, Both Foreign and Domestick*, and James Franklin's publication in the 1720s of his acerbic *New-England Courant* as milestones in the growth of press freedom. They preferred the view that the adoption of the First Amendment vindicated the righteous struggle of the colonial newspapers against authority. Frank Luther Mott's *Jefferson and the Press* (1943), one of the most detailed early studies by a media historian, epitomized the libertarian interpretation of Jefferson as the foremost American libertarian thinker on freedom of the press. In describing his views on freedom and his relationship with journalists, Mott presented Jefferson as a purist philosopher on press freedom who could do little wrong despite the fact that on many occasions journalists treated him harshly and unfairly.

The libertarian theory and history of the First Amendment are arguably the prevailing justification for the modern state of freedom of the press. The libertarian historians' work did not end in 1960, but they were put on the defensive after that point.

Levy and the Revisionist School

Before Leonard Levy published *Legacy of Suppression* in 1960, only a few historians had attempted to explain early freedom of the press outside the libertarian interpretation, and those who did limited their studies to isolated episodes. They made no effort to examine the overall question of whether early American attitudes were truly libertarian or to provide a thoroughgoing revision of the traditional view. Their works stand out because they were among the very few to present divergent interpretations of the early American concept of liberty of expression. In attempting to revise the traditional interpretation, however, they had meager success.

Such was not the case with Levy's work. Indeed, *Legacy of Suppression* was one of the most influential works ever written in changing historical interpretation in journalism. Levy contended that the theory of freedom of expression in early America was narrow, that the First Amendment was not intended to supersede the existing common law against seditious libel, and that it was not until the debates over the Alien and Sedition Acts that a libertarian concept of freedom of expression got a solid foothold. As measured against Levy's libertarian standard, the early American view of freedom of expression fell short.

In colonial times, liberty was advocated in words but "dishonored in practice," according to Levy. English philosophers such as John Locke and John Milton did not disagree with the common law concept that made criticism of government a crime, and subsequent philosophers passed on to American leaders "in unaltered form an unbridled passion for a bridled liberty of speech." When America's proponents of revolution talked of freedom, they intended a freedom confined to themselves and for only those people on their side. Such a philosophy, Levy declared, "is not free speech at all, or at best is an extraordinarily narrow concept of it." Thus, colonial and revolutionary America had little experience with true freedom of expression "as a meaningful condition of life." During the Revolution itself, freedom of the press did not exist, because the trying times of a war are not ideal for nurturing freedom; and liberty existed only for the praise of the Patriot side. Criticism of the Patriot cause, which its supporters claimed was the cause of liberty, "brought the zealots of patriotism with tar and feathers."[4]

Even after the Revolution with the adoption of the Bill of Rights and its guarantee of press freedom, Levy argued, the common law on sedition remained in effect. Although it is uncertain what the writers of the First Amendment intended it to mean, they did not intend complete freedom, and they did not intend to protect criticism of government. Instead, the evidence suggests that they intended to leave the Blackstonian definition of freedom intact and the common law of seditious libel in force. It was not until the public outcry over the Sedition Act, Levy suggested, that American libertarian thought really emerged, although libertarian arguments of the time appear to have been presented primarily for political purposes rather than for the philosophical cause of freedom. The debate did, however, have the effect of casting off the Blackstonian concepts of press freedom and instituting a new American theory of the right of the individual to freedom of expression.

In the 1985 revision of his work, entitled *Emergence of a Free Press*, Levy fortified his interpretation with new evidence and new arguments that true freedom of the press did not exist in the United States until the Sedition Act debates, that the colonial assemblies were more suppressive than royal courts, that the First Amendment was more a consequence of federalism than libertarianism, that the whole Bill of Rights was a political accident, that free press theory was narrow until 1798, and that English libertarian theory was considerably advanced in comparison to American theory of press freedom. Levy revised himself only on the point that press freedom practice was limited in the colonies. After examining 33 colonial newspapers from 1704 to 1820, however, he would accede only that he "was puzzled by the paradox . . . of nearly unfettered press practices in a system characterized by legal fetters and the absence of a theory

---

[4]Leonard Levy, *Legacy of Suppression: Freedom of Speech and Press in Early American History* (Cambridge, MA: Belknap Press, 1960), 105, 87, 176.

of political experience that justified those press practices."[5] In several related works, Levy has also suggested among other things that Thomas Jefferson's attitude toward freedom was restrictive rather than libertarian and that the Zenger verdict was more the result of the forensics of his lawyer, Andrew Hamilton, than a milestone in the development of freedom from the common law of seditious libel.

Another one of the most pointed critiques of traditional assumptions was C. Edward Wilson's "The Boston Inoculation Controversy: A Revisionist Interpretation" (1980). Wilson argued that James Franklin's *New-England Courant*, which had a reputation among historians as the first American newspaper to publish outside governmental authority and the first to conduct an editorial crusade, does not deserve credit for either. The *Courant* campaigned against inoculation for smallpox during an epidemic in Boston in 1722. Franklin opposed inoculation in part because Increase and Cotton Mather, New England's religious leaders, advocated it. Contrary to the traditional historical view that Franklin was the first editor to take up the issue, Wilson argued that the press debate over inoculation already was being waged before the *Courant* began publication, the people of Boston generally shared Franklin's anti-inoculation position (thus making his opposition less significant than it might have been if he had been either the originator or leader of the campaign), and Franklin's campaign had little meaning as a challenge to authority because "the colonial government was either neutral or impotent in respect to newspapers of the time."[6] Neither did Wilson picture Franklin as a defiant, certain advocate of press freedom. Franklin, Wilson concluded, was unsure of his view on freedom of the press and tended to waiver and backpedal on the issue when confronted by authorities.

Although, like Levy, challenging the Libertarian interpretation, a conservative legist argued that Levy naively assumed that the Jeffersonians deserved credit for advances in the American concept and practice of freedom of expression. In "Freedom of the Press and the Alien and Sedition Laws: A Reappraisal" (1970), Walter Berns suggested that Jefferson and his followers were unable to fashion a libertarian philosophy of freedom because they were tied to the Southern system of slavery. Contrary to Levy's assumption, Berns declared, "it was not really a 'broad libertarian theory' that emerged during the fight against the Alien and Sedition Laws," for the principle on which Republicans based their Virginia and Kentucky Resolutions in opposition to the laws was not a liber-

[5]Leonard Levy, *Emergence of a Free Press* (New York: Oxford University Press, 1985), xvii.

[6]C. Edward Wilson, "The Boston Inoculation Controversy: A Revisionist Interpretation," *Journalism History* 7 (1980): 16.

tarian "version of civil liberties but the doctrine of states' rights, or nullification, or disunion." Primarily responsible for the "development of a liberal law of free speech and press—for fashioning a remedy for the deprivation of the constitutional rights of freedom of speech and press—" Berns argued, "were the Federalists Alexander Hamilton and James Kent, who were able to do this because, unlike Jefferson and his colleagues and successors, they were not inhibited by an attachment to the institution of slavery."[7]

The Neo-Libertarian School

Libertarian reactions to Levy came in three forms. One group of historians argued that even if Levy were correct in his conclusion that the philosophy of freedom was limited, real practical advances in freedom did occur. The second confronted Levy's interpretation directly and argued that the weight of early American philosophy was truly libertarian. Finally, a group of legal scholars conducted a spirited defense of the 20th century jurisprudential approach to press freedom, while building an even stronger historical basis for it.

The first group, which was made up almost exclusively of journalism professors, including several at the University of Wisconsin, explained the growth of freedom of the press as a result of political pragmatism, as an outcome of partisan conditions in which certain groups or individuals viewed freedom as beneficial to their causes. Although their arguments for press freedom were motivated largely by selfish interests, their advocacy of freedom often promoted the growth of freedom as a concept and its extension to other members of society. The view of this group was epitomized in the work of Dwight Teeter, a journalism professor specializing in media law. Drawing on research from his doctoral dissertation at the University of Wisconsin, revealingly entitled "Legacy of Expression," he elaborated in a number of studies the thesis that the development of early freedom of the press sprang from freedom's usefulness in practical politics. In "Press Freedom and the Public Printing: Pennsylvania, 1775-83"[8] (1968), he concluded that Philadelphia journalists, although getting financial support through government printing, still criticized the government. They believed newspapers should carry conflicting opinions and that criticism of the government served the public good. In their criticism, they were protected by the maneuvering of political factions and were free from excessive reliance on government's economic support. In a study of an individual journalist, "The Printer and the Chief Jus-

---

[7]Walter Berns, "Freedom of the Press and the Alien and Sedition Laws: A Reappraisal," *Supreme Court Reports* 1970 (1970): 109-159.

[8]Dwight Teeter, "Press Freedom and the Public Printing: Pennsylvania, 1775-83," *Journalism Quarterly* 45 (1968): 445-451.

tice: Seditious Libel in 1782-83" (1968), Teeter concluded that although Philadelphia's Eleazer Oswald's arguments for press freedom "sprang more from practical politics and the desire to avoid punishment than from libertarian principle . . . by asserting a right to criticize government and government officials," his newspaper, the *Gazetteer*, struck at the heart of the law of seditious libel. Although his struggle was "for a one-sided freedom—his own—Oswald anticipated, in part, the broader freedom that the Jeffersonians helped create during their struggle against the Sedition Law of 1798."[9]

Other historians, in studies ranging in subject matter from isolated episodes to the development of philosophies of freedom of the press, filled in details of this interpretive approach. They concluded, among other explanations, that colonial editors began to speculate on freedom of the press as new newspapers tried to break press monopolies; that James Alexander, a key figure in the Zenger case who developed his ideas of press freedom because of his feud with Governor Cosby, thought of the press as a political weapon and therefore developed his concepts of press freedom—which became important to the ideology of press freedom—for their usefulness in political battle; that a libertarian concept of freedom of the press developed from bitter partisanship that existed among factions; that a theory of press freedom, although not well conceptualized or coherently stated, was emerging in the decade preceding the adoption of the First Amendment; that editors in the 1780s freely criticized government, confident that they would not suffer punishment; that a tradition of a free American press had developed by the 1790s, if not in the body of law at least as the expected and accepted practice; that Republicans, when finding that procedural safeguards were not effective in combatting Federalist efforts to enact the Alien and Sedition Acts, championed a broader definition of freedom of the press; and that the Croswell case in 1804 resulted in greater press freedom by establishing truth as a defense and vitiating the argument that libels tend to cause breaches of the peace by libeled individuals seeking revenge.

Perhaps the most ambitious confrontation with Levy by a journalism historian, however, was conducted by Jeffery A. Smith, whose doctoral dissertation from the University of Wisconsin was published in 1988 as a book with the title *Printers and Press Freedom: The Ideology of Early American Journalism*. It explored the English radical Whig and Enlightenment arguments against oppression which the colonists imported to cope with their own similar difficulties. Various journalists in the 18th century employed these

---

[9]Dwight Teeter, "The Printer and the Chief Justice: Seditious Libel in 1782-83," *Journalism Quarterly* 45 (1968): 260.

arguments in political and legal defenses against censorship and subsequent punishment for their publications. Smith animated the issues involved by following the publishing career of Benjamin Franklin and his respected and prosperous network of editors and printers throughout the colonial, revolutionary, and constitutional periods. "The study as a whole," Smith said, "offers evidence that colonists were publishing and justifying aggressive journalism for decades before the Revolution" and that "Americans had forged a general libertarian press ideology that was incompatible with the idea of seditious libel."[10]

Another recent school in historiography attempted to refute Levy's conclusions simply by restating the traditional Libertarian interpretation of freedom of the press. One group of historians, strictly journalistic in outlook, concluded that the early period of journalism provided the basis for later trends in press freedom. The present-day libertarian concept of freedom of the press, they argued, is in large part the handiwork of the colonial and revolutionary journalists.

More critical scholarship, however, was provided by a number of historians who propounded the Libertarian interpretation but documented their studies more thoroughly. A close scrutiny of the attitudes led them to the conclusion that the prevailing philosophy was libertarian. Edward G. Hudon, in *Freedom of Speech and Press in America* (1963), attempted to show that the U.S. Constitution and Bill of Rights arose from a "natural law environment" which provided a historical basis for today's libertarian belief in the need for freedom of expression in a complex society. Hudon's extensive study analyzed the British law of speech and press as it existed in England and colonial America and the "theories of law and sovereignty which permitted this English and Colonial law to follow the course that it did." The guarantees of the First Amendment were "intended as more than instruments of political expediency," for their "purpose was to protect the rights of the minority from the whims of the majority." The First Amendment, Hudon concluded, was intended to break away from the repressive concepts of British law and fulfill the Declaration of Independence statement that "all men are created equal, that they are endowed by their creator with certain inalienable rights."[11]

In another study of the background of the First Amendment, *The Bill of Rights: Its Origin and Meaning* (1965), Irving Brant concluded that the framers were libertarians and intended to reject the

---

[10]Jeffery A. Smith, *Printers and Press Freedom: The Ideology of Early American Journalism* (New York: Oxford University Press, 1988), 13.

[11]Edward G. Hudon, *Freedom of Speech and Press in America* (Washington, DC: Public Affairs Press, 1963), ix, 168.

restrictive 18th-century English common law of freedom of the press. Narrating a collection of historical incidents related to the Bill of Rights, Brant argued that the Alien and Sedition Acts—whose passage Levy considered evidence that a suppressive concept of freedom prevailed during the early years of the new nation—were a "perversion of the Constitution" passed in a time of "super-patriotic jingoism." They were enforced only against political opponents of the Federalists and, he declared, with as little regard for justice as the passage of the laws had shown for constitutional rights.[12]

Other historians made similar arguments. Early American editors, they claimed, based their views on a libertarian background that grew out of the influence of the concepts of England's "Commonwealthmen," who promoted the ideas of freedom, equality, and autonomy in the colonies. The editors adopted the natural rights arguments of libertarian writers such as John Trenchard and Thomas Gordon to express their own political arguments. Although there were many obstacles to freedom, these historians argued, early Americans viewed freedom as a good ideology. In practice, however, freedom was not unbounded because the dominant ideology held also that freedom should be used for the public good. Thus after the Revolution, even the Federalists' views on restricted freedom were not inconsistent with their belief that licentiousness would endanger the nation. Despite such limitations in philosophy, colonial and revolutionary journalists took impressive steps toward formulating and implementing libertarian ideals of freedom of the press.

The Libertarian view also has dominated the law schools and law journals since 1960. George Anastaplo in *The Constitutionalist: Notes on the First Amendment* (1971) emphasized early and contemporary linguistic analyses of the First Amendment and other relevant sections of the Constitution within the context of the beginning and initial development of the republic and the part played by freedom of speech and press. Rejecting both Holmes' "clear and present danger test" as too limiting on freedom of expression and Levy's historical research as unappreciative of the republican culture that created the language of the First Amendment, Anastaplo advocated broader freedom of expression than the Supreme Court had allowed. Other legal historians have argued that the framers of the First Amendment intended that the press would act as one of the checks on the federal government, which consequently requires a distinctive, if not elevated, protection for the press under the Constitution.

---

[12]Irving Brant, *The Bill of Rights: Its Origin and Meaning* (Indianapolis: Bobbs-Merrill, 1965), 247-248.

Others proposed a "new" understanding of the scope of liberty of the press by insisting that the First Amendment's ratification process clearly broke from the English notions of seditious libel and constructive treason. According to this argument, the intellectual reaction to the suppression of speech and press in England formed a novel influence on the framers of the First Amendment. Similarly, other legal historians have focused not on the persistence in belief by the framers in seditious libel but rather on how far beyond Blackstone's definition of freedom of the press, which was Levy's maximum definition, the framers actually were willing to allow. Most of the writers of the Constitution—although limited in their philosophical vision—recognized that freedom of the press was integrally related to the American concept of government and was necessary to be protected. These historians coupled their attacks on Levy's interpretation with an assault on his scholarship, accusing him of anachronism, ahistoricism, distortion, and misconstruction. Among their points was a claim that Levy refused to concede that only the refutation of seditious libel by prevailing political leaders could mean the achievement of the modern conception of freedom of the press.

Discussion
Freedom of the press not only has been a topic of major interest to generations of historians; but it remains today, as the activity of recent scholarship indicates, a topic of ardent debate. It is ironic that the area of most intense controversy in media historiography today is the one area in which the previous century and a half had witnessed uniform consensus. The debate raises several questions about historical research. The first, perhaps, is a question of definition of terms.

1. Is it possible for historians to come to an agreement without a clear and accepted definition of the term *libertarian*? What did the term mean to 19th-century historians, and what does it mean to historians on the differing sides of the historiographical debate today?

2. What role should and does *evidence* play in historical study? How is it that various historians have the same evidence available to them and can come to very divergent interpretations of it?

3. Should historians attempt to find evidence in history, as the Libertarian historians have been prone to do, with the motivation of justifying present-day attitudes and values?

4. How difficult is it for historians to explain the past without reference to their own values?

5. All the previous questions point to the central question about early American attitudes toward freedom of the press: Were they truly libertarian, or were they limited?

Readings

Nationalist School

Lossing, Benjamin J., "Freedom of the Press Vindicated," *Harper's New Monthly Magazine* 57 (July 1878): 293-298.

Rutherford, Livingston, Ch. 3, "The Trial—Its Effect—Zenger's Subsequent Career," pp. 60-131, *John Peter Zenger, His Press, His Trial and a Bibliography of Zenger Imprints*. New York: Dodd, Mead, 1904.

Progressive School

Anderson, Frank M., "The Enforcement of the Alien and Sedition Laws," *Annual Report of the American Historical Association, 1912* (1914): 113-126.

Malone, Dumas, Ch. 4, "Republican Politics and Seditious Libel," pp. 111-149, *The Public Life of Thomas Cooper, 1783-1839*. New Haven, CT: Yale University Press, 1926.

Professional / Developmental School

Miller, John C., Ch. 10 (untitled), pp. 160-181, *Crisis in Freedom: The Alien and Sedition Act*. Boston: Little, Brown, 1951.

Mott, Frank Luther, Ch. 2, "The Basic Principles," pp. 4-8, *Jefferson and the Press*. Baton Rouge: Louisiana State University Press, 1943.

Rutland, Robert, Ch. 5, "Personal Freedom in the New Republic," pp. 78-105, *The Birth of the Bill of Rights, 1776-1791*. Chapel Hill: University of North Carolina Press, 1955.

Smith, James Morton, Ch. 18, "The Sedition Law, Free Speech, and the American Political Process," pp. 418-433, *Freedom's Fetters: The Alien and Sedition Laws and American Civil Liberties*. Ithaca, NY: Cornell University Press, 1956.

Revisionist School

Berns, Walter, "Freedom of the Press and the Alien and Sedition Laws: A Reappraisal," *Supreme Court Reports* (1970): 109-159.

Blanchard, Margaret, Ch. 4, "Freedom of the Press, 1690-1804," pp. 91-118, Wm. David Sloan, James G. Stovall, and James D. Startt, eds., *The Media in America*. Worthington, OH: Publishing Horizons, 1989.

Carroll, Thomas F., "Freedom of Speech and the Press in the Federalist Period: The Sedition Act," *Michigan Law Review* 28 (May 1920): 615-651.

Levy, Leonard, Ch. 5, "From the Revolution to the First Amendment," pp. 176-248, *Legacy of Suppression: Freedom of Speech and Press in Early American History*. Cambridge, MA: Belknap Press, 1960.

Smelser, Marshall, "George Washington and the Alien and Sedition Acts," *American Historical Review* 59 (January 1954): 322-334.

Neo-Libertarian School

Brant, Irving, Ch. 19, "Congress Shall Make No Law," pp. 223-236, *The Bill of Rights: Its Origin and Meaning*. Indianapolis: Bobbs-Merrill, 1965.

Hudon, Edward G., Ch. 3, "British Concepts of Law and Sovereignty: Their Rejection in Colonial America," pp. 20-36, *Freedom of Speech and Press in America*. Washington, DC: Public Affairs Press, 1963.

Smith, Jeffery, "Introduction," pp. 3-13, *Printers and Press Freedom: The Ideology of Early American Journalism*. New York: Oxford University Press, 1988.

Stevens, John D., "Congressional History of the 1798 Sedition Law," *Journalism Quarterly* 43 (1966): 247-256.

Teeter, Dwight, "Press Freedom and the Public Printing: Pennsylvania, 1775-83," *Journalism Quarterly* 45 (1968): 445-451.

7

Women in Media, 1700-Present: Victims or Equals?

Women have been involved in American media almost from the very start. Wives, widows, and spinsters in the American colonies were expected to work as hard as the men, although they did not have the same political status as men. Women could not vote, but they could operate businesses. Colonial women were landladies, operated millinery shops, ran jewelry stores, taught school, sewed for the public, sold slaves, handled busy households, conducted horse racing, and owned and sold land.

It was not out of place, then, when America's first woman newspaper editor took her post in 1739. Elizabeth Timothy of Charleston took over the *South-Carolina Gazette* when her husband died. Women have been involved as workers in the media ever since. Despite the fact that colonial America was not shocked by women working as journalists, Americans of later eras gradually grew to think of journalism and other media jobs as man's work. Women in media came to be viewed, in general, with some amazement and some skepticism. But more and more females became journalists, broadcasters, and other media workers over the years, convincing the dubious industry and public that they could, indeed, handle the jobs.

Of course, women had been involved in the news in another way long before Elizabeth Timothy, for women had always been subjects of the news. Queens gave birth to heirs, and the press proudly recounted that fact. Female victims of disaster, religious persecution, and crime found their way into news reports. But there were some issues that seemed to be of more interest to women than to men. Early newspapers, for example, published stories about single motherhood and the dangers, for women, of dating. That early treatment of women's news evolved over time to become the "women's pages"

By Julie A. Hedgepeth
University of Alabama

of newspapers and special magazines or broadcast shows geared toward women. From time to time over the years, women rebelled at the notion that women's news was somehow divorced from men's news and that women should not be interested in "male" spheres. The rebellion became more popular in the 1960s, and women's pages began disappearing. Issues of interest to women began being treated as front-page fare.

Historians' work on the feminine contribution to the mass media reflected the dual role women played in the American media. Many historians were fascinated by women such as Elizabeth Timothy and her sister employees in the media. Others explored the treatment of women and women's issues as subjects in the media. Historians debated whether women, both as media subjects and as media employees, were victims of a masculine industry or whether they were treated professionally. In their efforts to answer those basic questions about women in media, historians wrote from varying schools of interpretation.

The Romantic school lauded great media women and praised great achievements in women's media. Analyzing women in the media from a different angle, historians of the Developmental school were interested in the process women went through to become true professionals in the media. That school also studied the developing maturity of the media in covering women's issues. Another group of historians, those from the Cultural school, looked at how external influences shaped women's careers in the media. A fourth school and the largest of all, the Feminist school, focused on the discrimination women faced and overcame. Historians in that school were also especially interested in the feminist media.

The Romantic School

The earliest historical works about women in the media took a Romantic point of view. To the Romantic historians, the description of the past was an art. History was to be painted in florid pictures of past grandeur, bygone glory. Romantics were especially fascinated with great women of the media, lauding them for their unusual achievements and noble characters. As the Romantic historians saw it, the public in general was unfortunately unaware of these great women who had helped chart the course of American media—and, indeed, the course of American civilization. American civilization was all-important to Romantics, who felt that America played a unique part in the liberation of mankind. Writers in the Romantic school sought to praise great women who had had such a glorious role in history, so that the public would become aware of their contributions.

Of course, great women as individuals were not the only subjects the Romantic historians praised. They also admired women's media. Therefore, they praised great publications geared toward femininity, lauding those works for their moral guidance and their dignified aid to the female gender. To the Romantic historian, these media achievements, no less than the great women themselves, helped furnish guiding lights for society to follow. Without these great women and great periodicals, the media and the nation would surely have suffered.

The Romantic school was evident as early as 1872; and by the early 1900s, the school was quite popular. It flourished into the 1940s. Although other schools of interpretation of women in the media grew more common later, the Romantic school never really died. As historians after the 1940s "discovered" pioneer women journalists, broadcasters, and so on, they often wrote of these women's accomplishments in the spirit of the Romantic "great woman" ideal. Later writers gave up the flowery prose popular in the 1920s, 1930s, and 1940s, but they still looked with admiration on great women and recounted their great achievements, wishing to bring these exceptional women into the public view.

The earliest historic work on female journalists was Jessie E. Ringwalt's 1872 article, "Early Female Printers in America." Ringwalt praised women printers for their exemplary womanhood as well as their journalistic capabilities. For instance, Ringwalt quoted an "exquisite and elaborate" contemporary account of printer Elizabeth Green, calling her a "model woman, wife and mother" who was equally skillful at home and at her print shop. Ringwalt romantically idealized the struggle for American independence. Writing of pro-British printer Margaret Draper, for instance, Ringwalt said that Draper's Boston *News-Letter* "could not recognize the new light kindled on Bunker Hill, and ignominiously closed its long career" by collapsing along with the British colonial government.[1]

Likewise, Richard Fay Warner wrote of Romantic ideals in his 1924 article "Godey's Lady's Book." He praised *Godey's Lady's Book* and the exceptional people who published it, making it a popular magazine for ladies from 1830 to 1876. The magazine was "the guiding star of female education, the beacon light of refined taste, pure morals and practical wisdom." Each issue of *Godey's* contained "the same sweet and uplifting stories, worded a little differently each time, to be sure, but still always the same." Such stories, Warner said, gave female readers "pious sermons on correct behavior, on the joys of the domestic hearth, on a mother's love, a sister's sorrow . . . ." Warner lauded Louis Antoine Godey, the magazine's founder, and its editor, Sarah Hale. Godey had supreme con-

---

[1]Jessie E. Ringwalt, "Early Female Printers in America," *Printer's Circular and Stationer's and Publisher's Gazette* 7 (October 1872): 284-285.

fidence in his magazine for women, and he had excellent business sense, Warner said. Hale was truly "the guiding star of female education." Warner described her glowingly as a lady who told her readers that they, too, must be ladies.[2]

The Romantic interpretation of women in journalism was epitomized in Kent Cooper's 1946 work, *Anna Zenger, Mother of Freedom*. Cooper freely admitted that his biography of John Peter Zenger's wife was "novelized," but he said the detail of his story corresponded to actual events "that I believe were the genesis of freedom in this land." The biographical novel portrayed Anna Zenger as the true power behind her husband, who was famous for helping establish the right of the press to criticize the government. John Peter Zenger was jailed and then tried by colonial New York authorities for printing accusations against them. His victory helped establish broader powers than the press had ever before enjoyed.

Cooper was convinced that Anna was far greater than her husband. He called her a "genius who first sowed the seed of freedom in this land." He based his argument on his contention that John Peter Zenger was not educated and could not write, whereas his wife freely operated his New York *Weekly Journal* during his imprisonment and again after his death. Cooper said, in fact, that John Peter Zenger had amounted to nothing until he married Anna. Cooper contended that Zenger went to prison "for no other reason than to shield [Anna]."[3]

The Developmental School

By the time the Romantic interpretation neared its apex, the Developmental explanation of media history already had become the dominant one. By the mid-1930s, women had been involved in journalism in substantial numbers and had gained sufficient acceptance for historians to begin judging their professional development over time. That sense of professional development was the foundation of the Developmental school.

Developmental historians had specific standards of media professionalism in mind when they wrote. With that frame of reference, they then compared the performance of women in the media to those professional standards. Some writers lauded women for achieving professional goals after passing through painful stages of development. Others criticized women for not meeting professional objectives.

The Developmental school did not, however, confine itself to in-

---

[2]Richard Fay Warner, "Godey's Lady's Book," *American Mercury* 2 (August, 1924): 339, 401.

[3]Kent Cooper, *Anna Zenger, Mother of Freedom* (New York: Farrar, Strauss, 1946), 1, 329.

dividual women journalists and their professional achievements. The school also had an interest in how the media wrote about women and how the media treated issues of interest to women. Some historians saw signs of professional immaturity in the media's handling of women. They decried the media for shrinking from women's issues or for coddling women in the press, substituting society's traditional protection of women for good media standards. Other Developmental historians saw a growing maturity of the media in the handling of women's issues and women in the news. Some said that the growing sophistication of the media in regard to women allowed female reporters to prove themselves by covering women as news.

The Developmental school, although not as prolific as the Romantic and the later Feminist schools, nevertheless did not go out of fashion. In fact, some of the later Feminist writers injected Developmental tones into their work as they explored feminist issues as factors in the professional development of women in the media.

Ishbel Ross made professional development the central theme in *Ladies of the Press* (1936). She attempted to fit female writers into a series of categories, tracing the development of professionalism over time. She described the professional goal toward which women journalists were working. As she put it, "The highest compliment to which the deluded creatures [women journalists] respond is the city editor's acknowledgment that their work is just like a man's. This automatically gives them a complacent glow, for they are all aware that no right-minded editor wants the so-called woman's touch in the [front page] news."[4]

Ross traced the evolution of women journalists toward that goal of writing like men. According to Ross, 1890-1900 was the stunt era for women reporters. Females in journalism did outrageous, sometimes dangerous, stunts in order to attract readers and attract attention of editors. The next era in the development of women journalists involved more pre-existing news, rather than trumped-up stunts. Ross called the 1900-1910 decade the "sob" era, when female reporters covered trials and other news with vivid, personal, feminine writing designed to play on the emotions. Next, women journalists turned toward a topic of vital concern to women in the attempt to effect social change. This era, 1910-1920, saw the rise of the women's suffrage press, dedicated to the fight to give women the right to vote. After women won the vote, female journalism developed into the 1920-1930 tabloid era, when undercover reporters were able to interview royalty and other glittering, hitherto aloof subjects for the flourishing tabloid industry.

Ross said women in 1930s journalism had moved closer to their

---

[4]Ishbel Ross, *Ladies of the Press* (New York: Harper, 1936), 13.

goal after their 44-year period of development. They had become more and more accepted as writers, more in line with males in journalism. "[Women] no longer have to climb skyscrapers by rope or wear false faces to get their stuff in the papers," she wrote. "They do it on a workmanlike basis."[5]

Similarly, Sidney Kobre, an historian with a deep interest in sociological influences on the press, used a Developmental interpretation in studying how newspapers reacted when confronted with the novelty of a sensational female criminal. In "New York Newspapers and the Case of Celia Cooney" (1937), Kobre described the young bandit who terrorized New York City as she and a male companion robbed businesses in 1924. The press tended to sentimentalize her, calling her the "bobbed-haired girl robber."

Kobre criticized the press for falling short of what he called a professional ideal in covering Cooney. He argued that all good newspaper editors and reporters should explore *why* crimes took place in order to help society. In this case, the press had a professional duty to explore Celia Cooney's motives, but it failed dreadfully. "Since no reporting in the best sense of the tradition had been undertaken," he said, "there would have been no intelligent revelation [by the press] of the cause and effect involved in the story of Celia Cooney." He asserted that it was the professional duty of editors and reporters to look for the cause and effect, rather than romanticizing a "girl bandit" or any other subject in the news. "It is this faculty of linking the news with the 'background story' that distinguishes the alert, intelligent editor from the run-of-the-mine news executive who is nailed to his swivel-chair," Kobre said.[6]

A more recent historian, Kathleen Endres, shed another Developmental light on women in the media in "The Symbiotic Relationship of Eleanor Roosevelt and the Press: The Pre-War Years" (1979). Endres said that the female reporters covering Eleanor Roosevelt benefited from the First Lady. Mrs. Roosevelt invited women to cover her press conferences. These conferences, in turn, became an important step in the professional development of women, for women were thus allowed to cover one of the most important individuals in the country. Female reporters had access to some of the most important news events in the nation. The newswomen, as a result, took another vital professional step: they got major bylines, and when their names appeared on news pages, they gained more acceptance as committed newswomen.

According to Endres, Mrs. Roosevelt's encouragement of female reporters propelled media women through professional ado-

---

[5]Ibid., p. 14.

[6]Sidney Kobre, "New York Newspapers and the Case of Celia Cooney," *Journalism Quarterly* 14 (1937): 134, 141, 143.

lescence and helped them reach a businesslike level. By the time the Roosevelt administrations ended, females in journalism had been elevated to professional standards beyond their previous level.[7]

The Cultural School

In contrast to Developmental historians, historians of the Cultural school were not so much interested in the professional relationship of women and media, but in the external forces that caused media women to do what they did. The media, after all, seemed historically to be hostile to female employees. Women as a group had had to work hard to gain acceptance as members of the media. Why did they bother? Cultural historians, interested in the environmental influences that shaped women journalists, tried to answer that question.

Cultural historians looked at a wide array of factors which left their mark on media women. In some cases, events that had happened to women propelled them into media work. In other cases, people played a large role: deadbeat husbands, unable to earn a living, caused wives to seek employment; children caused financial hardship, which sent women to the office; fathers encouraged daughters to think and read, in opposition to the notions of their era that women should be more docile than educated.

Another branch of the Cultural school was interested in exactly how environmental factors shaped women's work in the media. Historians writing from this viewpoint looked at how geography, social attitudes, traditional feminine upbringings, or other factors compelled media women to communicate various ideas in certain ways to the public.

The Cultural school became popular in the 1970s. Like the larger Feminist school, which was coming into its own at the same time, Cultural historians recognized that women had faced discrimination. They centered their studies, however, more on environment, with only a passing nod to the existence of the discrimination that so fascinated Feminists.

The Cultural outlook was evident in the work of Madelon Golden Schilpp and Sharon M. Murphy. In *Great Women of the Press* (1983), they analyzed the external factors that had influenced a number of great press women. Margaret Bourke-White, for instance, a pioneer photojournalist who lived from 1904-1971, was heavily influenced by outside factors. "Her career was simultaneous with the advent of photojournalism, a word coined in her youth, as a result of advances in photography and magazine production,"

---

[7]Kathleen L. Endres, "The Symbiotic Relationship of Eleanor Roosevelt and the Press: The Pre-War Years," *Midwest Communications Research Journal* 2 (1979): 57-65.

the authors said. "Her life cannot be considered apart from the heyday of picture magazines, when the great events of the 1930s, 1940s, and 1950s entered homes through the print media and radio."

Besides being influenced by society's growing interest in photography as an integral part of news, Bourke-White was shaped by personal events as well. Her father taught her to do everything she did better than anyone else, advice that perhaps helped her hold her own in a field dominated by men. She married young, but her marriage fell apart. Due to the failed marriage and the early death of her father, she returned to her mother's home and tried to support them both. Having never intended to be a photographer, she turned to her camera and took a few pictures to sell for ready cash. A career was born.[8]

Barbara Belford's *Brilliant Bylines: A Biographical Anthology of Notable Newspaper Women in America* (1986) was also rooted in the Cultural perspective. "The object of this book . . .," she stated, "is not to examine whether women journalists wrote any differently—or even better or worse—than men. It is to show how the careers of women who became journalists . . . and what they wrote were shaped by both personal and economic necessity and by the demands of the newspaper editors of their era."

One of the journalists Belford covered was Jane Grey Swisshelm, who lived from 1815-1884. She had an unfortunate marriage that shaped her career. Her husband clung to his mother, and his mother in turn expected Swisshelm to act as a maid. Unhappy, Swisshelm moved to a house behind her mother-in-law's, leaving her husband with his mother, and proceeded to forget her troubles by becoming interested in various creative pursuits. Her husband seemed unable to make a successful living; so he eventually looked the other way when she became a journalist and began working side by side with another man. Although such an arrangement was considered scandalous in its day, Swisshelm's husband seemed eager to have the income she brought in. Thus, Belford said, Swisshelm managed to get into the "forbidden" profession of journalism.[9]

The Feminist School

As the Cultural school was gaining strength as an explanation of general media history, change was sweeping American society. The women's movement of the 1960s was reshaping women's lives. It also was shaping a new Feminist movement in historiography of women in the media. Starting in the 1960s, more and more women

---

[8]Madelon Golden Schilpp and Sharon M. Murphy, *Great Women of the Press* (Carbondale: Southern Illinois University Press, 1983), 179-182.

[9]Barbara Belford, *Brilliant Bylines: A Biographical Anthology of Notable Newspaper Women in America* (New York: Columbia University Press, 1986), x, 20-30.

sought higher education and expected to enter the work force. More and more of them became scholars and historians. Many of these female historians had a natural interest in women's roles and achievements. They began to discover that women had long worked in the media, even though the lengthy historic involvement of females was not always readily apparent in existing works by historians.

Due to such growth in scholarship by women, the 1970s saw an explosion of historic writings on women in the media, with works from the Feminist perspective surpassing those from any other school. A great deal of those writings reflected the women's movement which had caused the upsurge in women's scholarship, resulting in a Feminist interpretation of women in media history. Many Feminist writers had a fascination with feminist issues as portrayed in the media. They studied the feminist media, as well as feminist actions in the media. But their work was by no means limited to a study of the feminist movement as shown in the media. A number of Feminist historians explored with admiration how various women managed to overcome the discrimination in their path toward becoming accepted, valued members of the media. Other historians were more hard-hitting; they criticized society for overlooking media women and the media for overlooking women's issues.

That sense of correcting discrimination separated Feminist historians from historians of other schools. Whereas other historians had looked with awe at the fact that women had made gains in a profession historically dominated by men, Feminist historians focused more on the existence of discrimination against women. The natural abilities of women had either conspiratorially or ignorantly been hidden from view, Feminists said. To rectify the lack of information on women, Feminist writers uncovered and wrote about a wide array of little-known female journalists, broadcasters, and other women in the media.

Addressing history's blindness toward women, Susan Henry pleaded for historians to revise their methods and begin digging up long-forgotten facts on women and minorities. In "Colonial Woman Printer as Prototype: Toward a Model for the Study of Minorities" (1976), she decried historians for paying little attention to colonial women printers, saying historians' inaction "reveals . . . much about American historiography." Historians, she said, often looked at power struggles as proper historic subjects. "Thus, because colonial women as a whole could not vote, had little say in government or politics, and only occasionally wielded extensive economic or intellectual influence, they have often been pictured as oppressed and restrained members of colonial society." In reality, she said, colonial businesswomen were accepted as part of society. Other than female printers, few colonial women in business could read or write; so they did not leave their own records. Because they were considered a normal part of society, they were rarely written about by their colleagues. Henry said that historians had to dig to find records of them, and historians had just not done the work.[10]

Marion Marzolf, in *Up From the Footnote: A History of Women Journalists* (1977), repeated Henry's complaint about historians in their treatment of women. "Historians," she said, "skip over these early women printer-editors, usually passing them off as accidents created by the early deaths of husbands or fathers." She traced the experience of women in media from widow colonial printers to city reporters to war correspondents to broadcasters. She gave examples of women who faced discrimination based on gender. For instance, women took over male media posts during World War II, but afterward they were forced back into the writing of "women's" news. "Once again you could count the number of women in the newsroom on one hand and their beats were likely to be education, health, welfare or features," Marzolf said. "The wartime lesson that 'women could do anything' had contained an unspoken but powerful tag end—'in an emergency.'"[11]

Like Marzolf, Maurine Beasley explored discrimination against female journalists. Beasley's "Lorena A. Hickok: Woman Journalist" (1980) chided historians for focusing exclusively on gossip about Hickok. Letters between Hickok and her friend Eleanor Roosevelt perhaps suggested a lesbian relationship, denied by the Roosevelt family. Beasley said the focus on such gossip obscured Hickok's true importance as a reporter who wrote of the extreme suffering of everyday people for the Franklin Roosevelt administration as it struggled to cope with the Great Depression of the 1930s.

Had Hickok not written of the Depression for the administration, however, she would have been notable anyway, Beasley said, "for she was one of the relatively few women to achieve success in the rough-and-tumble world of New York journalism in the early 1920s and 1930s." Hickok experienced the "customary sex discrimination" of her era but was able to overcome it. As Hickok herself put it, "When I first went into the newspaper business I had to get a job as society editor—the only opening available to women in most offices." Then she volunteered to cover night assignments, which pleased the city editor. "[Then I would] get into trouble with some dowager who would demand that I be fired, and finally land on the

    [10]Susan Henry, "Colonial Woman Printer as Prototype: Toward a Model for the Study of Minorities," *Journalism History* 3 (1976): 20.

    [11]Marion Marzolf, *Up From the Footnote: A History of Women Journalists* (New York: Hastings House, 1977), 3, 74, 75.

straight reportorial staff, which was where I had wanted to be from the beginning."

Her reports for the Roosevelt administration drew on her journalistic strength, going beyond statistics. "She looked for human interest stories," Beasley wrote, "vignettes on victims of the Depression: the black woman in Philadelphia who walked eight miles a day in an unsuccessful hunt for cleaning work at 15 cents an hour; the 8-year-old Mexican girl in Colorado who had already worked two summers 'in the beets' . . . ."[12]

Taking a different slant, Sherilyn Cox Bennion discussed in a large number of studies feminism in the American frontier press. In "Woman Suffrage Papers of the West, 1869-1914" (1986), she explored why the Western United States was more accepting of women as equals to men than the more rigid East. She suggested that a "frontier spirit promoted a sense of equality" in the West and that Westerners respected women simply because they were scarce. Historians in general, she added, had overlooked Western suffrage newspapers, which all seemed based on the idea that women had a natural right to vote.

She concluded that the suffragist press was morally right in the fight for equality as well as highly successful in helping give shape to the suffrage movement. "The papers led the way in the campaigns for suffrage wherever they were published," she said. "They helped develop ideas and organizations. They provided a forum for a cause which had time—and justice—on its side."[13]

Discussion

The historiography of women in the media continually runs into unique problems. Society still has not successfully wrestled with the need for women both at home and in the workplace. Thus, attitudes toward women's roles remain volatile, with societal opinions toward women and the women's movement changing from decade to decade. Given such an ever-changing setting, varying language used by historians studying women in the media goes out of fashion quickly, by turns seeming too archaic for the times or too militant. Thus, although historic works of previous eras may contain valid basic information, each new generation of historians who write of women in the media may feel compelled to start over, telling the basic historical story in fresh terms acceptable to the decade. Because of this continual rewriting of the most basic information, historiography of women in the media often tends to stagnate at the basic

---

[12]Maurine Beasley, "Lorena A. Hickok: Woman Journalist," *Journalism History* 7 (1980): 92, 94.

[13]Sherilyn Cox Bennion, "Woman Suffrage Papers of the West, 1869-1914," *American Journalism* 3 (1986): 129, 140.

level. Add to that the fact that less seems to be known in general about early media women than about their male counterparts, and historiography of women in the media at times seems to be in an infant stage, still exclaiming with delight over the very existence of women in important media roles without exploring women's contributions on a deeper level. Is there anything more to say about these women than the Romantic school's rightful proclamation that these were, indeed, great women? Even though the number of works on women in media have proliferated, a number of questions remain.

1. Did these women leave lasting impressions on the media?

2. How did they treat various subjects? How much did gender have to do with their treatment of these subjects?

3. Did the outside world exercise a major influence in their lives, as Cultural scholars argue? Or did their careers come about because they were exceptional people?

4. How has the concept of "women's news" metamorphosed over time?

5. Why exactly did most "women's pages" die, while women's magazines flourished?

6. Is the explanation for a separation between men's and women's media rooted in a discriminatory attitude, as Feminist historians claim, or have the media responded to genuine interests of women?

7. To what degree did discrimination influence women's work in the media? Did women write any differently because men dominated the field?

8. As the media have allowed more and more women employees and as they have defined more and more "women's news" as "hard" news, have the professional standards and expectations of the media changed? Has the public or the media viewed women's issues any differently over time as women became more accepted members of the media?

9. With all of these questions still in need of examination, the overriding disagreement among historians has been over the nature of the relationship of women and the media. Have women performed as equals to their male counterparts, and been treated as such; or have they been victims of a profession traditionally dominated by males?

Readings

Romantic School

Jackson, George Stuyvesant, "Anne Royall vs. Washington, D.C.," pp. 90-131, *Uncommon Scold: The Story of Anne Royall.* Boston: Bruce Humphries, 1937.

Ringwalt, Jessie E., "Early Female Printers in America," *Printers' Circular and*

Stationers' and Publishers' Gazette 7 (October 1872): 284-285.

Warner, Richard Fay, "Godey's Lady's Book," *American Mercury* 2 (August, 1924): 399-405.

Developmental School

Endres, Kathleen L., "The Symbiotic Relationship of Eleanor Roosevelt and the Press: The Pre-War Years," *Midwest Communications Research Journal* 2 (1979): 57-65.

Olasky, Marvin, "Opposing Abortion Clinics: A New York *Times* 1871 Crusade," *Journalism Quarterly* 63 (1986): 305-310, 321.

Ross, Ishbel, Ch. 1, "Front-page Girl," pp. 1-13, *Ladies of the Press*. New York: Harper, 1936.

Cultural School

Belford, Barbara, "Introduction," pp. ix-xiv, and Ch. 2, "Jane Grey Swisshelm," pp. 20-30, *Brilliant Bylines: A Biographical Anthology of Notable Newspaper Women in America*. New York: Columbia University Press, 1986.

Schilpp, Madelon Golden, and Sharon M. Murphy, Ch. 17, "Margaret Bourke-White," pp. 179-190, *Great Women of the Press*. Carbondale: Southern Illinois University Press, 1983.

Stinson, Robert, "Ida M. Tarbell and the Ambiguities of Feminism," *Pennsylvania Magazine of History and Biography* 101 (April 1977): 217-239.

Feminist School

Beasley, Maurine, "Lorena A. Hickok: Woman Journalist," *Journalism History* 7 (1980): 92-95, 113.

Bennion, Sherilyn Cox, "Woman Suffrage Papers of the West, 1869-1914," *American Journalism* 3 (1986): 125-141.

Henry, Susan, "Colonial Woman Printer as Prototype: Toward a Model for the Study of Minorities," *Journalism History* 3 (1976): 20-24.

List, Karen K., "The Post-Revolutionary Woman Idealized: Philadelphia Media's 'Republican Mother,'" *Journalism Quarterly* 66 (1989): 65-75.

Marzolf, Marion, Ch. 1, "Widow Printer to Big City Reporter," pp. 1-31, *Up From the Footnote: A History of Women Journalists*. New York: Hastings House, 1977.

8

The Frontier Press, 1800-1900:
Personal Journalism or Paltry Business?

The 19th century witnessed a dramatic and steady increase in the number of newspapers published on the western frontier. As settlement moved from the original colonies over the Allegheny Mountains across the Mississippi River through the Great Plains and on to the Pacific Coast, newspapers sprang up with the towns. By the end of the century, more than 700 papers were publishing west of the Mississippi.

A number of features were evident among the newspapers. Editors had an interest in the growth of their towns and, as a result, often served as town boosters or advocated civic improvement. Some of them were tied to partisan politics, whereas others served special interests such as religion or agriculture. Most faced difficulties, ranging from transporting heavy printing equipment to collecting payments from subscribers. Their views on the frontier itself varied. Most advocated the removal of Indians, although they disagreed on the imposition of "law and order" in an effort to civilize frontier society.

By the end of the 19th century, however, frontier newspapers "began showing," one historian has observed, "the conformity of industrialism evident in their urban counterparts. Like the urban paper, which moved toward stricter standards of news, the weekly newspapers became businesses; many publishers showed little resemblance to the early printers who took pride in their printing craft and their bombastic political essays."[1]

The central questions that historians have confronted about the frontier press deal with the essential character of the press and its editors. Were journalists rugged, colorful, admirable individualists; or were they small-time businessmen barely able to eke out a living? Were they promoters of civilization and progress, or were

---

[1]William Huntzicker, "The Frontier Press, 1800-1900," in Wm. David Sloan, James G. Stovall, and James D. Startt, eds., *The Media in America: A History* (Worthington, OH: Publishing Horizons, 1989), 189.

they advocates of bigotry and violence? How historians answered those questions depended on their views broadly about the nature of the American frontier, American society, and, most fundamentally, the American character.

The earliest works on the frontier press were produced by Romantic historians beginning near the middle of the 19th century. These historians held a generally favorable view of frontier editors. They presented the editors as rugged, colorful individualists who made major contributions to the progress of American civilization. In similar fashion, a small group of Developmental historians beginning in the early part of the 20th century presented the contributions that frontier editors had made to the progress of journalism. In contrast, Cultural historians began in the 1930s to question the character of editors, their reasons for starting newspapers, and the conditions under which they operated. Rather than colorful individualists, the editors were transformed under the scrutiny of Cultural historians into secondary players. More important were the conditions of the frontier that molded the newspaper. Rather than being brilliant, bold operators of newspapers, Cultural historians declared, editors were small-time businessmen who ran their papers under pervasive difficulties imposed by frontier conditions and who barely were able to scratch out a living. Whereas the Cultural historians explained the nature of editors and newspapers as a result of the conditions on the frontier, Progressive and other ideological historians presented a more critical assessment. In their hands, the Romantic historians' image of the bold editors who contributed to civilization and progress was transformed into one of bigots and racists who were as limited and regressive in their thinking as the American frontier itself generally was.

The Romantic School

Romantic historians, the first chroniclers of the frontier press, saw in editors two primary characteristics. One was their colorful individualism. The other was their contribution to the progress of American civilization. These historians reflected the outlook of Americans of the 19th century. They had an expansive view of the American nation, and they saw in the frontiersman the praiseworthy features that made Americans distinctive from citizens of European and other countries. On the frontier, 19th-century Americans believed, one could find the true American. On the frontier one could find rugged individualism, versatility and self-reliance, determination, and egalitarianism. The frontier, unsoiled by the blights of urbanism, provided the natural environment where the individual could find true expression. The frontier, untamed by society, required, however, a certain type of individual—one who could confront harsh conditions and prevail. It was this type of individual who eventually would tame the frontier and bring civilization to it.

Despite their boisterousness, whimsy, and a generally erratic lifestyle, frontier editors nevertheless played an important role in their communities and exercised considerable authority, Romantic historians argued. They were a key feature in the expansion of western towns and were courageous in speaking out on issues and problems. The frontier required sturdy settlers to break the land and preserve liberty. Editors needed to be both rugged and brave, willing to speak plainly and boldly. Typically, they were ambitious, romantic but practical, honest, and stubborn when principles required. Useful, public-spirited, and trustworthy citizens, they became spokesmen for their towns, were leading figures in the cultural life of the frontier communities, and literary figures as well, and sometimes served as political office holders.

Historians of the press identified in frontier editors the same rugged characteristics found in frontier life. Frederick Follett's *History of the Press of Western New York* (1847), the first important book on the history of rural weekly newspapers, exemplified the Romantic approach, providing details and anecdotal stories about the newspapers and their printer-editors. Similarly, Edward C. Kemble's 1858 series of articles entitled "A History of California Newspapers 1846-1858" provided an antiquarian record of the early press, with names, dates, and places of publications. Kemble's history originally appeared in the Sacramento *Union* in 1858 and was published in book form in 1962.[2] These early Romantic historians and the ones who followed them presented frontier editors as colorful, creative journalists who served as promoters of their communities, were skilled in a variety of tasks, worked hard, and frequently—as the exploits of some gunfighting editors in the western frontier demonstrated—engaged in personal, vituperative clashes. Boisterousness was one of the key characteristics, a result of newspapers' interaction with frontier society. Although the newspapers abounded with political arguments, violent accusations, tasteless personal attacks, and promotion of schemes, they exhibited the features of American democracy which marked the frontier as a distinctive American feature. Editors led an uninhibited way of life, ready even to fabricate the content in their newspapers, including wild tales, exaggerated details of mining prosperity, comic episodes, and so forth, mostly in good humor.

This 19th-century view of frontier editors was summed up in a popular article published near the end of the century, Z. L. White's "Western Journalism" (1888). In the 1830s west of the Allegheny Mountains, White declared, many "restless, erratic geniuses

---

[2]Edward C. Kemble, *A History of California Newspapers 1846-1858*, Helen Harding Bretnor, ed. (Los Gatos, CA: Talisman, 1962).

drifted into journalism, and the frontier newspapers they made, often written and printed under great difficulties, possessed the merit of having at least a positive and unmistakable individuality. They were crude in style and in moral tone as well as in mechanical construction . . . but the papers were made for a constituency that was as peculiar in its tastes as it was independent in its habits and thought, and cared less for the form than for the substance of what it had to read."[3] Later successful western newspapers, such as the Cincinnati *Commercial* and San Francisco *Daily Examiner*, were a legacy from the pioneer press, White concluded.

Along with the rugged characterization of frontier editors, Romantic historians also detailed their contributions to civilization. Frequently written as commemorative histories, many such works celebrated anniversaries of events in territories or states. Henry O'Reilly's 1867 article, "The First Daily Newspaper in the West, and the First Telegraph Line between the Atlantic and the Mississippi Valley," for example, was written in commemoration of the 40th anniversary of the founding of the Rochester (N.Y.) *Daily Advertiser*, an "epoch," O'Reilly commented, "in the history of our Continent."[4]

In a similar vein, the *Missouri Historical Review* published a series of articles in 1919-1920 celebrating the centennial of journalism in its state. In one of the articles, Anna Lee Brosius Korn lauded the founder of the *Missouri Intelligencer* and Boone's Lick *Advertiser* as a "typical gentleman of the 'Old South' of Democratic politics" who "encouraged all matters pertaining to the public good."[5] In a second article, William Vincent Byars attributed to Missouri's first newspapers a role that rivaled religion and education in importance. In the 1820s, he wrote, Missouri pioneers "looked to the church, the school and the press . . . for enlightenment, to save them and their posterity from calamities . . . .The county newspaper was thought of as not less necessary than the county courthouse."[6] Throughout the century, the best Missouri newspapers kept the people enlightened so that they could maintain their excellent characteristics. The same view could be found in states other than Missouri, as Romantic historians glowed over the quality and character of life and journalism in their home state. George W. Purcell, for exam-

---

[3]Z. L. White, "Western Journalism," *Harper's New Monthly Magazine* 77 (1888): 678.

[4]Henry O'Reilly, "The First Daily Newspaper in the West, and the First Telegraph Line between the Atlantic and the Mississippi Valley," *Harper's Monthly* 1 (January 1867): 22.

[5]Anna Lee Brosius Korn, "Major Benjamin Holliday, 1786-1859," *Missouri Historical Review* 14 (October 1919): 28.

[6]William Vincent Byars, "A Century of Journalism in Missouri," *Missouri Historical Review* 15 (October 1920): 53.

ple, in 1924 wrote that "the early history of newspapers in this vast territory [Indiana]," dating from 1787, "reads like a novel of heroic characters, and brave men—the torchbearers of the gospel of liberty to light civilization's path over the prairies and in the fertile valleys of the Ohio, Mississippi and Missouri rivers."[7] Such a positive, Romantic view remained popular with some historians until only recently.

Unlike the historiography on many other media topics, in historical work on the frontier press a well-defined Romantic approach continued to be strong well into the 20th century. The endurance of that interpretation was accounted for by the pervasive image of the American west in the nation's view of its past. As demonstrated, for example, by motion films' glamorized treatment of the American cowboy, the Romantic view of the frontier kept a tenacious hold on Americans' thinking.

That the Romantic view was little changed with the beginning of the 20th century was indicated with the work of R. G. Thwaites. In "The Ohio Valley Press before the War of 1812-1815" (1909), Thwaites wrote that although frontier editors faced unfavorable conditions and problems, they were optimistic, innovative, hardworking, and enterprising—though not prudent or conservative. Although they were politically trenchant, their partisanship and vituperation were "quite in line with prevailing tastes." They reflected, Thwaites summarized, "credit on the profession of journalism, and did admirable service in the early development of the Middle West."[8]

Among recent historians, the Romantic interpretation of the frontier press has been presented most fully by Robert F. Karolevitz, the author of two books on the subject. In *Newspapering in the Old West: A Pictorial History of Journalism and Printing on the Frontier* (1965), Karolevitz presented an anecdotal, illustrated treatment of newspapers from 1840 to the latter part of the 1800s. Frontier journalism, he concluded, was rough and tumble; and newspapermen were individualists, not fitting any common characteristics or stereotype. In *With a Shirt Tail Full of Type: The Story of Newspapering in South Dakota* (1982), Karolevitz presented a chronological narrative from 1859 to the present, illustrated profusely with photographs. Concentrating especially on the discovery of gold in the Black Hills, he observed that the discovery led to a newspaper boom and that editors' boisterous approach to running their newspapers mirrored the rollicking conditions on the gold-mining frontier.

---

[7]George W. Purcell, "A Survey of Early Newspapers in the Middle Western States," *Indiana Magazine of History* 20 (December 1924): 347.

[8]R. G. Thwaites, "The Ohio Valley Press before the War of 1812-1815," *American Antiquarian Society Proceedings* 19 (April 1909): 352, 353.

The Developmental School

The frontier press is one of the few topics in media history not dominated by historians from the Developmental school. The reason is twofold. First, the distinctiveness of the frontier character and the influence of frontier conditions were especially evident to historians. Thus, it was those features—rather than the practice of journalism as a profession on the frontier—that seemed to account for the essential nature of the frontier press. Second, historians considered the practice of frontier journalism to be crude as compared with its metropolitan counterpart. Because the frontier press remained in a rudimentary state, historians thus found little in its progress and professional practice that enticed them to view it in terms of its journalistic development. Despite such conditions, there still were a number of historians who approached the frontier press from the Developmental perspective.

Developmental historians studied the frontier press within two structural frameworks. One was the history of journalism within states, whereas the other was comprised of biographies of editors. Thus, they produced narratives of the newspapers in such places as Ohio, Florida, Oregon, Texas, Tennessee, and so on, emphasizing the journalistic development and progress in those states. Typical of this approach was Fred W. Allsop's *History of the Arkansas Press for a Hundred Years and More* (1922), a chronology (composed mainly of brief sketches of newspapers) of journalism in the state from the time of the founding of the *Arkansas Gazette* in 1819. Mixing a strong, pervasive Romantic view of editors with the Developmental concern in newspaper progress, Allsop wrote that Arkansas newspapers "have grown more impersonal with the years, not that editors lack the personality and force of early day newspaper workers, but because conditions and the practices of journalism have changed. The newspaper of the early days was the personal product of the editor, and he breathed his spirit into it. The product of today is more impersonal because it caters to a wider field and is made by a greater number of minds."[9]

The state accounts normally began with discussions of the first newspapers in the region and traced their development from small, short-lived weeklies to well-established dailies or, at the least, to large, prosperous weeklies. Usually descriptive and antiquarian, these accounts chronicled the crude conditions under which the first newspapers operated and their subsequent development into newspapers concerned with getting news, serving their readers with the latest information, and publicizing the activities of their communities.

---

[9]Fred W. Allsop, *History of the Arkansas Press for a Hundred Years and More* (Little Rock: Parke-Harper, 1922), 20.

Within this chronology, individual editors played major roles. Developmental historians gave considerable emphasis to them not only as originators of journalism in their communities, but also as sincere, articulate journalists with a real concern for how they practiced their profession and who contributed to the progress of journalism in their communities or regions.

The most prolific historian of the frontier press from the Developmental school—and, indeed, from any school—was Douglas C. McMurtrie, the author of more than 200 books, articles, and pamphlets on the subject written mainly during the 1920s and 1930s. Although his primary interest was printing rather than particularly newspapers, he provided an exhaustive record of the westward progress of both printing and newspapers. Taking an antiquarian approach, he chronicled the "beginning of . . .," "first," "early," and "pioneer" printing and newspapers in most territories and states and in numerous towns. One can trace in his works the westward movement of the press from North Carolina to Kentucky to Tennessee, Wisconsin, South Dakota, Montana, Wyoming, Colorado, New Mexico, Arizona, Nevada, and finally to California. Although McMurtrie's concern was not the professional journalism of the traditional Developmental historian, like historians of that school he was especially interested in the origins and development of practices of the trade, and one sees in his interest in newspaper printing a focus that mirrors Developmental journalism historians' attention to progress in their field.

The Cultural School

Whereas Romantic and Developmental historians found much to be admired in the character and contributions of frontier editors, Cultural historians downplayed those individuals and instead lifted to preeminence the surrounding conditions in which the editors operated. The Cultural interpretation of the frontier press came into prominence, by no coincidence, in the 1930s. Its reinterpretation was the result primarily of two factors. The first was the change in conditions in rural America brought about by the Great Depression and by the dust bowl that drought created. The second was the increased study of the frontier press being done by journalism historians trained as academic scholars.

In the 1930s, historians became more aware of the harsh conditions of life in rural areas and on the frontier. The drought and the resultant rural poverty made historians reassess the picture that Romantic historians had painted of frontier editors as colorful individuals succeeding against the rugged frontier. It was the environment, Cultural historians argued, that was stronger; and the conditions of the frontier, they declared, exercised a major influence on the character of the frontier press. Forces included a variety of features such as the environment, the level of culture, the regional heritage, religion, geography and geographic location, agriculture, the restricted means of transportation and communication, and most important, several Cultural historians believed, economics.

Frontier conditions influenced the character of journalists, and the content and operation of publications as well. With transportation not highly developed, newspapers received news and information by whatever means was available—including the postal system, express riders, and general travelers—rather than by organized news systems such as wire services or reporting staffs in distant places. Neither were printing operations as advanced as on eastern newspapers. Newspapers placed a strong emphasis on the editorial function, and they were involved in political and social debates, notably including the conflicts between Whites and Indians.

The key historian in the reassessment of the frontier press was Robert Housman. A doctoral graduate from the University of Missouri, he was the individual scholar primarily responsible for providing the impetus for the Cultural reinterpretation. He was the first person to complete a doctoral program in journalism in the United States, receiving, according to the University of Missouri, his degree in 1934. From his dissertation—entitled "Early Montana Territorial Journalism as a Reflection of the American Frontier in the New Northwest"—he published a number of articles, becoming one of the most prolific historians of the frontier press. Although he argued—as Romantic historians had done—that a distinctive feature of frontier editors was their individualism, he also noted "the hardships of pioneer newspaper making: the long hours, the irregular routines, the work with inadequate equipment."[10] Although much of his writing took merely an antiquarian approach to chronicling early publishing in Montana, he presented his Cultural explanation clearly in a 1935 article entitled "The End of Frontier Journalism in Montana." The press in the 1870s, he wrote, was a mirror of the political, social, and economic frontier. Editors brought with them the "tradition of personal journalism characteristic of the general newspaper work of the period,"[11] but in regard to politics, racial problems, law and order, and other topics, the frontier press was a reflection of its environment. Its emphasis was on agriculture (the primary concern in Montana) and other conditions dominant on the frontier.

Along with Housman, the leading advocate of the Cultural in-

---

[10]Robert L. Housman, "Boy Editors of Frontier Montana," *Pacific Northwest Quarterly* 27 (July 1936): 219.

[11]Robert L. Housman, "The End of Frontier Journalism in Montana," *Journalism Quarterly* 12 (1935): 133.

terpretation of the frontier press was William H. Lyon. In *The Pioneer Editor in Missouri, 1808-1860* (1965) he analyzed frontier journalism in Missouri with a primary emphasis on outside factors such as the environment, newspaper purposes, economics, content, news values, freedom, and professional relationships among journalists. Four agents, he found, fostered the founding of pioneer papers: government, politicians, the literate citizenry who wanted reading matter, and the editor-printer himself. The frontier press had certain general characteristics. Editors, Lyon noted, proclaimed their independence from parties rather consistently, although some of their writings were marked by rabid partisanship and editors apparently seldom equated independence with neutrality. They also were concerned that they fulfill their obligation to social responsibility—although their ideas of such responsibility were not the same as those of professional journalism today. Lyon also took issue with the tendency of historians to concentrate "on the bizarre or the bland, on the poison pens or the place of publication" of newspapers.[12] He argued that historians should be concerned instead with the significance of newspapers in American frontier life. That significance could be found, he said, by examining newspapers within the context of the frontier environment.

The harshness of the frontier that Cultural historians recognized during the dust bowl of the 1930s encouraged a reassessment of publishing conditions. Rather than the glamorized life that Romantic historians had envisioned, Cultural historians began to paint a picture of frontier publishing filled with difficulties. Most newspapers, they found, had short lives, and few editors prospered. The weather was harsh, money was scarce, transportation was unpredictable and slow, Indians were hostile, there were difficulties in getting news from the outside because of geography, political opponents sometimes presented physical threats—times in general were hard. One editor, describing his trials and tribulations in Illinois, proclaimed, "I am in purgatory now."[13] It was these features of frontier publishing that Cultural historians began to note and to emphasize.

Generally, Cultural historians were sympathetic to the difficulties that frontier editors faced. Milton W. Hamilton, one of the earliest Cultural historians, epitomized that concern. Taking as his subject the rural press of New York, he described the progress of its westward movement, which corresponded to the spread of civilization at the edge of the frontier, as "a natural development, following

---

[12]William H. Lyon, "The Significance of Newspapers on the American Frontier," *Journal of the West* 19 (April 1980): 3-13.

[13]Everett W. Kindig, "'I am in purgatory now': Journalist Hooper Warren Survives the Illinois Frontier," *Illinois Historical Journal* 79 (Autumn 1986): 185-196.

trade and population."[14] In *The Country Printer: New York State, 1785-1830* (1936), he detailed a sympathetic study covering the various aspects of frontier publishing, including such topics as apprenticeships, freedom of the press, early development of newspaper ethics, political partisanship, financing of papers, the fierce independence of pioneer printers, circulation, newspaper influence, and finally the encroachment of city papers. At the forefront of Hamilton's explanation was a description of the numerous problems that publishers confronted. They included such things as shortage of capital, meager public support, the inadequacy of printers' education, difficulties in obtaining news, angry readers, and subscribers who failed to pay. The picture of the frontier newspaper that emerged from Hamilton's chronicle was that of a small enterprise that struggled to make ends barely meet.

The most common difficulties, according to many Cultural historians, were economic ones. Financial problems, including difficulties in collecting payments from subscribers, were severe, although some papers apparently made a modest profit. This aspect of publishing was presented most fully by Alfred L. Lorenz. In studies of journalism in frontier Wisconsin, he presented a picture of newspapers as founded and maintained under difficult circumstances. In "Harrison Reed: an Editor's Trials on the Wisconsin Frontier" (1976), he concluded that nearly all printer-editors of Wisconsin Territory in the 1830s and 1840s—as exemplified by Reed, editor of the *Wisconsin Enquirer*—faced financial, social, and political pressures. Reed left journalism, Lorenz wrote, because "he had endured more financial deprivation, political double-dealing and personal abuse . . . than he could any longer bear . . . . Men like Reed usually established their presses with the financial support of town speculators and promoters who wanted to use the newspapers to attract immigrants to Wisconsin or by politicians who wanted a platform from which to advance their political ambitions. In neither case, however, was the support generous, and the printer-editor's position was nearly always insecure. In the one instance, his ability to stay in business depended on whether his backer held to his vision of the community's future, his enthusiasm for the project, and his money. In the other, the editor who supported a political party or leader could at almost any time find himself a casualty of the treacherous, anything-goes inter-party and intra-party battles which were part and parcel of frontier politics."[15]

---

[14]Milton W. Hamilton, "The Spread of the Newspaper Press in New York Before 1830," *New York History* 14 (April 1933): 143.

[15]Alfred Lawrence Lorenz, "Harrison Reed: An Editor's Trials on the Wisconsin Frontier," *Journalism Quarterly* 53 (1976): 417. See also Lorenz, "'Out of Sorts and Out of Cash': Problems of Publishing in Wisconsin Territory, 1833-1848," *Journalism History* 3 (1976): 34-39, 63.

Whereas Cultural historians such as Lorenz detailed the difficulties that financial matters presented to frontier editors, another group of Cultural historians were more concerned with analyzing the key role that economics played in newspaper operations. With such a view, they could more properly be considered Economic historians than general Cultural historians, for their interest clearly focused on that one topic. Although Karl Trever in his 1948 study "Wisconsin Newspapers as Publishers of the Federal Laws, 1836-1874"[16] presented an early discussion of the economics of frontier publishing and the patronage system of awarding federal printing contracts, the mantle of the Economic group of historians has been worn by two more recent historians, Carolyn Stewart Dyer and Barbara Cloud. Both painted a picture of frontier editors motivated and influenced mainly by financial concerns.

In "Economic Dependence and Concentration of Ownership Among Antebellum Wisconsin Newspapers"[17] (1980), Dyer explained newspapers as generally not capitalized exclusively by their operators—that is, they received financing from outside people or agenices—and argued that the forms of capitalization posed threats to the operators' independence. Approximately one-fourth of newspapers were parts of chains or groups, which, among other effects, reduced the amount of content diversity. She followed that study with another, "Political Patronage of the Wisconsin Press, 1849-1860: New Perspectives on the Economics of Patronage" (1989), which analyzed the system of financing newspapers through political patronage. Patronage, she argued, provided a major source of income for political newspapers and thus was used, either as reward or punishment (through its withdrawal), by partisans to influence editors. "Party politics and political patronage," she explained, "were the primary currencies of exchange that made the newspaper possible in new Wisconsin communities of a few hundred or thousand settlers . . . . [P]olitical patronage of the press . . . was both more diverse and more diffuse than many other studies of patronage have revealed . . . . [It occurred] in a broader context of the economics of the nineteenth century press. . . .[T]he economic and political foundation supported a two-tiered, statewide political press system or network." The system had "built-in mechanisms for awarding substantially greater amounts of patronage to a party's

---

[16]Karl Trever, "Wisconsin Newspapers as Publishers of the Federal Laws, 1836-1874," *Wisconsin Magazine of History* 31 (March 1948): 305-325.

[17]Carolyn Stewart Dyer, "Economic Dependence and Concentration of Ownership Among Antebellum Wisconsin Newspapers," *Journalism History* 7 (1980): 42-46. This article, along with Dyer's other publications, grew out of her doctoral dissertation, "The Business History of the Antebellum Wisconsin Newspaper, 1833-1860: A Study of Concentration of Ownership and Diversity of Views," University of Wisconsin, 1978.

most important and most needy newspapers."[18]

Writing at the same time as Dyer, Barbara Cloud also emphasized the economic basis of frontier newspapers, but with a focus on publications in Washington state rather than Wisconsin. She came to conclusions similar to Dyer's. In "A Party Press? Not Just Yet! Political Publishing on the Frontier" (1980), she found that in most Washington towns from 1852 to 1882, the first newspaper was started primarily for economic reasons. "Subsequent newspapers in each town, however, sometimes were started," she wrote, "in order to disseminate a message. In the 1850s and 1860s this message tended to be political; in the later period it varied from religious to theatrical." To support a newspaper, a community needed to have a minimum stable population and per capita income, profitable agriculture in the surrounding area, some manufacturing, and a formal government. In most towns, the pattern of development was nonpartisan first newspaper, emerging partisanship, and then competing partisan papers.[19]

To Cultural historians such as Dyer and Cloud, the Romantic view of editors was a myth. Cultural historians agreed with their Romantic predecessors that the frontier press did indeed exhibit the characteristics of the frontier; but—rather than providing instances of rugged, colorful individualism, as Romantic historians had argued—the character of the press, Cultural historians declared, was typical of the routine, socialized conditions that dominated the frontier. Editors were not the stereoptypical, glamorized heroes that Romantic historians described, but printers committed to their craft and to making a living whose nature mirrored and to some extent was determined by the forces of the frontier. Although some historians from other, especially ideological schools condemned editors for their attitudes, Cultural historians generally tended to justify them because they, like other inhabitants of the frontier, were susceptible to surrounding environmental and cultural forces. Overall, however, the image of frontier journalism that emerged from Cultural studies was that of ordinariness, banality, lack of individuality, excessive partisanship, town boosterism, and bare financial subsistence.

---

[18]Carolyn Stewart Dyer, "Political Patronage of the Wisconsin Press, 1849-1860: New Perspectives on the Economics of Patronage," *Journalism Monographs* 109 (1989): 1, 31.

[19]Barbara L. Cloud, "A Party Press? Not Just Yet! Political Publishing on the Frontier," *Journalism History* 7 (1980): 54-55, 72-73. The quoted material is from her doctoral dissertation, "Start the Presses: The Birth of Journalism in Washington Territory," University of Washington, 1979. She presented additional material on her economic explanation in "Establishing the Frontier Newspaper: A Study of Eight Western Territories," *Journalism Quarterly* 61 (1984): 805-811.

This revised description of the editor's character was presented first by Philip D. Jordan in 1930 in "The Portrait of a Pioneer Printer." His subject was James G. Edwards, a printer in Illinois in the 1830s. Edwards, Jordan said, "has few claims to prominence and practically all the claims to obscurity. He is of interest only because of his supreme normality. A typical frontier newspaperman who set his type by hand, pulled the galley proofs, ran off the edition, delivered it, and then attempted to collect from his subscribers—this was Edwards and in these chores he was no different from other printers who were hoping to build up a publishing business on the frontier."[20]

Although Jordan's assessment was relatively neutral, that of some Cultural historians was definitely critical. Among those historians, Thomas H. Heuterman provided the fullest and most sustained attack on the Romantic image of frontier editors. He argued that one of the primary characteristics of the frontier editor was racism. In "Assessing the 'Press on Wheels': Individualism in Frontier Journalism" (1976),[21] Heuterman wrote that because of the western characteristic of "individualism," the newspaper the *Frontier Index* cannot be considered necessarily typical of western papers or to have mirrored western society. It was, however, partisan, boosterish, and financially successful and carried colorful tales from the west. Its editor, Legh Freeman, was important socially and politically on the local level and believed in rugged individualism. Heuterman followed that article with a book-length study of Freeman and his newspaper, *Movable Type: Biography of Legh R. Freeman* (1979). It provided a hard, unglamorized picture of the roving frontier editor. "[F]rontier newspapers by their mere existence," Heuterman wrote, "are said to have raised the educational level of society, civilized the West and been an agent of literacy. Frontiersmen were avid readers, but whether racist, anti-Grant editorials or land promotion schemes achieved such enlightenment is questionable . . . . Freeman hardly helped to civilize the West [through] his inflammatory vigilante or political editorials." Publishing in various states, he left a legacy of "tall tales, boosterism, and even racism."[22] Readers received Freeman's racist writings enthusiastically, thus providing another indication of the violent nature of the frontier.

---

[20]Philip D. Jordan, "The Portrait of a Pioneer Printer," *Journal of the Illinois State Historical Society* 23 (April 1930): 175.

[21]Thomas H. Heuterman, "Assessing the 'Press on Wheels': Individualism in Frontier Journalism," *Journalism Quarterly* 53 (1976): 423-428.

[22]Thomas H. Heuterman, *Movable Type: Biography of Legh R. Freeman* (Ames: Iowa State University Press, 1979). See also Thomas Heuterman, "Racism in Frontier Journalism: A Case Study," *Journal of the West* 19 (April 1980): 46-50.

The Ideological Schools

The image of the frontier editor suffered even further in the hands of a number of historians writing from ideological perspectives. Some of those historians were Progressive in their outlook, whereas others simply had an interest in particular topics of social concern. The Progressive historians were concerned primarily about the liberalism of editors, whereas other historians were mainly interested in media treatment of minorities or special groups, particularly American Indians and women. These ideological historians took several approaches. Some Progressive historians praised liberal, reform-oriented editors, especially abolitionists, Populists, and crusaders. Others criticized conservative, reactionary editors. Historians of American Indians and women normally praised members of those groups who edited newspapers, or condemned Anglo-Saxon and male editors for neglecting or mistreating them. The picture of the typical frontier editor that emerged from these historians generally was a critical one. The praiseworthy white, male editor of the Romantic historians became a racist and sexist who urged repression and advocated violence.

The critical assessment of frontier editors was particularly evident in the works of historians writing about newspaper treatment of Indians. These historians claimed that editors' belief in racial superiority toward and hatred of Indians encouraged violence toward them. Elmo S. Watson, who first articulated the reevaluation of editors' attitudes toward Indians, declared that newspapers were responsible, because of their intentionally distorted accounts, for fomenting wars that finally wiped out Indian culture. Newspapers, he wrote, exaggerated, twisted, and faked news stories about the peaceful activities of the Sioux Indians in North and South Dakota, making it appear as if the Indians were beginning an uprising. Whites' misunderstanding of the Sioux actions led to war. In "The Indian Wars and the Press, 1866-1867" (1940), Watson argued that the "kind of news from the 'Wild West' which the newspapers east of the Mississippi began publishing in 1866 reflects little credit upon American journalism. Depending mainly upon volunteer correspondents more gifted in imaginative writing than in accurate reporting, they spread before their readers the kind of highly-colored accounts of Indian raids and 'massacres' that the most sensational yellow journals of a later period might have envied."[23]

A number of other historians followed Watson's lead, whereas others, believing American Indians generally had been neglected by historians, began to shift the focus of research from Anglo-Saxon

---

[23]Elmo S. Watson, "The Indian Wars and the Press, 1866-1867," *Journalism Quarterly* 17 (1940): 302. See also Watson, "The Last Indian War, 1890-91—A Study of Newspaper Jingoism," *Journalism Quarterly* 20 (1943): 205-219.

to Indian editors. Historians produced works on Indian journalism as early as the 1930s, but the explosion in the interest in the subject came in the 1970s. During that decade, Americans became especially aware of minority groups in society, and historians began to devote more attention to them. The most prominent historians of Indian journalism were Sharon Murphy and Sam Riley.

In a series of articles and the book *Let My People Know: American Indian Journalism* (1981), Murphy criticized the White press along the lines Watson had laid out, explained the reasons for the origins of Indian journalism, and described its functions. "Long before television and films," she declared, "the print media of the 19th Century did their part to foster inaccurate images of Indians. In fact, much of news reporting about Indians was done in advocacy fashion, encouraging or at least condoning the savage treatment of Indians."[24] Indian journalism developed in response to stereotypes presented in the White press and as an attempt to provide communication channels for Indians themselves. Indian newspapers "served as watchdog, teacher and advocate, promoting literacy, reporting on encroachments by white civilizations and commending the heritage and accomplishments of the Indians."[25]

Sam Riley held a similarly sympathetic view of Indian journalists,[26] but at the same time he cautioned that historians should be wary about attributing narrow prejudice exclusively to White editors. Although recent White journalism historians, he wrote, have tended to be sympathetic toward American Indians and critical of Anglo-American treatment of them, critics need to recognize that "the Indian was and is no more inherently egalitarian than the whites who engulfed him . . . . Though Cherokees were themselves the victims of intense racial discrimination, an examination of the *Phoenix* [edited by Elias Boudinott] reveals that the tribe had prejudices of its own."[27]

As with Indian journalism, historians in the 1970s began to spotlight the work of women and Black journalists and foreign-language newspapers on the frontier. As a general rule, these histori-

---

[24]Sharon Murphy, "American Indians and the Media: Neglect and Stereotype," *Journalism History* 6 (1979): 39.

[25]Sharon Murphy, "Neglected Pioneers: 19th Century Native American Newspapers," *Journalism History* 4 (1977): 79.

[26]See Sam G. Riley, "*The Cherokee Phoenix*: The Short Unhappy Life of the First American Indian Newspaper," *Journalism Quarterly* 53 (1976): 666-671; "*Indian Journal*, Voice of Creek Tribe, Now Oklahoma's Oldest Newspaper," *Journalism Quarterly* 59 (1982): 46-51, 183; and "Alex Posey: Creek Indian Editor/Humorist/Poet," *American Journalism* 1, 2 (1984): 67-76.

[27]Sam G. Riley, "A Note of Caution—The Indian's Own Prejudice, as Mirrored in the First Native American Newspaper," *Journalism History* 6 (1979): 44-47.

ans—like those of the American Indian press—were critical of the White, male-dominated press' traditional or reactionary views. They provided a favorable assessment of female and minority editors as advocates of women's interests and of civil rights and as defenders of equality and minority culture.

The most prolific historian on any of these topics was Sherilyn Bennion. In numerous articles she pointed out the importance of the female frontier journalist for historical study. Although receiving little attention from historians, frontier newspapers and magazines that were published for women, Bennion said, were "not only well read but were also recognized as shapers of community opinion." Editors generally were "articulate, self-sufficient and committed, occasionally slightly eccentric, but very rarely dull."[28] Suffrage newspapers were especially prominent. They articulated the ideas of the movement for women's right to vote, helped win adherents to the cause, and "enabled suffragists to solidify a base from which to extend their efforts . . . . The papers led the way in the campaigns for suffrage wherever they were published. They helped develop ideas and organization. They provided a forum for a cause which had time—and justice—on its side."[29] They were, Bennion concluded, "ardent voices in favor of women obtaining the right to vote . . . [demonstrating] that women's concerns found published expression in the West, as well as in the East, very early in the struggle for suffrage."[30]

Discussion

The historical view of the frontier press and its editors has ranged widely. One sees in the evaluations offered by Romantic and ideological historians, for example, greatly differing pictures. According to which school one accepts, editors may be viewed in terms running from the glowingly positive to the harshly negative. Historians have presented a number of questions about the character of editors.

1. Were editors, as Romantic historians assumed, rugged individuals and the creators of civilization on the frontier?

2. Were Romantic historians influenced too greatly by the national views of their own time to allow them to provide an accurate assessment of frontier editors from their own time period?

3. Is it appropriate to impose the standards of journalism deriving mainly from metropolitan newspapers on the small weekly pub-

---

[28]Sherilyn Cox Bennion, "Early Western Publications Expose Women's Suffrage Cries," *Matrix* 64 (Summer 1979): 6-9.

[29]Sherilyn Cox Bennion, "Woman Suffrage Papers of the West, 1869-1914," *American Journalism* 3 (1986): 140.

[30]Sherilyn Cox Bennion, "*The New Northwest* and *Woman's Exponent*: Early Voices of Suffrage," *Journalism Quarterly* 54 (1977): 286.

lications that were operating on the frontier?

4. Were editors less important and benign than Romantic historians described them as being? Were they really insignificant figures buffeted by the exigencies of the frontier or, at best, small-time businessmen concerned mainly with surviving, as Cultural historians described them?

5. Did the conditions of Cultural historians' own age—such as the dust bowl and the recent emphasis on newspapers as money-making businesses—too greatly affect their assessment of the frontier press? Is it appropriate, as Cultural historians may have done, to project present conditions back on the frontier press?

6. Which is more important as a factor in history: the environment, as Cultural historians argued, or the individual? What is the relationship between the two?

7. Can editors be explained best in ideological terms: as liberal social reformers, as some ideological historians have presented them, or racists, as others have declared?

8. Have ideological historians unfairly condemned frontier editors for holding the social views that may have been general for their time rather than the later, enlightened views of the historians' time?

Readings

Romantic School

Beebe, Lucius, "Season in the Sun," pp. 21-39, *Comstock Commotion: The Story of the Territorial Enterprise*. Stanford, CA: Stanford University Press, 1954.

Gregory, John G., "Early Wisconsin Editors: Harrison Reed," *Wisconsin Magazine of History* 7 (June 1924): 459-472.

Karolevitz, Robert F., "Quills, Type Sticks and Six-Guns," pp. 11-15, and "Colorado: Horace Greeley's West," pp. 59-69, *Newspapering in the Old West: A Pictorial History of Journalism and Printing on the Frontier*. Seattle, WA: Superior Publishing, 1965.

Lent, John A., "The Press on Wheels: A History of *The Frontier Index*," *Journal of the West* 10 (1971): 662-699.

Thwaites, R. G., "The Ohio Valley Press before the War of 1812-1815," *American Antiquarian Society Proceedings* 19 (April 1909): 309-368.

White, Z.L., "Western Journalism," *Harper's New Monthly Magazine* 77 (1888): 678-699.

Developmental School

Allsop, Fred W. Part I, pp. 15-41, *History of the Arkansas Press for a Hundred Years and More*. Little Rock: Parke-Harper, 1922.

Davis, Horance G., Jr., "Pensacola Newspapers, 1821-1900," *Florida Historical Quarterly* 37 (1959): 419-445.

McMurtrie, Douglas C., "The Pioneer Press in Montana," *Journalism Quarterly* 9 (1932): 170-181.

Turnbull, George, "The Schoolmaster of the Oregon Press," *Journalism Quarterly* 13 (1938): 359-369, 382.

Cultural School

Cloud, Barbara L., "A Party Press? Not Just Yet! Political Publishing on the Frontier," *Journalism History* 7 (1980): 54-55, 72-73.

Dyer, Carolyn Stewart, "Political Patronage of the Wisconsin Press, 1849-1860: New Perspectives on the Economics of Patronage," *Journalism Monographs* 109 (1989).

Ellison, Rhoda C., "Newspaper Publishing in Frontier Alabama," *Journalism Quarterly* 23 (1946): 289-301.

Garcia, Hazel, "'What a Buzzel is This. . . about Kentuck?' New Approaches and an Application," *Journalism History* 3 (1976): 11-15, 19.

Hamilton, Milton W., "The Spread of the Newspaper Press in New York Before 1830," *New York History* 14 (April 1933): 142-151.

Heuterman, Thomas H., "Assessing the 'Press on Wheels': Individualism in Frontier Journalism," *Journalism Quarterly* 53 (1976): 423-428.

Housman, Robert L., "The End of Frontier Journalism in Montana," *Journalism Quarterly* 12 (1935): 133-145.

Huntzicker, William, Ch. 8, "The Frontier Press, 1800-1900," pp. 165-190, Wm. David Sloan, James G. Stovall, and James D. Startt, eds., *The Media in America: A History*. Worthington, OH: Publishing Horizons, 1989.

Jordan, Philip D., "The Portrait of a Pioneer Printer," *Journal of the Illinois State Historical Society* 23 (April 1930): 175-182.

Katz, William A., "The Western Printer and His Publications, 1850-90," *Journalism Quarterly* 44 (1967): 708-714.

Kindig, Everett W., "'I am in purgatory now': Journalist Hooper Warren Survives the Illinois Frontier," *Illinois Historical Journal* 79 (1986): 185-196.

Knight, Oliver, "*The Owyhee Avalanche*: The Frontier Newspaper as a Catalyst in Social Change," *Pacific Northwest Quarterly* 58 (April 1967): 74-81.

Lyon, William H., "The Significance of Newspapers on the American Frontier," *Journal of the West* 19 (April 1980): 3-13.

Ideological Schools

Bennion, Sherilyn Cox, "The Woman's Exponent: Forty-two Years of Speaking for Women," *Utah Historical Quarterly* 44 (1976): 222-239.

Blankenburg, William B., "The Role of the Press in an Indian Massacre, 1871," *Journalism Quarterly* 46 (1969): 61-70.

Murphy, Sharon, "American Indians and the Media: Neglect and Stereotype," *Journalism History* 6 (1979): 39-43.

Reilly, Tom, "A Spanish-Language Voice of Dissent in Antebellum New Orleans," *Louisiana History* 23 (1983): 325-339.

Riley, Sam G., "A Note of Caution—The Indian's Own Prejudice, as Mirrored in the First Native American Newspaper," *Journalism History* 6 (1979): 44-47.

Watson, Elmo S., "The Last Indian War, 1890-91—A Study of Newspaper Jingoism," *Journalism Quarterly* 20 (1943): 205-219.

Williams, Nudie, "The Black Press in Oklahoma: The Formative Years, 1889-1907," *Chronicles of Oklahoma* 61 (1983): 308-319.

9

The Penny Press, 1833-1861:
Product of Great Men or Natural Forces?

No matter what their interpretive stance, historians of the penny press era agree that the time was a pivotal one in the history of American journalism and the mass media. The era was, they believe, when the modern "mass media" emerged. American journalism changed profoundly between 1830 and 1861—as did American society itself. Because the changes in the mass media were so extensive, historians have struggled—with partial success and little agreement—to describe, explain, and interpret the era.

Some of the changes during the period are indicative of what occurred and easy to document. The number of daily newspapers published in the United States grew from 65 in 1830 to more than 350 in 1861. Total circulation increased from 78,000 to 1,478,000. This growth far outpaced the nation's population, suggesting that Americans' reading appetite and habits had changed. Newspapers were reaching audiences numbering in the tens of thousands, rather than the hundreds, and their audiences were not always local ones. A few papers, such as Horace Greeley's New York *Tribune* and Samuel Bowles' Springfield *Republican*, had national circulations.

Many of these papers were large enough to employ staffs of news reporters, editors, engravers, and printers, unlike the one-person operations of the previous decades. The big-city papers were supported by single-copy sales and subscriptions that people paid for in advance. Most importantly, they were run by men who were independent entrepreneurs, interested in politics and public issues but not dependent on the goodwill of politicians and political parties. Furthermore, the content and structure of the American newspaper also underwent change. By 1861 newspapers were publishing more news, human interest, and items not seen in the newspapers of the 1820s.

In short, the newspaper of 1840 was much more like that of the

By James G. Stovall
University of Alabama

1990s than the newspaper of 1825. Quickly and profoundly, the American newspaper had become "modern."

What happened? And why did it happen? These are the questions that journalism historians have tackled. In taking on these questions, they have revealed their own profound differences in interpretive orientations toward this important period.

The penny press era got its name from the idea, put into practice in New York and a few other large cities, that newspapers could be profitably produced and sold for one penny. Before 1833 newspapers were not sold as single copies. Readers subscribed to them for longer periods, usually a year. A single copy—if purchased at the printer's shop—might be six cents, and a year's subscription might be as much as eight or ten dollars, the equivalent of a laborer's weekly salary. It was a price that relatively few could afford. The name "penny press" does not, however, adequately describe the changes that occurred in journalism.

The first successful penny paper was the New York *Sun*, whose first edition appeared on September 3, 1833. What made the *Sun* different was not just the price but the content. The seriousness and pomposity that pervaded party newspapers were absent. James Parton's eyewitness description of a "respectable New Yorker" taking his first look at a penny newspaper is indicative of its content. "[H]e gazed at it," Parton wrote, "with a feeling similar to that with which an ill-natured man may be supposed to regard General Tom Thumb, a feeling of mingled curiosity and contempt; he put the ridiculous little thing into his waistcoat pocket to carry home for the amusement of his family; and he wondered what nonsense would be perpetrated next."[1]

The publishers of penny newspapers, however, were serious about what they were doing. Benjamin Day, publisher of the *Sun*, wrote a prospectus that read, in part, "The object of this paper is to lay before the public, at a price within the means of everyone, ALL THE NEWS OF THE DAY, and at the same time afford an advantageous medium for advertising."[2]

This "all the news of the day" concept was a radical one that even Day might not have fully appreciated. One of the great contributions of the penny press was the definition it gave to "news." Penny papers paid attention to local news of politics, government, the courts, society, and business. Private calamities and triumphs became public because of this new definition of news. Not only did the concept of news expand, but it also took on the characteristic of

---

[1]James Parton, *Life of Horace Greeley* (New York: Mason Brothers, 1855), 141-142.

[2]Quoted in Frederic Hudson, *Journalism in the United States, From 1690 to 1872* (New York: Harper and Row, 1873), 417.

timeliness. Because the penny press operated in a world where speed—speed of travel and speed of communication—was making sharp increases, information in the newspaper became more contemporary than it had ever been.

The man who advanced this definition of news farther than anyone else in his age was James Gordon Bennett. He founded the New York *Herald* in 1835 and, along with Horace Greeley, was one of the two most controversial and influential journalists of the time. The *Herald* hit the streets of New York City with Bennett vowing to take its readers to "wherever human nature and real life best display their freaks and vagaries."[3]

Bennett developed many enemies, including financiers on Wall Street, leaders in the Catholic and Protestant churches, and most especially publishers of other newspapers in the city. These enemies were so numerous that they organized the Great Moral War in 1840. It was a concerted effort to take readership and advertising away from the *Herald* and to induce Bennett to curb his attacks on others.

The New York *Herald*, in the eyes of contemporaries, may have lacked taste, morals, and restraint, but it did not lack for readers. Within two years, it had 20,000 regular buyers. Over the next two decades, it pioneered innovations that included Sunday editions, paid foreign correspondents, news of sexual scandals, sports news, prepaid subscriptions, reports on political conventions, the use of pictures, appeals to women readers, and the use of the telegraph, pony express, and any other means to get information ahead of the *Herald's* rivals.

Despite his huge influence on the future of journalism, Bennett did not emerge from the penny press era as the most noted journalist. That mantle fell instead to Horace Greeley. His journalistic career during the 1830s was unremarkable, but in 1841 he produced the first issue of the New York *Tribune*. Originally designed to be a cheap Whig paper to counterbalance the Democratic tendencies of the *Herald*, the *Tribune* soon became a reflection of its owner's energy, openness to new ideas, and hard work.

Like the *Herald*, the *Tribune* emphasized news and spared few efforts to attain it, but it went beyond the *Herald* by establishing a strong editorial voice. That voice was the voice of Horace Greeley, who opposed slavery, alcohol, and capital punishment while advocating labor unions, westward expansion, and a variety of "isms" that made the *Tribune* interesting, if not always instructive, to read.

Greeley, besides being the paper's chief editorial writer, was a noted lecturer and traveler. He supported the Republican Party and Abraham Lincoln during the war years, but afterwards he broke

---

[3]New York *Herald*, May 7, 1835.

with the party. His career culminated in an unsuccessful run for the presidency as the nominee of the Democratic Party and Liberal Republicans in 1872.

The other major personality to emerge in New York City during this time was Henry Raymond. His newspaper was the New York *Times*. Founded in 1851, the *Times* took advantage of the weaknesses of some of the other papers. It sought to be more interesting than the partisan *Courier and Enquirer*, less sensational than the *Herald*, and more politically stable and middle of the road than the *Tribune*. The fact that it was successful in these efforts was a tribute to Raymond, who set the tone editorially and who guided the paper through early financial straits.

The penny press era has been fertile ground for historians to apply their own explanations for the nature of American journalism and the underlying reasons for its characteristics. Nearly all historians agreed that major changes occurred during the period. The question of primary disagreement was over the nature of the changes and the reasons behind them. Were the changes mainly journalistic in nature, or were they broader? Were they brought about by individual genius and an innate recognition of what proper journalism should be, or did the causes arise from impersonal forces within the surrounding social environment? Romantic historians, who were writing at the time that the penny press dominated journalism, believed the changes originated with individual editors. They considered penny newspapers among the great instruments of American civilization and found the personalities of the period fascinating. They therefore concentrated their efforts on describing the lives of those great individuals and their contributions to the advance of the press. Although Developmental historians agreed with the idea of progress that Romantic historians emphasized, they assumed that the appearance of the penny press was a natural, perhaps inevitable, step in the progress of journalism. They saw the penny press era not primarily in terms of national progress but as a major development in the advance toward modern journalistic practices and professionalism. Progressive historians, on the other hand, politicized history and explained the penny press era in ideological terms. To a large degree, they argued that the penny press represented the emergence of a new voice in support of the interests of the common people and democracy. Especially favored by these historians was Horace Greeley, whom they described as an advocate of the great mass of Americans, of reform, and of economic and democratic equality. Cultural historians, comprising a fourth school of interpretation, explained the penny press not primarily in ideological or professional journalistic terms but as a response to the great sociological and cultural forces of the age. Each school found in the penny press evidence to support its own historical perspective.

The Romantic School

It is easy for the modern reader to denigrate the writings of the Romantic historians of the penny press. They were, after all, not "real" historians in the modern sense, as they evidenced little of the critical thinking and analysis that scholars demand of historical writings today. They were either men of leisure who were fascinated by the lives and times of their subjects or were veterans of the events of the time who sought to set the record straight about what they had lived through. Their writing often was flowery and full of tangents. It often took an instructive or prescriptive tone, exhorting readers to learn from their subjects and to become better persons for knowing about them. Yet for all of these objections, the Romantic historians produced a valuable body of literature about the penny press era—literature that modern historians find extremely useful.

Exemplary of all of these traits was James Parton's *Life of Horace Greeley* (1855). Known elsewhere as the father of American biography, Parton looked upon Greeley as the dominant personality of his age. He kept his admiration of Greeley somewhat in check by acknowledging that intellectually Greeley was no genius and that many of his ideas were unconvincing. Yet Parton used even these shortcomings to heap praise upon Greeley. "Genius?" Parton asked. "No," he answered:

> That is not the word. Dr. Arnold was not a man of genius. Carlyle is not a man of genius. But Great Britain owes more to them than to all the men of genius that have lived since Cromwell's time. Such men differ from the poets and authors of their day, precisely in the same way, though not, perhaps, in the same degree, as the Apostles differed from Cicero, Seneca, and Virgil. Between the Clays and the Websters of this country and Horace Greeley, the difference is similar in *kind*. Horace Greeley, Thomas Carlyle, and Dr. Arnold, have each uttered much which, perhaps, the world will not finally accept. Such men seem particularly liable to a certain class of mistakes. But, says Goethe's immortal maxim, "The *Spirit* in which we act is the highest matter"—and it is the contagious, the influencing matter. "See how these Christians love one another." *That* is what made converts![4]

Parton continued along these lines at one point for two full pages, without mentioning Greeley. He finally returned to his subject by observing that "[f]rom the general tenor of Horace Greeley's words

---

[4]Parton, pp. 435-436.

and actions, during the last twenty years, I infer that this is something like his habitual view of life and its duties. Shall he be praised for this? Let us envy him rather. Only such a man knows anything of the luxury of being alive. 'Horace Greeley,' said an old friend of his, 'is the only happy man I have ever known.'"[5]

The view that Isaac C. Pray took of his subject in *Memoirs of James Gordon Bennett and His Times,* written in the same year as Parton's biography of Greeley, 1855, was equally admiring. An employee of Bennett's who wrote and published his biography during Bennett's lifetime, Pray staunchly defended Bennett against detractors. He also attributed much that was good about the world of journalism to the admirable actions of the New York *Herald* and its owner. The kind of journalism they practiced provoked readers "to thought and action, not in the old beaten track of political dictators, but on the broad ground of justice and the common welfare." Pray particularly delighted in the way Bennett turned aside the attacks made upon him by lesser men. Those attackers, he wrote, "were chagrined and maddened to see [Bennett's] jocose, quizzing and lampooning paragraphs maintaining favor in the public mind, while their own carefully written, and sometimes brilliant essays, were wholly ignored."[6]

Pray's view of journalism was typically romantic. Journalists, he declared, had a higher public duty to perform than earlier partisan editors had done. "May journalists," he urged, "ever keep glowing in their minds those words in which they may find a manual of practice as efficient for the country and for the elevation of their own profession, as any conventional usages, or any codes of maxims or laws: IRREPROACHABLE TASTE—CHARITY—FRATERNITY —JUSTICE—THE PUBLIC GOOD."[7]

Despite the weaknesses that Romantic historians exhibited from a modern point of view, they made a valuable contribution to the study of the penny press. Their contemporary and sometimes eyewitness accounts of events provided subsequent historians with much of the material currently in use to interpret this period. The openness with which they expressed their own attitudes about journalists and journalism also provided later historians ideas about the contemporary views of these subjects. Finally, their emphasis on writing about the major personalities of the day, rather than the events that surrounded them, firmly entrenched the "great man" perspective with which many later historians continued to view this era of history.

---

[5]Ibid., pp. 436-437.

[6] Isaac C. Pray, *Memoirs of James Gordon Bennett and His Times* (New York: Stringer and Townsend, 1855), 418, 264.

[7]Ibid., p. 488.

The Developmental School

With the arrival of the penny press, journalism historiography gained a new school of interpretation. Frederic Hudson, the first and perhaps the most important Developmental historian, introduced the new perspective. It was one which declared that the press was advancing—away from the dark days of the economic and ideological alliance with political faction and toward an independent professionalism that should be journalism's ideal. Hundreds of later historians accepted the Developmental perspective in assessing various episodes in media history, but nowhere were they more in evidence than when talking about the changes that occurred in American journalism during the 1830s.

Developmental historians were, in some sense, the natural successors to the Romantic historians. While eschewing the language of the Romantic historians, they used much of the literature that the Romantic historians had produced, and more importantly, they refined the attitudes that many of them had exhibited. Like the Romantic historians, they felt the press was best when it served the public good, but they narrowed their main concern in the press from its broad interaction with American progress to its introduction and development of journalistic practices. Reasoning that the journalism as practiced by the penny press was the proper kind, they assumed that the proper explanation of journalism history was the origin and progress toward penny press practices.

One attitude that Developmental historians inherited intact from the Romantic historians was the emphasis on the importance of the personalities that shaped the history of the American press. Developmental historians found much to like and dislike about Day, Bennett, Greeley, and Raymond. Each made contributions to the advancement of the press, and each had his shortcomings.

Developmental historians, unlike their Romantic predecessors, paid little attention to the politics of the time as an influence on the press. Politics, they believed, was of little importance in the changes that took place. Instead, they reasoned, journalism's declaration of independence from political influence was the essential political event. Rather than political affiliation what was important to the Developmental historians was the change that was occurring in the content and structure of the newspapers themselves.

Finally, Developmental historians offered few, and usually unsatisfying, explanations about why the changes occurred. Readers of these histories might infer from the large body of Developmental literature that the changes in the press occurred "naturally" as part of the inevitable progress toward proper journalistic practices or, more substantively, that they were the results of the forceful personalities that dominated the era.

Frederic Hudson, the originator of the Developmental interpretation, spent most of his working career with the New York *Herald* and served as managing editor during its heyday under James Gordon Bennett. It is not surprising that he devoted the penny press chapters of his monumental work, *Journalism in the United States, From 1690 to 1872* (1873), to a sympathetic recounting of the character and actions of his publisher.

Hudson's work was, however, more than a brief for Bennett. He argued that the contribution that Bennett, and others of his age, made to the advancement of journalism was largely positive in that they began the movement away from the party-dominated newspapers that existed in the 1820s. The history of journalism up to 1872 was a natural progression toward what Hudson called the "independent press," which emphasized, along with political independence, the gathering of news and mass popular appeal. "Politics," he argued, "had sustained the old Party Press and had become a tyranny."[8] Transportation improvements—most notably the steamship and telegraph—and a growing body of literate readers provided the impetus for a modern press. Penny newspapers then were able to break free of the bondage to political patronage, escape their subservience to parties, and assume their proper role as informers of the public. The earliest penny papers educated a generation of journalists, who then were able to do an even better job of appealing to a mass reading public. The *Herald*, Hudson declared, was the most important originator of the modern journalism, that is, as practiced in 1872.

Hudson revealed an attitude of inevitability in the first paragraph of the chapter about this new era in American journalism. "It was now necessary," he declared, "to have a revolution in the Press. Those in existence were too large, and too much under the influence and control of politics. Something new was needed. Something fresh and vigorous."[9] That something was James Gordon Bennett and others like him. Hudson cast Bennett as the leading light of American journalism—a publisher whose many innovations and farsightedness were matched by the recalcitrance and pigheadedness of his contemporary New York publishers. Bennett exemplified the publisher who put news ahead of party affiliation, who contributed multiple innovations to the development of newspaper practices, who stood up for the public against monied interests, and who turned aside personal attacks with pithy and pointed paragraphs.

Although Hudson loved Bennett, he clearly admired Greeley and Raymond. His emphasis on the importance of the "great men" of this time can be found in his opening paragraph on Greeley. "If James Gordon Bennett and the New York *Herald* are synonymous

---

[8]Hudson, pp. 427.
[9]Ibid., p. 408.

terms," he observed, *"Horace Greeley* and the *New York Tribune* are equally so. If, in writing of these men and these institutions, we become somewhat mixed in the use of names, the matter will be clear to the reader whether we mention Greeley for the *Tribune,* or the *Herald* when we have to say a word of Bennett."[10]

What Hudson did for Bennett, Frank O'Brien attempted to do for Benjamin Day, founder of the New York *Sun,* in his history of the paper, *The Story of the Sun* (1928). O'Brien, like Hudson, subscribed to the "great man" approach in the Developmental explanation of the changes that occurred with the penny press. It was the *Sun* that provided the genesis of modern journalism, and it was Day who was its founder. Day, O'Brien explained, "found New York journalism a pot of cold, stale water, and left it a boiling cauldron; not so much by what he wrote as by the way in which he made his success . . . . Most [of the other New York publishers] are better known to fame than Day is, but no one of them did anything comparable to the young printer's achievement in making a popular, low-priced daily newspaper—and not only making it, but making it stick. . . . Bennett may have written the constitution of popular journalism, but it was Day who wrote its declaration of independence."[11]

Hudson's and O'Brien's attitude of inevitability in the development of journalism was echoed in other works on individual newspapers or particular journalistic practices. Victor Rosewater took such an approach to explaining the development of news practices in *History of Cooperative News-Gathering in the United States* (1930). Like Hudson, he credited much of the early progress in cooperative news gathering to Bennett, who, he said, appeared "as if directed by the stars." He also viewed the founding of cooperative news as a natural occurrence. "It was," he said, "inevitable that the gathering of news, the worth of which so plainly hinges on promptness and accuracy and which possesses an immediate commercial value only when undertaken with regularity and reliability, should become a function of the newspaper . . . . What was needed was the development of a daily newspaper as distinguished from the preceding weekly or semiweekly papers."[12]

This sense of inevitability that Hudson fostered and others took up provided the framework for *American Journalism* (1941) by Frank Luther Mott. That work, which was the most widely used textbook on mass communication history until the early 1970s, provided the apex for the Developmental interpretation. While criticizing Hudson's work as at times unreliable, Mott nevertheless accepted

---

[10]Ibid., p. 522.

[11]Frank M. O'Brien, *The Story of the Sun* (New York: Appleton, 1928), 129-132.

[12]Victor Rosewater, *History of Cooperative News-Gathering in the United States* (New York: Appleton, 1930), 11.

Hudson's implicit underlying assumptions about the essential framework of history. However, he went even further than Hudson in offering explanations for the changes that occurred. Mott constructed a paradigm that defined journalistic progress as increasing professionalism, an emphasis on news and objectivity, political independence, and mass popular appeal. Hudson wrote as if the changes that had occurred in American journalism resulted largely from the strong personalities who populated the times. Mott accepted this view to a certain degree, but he refined the descriptions of the individuals as gaining their greatness to the extent that they recognized proper journalistic practices and performed them well. The changes that had occurred with the penny press were not simply the results of imaginative thinking by creative individuals. Instead, they grew from a natural demand by the reading public for more professional-quality newspapers and the recognition by certain newspaper editors of what proper journalism was supposed to be.

Early in his book, Mott referred to the "dark ages" of the party press era. His first chapter on the penny press era was entitled "Sunrise" (a reference also to the advent of the New York *Sun*). Clearly, Mott was relieved that American journalism was changing, and his Developmental attitudes were pervasive in his writing about the three decades before the Civil War. He was not completely satisfied, however, with the press' performance. Many newspapers did not abide by the proper standards demanded by good journalism. Most publishers, he said, "with the exception of Bennett, . . . were printers looking for profitable opportunities in the line of their trade." Although the penny press contained much "healthy food, . . . [a]t the same time, the penny-press revolution was itself attended with great abuses. Bad taste, coarseness which sometimes became indecency, overemphasis on crime and sex, and disreputable advertising were outstanding sins of these papers."[13]

Mott provided little analysis of why these changes occurred. He simply assumed that they were part of the natural, inevitable advance of journalism. Other factors were secondary. Thus, he did not attempt to provide a critical analysis of them. As reasons for the mighty increases in circulation that the penny papers experienced, for example, he simply listed growth in population, increased literacy, better lighting in homes offering more reading time, a democratic system that made working-class individuals important, and a drop in newspaper prices. He uncritically accepted the conventional wisdom that the penny press appealed to the poorer segments

---

[13]Frank Luther Mott, *American Journalism: A History of Newspapers in the United States Through 250 Years, 1690 to 1940* (New York: Macmillan, 1941), 242, 243.

of society and that "newspapers for the uneducated draymen and porters must necessarily be different from those prepared for the rich merchants."[14]

The Progressive School

The Progressive school of interpretation, which emerged in the early 20th century, found much in the penny press era to study. Progressive historians viewed history as a struggle between freedom and reform on the one hand and wealth and privilege on the other. Those who concentrated on the mass media saw them as a means of exposing the vices of conservative forces, contributing to progressive political ideas, and influencing the general public into accepting ideas for political and social reform. They took little notice of the development of American journalism in and of itself. The press, they argued, should be judged on the contributions it made to the advancement of progressive political and economic ideologies. Their focus thus was on ideology and how the press contributed to the ideological atmosphere of the times. Consequently, many of them selected for study such topics as personal relationships such as those between Karl Marx and Greeley or political relationships between publications and various political movements.

Progressive historians did share some of the traditional concepts of the penny press. Like Romantic and Developmental historians, they, too, emphasized the "great men" of the era, studying their actions and ideas. Progressive historians, however, measured editors by their contributions to political and social ideology rather than to standard professional practices. Editors' stature depended on how they advanced democracy and economic conditions for the working masses. If Developmental historians loved Bennett, then Horace Greeley was the Progressives' hero.

Progressive historians differed from other historians in several other ways as well. Many preferred to emphasize the periodical press rather than newspapers in their study, apparently believing that it was often the periodicals, more than newspapers, that fostered and developed the liberal political ideas of the time. Progressive historians made more assumptions about the direct influence of the mass media on readers than did other historians. In this regard, for example, they credited Greeley with making many of the exotic ideas of the time acceptable to the general public. Finally, Progressive historians were not so much interested in the changes in journalism that took place but in the changes in the outlooks of journalists. The discipline of journalism often was a secondary or minor consideration in their study.

One of the earliest Progressive studies of the penny press era

---

[14]Ibid., p. 242.

was John Commons' tracing of the development of the Republican Party as the party of the working class. In "Horace Greeley and the Working Class Origins of the Republican Party" (1909), Commons—whose main interest was, incidentally, labor history rather than the media—focused on the role that Horace Greeley played in the party's development. He gave Greeley a premier place in the history of the period. "Greeley was to the social revolution of the forties," he declared, "what Thomas Jefferson was to the political revolution of 1800. He was the *Tribune* of the People, the spokesman of their discontent, the champion of their nostrums." For Commons, Greeley personalized and personified the struggles of the working class. Greeley's life "was itself a struggle through all the economic oppressions of his time."[15]

As editor of one of the most widely circulated newspapers in the nation, Greeley became a defender of labor unions and laborers. The cornerstone of his ideology was protective tariffs that would elevate the country's wage earners. Greeley's *Tribune*, prior to 1854, was "the first and only great vehicle this country has known for the ideas and experiments of constructive democracy." According to Commons, Greeley and the *Tribune* thus played a decisive role in the development of the basic ideology that was to undergird the liberal Republican party in its beginnings.

The idea of the influence of Greeley and the *Tribune* was taken up by William H. Hale in his 1950 biography *Horace Greeley: Voice of the People.* Greeley exemplified the nation's political leaders during the era of the penny press. "The man who barged so broadly through that age at the head of the New York *Tribune*," Hale wrote, "was like many other mentors of his time—by turns dizzy with American success and laid low by the persistence of evil. As knights of progress these men traveled light and carried little armor for self-defense. But they remained moralists even while serving as promoters, and so their personal crises came when they encountered oppression hand in hand with triumph."[16] Hale described Greeley's purpose as two-fold: to build an alliance between American progressives and businessmen and to voice his disillusion when he viewed the results of such an alliance.

The Cultural School
Since the 1950s, the Cultural school has provided a number of major studies that have departed significantly from the explanations given by previous schools. Cultural historians primarily were con-

---

[15] John R. Commons, "Horace Greeley and the Working Class Origins of the Republican Party," *Political Science Quarterly* 24 (1909): 469, 470.

[16] William Harlan Hale, *Horace Greeley, Voice of the People* (New York: Harper and Row, 1950), v.

cerned with the interrelationship of the mass media and the environment. Although most considered the penny press to be the beginning of the modern forms and attitudes of the media, they set themselves apart from other schools of interpretation in a variety of ways.

Like Developmental historians, Cultural historians looked at the penny press to find the roots of modern journalistic practices. Unlike the Developmental historians, however, they were willing to challenge the assumptions, and sometimes the reverence, that Developmental historians held for these modern practices. For example, whereas Developmental historians hailed the emergence of objectivity as a noble standard for journalists, Cultural historians found pragamatic and sometimes questionable reasons for its emergence.

Cultural historians were the most successful of all the schools of interpretation in freeing themselves of the "great men" prism through which to look at the penny press. With a few exceptions, Cultural historians placed relatively little importance on the personalities of men such as James Gordon Bennett, Horace Greeley, and Henry Raymond. Their focus was more on the social, economic, and political factors that led these men to make the decisions they did about their publications.

Cultural historians, like the Progressives, were interested in ideology, but their emphasis was a different one and their definition of ideology much more expansive. Whereas Progressive historians concentrated on the great ideological and political movements of the time, Cultural historians saw ideology in less idealistic and more economic terms.

One of the first historians to take a Cultural approach to the penny press was Sidney Kobre in *Foundations of American Journalism* (1958). He argued that the most important task of historians was to look at the social and economic factors that surrounded the emergence of the penny press, and he devoted an entire chapter to describing these factors. They included population growth and movement, changes in agriculture, institution of the public education system, growth of the post office, scientific and technical advances, and others. In his subsequent description of the penny press, he did not make clear the relationship of these factors to the emergence of the penny press, and he was not successful in explaining how they contributed to the development of the press. In fact, at the end of several chapters on the various newspapers he examined, Kobre slipped into the Developmental mode of describing the "contributions," both positive and negative, that newspapers made to the development of modern journalism.

Another attempt to relate social and economic factors to the development of the press was Michael Schudson's *Discovering the*

News: A Social History of American Newspapers (1978). Adopting the "symbolic meaning" perspective of some recent Cultural historians, Schudson believed that newspapers were a manifestation of the main ideas of a culture rather than the result of journalists' efforts to make them into models of professionalism. He thus challenged the assumption that objectivity in news reporting developed with the penny press because it was the natural professional standard or because of the wire services and the sharing of reports that had to take place with a cooperative news gathering effort. Instead, he said, the penny press' emphasis in writing was on sensationalism and "telling a good story." This emphasis continued through the 19th century and into World War I. It was only after World War I that "objectivity" became the guiding principle of news reporting.

Newspapers during the penny press era, Schudson reasoned, reflected the egalitarianism of the age. They contributed to the expanding economy by making advertisements available and by transforming themselves from a fairly rare cultural artifact (something that could be borrowed occasionally) to a household item. They were, he declared, an integral part of the "democratization of economic life."[17]

Daniel Schiller, in *Objectivity and the News: The Public and the Rise of Commercial Journalism* (1981), though also writing from a Cultural perspective, challenged Schudson's thesis on a number of points. He said that advertisements from tradesmen were abundant in newspapers before the 1830s, and that these tradesmen formed the bulk of penny press readers. They should not, however, be considered a "middle class" with a distinct set of values and attitudes, as Schudson had claimed. Schiller sought to demonstrate that the success of the penny press stemmed "largely from its remarkably fluent use of the idiom prevalent among its public of tradesmen. In the eyes of many readers, the cheap papers turned to defend the rights of many, through crime news especially, at a time when those rights seemed to be threatened by changing social relations, and when other institutions only turned their backs on cardinal republican values."[18]

Discussion

The penny press era is an important period in American journalism and has produced a large body of historical literature: biographies, reminiscences, surveys, and analyses. Although historians have presented a variety of explanations of the period, most agree on

---

[17]Michael Schudson, *Discovering the News: A Social History of American Newspapers* (New York: Basic Books, 1978), 21.

[18]Daniel T. Schiller, *Objectivity and the News: The Public and the Rise of Commercial Journalism* (Philadelphia: University of Pennsylvania Press, 1981), 10.

certain assumptions. They recognize it as the beginning of modern journalism, they place an emphasis on the New York City press, and they emphasize the development of newspapers and journalistic practices. Despite these agreements, a number of questions central to the study of the penny press remain in dispute.

1. What was the essential nature of the penny press?

2. Did the penny press provide a model of proper journalistic practices, as Developmental historians argued, or did it gain its value by advocating the ideological cause of the common man, as Progressive historians declared?

3. What were the reasons for the appearance of the penny press: the insight of great, creative men; the natural recognition by journalism of what proper newspapers should be; or great social forces that had come to the fore?

4. Other questions also confront historical study. Although we know much about what was happening in the large urban areas of the nation—particularly New York City—what changes were occurring in the journalism of the smaller cities and rural areas? Were the changes a reflection of those that were occurring in the larger urban areas?

5. The whole question of newspaper readership has not been fully answered by any school of historians. Who were the newspaper readers of the day? Why did they read? What effect did their reading have on the individuals and society at large?

6. Questions can also be raised about the various interpretative schools. Why does the emergence of the penny press seem to be a "natural" occurrence for Developmental historians?

7. What could be added to the Progressive interpretation if historians shifted some of their attention away from ideology and toward the changes occurring in the profession of journalism?

8. While attempting to recognize the importance of great impersonal forces, do Cultural historians err in avoiding exploration of the great personalities of the penny press era?

Readings

Romantic School

Maverick, Augustus, Ch. 13, "The Baltimore Convention," pp. 120-141, *Henry J. Raymond and New York Press for Thirty Years*. Hartford, CT: A. S. Hale, 1870.

Parton, James, Ch. 15, "Starts the Tribune," pp. 191-198, *Life of Horace Greeley*. New York: Mason Brothers, 1855 (rev. ed., New York: Arno, 1970).

Pray, Isaac C., Ch. 14, "The War of Journalism," pp. 197-213, *Memoirs of James Gordon Bennett and His Times*. New York: Stringer and Townsend,

1855.

Developmental School

Hudson, Frederic, Ch. 27, "The New York Herald," pp. 428-455, *Journalism in the United States, From 1690 to 1872.* New York: Harper and Row, 1873.

Mott, Frank Luther, Ch. 12, "Sunrise," pp. 215-227, *American Journalism: A History of Newspapers in the United States Through 250 Years, 1690 to 1940.* New York: Macmillan, 1941.

O'Brien, Frank M., Ch. 2, "The Field of the Little 'Sun,'" pp. 11-36, *The Story of the Sun.* New York: Appleton, 1928.

Rosewater, Victor, Ch. 7, "Newspaper and Telegraph," pp. 40-49, *History of Cooperative News-Gathering in the United States.* New York: Appleton, 1930.

Progressive School

Commons, John R., "Horace Greeley and the Working Class Origins of the Republican Party," *Political Science Quarterly* 24 (1909): 468-488.

Hale, William Harlan, Ch. 6, "Utopian," pp. 91-107, *Horace Greeley, Voice of the People.* New York: Harper and Row, 1950.

Stoddard, Henry L., Ch. 8, "Greeley's Isms," pp. 78-86, *Horace Greeley: Printer, Editor, Crusader.* New York: Putnam, 1946.

Cultural School

Kobre, Sidney, Ch. 12, "Expanding Democracy," pp. 220-235, *Foundations of American Journalism.* Tallahassee: Institute of Media Research, School of Journalism, Florida State University, 1958.

Olasky, Marvin, "Advertising Abortion During the 1830s and 1840s: Madame Restell Builds a Business," *Journalism History* 13 (1986): 49-55.

Schiller, Daniel T., Ch. 4, "Anchoring the Facts: The Pattern of Objectivity in the *National Police Gazette* 1845-1850," pp. 96-124, *Objectivity and the News: The Public and the Rise of Commercial Journalism.* Philadelphia: University of Pennsylvania Press, 1981.

Schudson, Michael, Ch. 1, "The Revolution in American Journalism in the Age of Egalitarianism: The Penny Press," pp. 12-60, *Discovering the News: A Social History of American Newspapers.* New York: Basic Books, 1978.

Shaw, Donald Lewis, "At The Crossroads: Change and Continuity in American Press News 1820-1860," *Journalism History* 8 (1981): 38-50.

10

The Antebellum Press, 1827-1861: Effective Abolitionist or Reluctant Reformer?

The 1820s marked the continuation of political democratization of the country, retaining some of the partisan control over the press that had been evident in previous years. Editors and publishers still maintained their political ties, but the strength of the affiliations was weakening. A press dominated by blind party loyalty was beginning to give way to a press also concerned with broader civic responsibility.

The country's preoccupation with moral and ideological issues established the basis for a reform movement which began with the antebellum press and continued well past the end of the Civil War. The rise of various benevolent societies and crusades for the improvement of the lifestyles of the common man, particularly for Blacks, resulted in a desire to alter many practices of the period.

Into this environment, crusaders introduced a sense of piety coupled with political activism. Americans focused on conditions surrounding the institution of slavery, and many had found it lacking in probity. Supporters of slavery attempted to defend their position by pointing out that the slaves were supplied with food, clothing, shelter, and security against sickness and old age—conditions far better than those many Whites endured. However, opponents of slavery were apt to stress the fundamental consideration the supporters frequently overlooked: The slaves were not *free*. They reasoned that no matter how benevolent the master, the slave did not possess the rights and privileges God intended man to have.

The antebellum press played a pivotal role in this quest for human rights. Newspapers and magazines served as platforms for self-expression, as well as for appeals to the masses. Editorials and published speeches became the backbone of the movement, as editors and publishers voiced their criticisms or positions on issues. Some favored reform, whereas others opposed it. Topics addressed ranged

By Bernell Tripp
University of Alabama

from suffrage to slavery to education.

For Blacks, the antebellum press signified the first opportunity to express their own opinions. The conditions of slavery were not the only concerns. Free Blacks living in the North lacked many of the rights their White counterparts enjoyed. Many were illiterate, and most suffered from prejudice and poor working conditions.

Those Blacks who were able to rise above these circumstances joined in the struggle to better their lives. *Freedom's Journal*, the first Black-owned and Black-operated newspaper, appeared in 1827 in New York City, followed by the first Black periodicals 11 years later. Blacks now had a literary voice in determining their own destiny and in attempting to correct the perceived wrongs in their communities. Black editors and publishers earned their livelihood in a variety of occupations. Many, like Samuel Cornish, were ministers, whereas others were businessmen and common laborers. Most received only the minimal amount of education, but their magazines and newspapers reflected the diverse measures Blacks were willing to take to alter their social status. Although many considered emigration as an alternative solution, there were those who determined that remaining in the United States and disproving the charges of Black inferiority was the only way to fight prejudice. In addition to a press sensitive to their needs, Blacks also banded together and established their own institutions, such as churches, schools, libraries, and labor organizations, in order to combat various forms of legal and extralegal discriminatory practices.

Participating in the reform movement was not an easy task. Editors, writers, and publishers faced many hardships. Caning and beating were nothing unusual. Editor Wilbur F. Storey had the dubious distinction of being publicly horsewhipped by a group of burlesque dancers for one of his particularly poisonous editorials on their virtue. The abolitionist editor Elijah Lovejoy was murdered. Presses were destroyed, and homes were burned. Mobs attacked the office of abolitionist Gamaliel Bailey's newspaper, *The Philanthropist*, three times.

Historians examining this period were unable to focus on the key concerns of the times without also taking note of the individuals who made major contributions to the movements. Publishers, clergymen, businessmen, as well as members of the general public, all formed segments of the movement as supporters or as adversaries. Historians tended to categorize the characters in the antebellum period as abolitionists, segregationists or secessionists, and humanitarians. Which group historians supported was dependent on what they considered to be the function of the media and which faction of the movement was right. Abolitionists were those individuals who reasoned that every moral and religious consideration demanded reform and the extinction of slavery. By contrast, segregationists and secessionists contended that conditions for Blacks were not as bad as the abolitionists would make circumstances appear, and Blacks were better off with their own kind, generally under the "benevolent protection" of the slaveowners. The third group, the humanitarians, concentrated less on the plight of Southern slaves and worked toward societal improvements for free Blacks and ex-slaves in the North.

Subsequently, historians were faced with the question of whether antebellum journalists were effective abolitionists or reluctant reformers. The answers they gave depended to a considerable extent on prevailing attitudes at the time they were writing, on their own individual values, and on their views of the function of the media. Historical treatments of the antebellum press fell into five schools of interpretation. The earliest, Romantic historians viewed journalists favorably as individuals of great personal virtue and courage. A second school of historians, writing from a Developmental perspective, pushed ideological considerations into the background. They argued that the most admirable journalists were those who viewed the situations "objectively" or who were willing to take positions without regard to outside influence. Thus, media autonomy and freedom of the press were among their major considerations. Progressive historians brought to their studies a stronger ideological bent and cast journalists as either heroes or villains, depending on whether they supported reform. Cultural historians, on the other hand, although sharing a concern for the conditions that Blacks faced, dealt with Black newspapers primarily in terms of how they served the needs of their constituency rather than with the general liberal vs. conservative conflict that Progressives found so attractive. Also differing with the Progressive approach were Consensus historians. Rather than conflict, they dealt with Americans' general agreement on basic principles. They believed that journalists served best in helping solve Black Americans' problems when they worked within the framework of fundamental American values rather than when they encouraged radical approaches.

The Romantic School

The first works by Romantic historians appeared in the late 1800s. Whether favoring abolitionists, segregationists/secessionists, or humanitarians, these historians depicted the editors and writers as individuals of great moral strength and intellect who were devoted to the causes they supported. The journalists, according to Romantic historians, were noble crusaders dedicated to arousing public support and serving the needs of the common man, whereas their opponents were greedy and cruel opportunists concerned only with oppression. Early Romantic historians usually knew the people about whom they wrote. This intimacy with the subject tended to influence their choice of who became the hero and who became the victim.

Oliver Johnson's *William Lloyd Garrison and His Times* (1880) exemplified hero-worship from the Romantic perspective. Johnson perceived the abolitionist editor as the sole deciding factor in the slavery controversy. Johnson was Garrison's contemporary and also served as temporary editor of the *Liberator*, Garrison's newspaper. He admitted his close association with Garrison and cited this intimacy as his primary qualification for the task of analyzing Garrison's character and philosophies. In Johnson's work Garrison, often depicted as a "dangerous radical" by later Romantic historians, appeared as a gentle intellectual, an individual whose "descriptions of slavery and of slaveholding were simply and scientifically accurate." According to Johnson, Garrison wrote "not a word . . . from malice or the love of severity, or with the purpose of making men angry. He wounded only to heal."[1] Johnson denounced Garrison's critics as timid Northerners who were afraid to antagonize "our Southern brethren" or as Southerners who feared the loss of their established lifestyle and inexpensive labor force. He concluded that the moral salvation of humanity had rested on Garrison's actions, which included direct opposition to secession and slavery.

Grace Greenwood presented a similarly favorable portrait of another abolitionist, Gamaliel Bailey. In her memorial tribute, "An American Salon" (1890), she equated both secessionists and slaveholders with the brutal mobs who spent their fury on newspapermen and innocent Blacks. She declared that Bailey always "conducted with rare talent, tact, and devotion" his abolitionist journal. She concluded that he maintained his paper's "moral and political influence" until his mission was accomplished. Bailey's devotion to his cause was the direct result of his love for humanity and "an almost morbid sense of responsibility." He had realized early the "national iniquity and disgrace of slavery," and continued to support the cause of abolition throughout his life.[2]

From the Southern perspective, a secessionist took on an equally larger-than-life persona in Laura A. White's *Robert Barnwell Rhett: Father of Secession* (1931). White declared that the lingering appeal of nationalism in 1827 first led Rhett into political activism as "the revolutionary leader who would ride the whirlwind of Southern resistance." She described Rhett, editor of the Charleston (S.C.) *Mercury*, as a remarkable man "whose eloquent and fiery preaching of the gospel of liberty and self government, and of the revolu-

---

[1] Oliver Johnson, *William Lloyd Garrison and His Times, or Sketches of the Anti-Slavery Movement in America, and of the Man Who Was Its Founder and Moral Leader* (Boston: B.B. Russell, 1880), 54.

[2] Grace Greenwood, "An American Salon," *Cosmopolitan* 8 (1890): 438, 437.

tion to achieve these ends, beat upon their [people of South Carolina] ears in season and out of season for over thirty years."[3] He was an individual thinker who "drove straight to the heart of a problem," and abolitionists were usurpers of Southern rights, concerned more with aggrandizement for the North than with the disenfranchisement of Blacks. White concluded that Rhett's support of secession was a viable method for maintaining South Carolina's rights of self-determination.

The Developmental School

Concerned less with the national and racial issues that Romantic historians confronted, Developmental historians based their evaluations of the press on the concept of the professional evolution of journalistic practices and standards for the antebellum press, rather than on journalists' advocacy of their section's interest or concern for the conditions of slaves. Although work from the Developmental school had begun with Frederic Hudson's survey history of journalism published in 1873, most historians of the latter part of the 19th century continued to be affected deeply by the recent war between the North and South. It was not until the 20th century, after sectional passions had cooled and concepts about journalism as a profession had become widely institutionalized, that works written from a purely Developmental perspective first appeared. In the 20th century, the functions of the press were rapidly changing. Newspapers were generally independent of political influences or sectional interests and were instead committed to certain standard journalistic practices. Developmental historians, thus, were especially interested in press freedom and an autonomous press unhampered by outside influences.

From this perspective, Russel B. Nye presented a picture of an antebellum press dedicated to preserving both free speech and press freedom. In "Freedom of the Press and the Antislavery Controversy" (1945), he reasoned that abolitionists were devoted to yet another cause, "the struggle to define and to maintain the traditional American civil rights and liberties" such as "free speech, a free press, the rights of petition, assembly and trial by jury."[4] Nye determined that slaveholders and slavery supporters feared that antislavery editorials would incite Blacks to violence, and local lawmakers wrote statutes aimed at restricting freedom of speech and of the press. He also detailed how several abolitionist Kentucky editors defied resistance in order to maintain their journals. Nye con-

---

[3]Laura A. White, *Robert Barnwell Rhett: Father of Secession* (New York: Century, 1931), 13, 10.

[4]Russel B. Nye, "Freedom of the Press and the Antislavery Controversy," *Journalism Quarterly* 22 (1945): 1.

cluded that this conflict over the abolitionist press and the slavery question marked a turning point in American journalism history. He explained that abolition became the first major issue in the struggle for a free press that the country had faced since the Revolution.

With a similar viewpoint, Justin Walsh's biography of Chicago *Times* editor Wilbur F. Storey exemplified the Developmental concept of the press remaining devoted to journalistic ideas rather than to a section or a social cause and dedicated to retaining the rights of unrestricted expression. In *To Print the News and Raise Hell* (1968), Walsh concluded that Storey epitomized the idea of a free press, printing "a brand of journalism calculated to bring him curses and infamy, money and circulation. At the same time his readers received news and sensation on a scale grander than the region had ever known." Storey believed the press reserved the right to criticize any action or organization without restriction. He, therefore, constantly lambasted abolitionists, temperance reformers, and politicians. Walsh explained that despite Storey's infamous reputation for savage attacks in print, he earned an important niche in media history for such innovations as establishing a female typesetters school and presenting the "widest coverage of up-to-date news from all over the world" that Chicago readers had ever seen. Disliked by many of his peers for his actions and philosophies, Storey, nevertheless, received praise for being a journalist who fought for his ideas "without regard for his life, his friends or his enemies."[5]

The Progressive School

Progressive historians displayed considerably more concern for ideology than Developmental historians did and, at the same time, more consistency than Romantic historians in choosing the heroes and villains of the reform movement. They clearly identified anti-slavery editors as reformers who faced a variety of obstacles, including slaveholders and big businessmen, in order to restore a sense of morality and democracy to the nation. Although the Progressive interpretation of both American and media history had been at its height in the first half of the 20th century, its influence in the study of the antebellum press appeared more often during the late 1960s and early 1970s—a time when 20th-century America was confronting a similar reform movement in the quest for civil rights. Progressive historians believed the primary purpose of the media was to champion the causes of the common man and to crusade for social and economic changes. On the one side were the forces of

---

[5]Justin E. Walsh, *To Print the News and Raise Hell* (Chapel Hill: University of North Carolina Press, 1968), 4., 7.

equality and reform, whereas on the other side were the wealthy and the politically influential.

This class-conflict perspective provided the basis of Curtiss Johnson's biography of New York *Evening Post* editor William Cullen Bryant. In *Politics and a Belly-full* (1962), Johnson emphasized the opposition of businessmen and government officials whom Bryant faced in his own reformist endeavors. He determined that while Bryant was known as a radical editor during his time with the *Post*, he would be considered a liberal editor by today's standards. According to Johnson, Bryant fought a variety of battles against big business, including support of free trade and collective bargaining for laborers. He also emphasized Bryant's conflict with the United States Bank, which Bryant insisted was being used "as an instrument to make the rich richer." However, Johnson concluded that "[o]f all Bryant's fundamental beliefs, none was held more deeply, and none so completely exemplified his sedulous humanitarianism and his liberal philosophy as his opposition to human bondage, his hatred of slavery."[6]

Aileen Kraditor employed a similar approach in *Means and Ends in American Abolitionism* (1967). She examined abolitionists' arguments and tactics from 1834 to 1850 and how they used the press as an instrument of reform. According to Kraditor, abolitionist editors represented liberty, civil reform, and equality, while struggling against various forms of repression. For instance, she cited numerous acts of repression, including the murder of Illinois editor Elijah Lovejoy, as well as Congress' opposition to a petition for the abolition of slavery and President Andrew Jackson's endorsement of the burning of abolitionist mail in Charleston. Abolitionist newspapers duly reported these acts to garner the support of the public. Kraditor determined that "[m]any Americans who did not feel strongly about slavery began to believe that if abolitionists could be mobbed with impunity and prevented from having their petitions considered by Congress, the rights of all Americans were in danger."[7] She decided that the abolitionist movement was interrelated with other liberal crusades of the period—issues such as religion and political action. However, in each of these confrontations, Kraditor reasoned, the abolitionists were always pitted against members of the ruling class or established institutions.

---

[6]Curtiss S. Johnson, *Politics and a Belly-Full: The Journalistic Career of William Cullen Bryant, Civil War Editor of the New York Evening Post* (New York: Vantage Press, 1962), 188.

[7]Aileen S. Kraditor, *Means and Ends in American Abolitionism: Garrison and His Critics on Strategy and Tactics, 1834-1850* (New York: Pantheon Books, 1967), 7.

The Cultural School

Although less intrigued with ideological conflict than were Progressive historians, Cultural historians nevertheless were concerned with the conditions that confronted Black Americans. As a result, they, unlike Developmental historians, showed little concern with the purely journalistic functions of the antebellum press. These historians looked beyond how the journalists performed as journalists *per se* to examine how well the press served its immediate audience. In the Cultural interpretation of the antebellum press, which emerged primarily over the last two decades, historians studied the interrelationship between the press and its operating environment, viewing the antebellum press from the perspective of how the needs of its readers influenced the press.

In "Negro Journalism in America Before Emancipation" (1969), Carter Bryan suggested that Black journalists in the antebellum period operated their newspapers based on their obligations to improve societal conditions for Blacks. He traced the Black press from its beginning in 1827 to just prior to the Civil War. Like other Cultural historians, he concluded that while Black editors promoted the antislavery cause, they also acted as spokesmen, advocates, chroniclers, and teachers of the race.[8] Bryan supported the idea that Black journalists were devoted to elevating the moral and intellectual level of free Blacks, while promoting a better understanding between the races. He theorized that more than 90% of America's Blacks were slaves in the South, where they were denied such basic opportunities as formal education and economic opportunities. While Blacks in the North were free, two-thirds were still illiterate and were refused basic human rights. Bryan inferred that those Blacks who were able to succeed despite the obstacles assumed the task of advocating the causes of those Blacks who could not speak for themselves.

This same interest in how the Black press responded to the concerns of Black Americans served as the basis for Kenneth Nordin's "In Search of Black Unity: An Interpretation of the Content and Function of *Freedom's Journal*" (1977-1978). Nordin proposed that the founders of *Freedom's Journal* were not only reforming abolitionists, but also were trying to build a sense of fraternity among Blacks, create guidelines for Blacks' self-improvement, provide Black readers with a sense of their culture, and furnish readers with significant and current news items.[9] According to Nordin, these goals were dictated by the problems and concerns of Northern

---

[8]Carter R. Bryan, "Negro Journalism in America Before Emancipation," *Journalism Monographs* 12 (1969): 29.

[9]Kenneth D. Nordin, "In Search of Black Unity: An Interpretation of the Content and Function of *Freedom's Journal*," *Journalism History* 4 (1977-1978): 128.

free Blacks and ex-slaves. He reasoned that *Freedom's Journal* co-editors Samuel Cornish and John Russwurm acknowledged that the lack of educational opportunities and poverty accounted for many of the problems that Blacks confronted daily. Therefore, a nationally circulated newspaper aimed at Blacks scattered in communities throughout the North might provide them with a sense of moral direction, as well as develop racial cohesiveness and Black consciousness. Most Black antebellum newspapers and magazines were established in locations where Black community life already existed. This way, the editors were assured of determining just what the Black readers needed.

The Consensus School

Consensus historians adopted a less radical approach than Progressive historians, or even Cultural historians, did in describing conflicts in society, whether between races or political factions. They believed that the press performed best when it worked toward national unity and aided in solving the problems the country faced. They argued that the press must act responsibly as part of society, and journalists should consider the welfare of the nation as a whole and not just the press alone. They advocated the idea that the press should work with the public and the government to solve threats to national unity rather than emphasizing conflicts in order to create divisions in society. Consensus historians also believed that key individuals in the antebellum press had logical and practical reasons for the way they conducted their newspapers.

One of the best examples of the Consensus approach was Stanley Harrold's biography of abolitionist Gamaliel Bailey. One of history's more obscure abolitionists, Bailey was less flamboyant and radical than abolitionists such as William Lloyd Garrison and New York philanthropist Gerrit Smith. Characterized by Garrison and Smith as "a compromiser who modified antislavery principles for the sake of popular approval," Bailey was pictured in Harrold's *Gamaliel Bailey and Antislavery Union* (1986) as "a person who worked desperately to balance his moral principles with his conviction that a powerful political movement was required to rescue the United States from the effects of slavery." Harrold reasoned that since Bailey had assumed the task of extending antislavery appeals into the lower North and the South, he was forced to adopt a style that was more moderate than that of the abolitionists who chose to campaign farther North. Bailey's moderate style allowed him to become a national leader at every stage of the expanding antislavery movement. Harrold concluded that Bailey's strategy was more effective than that of other abolitionists as he "worked to hold the movement to a middle course between opportunism and compromise on the one side and tactics he regarded as impractical or unpopular on the other."[10]

Another portrait of a reasonable and dominant figure who shunned the public eye while attempting to translate much-needed reforms into reality was painted in Horace Raper's *William W. Holden: North Carolina's Political Enigma* (1985). Raper described the journalist-turned-politician as both a visionary and a pragmatist. Holden generally "understood the needs of the people and of the state usually far in advance of other leaders."[11] Raper reasoned that many of Holden's journalistic actions failed to appeal to his Southern colleagues. In one such instance Holden displeased his critics when he cautioned for deliberation over the issue of secession. Raper theorized that Holden viewed secession from an academic standpoint, considering it as a weapon to be used only as a threat and not as a feasible and viable solution to the antislavery controversy. The threat of secession was to be utilized in uniting the South in order to speak with one voice and to gain the respect of the North for the rights of the slave states. Raper concluded that Holden possessed a determination to preserve the federal union, and Holden assured his critical colleagues that this policy made him a better friend to the Union than they were.

Discussion

For historians, the antebellum period has offered a chance to examine the philosophies of the individuals who contributed to the events leading to the Civil War. Because the country was in a major conflict with itself, each organization and individual in America was forced to choose sides. Even the press was in disagreement over right and wrong and its own role in the dispute. It is no wonder that numerous questions continue to spark lively debates among historians.

1. Should journalists have taken sides in the conflict and used their newspapers as tools for reform, as Progressive historians argued? Or should they have maintained their journalistic objectivity, as Developmental historians reasoned?

2. Who were the heroes of the antebellum press—the abolitionist editors, the secessionists, or the moderates?

3. Which approach was more successful in bringing about the end of slavery—the pragmatic approach of editors such as Bailey and Holden, as Consensus historians argued, or the outspoken and radical approach of Garrison and Bryant, as Progressive historians suggested?

---

[10]Stanley Harrold, *Gamaliel Bailey and Antislavery Union* (Kent, OH: Kent State University Press, 1986), X, XI.

[11]Horace W. Raper, *William W. Holden: North Carolina's Political Enigma* (Chapel Hill: University of North Carolina Press, 1985), XIII.

4. Were abolitionists really concerned with the treatment of Blacks, or were they more interested in further enrichment of Northern businessmen or in increasing circulation figures?

5. Were White abolitionists as sensitive to the needs of the Black community as Black journalists were?

6. How great an impact did the antebellum press make on the country's move toward civil war? Did the outspoken qualities of the editors aid in hastening the country into war? Did abolitionist propaganda encourage Southern secession?

7. Was the journalists' active involvement in the movement appropriate by the professional standards of Developmental historians?

8. Did the circumstances leading up to the Civil War force antebellum editors into the role of correcting the country's moral and political mistakes?

9. In addressing the overriding issue of slavery, were editors effective abolitionists or reluctant reformers?

Readings

Romantic School

Brewer, William M., "John B. Russwurm," *Journal of Negro History* 13 (1928): 413-422.

Cairns, William B., Ch. 19, "Later Magazines," pp. 299-318, William P. Trent, et. al., eds., *The Cambridge History of American Literature* Vol. 3. New York: Macmillan, 1933.

Greenwood, Grace, "An American Salon," *Cosmopolitan* 8 (1890): 437-447.

Johnson, Oliver, Ch. 3 (untitled), pp. 50-66, *William Lloyd Garrison and His Times, or Sketches of the Anti-Slavery Movement in America, and of the Man Who Was Its Founder and Moral Leader*. Boston: B.B. Russell, 1880.

White, Laura A., Ch. 2, "Nullification" pp. 10-31, *Robert Barnwell Rhett: Father of Secession*. New York: Century, 1931.

Developmental School

Coulter, Ellis Merton, Ch. 3, "Personal Journalism," pp. 35-52, *William G. Brownlow: Fighting Parson of the Southern Highlands*. Chapel Hill: University of North Carolina Press, 1937.

Gill, John, "Preface," pp. 1-10, and "Postscript," pp. 205-211, *Tide Without Turning: Elijah P. Lovejoy and Freedom of the Press*. Boston: Starr King Press, 1958.

Nye, Russell B., "Freedom of the Press and the Antislavery Controversy," *Journalism Quarterly* 22 (1945): 1-11.

Reilly, Tom, "Lincoln-Douglass Debates of 1858 Forced New Role on the Press," *Journalism Quarterly* 56 (1979): 734-743, 752.

Walsh, Justin E., Ch. 1, "To Print the News and Raise Hell," pp. 3-10, *To Print the News and Raise Hell*. Chapel Hill: University of North Carolina Press, 1968.

Progressive School

Bontemps, Arna, Ch. 1, "The Journey," pp. 5-29, *Free at Last: Life of Frederick Douglass*. New York: Dodd, Mead, 1971.

Chapman, John J., pp. 162-176, *William Lloyd Garrison*. Boston: 1913.

Dillon, Merton L., Ch. 4, "The Religious Editor," pp. 32-43, *Elijah P. Lovejoy, Abolitionist Editor*. Urbana: University of Illinois Press, 1961.

Holmes, J. Welfred, "Some Anti-Slavery Editors at Work: Lundy, Bailey, Douglass," *CLA Journal* 7 (September 1963-March 1964): 48-55.

Johnson, Curtiss S., Ch. 10, "Journalistic Accomplishments," pp. 169-189, *Politics and a Belly-Full: The Journalistic Career of William Cullen Bryant, Civil War Editor of the New York Evening Post*. New York: Vantage Press, 1962.

Kraditor, Aileen S., Ch. 1, "Introduction," and Ch. 2, "The Abolitionist as Agitator," pp. 3-38, *Means and Ends in American Abolitionism: Garrison and His Critics on Strategy and Tactics, 1834-1850*. New York: Pantheon Books, 1967.

Cultural School

Bryan, Carter R., "Negro Journalism in America Before Emancipation," *Journalism Monographs* 12 (1969): 1-29.

Flanders, Bertram Holland, Ch. 4, "Summary and Conclusions," pp. 179-208, *Early Georgia Magazines: Literary Periodicals to 1865*. Athens: University of Georgia Press, 1944.

Nordin, Kenneth D., "In Search of Black Unity: An Interpretation of the Content and Function of *Freedom's Journal*," *Journalism History* 4 (1977-1978): 123-128.

O'Kelly, Charlotte G., "Black Newspapers and the Black Protest Movement: Their Historical Relationship, 1827-1845," *Phylon* 43 (Spring 1982): 1-14.

Reynolds, Donald E., "Introduction," pp. 3-11, *Editors Make War: Southern Newspapers in the Secession Crisis*. Nashville: Vanderbilt University, 1966.

Snograss, J. William, Ch. 7, "The Sectional Press and the Civil War," pp. 143-163, Wm. David Sloan, James G. Stovall, and James D. Startt, eds. *The Media in America*. Worthington, OH: Publishing Horizons, 1989.

Consensus School

Harper, Robert S. Chs. 1-5, pp. 1-34, *Lincoln and the Press*. New York: Mc-Graw-Hill, 1951.

Harrold, Stanley, Ch. 1, "Benevolence," pp. 1-11, *Gamaliel Bailey and Antislavery Union*. Kent, OH: Kent State University Press, 1986.

Quarles, Benjamin, Ch. 4, "Pulpit and Press," pp. 68-89, *Black Abolitionists*. New York: Oxford University Press, 1969.

Raper, Horace W., Ch. 1, "The Making of a Newspaperman," pp. 1-26, *William W. Holden: North Carolina's Political Enigma*. Chapel Hill: University of North Carolina Press, 1985.

11

The Civil War Press, 1861-1865:
Promoter of Unity or Neutral Reporter?

The Civil War is one of the most studied periods of American history, and understandably so. It was fought entirely in American territory, more Americans died in that war than in any other, and it was the only American war in which other Americans were the enemy. For these and other reasons, American historians continue to be especially fascinated by the Civil War.

This fascination is shared by a number of historians who have dealt with the role of journalism during the war. Most of their studies have focused on one or both of two major issues: military censorship of newspapers and press performance during the war. The way historians dealt with these issues was usually dependent on what they considered to be the proper function of the press during wartime in general and during the Civil War in particular. Should the press have directed its efforts toward unifying its readers in support of the war effort? Or should the press simply have reported on the war as a detached nonparticipant, striving always to tell the truth, without considering whether news reports reveal military secrets to the enemy? Generally, historians who believed the primary duty of the press was to support the war effort accepted censorship as necessary for military security, whereas those who believed the press should remain neutral condemned censorship as a repressive and unwarranted violation of the First Amendment.

The Civil War imposed widespread hardships on the press. Some have argued that the extraordinary demand for news in time of war makes war desirable for newspapers. In spite of the public's desire for news, however, newspapers during war have to face high costs of paper and labor, heavy taxes, and restrictions on their freedom. They also must share in the confusion and hazards of war, and if they happen to be in captured territory, they may be destroyed. Even the circulation increases which frequently accompany war

---

By Thomas Andrew Hughes
University of Alabama

depend upon greatly increased expenditures for news gathering. Such was the case in the Civil War.

After the Confederates fired on Ft. Sumter in 1861, most Northern newspapers immediately took up editorial arms against the rebels and urged fast and decisive military action. Editors also recognized the extremely high degree of public interest in news of the war, and their newspapers soon had a large corps of correspondents dispatched into the field. Probably no war has been so thoroughly covered by eyewitness reporters as the Civil War. The conditions of that war allowed for more uncensored, on-the-scene reporting than did those of later wars.

Problems, however, were commonplace. News sometimes was tardy because telegraph facilities were not always available. Correspondents often had to journey on foot or horseback to get to a point where their accounts could be safely transmitted. Even then, use of the wires was sometimes denied them because of the government's need for the wire, military censorship, heavy use by commercial business, or breaks in service. Thus, correspondents, exhausted and looking like tramps, frequently brought their stories personally into their newspaper offices. Published reports from the fronts were frequently three or four days old, and sometimes much older. Because of the inadequacy of news transmission, many reports were based on rumor; and the heading "Important–if true" was common in newspapers.

A number of well-known, highly respected correspondents worked in the field, but most others faced demoralizing conditions. They were not recognized as noncombatants and were subject to the same dangers as soldiers. Among the best known was Albert D. Richardson of the New York *Tribune*. He reported a number of battles and, along with another correspondent, was captured by the Confederates after the military boat they were on was attacked. They were sent to several military prisons and suffered great deprivations before escaping in winter. On foot, they waded through icy streams making their way north. They were befriended by Negroes, mountaineers, bushwhackers, and "a nameless heroine" who appeared mysteriously to lead them through dangerous passes and then disappeared just as mysteriously. When finally reaching Union territory, Richardson saluted the American flag with tears in his eyes and rushed to the telegraph office to wire the *Tribune*: "Out of the jaws of death; out of the mouth of hell." Despite the presence of glamorized correspondents such as Richardson, most led a drearier and less exciting, perhaps even dismal life. One reporter declared that they were sometimes driven out of certain army camps and were "forced to hover around the rear of the armies, gathering up such information as they could . . . . The majority . . . were mere news scavengers."

In contrast to the correspondents' working conditions, press freedom was remarkably broad. The restrictions that did occur seem to have been sporadic and isolated. The Union government proscribed a number of pro-South newspapers from using the mails, while military commanders in the field sometimes prohibited use of available telegraph lines, censored copy before it was transmitted, or prohibited correspondents from covering their activities. The commander whom correspondents disliked most was Gen. William T. Sherman. He shared their animosity. When informed one afternoon that three correspondents had just been killed by an exploding shell, he is said to have replied, "Good! Now we shall have news from hell before breakfast." The cause for problems did not rest solely with the military. Correspondents bore much of the responsibility. Their most noted fault was their frequent efforts to cultivate the favor of military commanders, and as a result many of them became little more than press agents for the generals.

Most historical treatments of the Civil War press can be divided into four schools of interpretation: the Contemporary school, the Developmental school, the Consensus school, and the Southern Nationalist school. The Contemporary school spanned from soon after the war ended until around 1913. Most Contemporary works were written by Northern reporters who had travelled with the Union army and wrote newspaper accounts of battles. Their works usually sought to justify their own actions and the actions of the North in general while placing the blame for causing the war on the South. Most Union generals were depicted favorably. However, those who attempted to ban reporters from their camps or to control what they could and could not write, especially William T. Sherman, were singled out for special derision. Contemporary writers were usually proud of their own exploits and those of their colleagues, and most believed the Northern press performed admirably during the war.

A second group of historians, comprised of newspapermen who began their journalistic careers after the war had ended, began publishing evaluations of the Civil War press in the early 1900s. These Developmental writers were primarily interested in how the war led to modern journalistic practices and how well the Northern press performed as a profession during the war. When writing about censorship, they viewed it as part of a conspiracy to eliminate or at least weaken reporters' First Amendment rights. In their estimation, however, it did not and could not prevent the Confederates from discovering Union army secrets, nor would stricter censorship have shortened the war. Therefore, censorship should not have been practiced because of its ineffectiveness and because it led to peacetime repression of press freedom. When evaluating the performance of the Northern press, some Developmental historians were critical of reporters' partisan attitudes during the war, but most believed that they had performed well under difficult conditions.

The Southern Nationalist and Consensus schools both emerged during the 1930s. The Consensus school is best understood as a reaction to the Progressive interpretation of American history, although Progressive historians devoted little attention to the Civil War press. The Progressive school arose in the early 1900s as a part of the Progressive reform movement. Progressive historians were primarily concerned with explaining the causes and negative results of the war. The war was actually a class conflict between Northern labor and Southern aristocracy, Progressives believed, which led to America's industrialization and dehumanizing domination by abusive capitalists.

In reaction to the Progressive school, Consensus historians refuted the idea of the Civil War as a class conflict and ignored negative effects of the industrialization the war made possible. Rather, they emphasized that the war's outcome led to both the modernization of America and to a sense of national unity. Though they believed neither the North nor the South was solely to blame for causing the war, Consensus historians usually dealt only with the Northern press because modern American journalism nationwide was patterned after it. They argued that most Northern newspapers accepted the need for military security and conscientiously tried to determine what information they should not have published. Newspapers that printed sensitive military information, however, seriously damaged the national cause. Furthermore, newspaper criticism of the army and of the Lincoln administration embarrassed some generals into attacking before they had originally intended and undermined public confidence in the management of the war. Thus Consensus historians usually concluded that governmental or military control of the press would have shortened the Civil War, and that in future wars the United States should institute an effective system of press censorship.

As the Progressive school began to be challenged by the Consensus school during the 1930s, a number of Southern historians began reacting defensively to the negative portrayals of the South's role in the war which had dominated the writing of American history. They tried to shift blame for causing the war to the North. When writing about the Civil War press, Southern Nationalist historians attacked the reputations of prominent Northern journalists who had been depicted favorably by most other historians. They also praised the unity of the Southern press, as evident by its voluntary suppression of sensitive material, as a sign of the South's moral superiority.

The Contemporary School

Most of the works on Civil War journalism written in the 19th century were by Northern reporters who had served as correspondents during the war. Their books were usually personal reminiscences which attempted to justify their own actions, the actions of the Northern press in its conflicts with the Union army, and the Northern cause in general. They viewed the war as being caused by a Southern conspiracy to further the spread of slavery no matter what the consequences to the nation. The North, on the other hand, was simply defending itself and the Constitution against unprovoked aggression.

Union troops, then, were usually portrayed as courageous and totally devoted to the war effort, even after such terrible defeats as they suffered in the battle of Fredericksburg. Most Union generals were depicted as noble, statesmanlike heroes leading the fight for truth and liberty. This did not hold true for General William T. Sherman, however, who fought vigorously against the press throughout the war. He frequently banned reporters from his camps, and even tried to have one reporter executed after first having him court-martialled. It is not surprising, then, that most reporters believed for the duration of the war an early newspaper account that stated Sherman was insane.

The efforts of Sherman and other Union generals to control the press aroused harsh criticism from most Contemporary historians. They believed that the military had no right to prohibit reporters from travelling with the army or to censor their dispatches. Such efforts were not intended to prevent the publication of military secrets, as the generals claimed, but were really meant to spare generals the embarrassment of legitimate criticism before the public. Although admitting that some reporters had indeed acted with gross irresponsibility, Contemporary historians maintained that the entire profession had been unfairly judged on the basis of only a few transgressions. Most reporters, they argued, were conscientious men who had served both their profession and their country well under extremely trying conditions.

The first book to comment on Civil War journalism was Albert D. Richardson's *The Secret Service: The Field, The Dungeon, and the Escape* (1865), which was sent to press during the last few months of the war. Richardson's views were no doubt shaped by the fact that he was held for nearly two years before escaping from the Confederate prison camp at Salisbury, North Carolina, struggling 300 miles through snowbound mountains to Union-held Knoxville, Tennessee. Setting the tone for later books by other Northern correspondents, he praised the North while harshly criticizing the South. Some of his criticisms were nothing more than general insults directed at Southern women, with subsections of the book titled "Challenge from a Southern Woman," "Rebel Girl with Sharp Tongue," and the "Bloodthirstiness of Rebel Women."

Yet his devotion to the Northern cause was exceeded by his belief that the Union army had no right to exclude reporters from the army. When General Halleck did just that, Richardson decried the action as a shallow subterfuge to hide the general's fear of having his conduct described to the country in anything other than official reports. He believed the general's action represented "a grave issue between the Military Power and the rights of the Press and the People."[1]

Noting that many Union generals and some of the general public held war correspondents in low esteem, Richardson argued that they were being judged unfairly because of the irresponsible actions of just a few reporters. According to him, two accounts of the battle of Pea Ridge, Arkansas, by reporters who had not actually witnessed the battle were written "as a Bohemian freak," and were the only accounts fabricated by reputable journalists during the war. To prevent further such transgressions, he wrote, there should be a law authorizing reporters to accompany troops in the field which would hold them responsible for publishing anything that could aid the enemy.

Richardson also foreshadowed later works by other correspondents with his evaluation of General Ambrose Burnside's role in the Union defeat at Fredericksburg. Although Richardson was not present at the battle, he spoke at length with Burnside a few days afterward. He was impressed with how the general accepted full responsibility for the loss of more than 10,000 men. Burnside was, he wrote, "great in his earnestness, his moral courage, and perfect integrity."[2] When ordered, the general flung his army upon the Rebels, and the result was defeat. Yet according to Richardson, that policy was the Union army's salvation. Though every soldier knew the battle was a bloody mistake, their spirit was not broken and they would have gone cheerfully into battle again the following week. Most other Contemporary accounts of the battle followed Richardson's example.

A much more critical evaluation of war correspondence, however, appeared only a few months later. In a series of three articles published in *The Nation*, beginning on July 20, 1865, former war correspondent Henry Villard traced the qualitative rise and fall of army reporting during the course of the war. Born in Germany as Ferdinand Heinrich Gustav Hilgard and educated at the University of Munich and the University of Würzburg before coming to America, he edited a German-language newspaper in Wisconsin while teaching himself how to write in English. After Americaniz-

---

[1]Albert D. Richardson, *Secret Service, The Field; the Dungeon and the Escape* (Hartford, CT: American, 1865), 258.

[2]bid., p. 306.

ing his name, Villard became one of the most respected correspondents during the war, writing for both the New York *Herald* and the New York *Tribune*.

Villard argued that the quality of correspondence declined as the war progressed. He noted, for example, that some of the first accounts of the Bull Run campaign were quite good, and reports by the better correspondents steadily improved through 1862 and 1863. However, even then certain shortcomings were apparent that grew more glaring over the course of the war—incompleteness of information, inaccuracy of statement, and a resort to fiction to make stories more interesting. By the end of 1863, the decline was well under way. "From that time to the fall of the curtain in the grand national drama," Villard wrote, "a gradual depreciation in the value of army correspondence must have been noticed by every habitual reader of the daily papers."[3] This depreciation was caused by the succession of incompetent reporters into positions vacated by capable correspondents who were no longer able to withstand the extremely harsh rigors of the profession. Villard concluded that, overall, army correspondence had contributed a positive gain to journalism, as evidenced by the several former army correspondents who went on to hold important editorial positions at most of the leading newspapers in the country.

More representative of the Contemporary school were Villard's memoirs, published in 1904. This two-volume work took a realistic look at Civil War journalism, although Villard painted his own performance and the righteousness of the North's cause in an unquestioningly favorable light. Perhaps the most interesting feature of the memoirs was Villard's descriptions of his dealings with major journalistic figures of the day. He wrote disdainfully of New York *Herald* editor James Gordon Bennett's "shameful record as a journalist," and of the "sneaking sympathy of his paper for the Rebellion, and its vile abuse of the Republicans for their antislavery sentiments."[4] In another dramatic episode he explained how in the battle of Fredericksburg, in order to prevent his Boston *Journal* colleague Charles Carleton Coffin from beating him to press with a battle account, he defied an interdict from General Burnside prohibiting reporters from travelling north without a special permit from his headquarters. In light of Burnside's attempt to control the press, it is hardly surprising that Villard blamed him for the Union army's defeat at Fredericksburg.

Coffin wrote his own account of Civil War correspondence, enti-

[3]Henry Villard, "Army Correspondence: Its History," *The Nation* 1 (July 27, 1865), 115.

[4]Henry Villard, *Memoirs of Henry Villard: Journalist and Financier, 1835-1900*, Vol. 1 (Boston: Houghton-Mifflin, 1904), 161.

tled *Four Years of Fighting* (1866). His treatment of the war was not as detached as Villard's, nor was he as concerned with the performance of journalism as a profession. Instead, his book was a record of personal observations primarily concerned with justifying the actions and cause of the North. He interpreted the war as a mighty contest in which right triumphed over wrong, which resulted in the human race moving on to a higher civilization. He also condemned the South in no uncertain terms, writing that "the Rebellion was an attempt to suppress Truth and Justice by tyranny."[5]

Understandably, then, his interpretation of the battle at Fredericksburg was quite different from Villard's. What Villard viewed as an "appalling disaster" Coffin saw as only "disheartening to the army." The Union army lost the battle only because some of the officers failed to support Burnside's plans wholeheartedly, Coffin wrote. Though repulsed, the soldiers felt they were not beaten and had no thought of giving up the fight. Coffin did not mention his being "scooped" by Villard, either.

One contemporary evaluation of Civil War journalism stands out because its author served both as managing editor of one of the most important newspapers of the time and then as Assistant Secretary of War in the Union government. Charles A. Dana had worked closely with Horace Greeley at the New York *Tribune* for 15 years before Greeley asked him to resign in April 1862 because Greeley favored greater efforts to achieve peace whereas Dana supported a continuation of the war until the South's rebellion had been completely squelched. Lincoln's Secretary of War Edwin M. Stanton offered Dana a job in the war department soon after, and promoted him to Assistant Secretary in 1863. Dana was present at what has become an often cited example of tense relations between the Northern press and the Union army, when General Meade paraded a correspondent wearing a sign reading "Libeller of the Press" before the troops and expelled him from camp because he had published a report that Meade advocated retreat after the Battle of the Wilderness.

Directly contradicting negative evaluations of army correspondence by Villard and later historians, Dana wrote in *Recollections of the Civil War* (1898) that the preceding example of tense army-press relations was an exception rather than the rule. He argued it was not often that correspondents got into trouble with the army, because as a rule they were discreet. Yet this observation seems inconsistent with Dana's accounts of General Sherman's attitudes toward reporters. After notifying the general of an accurate report of his upcoming movements published in the Indianapolis *Journal,* Dana

---

[5]Charles Carleton Coffin, *Four Years of Fighting: A Volume of Personal Observation with the Army and Navy* (Boston: Ticknor and Fields, 1866; reprint, Arno Press, 1970), 557.

wrote, Sherman responded with two "characteristic" dispatches. The first read, "Dispatch of 9th read. Can't you send to Indianapolis and catch that fool and have him sent to me to work on the forts?"[6] In the second, Sherman ordered that when newspapers published information "too near the truth," Dana should attempt to counteract its effect by publishing contradictory reports of the same information calculated to mislead the Confederates. In accordance with Sherman's first request, Dana ordered a Union general in Indianapolis to determine who alerted the *Journal* to Sherman's movements and to arrest him. However, the person or persons responsible were never found.

The Developmental School

By the second decade of the 20th century, historians who had not worked as war correspondents began to provide more detached evaluations of press performance during the Civil War. A number of professional journalists who were also amateur historians tried to explain how the war had led to a revolution in journalism in the North, which established the modern standards of professional journalistic practice to which they had been indoctrinated. The war marked the end of editorially based journalism, they believed, and established unbiased news accounts as the primary function of newspapers. Even more important, it established the right to report as an essential element of the democratic process.

Developmental historians were also especially interested in how well the Northern press performed when evaluated against modern standards of journalism. Some believed that, even allowing for the problems of military censorship and dangerous battle conditions that war correspondents faced, most war reporting was of poor quality. Others believed that, on the contrary, most reporters performed surprisingly well despite these obstacles. Most agreed, however, that the quality of reporting did improve during the war.

Naturally, then, Developmental historians viewed military censorship as a threat to proper press performance. Some argued that censorship was simply unacceptable in a democracy, as the national cause was best served by a public well informed with truthful and accurate accounts. Others criticized censorship on more practical grounds, writing that attempts at censorship were futile as reporters always found ways around them. In fact, they argued, censorship actually damaged the war effort by confusing the Northern population while failing to prevent the Confederate army from learning Union military secrets. Furthermore, most concluded, none of the available evidence indicates that stricter censorship

---

[6]Charles A. Dana, *Recollections of the Civil War* (New York: Appleton, 1898), 216-217.

would have shortened the war.

One of the first Developmental interpretations of Civil War journalism was Frederick L. Bullard's *Famous War Correspondents* (1914), a collection of biographical sketches of representative war reporters from 1790 until the Spanish-American War in the late 1890s. Bullard believed that the most important duty of the press during wartime was to tell the truth. Publicity did the most to promote peace, he wrote, and military censorship was detrimental to humanity. Furthermore, attempts at censorship were ineffective because in time competent reporters always discover ways to tell what they saw.

The War of Secession, as Bullard called it, was extremely important in the development of war correspondence. No system of covering a war of such geographic magnitude existed at the war's beginning, but papers began organizing for the collection of war news upon an extensive scale "the instant the conflict began." Each important city had at least one newspaper with a correspondent in the field, and some journals in larger cities supported several war reporters. Yet these efforts were small compared to those of the three large New York dailies—the *Herald*, the *Tribune*, and the *Times*. These papers, led by Bennett's *Herald*, spent prodigious sums of money to establish and support their war departments.

Bullard, like Villard, observed that few correspondents could long endure the rigors of war reporting. Yet he was much more favorable to the profession overall. Although he admitted that some reporters were irresponsible adventurers prone to fabrication, he maintained that "far the greater number were as loyal and serious in their work as were the soldiers who fought the battles the reporters described."[7]

Arriving at a similar conclusion was Havilah Babcock's "The Press and the Civil War" (1929). Because no previous war of any magnitude had been covered as thoroughly, Babcock wrote, the Civil War contributed notably to the development of military correspondence. It also marked the end of "scurrilously personal journalism" as the newspaper institution became more important than individual editors. Newspapers became accustomed to spending huge sums of money to gather and present the news first, setting the precedent of breaking stories as soon after they occur as possible. In addition, the demand for a continuous chronicle of the war established the Sunday paper as a regular feature of the more important metropolitan dailies.

Babcock evaluated the effect of the war on journalistic development in both North and South. The war was unquestionably better reported in the North, but Southern papers were much more effective

---

[7]Frederick L. Bullard, *Famous War Correspondents* (New York: Beekman Publishers, 1974 reprint from the 1914 edition), 379.

in keeping military secrets out of the news and thus did a better job of promoting the interests of their section. Although the war stimulated journalistic development in the North, it stifled development in the South through the scarcity of materials and labor and through the constant danger of suspension or control by the Union army as it conquered Southern cities. "The effect of the Civil War upon the journalistic development of the South," he wrote, "unlike its effect upon that of the North, was almost uniformly discouraging."[8]

One of the most influential Developmental interpretations of Civil War journalism is found in Frank Luther Mott's classic textbook *American Journalism*, the first edition of which was published in 1941. This work served as the starting point for most historical study on the American press undertaken during the following 30 years. Mott viewed the past as the story of how journalism reached its modern state and thus was primarily concerned with documenting the progress of journalism and its practices. This assumption is evident in the book's chapters on Civil War journalism. No war before or since was as thoroughly covered by eyewitness correspondents, Mott wrote. Yet news was sometimes late because telegraph facilities were not always available, forcing reporters to travel great distances through enemy territory on horseback or even on foot to get their stories to press. Although newswriting was more direct than it had been immediately preceding the war, he wrote, modern news-story form had not yet been developed. Mott also criticized military censorship, arguing that it led some correspondents to curry favor from the generals they covered. Such reporters "thus became press agents for their generals and built up popular and even political reputations. Such promotion encouraged jealous rivalries and improper ambitions."[9]

Louis M. Starr argued similarly in *Bohemian Brigade: Civil War Newsmen in Action* (1954) that much Northern reporting was hackneyed and deficient, whether judged by modern standards or according to the prevailing view of the time. He explained that this was the result of the news revolution bursting upon journalism before concepts of accuracy and objectivity were completely formulated and because the work paid too poorly to attract many able men. Unlike Villard, however, Starr believed the quality of reporting improved during the course of the war. What was most important to Starr, though, was that reporters contributed to the development of journalism by satisfying the public's desire for news. This they accomplished by reporting the war so incessantly that it became an in-

---

[8]Havilah Babcock, "The Press and the Civil War," *Journalism Quarterly* 6 (1929): 5.

[9]Frank Luther Mott, *American Journalism: A History of Newspapers in the United States* (New York: Macmillan, 1941), 338.

escapable reality, thus helping news gain preeminence over editorials, and by establishing the right to report as essential to democracy. This right had to be fought for, as the First Amendment guaranteed only the right to print, not the right to report. "Against natural obstacles," Starr wrote, "against one another, against the many-sided obduracy of public officials, they have gradually established a quasi-legal right which is indispensable to a people who must be informed in order to govern themselves."[10]

The most ambitious and thoroughly documented Developmental interpretation was *The North Reports the Civil War* by J. Cutler Andrews (1955). He agreed with Mott that no other great war had been as thoroughly covered by eyewitness reporters. Although much of their reporting was full of errors, he wrote, most of the inaccuracies were not intentional but resulted from the haste and confusion involved in news gathering after a battle. Even the intentionally dishonest practices of some reporters were more the fault of their managing editors' low ethical standards than of the reporters themselves. Such editors were more likely to censure a reporter for being "scooped" by one of his colleagues than for including material of questionable truth in his accounts.

Andrews was more critical of the publication of sensitive military intelligence than were most other Developmental historians, writing that "the leakage of such information through the press was well-nigh scandalous." This does not mean, however, that he necessarily believed there should have been greater control of the Northern press during the war. Censorship was at times overly severe, he wrote, as those who administered it often interdicted wholesome criticism of the general execution of the war effort. However, censorship was most often utterly ineffectual, managing at best only to delay rather than to prohibit the public from learning of Union army defeats. Andrews concluded that although the profession was tarnished by irresponsible editors and overzealous reporters, though it faced erratic censorship and temperamental generals, the Northern press performed well during the war.

Andrews followed this work with the most extensively researched treatment of the Southern press, *The South Reports the Civil War* (1970). The war brought about many of the same changes in Confederate newspaper practice, Andrews wrote, that had occurred in the North. Among these were an increasing emphasis on news over editorial opinion and the use of special correspondents. However, wartime scarcities of materials and the loss of a large number of employees drafted into military service greatly limited the effectiveness of the Southern press. Yet in spite of these difficulties, the

---

[10]Louis M. Starr, *Bohemian Brigade: Civil War Newsmen in Action* (New York: Knopf, 1954), 40.

war stimulated greater public interest in news in the South than had ever been known before.

This greater interest in news did not necessarily lead to good reporting, however. Confederate battle accounts at their worst were extremely partisan, used an inflated style of writing, and down-played Southern defeats while greatly exaggerating victories. On the other hand, Andrews wrote, Confederate war reporting at its best was comparable to the best work by Northern correspondents. The better Southern reporters were acceptably accurate, grasped the larger significance of the events that they observed, and were will-ing to recognize and admit defeat at times. He concluded that the Southern press did its best to provide full coverage of the military and political events of the war, and performed remarkably well considering the great difficulties it faced.

Though he was critical of censorship in general, Andrews was less critical of voluntary censorship in the Confederate press than were other Developmental historians. Such restraint did impose a severe strain on the spirit of news enterprise, he wrote, but it was the inevitable consequence of an environment in which true freedom of the press had never been possible. Andrews also pointed out what many other historians had either ignored or failed to recognize: that the Southern press generally opposed attempts to broaden official powers of censorship. Furthermore, at least one paper, the Knoxville *Whig,* was shut down six months after the war began by Confederate authorities, who destroyed its press and types. Some other anti-se-cessionist papers in the South, Andrews wrote, might also have been suppressed had not public pressure forced them to change their edito-rial policies, had not changes in management been brought about, or had not lack of support forced them out of business soon after the war began.

Joseph J. Mathews was more critical of the partisan nature of Civil War journalism. He wrote in *Reporting the Wars* (1957) that as the war progressed, the distinction between war news and gen-eral news became meaningless. Political biases permeated every consideration; editors gave favorable coverage to pet generals and their strategies while blasting uncooperative military leaders, and some generals were partial to particular journalists. This resulted in numerous instances of reprehensible conduct by correspondents, who "reflected the prevailing low code of journalistic ethics."[11] Yet this was not entirely their fault, as reporters' accounts were usually governed by the biases of their employers.

The enduring concern over censorship was the focus for one of the best researched and well-written of recent Developmental inter-

---

[11]Joseph J. Mathews, *Reporting the Wars* (Minneapolis: University of Minnesota Press, 1957), 84.

pretations, John F. Marszalek's *Sherman's Other War: The General and the Civil War Press* (1981). Marszalek contended that the fundamental question of the press during war is still what it was during the Civil War: whether or not the government should impose restrictions upon the press, and if so, to what extent. Because this issue has not been conclusively resolved by the Supreme Court or by the U.S. Congress, he wrote, powerful generals such as Sherman imposed their own controls on the press as they saw fit. Therefore, "this nation of laws still depends on the whims of man in the crucial area of First Amendment rights in war."[12]

Marszalek explained the battles between Sherman and the press as personal conflicts rather than as a constitutional debate. Thus they were indicative of the historical tendency of press control in wartime to be an ad hoc rather than a constitutional reaction to immediate circumstances. Sherman's fears were misguided, Marszalek wrote, because whatever Union military intelligence reached the Confederates in Northern newspapers was usually so buried under details that it was hard to find and, therefore, of only limited value. Furthermore, stricter censorship would only have silenced essential criticism but would not have measurably shortened the war. "Sherman's battles with reporters," he wrote, "shows that grave danger exists to freedom of the press any time such a powerful public figure is able to put his anti-press ideas into practice."[13] He concluded, therefore, that these battles were obvious manifestations of a recurring movement toward repression in past wars and a warning of what will probably happen in future conflicts.

The Southern Nationalist School

By the 1930s, some Southern historians had become defensive in reaction to the vast body of Civil War literature that was critical of the South, and began to reevaluate relations between North and South before and during the war in order to vindicate their section. The result was a loosely defined and generally romantic movement which attempted to portray the agrarian Southern way of life as superior to the urbanized and industrialized lifestyle of the North. When writing about the war, Southern Nationalist historians usually exonerated the South while blaming the North for causing the war. They charged that the North considered itself the nation and destroyed the sectional balance of power by insisting on its own dominance. The cause of the war was not slavery, they argued, but the North's intent to destroy the superior Southern way of life.

When writing about Civil War journalism, Southern National-

---

[12]John F. Marszalek, *Sherman's Other War: The General and the Civil War Press* (Memphis: Memphis State University Press, 1981), 17.

[13]Ibid., p. 212.

ist historians accused prominent Northern editors of fanning the flames of aggressive hatred in the North against the South. Therefore, they attempted to refute prevailing views about the role of the Northern press in the war because they believed these views were accepted uncritically from self-serving accounts written by Northern journalists. They also ridiculed newspapers edited by occupying Union troops in defeated Southern towns.

Southern Nationalist treatments of the Confederate press, however, tended toward heroic depictions of Confederate editors and of the few known Confederate correspondents. They praised the voluntary censorship exercised by Southern newspapers, which resulted in far fewer breaches of military security than suffered by the Union army in the pages of Northern papers. This demonstrated that Southern papers more successfully served the interests of their section, they argued, implying that the publication of Union military secrets in Northern papers was indicative of the North's disunity and inherent moral weakness. Such views continued to appear as recently as 1969, when Hodding Carter wrote, "Whatever else may be said of the Southern press, the newspapers of the South have certainly demonstrated closer identification with the aspirations and turmoil and tragedy of their region than have those of any other part of the United States."[14]

One of the first Southern Nationalist interpretations of Civil War journalism was Lester J. Cappon's "The Yankee Press in Virginia, 1861-1865" (1935). Cappon ridiculed newspapers edited by Union personnel in defeated Virginia towns and cities. For instance, a single-issue paper entitled *The Connecticut Fifth* (produced by the Fifth Regiment of Connecticut Volunteers after their arrival in Winchester) "insulted the Confederate flag" although the "Yankees claimed to have maintained good order" in the city. Cappon wrote similarly of *The New Regime*, published by Major General Benjamin F. Butler in Norfolk, referring to it as "Butler's mouthpiece." *The New Regime* "lacked the comradery so characteristic of the cruder Yankee news-sheets" and was a business affair calculated to further the policies of the Union government.[15]

While Cappon attempted to discredit the North with his criticisms of occupation editors from the Union army, Richard Barksdale Harwell (1941) attempted to cast a favorable light on the South's role in the war by praising the books and magazines published in Atlanta during the war.[16] He noted that the necessity to publish

---

[14]Hodding Carter, *Their Words Were Bullets: The Southern Press in War, Reconstruction, and Peace* (Athens: University of Georgia Press, 1969), 1.

[15]Lester J. Cappon, "The Yankee Press in Virginia, 1861-1865," *William and Mary Quarterly* 15 (January 1935): 85.

[16]Richard B. Harwell, "Atlanta Publications of the Civil War," *Atlanta Historical Bulletin* 6 (July 1941): 165-200.

newspapers, government documents, and business records in the South was widely acknowledged. However, he challenged arguments that the publication of books to be read for pleasure was not necessary. Histories of the war, biographies of Southern leaders, and especially fiction were very important in maintaining Confederate morale. Thus Harwell tried to destroy stereotypes of the Civil War South as culturally inferior to or less literary than the North.

David M. Potter, on the other hand, minced no words in his condemnation of Northern Republican leaders. For instance, he wrote in "Horace Greeley and Peaceable Secession" (1941) that William H. Seward in the months preceding the war gave incessant expression to a "somewhat mystical conviction that the portentous and explicit acts of the South were evidences of a passing frenzy which would subside of itself."[17] Meanwhile Abraham Lincoln retreated into an impenetrable silence. Lesser Republicans, including New York *Tribune* editor Greeley, were "generally either blustering or vacillating, and, in either case, unrealistic" throughout the winter of 1860-1861.

Potter set out to destroy the predominant historical assumption which identified Greeley with peaceable separation. Although one well-known Greeley editorial said "we insist on letting them go in peace," Potter wrote, historians have ignored that expediency prompted Greeley to pretend to offer a separation that he did not expect the South to accept. Nor did historians recognize that the phrase and others like it were surrounded by conditions, reservations, and ambiguities that nullified its apparent meaning. Thus by concealing the fact that the nation had to choose between compromise and war until it was too late to prevent war, Greeley was at least partially to blame for causing the war.

The Southern Nationalist interpretation continues to appear occasionally, and in some cases has seemed to grow more bitter with the passage of time. One such example was William Stanley Hoole's *Vizetelly Covers the Confederacy* (1957). A warmly favorable biography of *Illustrated London News* correspondent Frank Vizetelly, who according to Hoole was the only special correspondent to cover the Confederate army, it also lashed out at the North nearly a century after the war ended. Hoole prefaced the book with memories of his father, born in 1860, who knew "the pain and the suffering and the bellyaching hunger that lay in Sherman's unholy swath across the South."[18]

---

[17]David M. Potter, "Horace Greeley and Peaceable Secession," *Journal of Southern History* 7 (1941): 145.

[18]W. Stanley Hoole, *Vizetelly Covers the Confederacy* (Tuscaloosa, AL: Confederate Publishing Co., 1957), 11.

The Consensus School

The Consensus School is best understood as a reaction to the Progressive perspective which dominated the study of American history for about 30 years of the first half of the 20th century. The Progressive school of American history originated during the domestic reform movement around 1900 and was concerned primarily with social problems resulting from an unfair distribution of wealth and power in American society. Progressive historians believed that the Civil War was actually a class conflict in which the industrialists, laborers, and farmers of the North destroyed the Southern planting aristocracy and eliminated its influence in national government. Yet Progressive historians usually condemned the war for leading American society to domination by ruthless capitalists concerned only for their own profit. As a result, reform was needed to achieve a fairer distribution of wealth and power.

In response to the Progressive perspective, Consensus historians argued that the Civil War was not a social war which led to an immoral domination of society by capitalists but rather a blessing in disguise that led to a modern and united America. The war was really an irrepressible conflict that grew out of sectional differences on issues of national policy, not the facade of a deeply rooted class conflict. Therefore, neither side was necessarily to blame for causing the war, although the South was clearly in the wrong for refusing to give up slavery and for seceding from the union.

Because of their attitude toward the South, Consensus historians usually wrote about the Northern press. They believed that most Northern newspapers agreed on the necessity for military security and sincerely attempted to avoid printing any information that could possibly aid the enemy. However, they were critical of newspapers that published reports about the locations and movement plans of Union troops. In so doing, these papers seriously damaged the national cause.

Although most historians who dealt with press censorship during the Civil War condemned it as an unwarranted and misguided act of repression, Consensus historians believed that there should have been stricter governmental control over what Northern newspapers could print. They argued that press censorship had been ineffective only because it was so randomly enforced, inflicting more damage to the Northern cause than if there had been no censorship at all. Therefore, stricter and more consistent censorship would have made the war effort more effective and might have shortened the war. The ultimate lesson to be learned from the role of newspapers during the war, then, is that in future wars the United States should control the press adequately enough to assure that it does not damage the national war effort. The national good, Consensus historians argued, is more vital than the practices of one institution.

Although the Consensus interpretation did not begin to acquire a sizable following until the 1940s, James G. Randall's "The Newspaper Problem in Its Bearing Upon Military Secrecy During the Civil War" (1918) was consistent with the Consensus perspective. Randall was critical of Northern newspapers for obstructing the war effort. They seriously harmed the national cause, he wrote, by frequently revealing military information and undermining public confidence in management of the war. Governmental intervention in the press, however, was relatively slight and, in any case, was much less effective than public opinion and the actions of private citizens. Editors suspected of disloyalty were threatened, sometimes run out of town, and newspaper offices were frequently attacked by mobs. As Randall wrote, "It may be said that the government did far less than the enthusiastic Union men of the time would have wished in the way of controlling the press."[19] As a result, there was no real suppression of opinion during the war.

Similarly, Adolph O. Goldsmith wrote in "Reporting the Civil War: Union Army—Press Relations"[20] (1956) that most Northern newspapers recognized the necessity for military security and made conscientious efforts to judge what should be omitted from news reports. Therefore, restrictions on handling of war news were generally very loose, but unnecessarily tight in some specific cases. This haphazardness of controls inflicted more damage on the war effort than if there had been no controls at all, Goldsmith wrote, whereas systematic and conscientious handling of news censorship might have shortened the war. Also, uninformed newspaper criticism of Lincoln's war strategies prodded some generals into striking before they were ready and did not contribute to an effective prosecution of the war. He concluded that in modern warfare rigid control of all news is essential to military success.

As Lincoln's most prominent critic, then, New York *Tribune* editor Horace Greeley was singled out by Consensus historians for special derision. James H. Trietsch, for instance, wrote in *The Printer and the Prince* (1955) that although Greeley was motivated by a fundamentally patriotic feeling, he was flighty and inconsistent. For example, immediately after the war he declared himself not for antagonism in peace but for lenient treatment of the South to encourage fraternal unity, apparently not realizing that his attacks on Lincoln's cautious military policies during the war had fanned the hatred that the North felt toward the South. Greeley would now

---

[19]James G. Randall, "The Newspaper Problem in Its Bearing upon Military Secrecy During the Civil War," *American Historical Review* 23 (January 1918): 332.

[20]Goldsmith, Adolph O., "Reporting the Civil War: Union Army Press Relations," *Journalism Quarterly* 33 (1956): 478-487.

have to abandon such campaigns, Trietsch wrote, in favor of a sober appeal for amnesty and for a genuine resumption of national citizenship. Trietsch concluded that only after Lincoln's death did Greeley realize how wise the president had been, and how his own misguided efforts had undermined what he now recognized as the common goals toward which each of them had worked.

Discussion

The Civil War has presented special difficulties for media historians because of the intense emotions arising out of the domestic nature of the war and because the role of the press during times of war always seems to raise strong opinions. Most historians who have studied Civil War journalism agree that the war led to a revolution in journalistic practices which for the first time established news, rather than editorial opinion, as the primary purpose of newspapers. What they disagree about is whether the press performed admirably or poorly and whether press censorship during the war should have been used at all or should have been utilized more extensively. The questions they have confronted involve essentially the issue of what the ultimate purpose of the press should be during wartime.

1. During the Civil War, to what did newspapers owe allegiance —to the unity of the nation, to their own sections, or to the journalistic precept of objectivity?

2. Was censorship during the Civil War acceptable? What are the fundamental principles that a historian should use in answering that question?

3. If the historian takes a Developmental approach, how does he or she justify placing journalistic practices above the national welfare?

4. Is it appropriate for historians to apply standards of journalistic practices of their own time in evaluating the Civil War press when standards then may have been different?

5. How well did the Civil War press perform? What standards are appropriate for use in judging its performance?

6. Which school of historians—the Contemporary or the Developmental, which wrote during times of differing journalistic standards—was best suited for judging newspaper performance during the Civil War?

Readings

Contemporary School

Richardson, Albert D., Ch. 22 (untitled), pp. 259-274, *Secret Service; the Field, the Dungeon and the Escape.* Hartford, CT: American, 1865.

Villard, Henry, "Army Correspondence: Its History," *The Nation* 1 (July 27, 1865), 79-82, 114-116, 144-146.

Developmental School

Andrews, J. Cutler, Ch. 2, "The Press Girds for the Conflict," pp. 6-34, *The North Reports the Civil War*. Pittsburgh: University of Pittsburgh Press, 1955.

Bullard, Frederick L., Ch. 14, "'Covering' the Civil War," pp. 375-408, *Famous War Correspondents*. New York: Beekman Publishers, 1974 reprint from the 1914 edition.

Marszalek, John F., Ch. 1, "The First Amendment in War," pp. 3-22, *Sherman's Other War: The General and the Civil War Press*. Memphis: Memphis State University Press, 1981.

Starr, Louis M., Ch. 1, "The News Revolution," pp. 3-29, *Bohemian Brigade: Civil War Newsmen in Action*. New York: Knopf, 1954.

Southern Nationalist School

Cappon, Lester J., "The Yankee Press in Virginia, 1861-1865," *William and Mary Quarterly*, 2nd ser., 15 (January 1935): 81-88.

Carter, Hodding, Ch. 1, "Introduction," pp. 1-18, *Their Words Were Bullets: The Southern Press in War, Reconstruction, and Peace*. Athens: University of Georgia Press, 1969.

Harwell, Richard B., "Atlanta Publications of the Civil War," *Atlanta Historical Bulletin* 6 (July 1941): 165-200.

Potter, David M., "Horace Greeley and Peaceable Secession," *Journal of Southern History* 7 (1941): 145-159.

Consensus School

Endres, Kathleen L., "The Women's Press in the Civil War: A Portrait of Patriotism, Propaganda, and Prodding," *Civil War History* 30 (March 1984): 31-53.

Goldsmith, Adolph O., "Reporting the Civil War: Union Army Press Relations," *Journalism Quarterly* 33 (1956): 478-487.

Randall, James G., "The Newspaper Problem in Its Bearing upon Military Secrecy During the Civil War," *American Historical Review* 23 (January 1918): 303-323.

Trietsch, James H., Ch. 10, "Aftermath," pp. 290-298, *The Printer and the Prince*. Boston: Beacon Press, 1955.

12

The Black Media, 1865-Present:
Liberal Crusaders or Defenders of Tradition?

The history of the Black media represents a sharp contrast to that of its White mainstream counterparts. Environmental, societal, and cultural obstacles all served to impede the progress of Black Americans who sought to establish an outlet for Black expression.

The first Black-owned and Black-operated newspaper was established in 1827 in New York City, the *Freedom's Journal*. The first Black periodicals appeared 11 years later, the *Mirror of Liberty* in New York City and the *National Reformer* of Philadelphia.

Following the Union victory in the Civil War in 1865, the atmosphere of depression and hopelessness that had surrounded Blacks changed to one of anticipation. Slaves were emancipated, and Blacks were promised full citizenship. Congressional actions such as the Civil Rights Act and the Fourteenth and Fifteenth Amendments attempted to grant Blacks more rights than they had ever received before in this country.

However, life as a free Black in the United States was not always perfect, or even adequate. Blacks discovered that they were still being denied many of the rights that Whites took for granted. When they sought to express their discontent—with governing bodies, White businessmen, White society—they were refused a voice in the White-dominated press. This lack of access to the mainstream press, in addition to a variety of societal obstacles and imbalances, led to the creation of a press devoted to the concerns of a Black readership. That resolve has continued through to today's Black media.

Like the White mainstream media, Black journalists were present during the most turbulent and exciting moments in U.S. history since the mid-1800s. Yet, those Blacks who wanted to create their own newspapers and magazines faced numerous obstacles. In most cases, the need for a press dedicated to serving the interests of

By Bernell Tripp
University of Alabama

the Black community was not enough to garner the support of a race that had only recently begun to show progress in educating itself. Financial difficulties plagued editors of the majority of the early newspapers and magazines of the 19th century and many of those operating in this century. The Black press of the latter 1800s still depended primarily on the generosity of Black and White businessmen for donations and what subscription fees they could collect from their poor Black readership. Few businessmen were willing to invest in ventures that were almost assured of failure, because most Black publications lasted only a short time. Blacks, they reasoned, could not afford to pay subscription fees, and the Whites who had the means were either hostile to the idea or reluctant to support the Black editors for a variety of reasons.

There was also a question of who would write the editorials and articles to be included in each edition. Editors and correspondents had to be literate individuals who were capable of making judgments on what was of interest to Black readers and of analyzing and interpreting key issues. They also had to be trusted members of the Black community, respected for their accomplishments and leadership abilities. Consequently, before the turn of the century, most Black correspondents were clergymen and businessmen— mainly those men who had received some formal education.

Despite these and many other difficulties, editors and writers had begun to produce publications in the 1820s and 1830s. When America's four and a half million Blacks were caught in the middle of the Civil War, Blacks sought leaders and spokesmen who would guide them through the troubled times. Since then, members of the Black media have managed to establish a collection of newspapers and magazines which began to rival their white competitors for the readership of both Blacks and Whites.

Most historians have viewed the history of the Black media since 1865 as a series of evolutionary stages characterized by a group of oppressed people who continuously endeavored to improve their voice. The result, Black people thought, would be a media that would not only help them improve their cultural and moral outlooks and lifestyles, but would also communicate the shortcomings of American society from the Black perspective. Within this overall view, historians can be divided into two categories: those historians who believed that Black newspapers, magazines, and their editors were predominantly instruments of change, dedicated solely to the universal elevation of the Black race and to their personal advancement; and those who agreed that the progress of the Black media was auspicious, but maintained that progress was reached not without a great deal of protest and reform. Historians in the first group believed that the item of top priority for the Black editors and publishers was to improve the status of all Blacks. They examined the Black media from the perspective of the contributions the journalists made to the moral, cultural, and social development of the race. These historians minimized the struggles against such opponents as the mainstream press, White businessmen, and the government, while emphasizing the achievements made toward reaching the goal of Black advancement. In contrast, the second group of historians emphasized the obstacles Black journalists faced and the rights and advantages for which they fought. Within these two broad perspectives, historians can be divided into five schools of interpretation: Romantic, Developmental, Consensus, Cultural, and Militant.

The Romantic School

Works by historians of the Romantic school spanned from the latter 1800s until the end of World War II. These historians depicted Black editors and correspondents as honest, noble intellectuals who sought to make the Black media more of a representative voice for their readership. Black journalists also served to encourage personal improvement through education and strict adherence to moral values. Romantic historians portrayed them as larger-than-life figures who acted as leaders and role models for Black Americans. By comparison, they depicted White opposition to the Black media less harshly than later historians would.

One of the earliest historical treatments from the Romantic school was Irving Garland Penn's *The Afro-American Press and Its Editors* (1891). The book documented not only a registry of early Black newspapers which had been established in America prior to the 1890s, but it included information on their editors, reporters, correspondents, and contributors. As a newspaper correspondent himself, Penn treated his former colleagues favorably. One of his more memorable descriptions of a Black journalist was a piece on Mary V. Cook, a columnist for the *American Baptist* and the *South Carolina Tribune*, whose life he described in these terms: "There is a divine poetry in a life garlanded by the fragrant roses of triumph."[1]

Frederick Detweiler was less florid in his descriptions, but equally enthusiastic about the performance of the Black press. In *The Negro Press in the United States* (1922), he viewed Black journalists and their Black readers as more educated and intelligent than Whites considered them to be. He described the "fearless personality" of William Calvin Chase of the Washington *Bee* as the primary attraction for selling his paper. Likewise, William Monroe Trotter's "reputation for bravery" led him to take up his race's cause. Detweiler also argued that it "is impossible not to picture the

---

[1]Irving Garland Penn, *The Afro-American Press and Its Editors* (Springfield, MA: Wiley, 1891), 367.

activity of the Negro press, while it was making such determined efforts to get a foothold after the Emancipation, as playing an important part in the process of educating the race."[2]

He minimized the conflict between the Black press and White
society by declaring it to be the same "atmosphere of conflict [from
which] the white man's press took its start and went on to grow and
thrive."[3] Indeed, Detweiler postulated, conflict breathed life into the
press and allowed it to prosper because the editor had something for
which to fight. Similarly, Detweiler argued that any "aggressive
tone" appeared after World War I and was probably more evident in
newspapers in the North than in the South.

By the 1930s, historians were beginning to take a less lofty view
of Black journalists, but opinions on the exalted virtues of the Black
press itself continued to be discussed in epic proportions. Although
these later historians, who might be termed "Neo-Romanticists,"
agreed with the idealism of the earlier Romanticists, they applied
these ideals to the newspapers and magazines and their development, rather than to the journalists themselves. The goals of the
media took on more glorified proportions than in the earlier perspectives.

In "'Freedom's Journal' and the 'Rights of All'" (1932), Bella
Gross declared that the goal of the Black press was the "universal elevation of man, the secret of which lay in the arts and sciences to be
cultivated by men working in harmony for the general good."[4] She
determined that a "Negro Renaissance" had begun with the creation
of the Black press, which emphasized the need for universal understanding among races. The Black press could only do this through
cooperation among enemies, as well as friends, in educating all the
people about the thoughts, hopes, and interests of Blacks. Like the
earlier Romantic historians, Gross reasoned that "only a strange
necessity" forced the Black press to stress race, and White opposition was no obstacle to its advancement.

Frederick J. Hoffman, Charles Allen, and Carolyn P. Ulrich
supported a similar opinion of Black magazines in New York City.
In *The Little Magazine* (1946), they examined small collegiate
magazines from 1891 to the 1940s. Their survey was one of the few
attempts at a study of Black magazines in the United States. They
considered the Black media in terms of the entire magazine movement, noting the powerful influence the magazines also had on the
development of poetry of the period. These Black periodicals also began to serve as a bridge to segregated communities, connecting

---

[2]Frederick Detweiler, *The Negro Press in the United States* (Chicago:
University of Chicago Press, 1922), 51.

[3]Ibid., p. 131.

[4]Bella Gross, "'Freedom's Journal' and the 'Rights of All,'" *Journal of Negro
History* 17 (July 1932): 246.

Blacks throughout a region by their shared needs and expectations.

Hoffman, Allen, and Ulrich also supported the idea that confrontations with racism and White opposition were secondary to establishing a Black press of which all Blacks could be proud. They advocated a press dedicated to teaching Blacks about their own culture and about issues endemic to Blacks in the United States.[5]

The Developmental School

Developmental historians evaluated the media from the perspective of journalistic practices and standards. By the turn of the century, the Black press had begun to establish itself as a viable component of the mass media. Black newspapers and magazines were enjoying a period of unparalleled growth with record circulation numbers and nationwide influence. Developmental historians saw the Black media as an instrument for race progress—an outlet for providing national and international news to meet the needs of a growing and increasingly diverse group of Black Americans. Most Developmental evaluations of the Black media appeared primarily within the last two decades of this century, which is understandable in the wake of the prominent role of Black correspondents during the nation's involvement in the wars and in the civil rights movement.

However, as early as 1928 one Developmental historian, Charles S. Johnson, viewed the Black press as an organization that not only gave the Black community what it wanted, but also what it needed—including a sense of group identity and an opportunity to help make changes. Johnson's "The Rise of the Negro Magazine" (1928) noted how the goals of the Black magazines changed. He determined that the *Anglo-African*, created in 1859 in New York City, was interested in supporting moral and human brotherhood. By the 1920s the magazine movement, according to Johnson, had altered its format to serve a more practical purpose. Blacks' informational needs had begun to change as the country's international relations and government policies changed after World War I. Rather than concentrating on features, poetry, and short stories, Black magazines provided concrete information from which readers could form their own opinions about specific issues. The *Opportunity*, for example, had shifted its emphasis from emotion in social situations to objective facts. It also attempted to stimulate creative self-expression and to educate Blacks and Whites about Black history and culture.[6]

Similarly, Lawrence D. Hogan emphasized how the Associated Negro Press developed into a quality reporting instrument that pro-

---

[5]Frederick J. Hoffman, Charles Allen, and Carolyn P. Ulrich, *The Little Magazine* (Princeton, NJ: Princeton University Press, 1946), 218-230.

[6]Charles S. Johnson, "The Rise of the Negro Magazine," *Journal of Negro History* 13 (January 1928): 7-21.

vided key information for Black readers. In *A Black National News Service: The Associated Negro Press and Claude Barnett, 1919-1945* (1984), Hogan focused on Barnett's efforts to build a reporting organization that would give the Black press access to a critical, comprehensive coverage of personalities and events relevant to Black Americans. Hogan reasoned that Barnett recognized the need for a Black-oriented news agency for a Black press "characterized by meager financial resources, lack of a strong tradition of cooperation among the publishers, and a limited understanding of what was required to reach a national audience." Hogan also credited Barnett's success to his reluctance to claim a share of his agency's attention and to his ability to recognize the components of a press that was responsive to a Black audience. Hogan detailed the ANP's contribution to a growing race consciousness. He noted how Black organizations promoted a thinking atmosphere among group members with "the competition between them, the issues they argued over, and the questions they raised that otherwise would not have been asked."[7] National newspapers drew on this consciousness, assuming a leadership and opinion-shaping role for a substantial number of Blacks.

Although Developmental historians generally focused on the evolution of the journalistic practices of the Black press, Leonard Ray Teel also considered the creation of the Atlanta *World* from a business standpoint. In "W.A. Scott and the Atlanta *World*" (1989), he argued that Scott's success with the *World* was largely due to its founding as a business venture and not as a "political experiment." He declared that "[a]lthough Scott believed the *World* could become an important, independent black voice, he focused his energies first upon creating a healthy financial venture." According to Teel, Scott also determined that political affiliations were a primary cause of the decline of financial support of the Atlanta weekly, the *Independent*. Scott resolved that the *World* would remain free of political loyalties. Teel also noted that although Scott's main interest was in building a successful *World*, he similarly remained responsive to his market. Scott "anticipated what the readers would want—even-handed coverage of the black community, not overloaded with news of political protest."[8]

However, political protest and social and cultural reform were key components in evaluations of the Black media by a second group of Developmental historians, who began their studies after World War II. They were also interested in the evolution of the

---

[7]Lawrence D. Hogan, *A Black National News Service: The Associated Negro Press and Claude Barnett, 1919-1945* (Rutherford, NJ: Fairleigh Dickinson University Press, 1984), 18-19.

[8]Leonard Ray Teel, "W.A. Scott and the Atlanta *World*," *American Journalism* 6 (1989): 158, 166.

Black media and analyzed their development. Like the first group, they agreed that the advancement of the Black media was a positive stage in the overall structure of American journalism. However, although the first group emphasized the progress of the Black media and minimized the difficulties, these historians pictured the Black media as having succeeded only after confronting a particularly hostile White press and American society.

Two of the best examples of this group of Developmental historians dealt with the Black press during World War II. Both authors, former working journalists, were college journalism professors who held a suspicious view of the government in its relationship with the news media. The Black press had undergone many changes after the first World War. Several Black weeklies had large national circulations, and the newspapers and magazines were beginning to focus on more national and international events of interest to Black readers. This focus shifted to war with the bombing of Pearl Harbor, and Black editors refused to "cover" World War II with reprints of government handouts and letters home—as they had in World War I. The larger Black newspapers were more secure financially than before, and the editors were determined to ensure their readers coverage unbiased by government interference.

In "From the Back of the Foxhole: Black Correspondents in World War II" (1973), John D. Stevens portrayed Black war correspondents as both reporters and advocates. He determined that the 27 Black correspondents he examined had dual roles: to report on the war and to chronicle the lives of Blacks contributing to the war effort, and to record mistreatment of Black soldiers and racial discrimination.[9] According to Stevens, this dual role caused the Black press to be compelled to do battle on two fronts—at home and abroad. Although the war correspondents did not usually suffer mistreatment, they were determined to push for equal opportunities and fair treatment for the Blacks they covered. As a result, Black editors were forced to defend their correspondents and their newspapers to government officials, service organizations such as the Red Cross, and government-contracted businesses when such exposés appeared. Stevens also noted a confrontation in 1942 in which the Justice Department wanted to indict a group of Black editors for sedition.

Patrick Washburn also addressed this topic in *A Question of Sedition: The Federal Government's Investigation of the Black Press During World War II* (1986). He attributed the conflict to the Black press' newly discovered outspokenness. According to Wash-

---

[9]John D. Stevens, "From the Back of the Foxhole: Black Correspondents in World War II," *Journalism Monographs* 27 (1973): 7.

burn, a shift in editorial content from ideological debates on achieving equality to front-page news of crime and discrimination created a mass-appeal publication that instilled in Black readers a sense of pride and interest. Reader approval and what Washburn referred to as "the combined criticism-and-support approach" of dealing with the government propelled the Black press into its first truly adversarial role. He argued that the threat of being suppressed was all too real for the Black press until the intervention of Attorney General Francis Biddle in 1942. A staunch believer in First Amendment rights, Biddle decided that he would not allow any Black publishers to be indicted for sedition during the war. Washburn argued that the Black press saw nothing wrong in pointing out injustices that Blacks suffered. He determined that it was the duty of Black journalists to challenge this attempt at government suppression of the Black press and to fight for racial equality during the war. With few exceptions, Washburn portrayed government officials, particularly J. Edgar Hoover, as domineering, paranoid, and overzealous in their attempts to locate violators of the Espionage and Sedition Acts. By contrast, Washburn depicted Biddle as a mild-mannered individual with a sharp mind and strong determination, whereas Black publishers and editors were pictured as diligent crusaders who represented an increasingly influential and disgruntled segment of American society.

The Consensus School
Consensus historians were not as adamant about the antagonistic relationship between the Black media and the government during World War II. They concluded that although the Black media were critical of many aspects of American society, they were avid supporters of the country's war effort. Realizing that this position could be beneficial for Blacks in the future, Black editors maintained a practical outlook on the situation. That stance, Consensus historians argued, was more successful than a dissenting or radical one would have been.

In *Forum for Protest* (1975), Lee Finkle denied that the war years were the start of the "Black revolution" of the 1960s as some historians had believed. With the outbreak of war, he explained, the Black press urged Blacks to demand the right to fight for their country. Editors reasoned that this wartime participation would dictate the status of Blacks in America after the war. Finkle contended that the Black press remained conservative in its editorial position on the war despite the resentment and anger of Black citizens over the treatment of Blacks at home and abroad. Black editors were agreeable to the idea of Blacks fighting in the war, with the hope that afterwards the White majority would end the caste system.[10]

Theodore Kornweibel Jr. presented a similar explanation of a Black editor who changed the editorial stance of his publication in order to achieve his goal. Kornweibel's *No Crystal Stair: Black Life and the Messenger, 1917-1928* (1975) detailed the 11-year operation of the radical magazine the *Messenger*. According to Kornweibel, the magazine became a successful advocate of the cause of Black Americans only after it gave up its early radical stance and moved toward the center of national politics. In the 1920s, Blacks received no help from government, the political right or left, industry, or labor. A. Phillip Randolph helped found the *Messenger* as a forthright Socialist magazine and tied its fate for the first five years to the American Socialist Party. Once Randolph realized, however, that the party offered no real hope for Blacks, he gradually changed the magazine's stance toward a pro-business one. Randolph's pragmatism—in contrast with an idealism which Progressive historians admired in American reformers but which Consensus historians argued was ineffectual in bringing about change—provided one of the prime factors in the magazine's surviving as long as it did. By the time the *Messenger* died in 1928, Randolph had moved it into the mainstream of American politics, where it sought accommodation with the Republican and Democratic parties and even with the mainline labor groups hated by Socialists.

The Cultural School

Not all historians described the history of the Black media in terms of the evolution of journalistic practices or of the advantages of cooperating with the country's war effort for the future good of all Blacks. Many in the last two decades were more concerned with society's effect on the press. These Cultural historians believed the Black press was influenced primarily by the status of Blacks in American society.

In "The Rise of the Black Press in Chicago" (1977-1978), Albert Kreiling characterized Black publications from 1874 to the late 1890s "from the standpoint of the unfolding patterns and styles of life, thought and consciousness manifest in their content."[11] According to Kreiling, Chicago's Black population and social structure were headed by an elite group of businessmen and tradesmen—a group that emerged in the pre-Civil War community and continued after the war. These elites took Black Republican politicians as their leaders and considered the Republican party to be "a moral force

---

[10]Lee Finkle, *Forum for Protest: The Black Press During World War II* (Rutherford, NJ: Fairleigh Dickinson University Press, 1975), 222-223.

[11]Albert Kreiling, "The Rise of the Black Press in Chicago," *Journalism History* 4 (1977-1978): 132.

and protector." The Black newspapers carried national political triumphs and disappointments and "outspoken protests against the worsening tide of oppression against blacks in the South." Therefore, Kreiling reasoned, the papers reflected a shared racial experience—an overall nationalization process and consciousness—as well as new developments, "as blacks, like other Americans, adjusted to the nascent industrial order."

Similarly, Penelope Bullock attributed the overall development of Black magazines primarily to political and social circumstances that played an important part in the lives of the Black population. In *The Afro-American Periodical Press, 1838-1909* (1981), she noted how Black magazines lay dormant after the Civil War while Blacks waited expectantly for their promise of full citizenship rights. However, from 1880 to 1909 adverse events of the post-Reconstruction years caused a proliferation of Black magazines to connect segregated communities and to promote integration into society.[12]

Some Cultural historians also emphasized how the needs of Black citizens influenced the media's actions. To these historians, it was not only the status of Blacks in American society, but Blacks' desires to be heard and the necessity of fighting to acquire that representative voice that helped formulate media practices. Roland Wolseley's *The Black Press, U.S.A.* (1971) examined the idea that Blacks still needed someone to fight the old societal battles, in addition to the currently developing new ones. According to Wolseley, Blacks, deprived of a variety of their rights, longed for a press that not only would protest these transgressions on their behalf, but also would keep Blacks informed about themselves. These demands helped shape a press to which Black readers could turn for leadership and guidance. However, Wolseley warned that if Black newspapers intended to survive, they could not "fall behind the educational growth and cultural development of their readers nor do they dare move too much in advance of them. At the same time, they must solve the difficult problem of crusading for causes important to black people while not alienating the business interests upon which they depend."[13]

Similarly, in *The Dissident Press: An Alternative Journalism in American History* (1984), Lauren Kessler concentrated on the influences of societal action on the Black press. However, she was primarily concerned with the necessity of creating an alternative to the conventional media marketplace which remained closed to

---

[12]Penelope L. Bullock, *The Afro-American Periodical Press, 1838-1909* (Baton Rouge: Louisiana State University Press, 1981), 11.

[13]Roland E. Wolseley, *The Black Press, U.S.A.* (Ames: Iowa State University Press, 1971), 330.

Blacks. She described a conventional White-dominated press, which—when it did not ignore the political, economic, and cultural goals of Blacks—"often stereotyped or ridiculed Black Americans." Thus, White society and the White press were sometimes patronizing, often thoughtless, and consistently cruel when dealing with the lives of Blacks. Kessler concluded that Black newspapers emerged as a result of this hostile American society and "grew to be independent forums that met the changing needs of their constituencies by providing information, education, and inspiration."[14]

The Militant School

Existing concurrently with the Cultural school was a growing group of historians who treated the Black media as part of the "Black revolution"—an idea in direct contrast to that of the Consensus historians. From the viewpoint of Militant historians, the Black media were instruments of political protest and societal reform. Battle lines were clearly drawn—on the one side, White politicians, editors, and businessmen who conspired to withhold from Blacks the rights and advantages enjoyed by White American citizens; and on the other side, the crusading Black publishers and editors dedicated to promoting political, as well as economic and cultural, equality.

James Tinney and Justine Rector presented the most fervent argument for a Black press immersed in American politics. In *Issues and Trends in Afro-American Journalism* (1980), they argued that the Black press "engaged in both non-electoral politics (seeking to pressure the white oppressor) and electoral politics (seeking to encourage black participation in voting and office-seeking)." Tinney and Rector noted the opposition these Black publishers faced and the subsequent problems, such as being arrested and having their homes burned and their offices dynamited. However, they also criticized the modern Black press for capitulating to "moderatism." Despite this accusation of a new conservatism, they admitted that the Black press had never given up in its "defense of equality and in its stand against white racism."[15]

Abby Arthur Johnson and Ronald Maberry Johnson presented a less belligerent viewpoint in their examination of Black magazines. In *Propaganda and Aesthetics: The Literary Politics of Afro-American Magazines in the Twentieth Century* (1979), the authors explained that magazine editors used Black literature, both creative and critical, in a variety of ways to articulate "the needs of a minority and historically oppressed people." These Black intellectuals

---

[14]Lauren Kessler, *The Dissident Press: An Alternative Journalism in American History* (Beverly Hills: Sage, 1984), 23.

[15]James S. Tinney and Justine J. Rector, eds., *Issues and Trends in Afro-American Journalism* (Lanham, MD: University Press of America, 1980), 1, 7.

and artists directed their periodicals to the protest for civil liberties—challenging the compromising doctrines of Booker T. Washington—and for "universal concerns" not addressed by the previous generations. By the 1960s, they reasoned, many young writers rejected the ideas of their elders and "utilized their periodicals, along with other efforts, not to gain admittance into the broader society but to attempt separation from Western ways."[16]

Discussion

Despite the contributions of Black publishers, editors, and writers, the Black media have failed to attract the attention or the interest of the majority of American media historians. Subsequently, many questions have been left to speculation or remain unanswered.

1. Is the idea of the Black media as the universal elevator of mankind too romanticized?

2. Were the goals of the Black media idealistic, or were they protest-oriented?

3. Whether idealistic or protest-oriented, was their approach less effective than a pragmatic, moderate approach would have been, as Consensus historians argued? Which approach—adapting to American society or militantly opposing its practices—was more effective in achieving the goals of Blacks?

4. Were the Black media concerned only with serving as role models and providing guidelines for self-improvement for their Black readers?

5. Were Black editors revolutionaries who struggled to achieve a set of ideals and to claim a rightful share of what American life had to offer?

6. Were Black publishers conservative or outspoken? If conservative, did they take this particular stand for the good of their Black readers, as the Consensus historians suggested, or did they become conservative for fear of losing White financial support, as Militant historians argued?

7. What was the motive of publishers and editors in making compromises: to benefit their race or to make their publications successful?

8. Did the Black media intend to become liberal crusaders or reformers seeking to challenge the powers of White society?

9. Can they be evaluated by standard journalistic criteria, as Developmental historians have tried to do?

10. Did the Black media help to shape the lives of their readers, or did their Black readers determine which course the newspapers

---

[16]Abby Arthur Johnson and Ronald Maberry Johnson, *Propaganda and Aesthetics: The Literary Politics of Afro-American Magazines in the Twentieth Century* (Amherst: University of Massachusetts Press, 1979), 202.

and magazines would follow?

Readings

Romantic School

Detweiler, Frederick, Ch. 6, "The Demand for Rights," pp. 130-157, *The Negro Press in the United States*. Chicago: University of Chicago Press, 1922.

Gross, Bella, "'Freedom's Journal' and the 'Rights of All,'" *Journal of Negro History* 17 (July 1932): 241-286.

Kerlin, Robert T., Ch. 1, "The Colored Press," and Ch. 2, "The New Era," pp. 1-29, *The Voice of the Negro*. New York: Dutton, 1920.

Onley, D. Watson, Richard W. Thompson, and Walter M. Wallace, Ch. 23, "Negro Newspapers," pp. 347-355, *Twentieth Century Negro Literature or a Cyclopedia of Thought on the Vital Topics Relating to the American Negro*. Naperville, IL: J.L. Nichols, 1902.

Penn, Irving Garland, pp. 350-368, *The Afro-American Press and Its Editors*. Springfield, MA: Wiley, 1891.

Developmental School

Hogan, Lawrence D., Ch. 1, "An Idea Whose Time Had Come," pp. 15-37, *A Black National News Service: The Associated Negro Press and Claude Barnett, 1919-1945*. Rutherford, NJ: Fairleigh Dickinson University Press, 1984.

Johnson, Charles S., "The Rise of the Negro Magazine," *Journal of Negro History* 13 (January 1928): 7-21.

Stevens, John D., "From the Back of the Foxhole: Black Correspondents in World War II," *Journalism Monographs* 27 (1973).

Teel, Leonard Ray, "W.A. Scott and the Atlanta *World*," *American Journalism* 6 (1989): 158-178.

Washburn, Patrick S., Ch. 1, "Civil Liberties Are the Essence of the Democracy We Are Pledged to Protect," pp. 3-10, *A Question of Sedition: The Federal Government's Investigation of the Black Press During World War II*. New York: Oxford University Press, 1986.

Consensus School

Finkle, Lee, Ch. 6, "The Black Press and World War II" and "Conclusion," pp. 191-223, *Forum for Protest: The Black Press During World War II*. Rutherford, NJ: Fairleigh Dickinson University Press, 1975.

Jones, Lester M., "The Editorial Policy of Negro Newspapers of 1917-18 as Compared with That of 1941-42," *Journal of Negro History* 29 (January 1944): 24-31.

Kornweibel, Theodore, Jr., Ch. 4, "The *Messenger* and the Harlem Renaissance," pp. 105-131, *No Crystal Stair: Black Life and the Messenger, 1917-1928*. Westport, CT: Greenwood Press, 1975.

Cultural School

Bullock, Penelope L., Ch. 1, "Perspective," pp. 1-12, and Ch. 5, "In Retrospect," pp. 205-221, *The Afro-American Periodical Press, 1838-1909*. Baton Rouge: Louisiana State University Press, 1981.

Kessler, Lauren, Ch. 2, "The Freedom Train," pp. 21-47, *The Dissident Press: An Alternative Journalism in American History*. Beverly Hills: Sage, 1984.

O'Kelly, Charlotte G., "The Black Press: Conservative or Radical, Reformist or Revolutionary?" *Journalism History* 4 (1977-1978): 114-116.

Wolseley, Roland E., Ch. 16, "Pro and Con on the Black Press," pp. 298-320, *The Black Press, U.S.A.* Ames: Iowa State University Press, 1971.

Militant School

Fox, Stephen R., "Epilogue," pp. 273-282, *The Guardian of Boston: William Monroe Trotter*. New York: Atheneum, 1970.

Lunardini, Christine A., "Standing Firm: William Monroe Trotter's Meetings With Woodrow Wilson, 1913-14," *Journal of Negro History* 64 (Summer 1979): 244-265.

Meier, August, Ch. 12, "Booker T. Washington and the 'Talented Tenth,'" pp. 224-236, *Negro Thought in America, 1880-1915: Racial Ideologies in the Age of Booker T. Washington*. Ann Arbor: University of Michigan Press, 1969.

Thornbrough, Emma Lou, Ch. 9, "Fortune Breaks," pp. 287-321, *T. Thomas Fortune: Militant Journalist*. Chicago: University of Chicago Press, 1972.

Tinney, James S., and Justine J. Rector, eds., Ch. 1, "Introduction," and Ch. 2, "Black Newspapers and Other Journals," pp. 1-24, *Issues and Trends in Afro-American Journalism*. Lanham, MD: University Press of America, 1980.

13

The Industrial Press, 1865-1883: Professional Journalism or Pawn of Urbanism?

In the years after the Civil War, the press underwent several major changes. In times of war, innovation and new ideas often replace old values and institutions. This was true in the case of the American press. Many innovations begun during the Civil War had been adopted almost universally by the end of the war. Instead of reverting to pre-war status, these innovations not only remained, but became more widespread.

Perhaps the most striking change was newspapers' break from control by political parties. Before the war, many papers were little more than house organs for a particular political party. Editorials reflected this bias most obviously, but the news was also reported with a political slant that favored the paper's party. The number of independent papers rose significantly after the war. Editors remained involved in partisan politics but did not enjoy the same status they did in the pre-war era.

The desire for more news considerably boosted the status of the reporter and encouraged new newspaper practices. Post-war journalists were much more likely to have a college education. At some papers, almost all of the reporters had some.

As independence from party bonds allowed more freedom in newspaper content, feature material appeared more often, usually in the form of "human interest" stories. Wit and humor columnists grew in number and popularity. Although they wrote primarily for one paper, some of them had pieces reprinted in so many papers that they became known across the nation.

Newspapers grew in number and in size. Another indication of newspaper growth was the increase in the number of Sunday editions of daily papers. During the war, readers were so eager for news that Sunday editions became commonplace, even though religious leaders frowned upon them. Gradually, the content of Sunday

By Jana Hyde
University of Alabama

editions began to focus less on news and to include more diverse reading, such as feature items.

Newspapers also began to take on crusades. These were not the party crusades of previous years, but were more socially oriented: cleaning up governmental corruption and promoting social welfare.

Several schools of interpretation are represented in the histories of the Industrial Press. Romantic historians concentrated on the most prominent individuals in journalism and their accomplishments. They gave attention to both the personal and professional sides of their subjects. Developmental historians focused more on the professional improvements journalism made. Progressive historians examined the press in terms of the ideological conflict between the wealthy few and the poor masses. Business historians, especially concerned about the changing character of the press as the nation became increasingly industrialized after the Civil War, believed institutional decisions related to the financial matters of newspapers provided the main force in determining the character and practices of the press. Cultural historians, however, argued that the influence was broader than simply the economic factor and that, instead, a combination of economic, sociological, psychological, and political factors played the largest role.

The Romantic School

The Romantic historians, though prolific in the latter half of the 19th century, continued in the early 1900s to make contributions to the historiography of the Industrial Press. They usually took as their subjects prominent individuals in the newspaper business. Often, they wrote about people they had known. Whereas some historians such as those from the Developmental school concentrated on the individuals as journalists and on their skills of the craft, Romantic writers glorified the whole personality of their subjects. Sometimes they credited them with superhuman qualities.

Romantic historians generally were not professional journalists, and therefore were not mainly interested in the limited journalistic role of their subjects. Although many had worked for newspapers, most often they were well-to-do, well-educated people who enjoyed history as a hobby. They were not trained in historical research or writing, but their work was usually of a high quality. Historical writing, to them, was an art; and they wrote not for an audience of journalists only, but also for the literate public.

Rollo Ogden's two-volume biography *Life and Letters of Edwin Lawrence Godkin* (1907) epitomized the Romantic approach. Godkin was the editor of the weekly *Nation* and also of the New York *Evening Post*. Ogden liberally interspersed his observations with illustrative letters to and from Godkin. He praised Godkin as a talented writer, a patriotic American citizen (even though he was born and died in Great Britain), and a valuable friend.

Many considered Godkin a gifted writer. In explaining why, Ogden wrote, "In verbal or written expression, Mr. Godkin's humor had a great range and variety. He was remarkable for unexpected turns of phrase . . . . He fell naturally into comic exaggeration, and abounded in original epithet."[1] Ogden illustrated Godkin's writing ability with profuse samples of his clever columns and letters.

Ogden's biography displayed another feature characteristic of the Romantic approach. Although suspicious of radical ideology, Ogden admiringly pointed out that Godkin did hold to the views of classic 19th-century liberalism, believing, for example, in freedom, the civic duty of an educated citizenry, proper standards of conduct in public affairs, and other ideas associated with public responsibility of the individual in a democratic society. Although a native of Ireland, Godkin had an early fascination for the American democratic system. When he became a citizen of the United States, he tried to use his writing talent to better the system. As one of his causes, he adopted the reform of civil service, and he used his position with the *Nation* to promote the cause. Here, too, Ogden found much to praise. "The ardor and argumentative power and statesmanlike prescience," he wrote, "with which Mr. Godkin pushed this reform year after year in the *Nation*, and labored for it through organization and correspondence and political appeal, can scarcely be given a right estimate by those who have lived since the battle was won."[2]

According to Ogden, many admired Godkin and considered him a loyal friend. He had the good fortune to be blessed with the friendships of intelligent and cultured women. "His manner with them was perfection," Ogden observed. "He knew how to be playful, mock heroic, sympathetic, gallant, paying to a woman the double compliment of being wholly at ease with her and giving her of his best."[3]

Resembling Ogden's portrait of Godkin as an exemplary man was Elizabeth Bisland's characterization of Lafcadio Hearn. In *The Life and Letters of Lafcadio Hearn* (1906), Bisland created a rosy picture of the New Orleans editor by mixing letters and examples of his own work with her few comments. In the preface she stated that the discovery of several autobiographical pieces "narrowed [her] task to little more than the recording of dates and such brief comments and explanations as were required for the bet-

---

[1] Rollo Ogden, ed., *The Life and Letters of Edwin Lawrence Godkin* (New York: Macmillan, 1907), vol. 2, 3.

[2] Ibid., pp. 41-42.

[3] Ibid., pp. 13-14.

ter comprehension of his own contributions to the book."[4]

Bisland knew Hearn, as other Romantic historians frequently had known their subjects, and so was able to write from her personal reminiscences. She used her first-hand knowledge to carefully turn criticism of his "neurotic" behavior into a compliment. She explained that Hearn's eccentric behavior was merely extreme sensitivity combined with a "vigour of mind and body to an unusual degree." Working first in Cincinnati, Hearn found New Orleans receptive to his work, which had a lyrical, ethereal quality. In recognizing his talent, Bisland wrote that he "was finally able to find his outlet in the direction to which his preparatory labours and inherent genius were urging him."[5]

The Romantic, flowery language that Bisland used to describe Hearn personally and professionally was echoed in his own letters to friends and in excerpts from his fiction. When Hearn moved to Japan, Bisland felt he reached the pinnacle of his talent. "I think it was at *Kobe* [a Japanese newspaper] he reached his fullest intellectual stature. None of the work that followed in the next eight years surpassed the results he there achieved. . . ." Bisland believed even Hearn's common correspondence was valuable as examples of his talent. She wrote that his letters "will bear comparison with the most famous letters in literature." Complaining about the limits space imposed on her selection, she wrote that the compression of letters "has obliged me to abandon all temptation to dwell upon his more human side, his humour, tenderness, sympathy, eccentricity, and the thousand queer, charming qualities that made up his many-faceted nature."[6] But this is just what her selection of letters did— they allowed the reader to see Hearn's personality.

The Developmental School

Developmental historians did not ignore the important individuals involved in media history, but they looked more at how the press matured and developed as a profession. They were interested in tracing the path journalism took to get to the state in which it existed in the historian's time, and often they evaluated past progress in terms of how it contributed to present-day journalism. According to Developmental historians, innovations in the age of the Industrial Press in printing processes, reporting, editorializing, and management organization were steps in the evolution of journalism as a profession.

For Developmental historians, how well journalists performed

---

[4]Elizabeth Bisland, *The Life and Letters of Lafcadio Hearn* (Boston: Houghton, Mifflin, 1906), vol. 1, vi.

[5]Ibid., pp. 80, 72.

[6]Ibid., pp. 132, 161-162, 161.

as journalists *per se* was an essential part of the history of progress. Thus, one finds among their works a number of biographies of leading figures. As applied to biography, that perspective can be seen in Isaac Marcosson's *Marse Henry* (1951), an account of the editor of the Louisville *Courier Journal*. Henry Watterson's approach to editorial writing embodied "personal journalism," which evolved from the editorial styles of the partisan press. In the period following the Civil War, editorials strongly reflected the intelligence and personality of their authors, and readers associated editorials more with the writer than with the paper in which they were printed. According to Marcosson, during Watterson's time "people read men instead of newspapers." He considered Watterson a master of editorial writing who displayed "courageous disregard of consequences for printing the truth,"[7] and his colorful editorials influenced many younger editors in a day when the influence of editors was waning.

Another such subject was Joseph B. McCullagh. His major contribution to the profession of journalism was, however, just the opposite of Watterson's. In *Little Mack: Joseph B. McCullagh of the St. Louis Globe-Democrat* (1969), Charles Clayton stated that although McCullagh was accomplished in many areas of newspaper practices, his biggest contribution to the profession was in leading journalism from the biased reporting of an early era influenced greatly by partisanship to the impartial reporting of "new journalism." He claimed that although McCullagh is not generally given credit, he actually pioneered the new journalism. His successful *Globe-Democrat* used innovations for which Joseph Pulitzer, who learned his approach to newspapering in St. Louis and later applied it successfully in New York City, usually is given credit. These innovations included aggressive news gathering for local and national news; adoption of crusades; an active, unabashed editorial page; frequent use of illustrations; and continuous promotion for the paper. Clayton also gave McCullagh credit for inventing the interview.

Clayton pointed out that McCullagh's newspaper colleagues regarded him highly. Pulitzer and William Randolph Hearst may have made larger fortunes and become more familiar names, but many other newspapermen felt that the two media tycoons imitated McCullagh for their success. McCullagh's own success did not come at the price of ethics, as Pulitzer and Hearst's did. McCullagh, Clayton said, "set the pattern for modern courage of political conventions."[8] He crusaded wholeheartedly, but not to the exclusion of

---

[7]Isaac Marcosson, *Marse Henry: A Biography of Henry Watterson* (New York: Dodd, Mead, 1951), 4, 2.

[8]Charles G. Clayton, *Little Mack: Joseph B. McCullagh of the St. Louis Globe-Democrat* (Carbondale: Southern Illinois University Press, 1969), 235.

other concerns, and he promoted the belief that a newspaper should become involved in its community's issues. Through successful implementation of his innovations he helped propel the newspaper industry into a new age of journalistic professionalism.

The Progressive School

Like the Developmental historians, Progressive historians studied the evolution of the press, but they were more interested in its relationship to "big business" and government. In the conflict between those two powerful entities and "the people," they placed journalists and papers on the side of the common man and against the wealthy industrialists, who tried to maintain control of the government for their own self-interest. Progressive historians viewed positively crusades against corrupt government practices and profit-hungry industrialists. They particularly admired cartoonists such as Thomas Nast, whose incessant lampooning of the Tweed Ring in New York City helped bring to justice one of the most corrupt political machines in history. In the same vein, Progressive historians looked favorably upon editors and columnists who used their columns to urge reform, such as Finley Peter Dunne's crusade for reform in the civil service system. In general, Progressive historians held the press in good light, because they selected for study, for the most part, newspapers that were exercising their independence from political parties and taking up crusades against corruption in both government and big business.

The Progressive concept of the journalist as reformer served as the basis for John M. Harrison's portrait of David Ross Locke in *The Man Who Made Nasby* (1969), a columnist whose stinging satire furthered his personal crusades for liberal social reform. The fictional character "Petroleum Vesuvius Nasby," whom Locke created, was an ignorant, bigoted, and coarse citizen who constantly wrote letters to the editor concerning public events. He wrote in dialect, misspellings, and all, a popular form of editorial humor at that time. Although the Nasby letters have been categorized as humor, that humor was only superficial, argued Harrison. He declared that Nasby was "the agent through which [Locke] created some of the most devastatingly effective satire written by an American."[9] Locke used an overwhelming majority of the letters in support of crusades he was promoting. In addition to the Nasby letters, he also wrote editorials that addressed the issues of his day. They covered such diverse subjects as slavery, the troubles of the Reconstruction period, prohibition, and civil rights for Negroes.

The years following the Civil War were rife with governmental

---

[9]John M. Harrison, *The Man Who Made Nasby, David Ross Locke* (Chapel Hill: University of North Carolina Press, 1969), 4.

problems. Locke, true to form, formed definite opinions about these issues, explained Harrison, and used editorials and the Nasby letters to advance his opinions. For example, he began supporting President Andrew Johnson's reconstruction policies, but a rift occurred in their beliefs and Locke reversed his position. With strongly worded editorials and Nasby letters, Locke withdrew his support from the President. By 1867, Nasby had become so popular that Locke took speaking engagements in which he spoke as the character of Petroleum V. Nasby. He also used the Nasby character in speeches and letters to support his campaign for the prohibition of liquor.

Barbara Schaaf presented a similar portrait of another columnist in *Mr. Dooley's Chicago* (1977). Chicago editor and columnist Finley Peter Dunne created the fictional "Mr. Dooley." The observations and experiences of this Irish immigrant and saloon-keeper reflected those of Chicago readers. In creating Dooley and his friends, Dunne drew on his experiences as a middle-class, street-smart, Irish Catholic Chicagoan. He used the Dooley columns to attack corruption and promote social progress in Chicago, and he found satire an ideal weapon with which to lampoon city bigwigs and local events. Mr. Dooley's attention was particularly drawn to politicians and corrupt figures.

Dunne fit in well with the reform era, according to Schaaf, "but he did not consider himself a card-carrying reformer, although he was quick to expose the evils he saw around him. . . ."[10] As editor of the Chicago *Post*, Dunne took up a variety of reform efforts. He wrote editorials urging the riddance of political corruption in the city and used the "Mr. Dooley" columns as an additional aid in this campaign. When it became apparent that the large businesses were consolidating into huge trusts, public outcry and antitrust legislation accompanied indignant articles and columns in newspapers and magazines. Dunne's "Mr. Dooley" columns were no exception. Although Mr. Dooley was not highly educated, he understood the economics involved and launched an attack on the trusts and their personages, especially Standard Oil and John D. Rockefeller.

During the height of Mr. Dooley's popularity, Chicago's city council was particularly corrupt. Dunne, through Mr. Dooley, aided the growth of a reform group called the Municipal Voters League. Again, Dunne used his editorial columns, along with the Dooley columns, to attack the corrupt government. The League competed against the established political parties and managed to elect enough aldermen to the council so that the government became much more honest.

---

[10]Barbara C. Schaaf, *Mr. Dooley's Chicago* (New York: Anchor Press/Doubleday, 1977), 32.

As indicated by the various crusades, Schaaf declared, Dunne was a true reformer. He attacked not only the corrupt politicians, but muckrakers, too, when "he felt they were getting too puffed up and preoccupied with sensationalism." He was motivated by a sincere interest in improving conditions and had no particular loyalties to any person or group. Instead, he wrote what he felt without fear of repercussion from his victims.

The Business School

While Progressive historians examined newspaper ideology and the press' relationship to the conflict between "big business" and the common man, Business historians studied the actual business practices of the press and how these practices affected its growth. Historians writing from this viewpoint generally perceived newspaper owners favorably for their contributions to the quality of journalism. The Business school interpreted the success and growth of the newspaper industry as the result of clever business decisions. Although historians recognized that the prime motivation for developing innovations and facilitating growth was the desire for profits, they did not consider making money to be evil, but part of the makeup of a successful American businessman.

Business historians particularly admired Joseph Pulitzer, who built one of the largest fortunes in the newspaper business. In *Pulitzer's Post-Dispatch, 1878-1883* (1967), Julian S. Rammelkamp investigated Pulitzer's press ownership beginnings in St. Louis. He pointed out that although Pulitzer crusaded for the public good, his crusades helped increase the circulation of his paper, and therefore made good business sense. Rammelkamp argued that even though Pulitzer preferred not to think of himself as a businessman, he "was preeminently a businessman who happened to be in the business of journalism."[11] Pulitzer participated in the reform movement by encouraging clean government, improved urban conditions, and the break-up of monopolies. These problems threatened not only the common man, but also the small businessman. At this time, Pulitzer, too, was a small businessman, and solving these problems made good business sense for him.

Pulitzer made changes in the *Post-Dispatch* to make it more attractive and successful. He changed the appearance of the front page and the size and the contents of the pages in order to improve circulation. He offered free want ads for the same reason. The news offered in the *Post-Dispatch* grew more sensational to attract readers: the "well known citizen" who died in the arms of his mistress was really a simple salesman; a reporter once played detective, hunting

---

[11]Julian S. Rammelkamp, *Pulitzer's Post-Dispatch, 1878-1833* (Princeton, NJ: Princeton University Press, 1967), vii.

for a fugitive the police could not catch, and claimed sightings of the man almost every day for a week. Although the truth of the *Post-Dispatch's* stories was often stretched, the sensationalism was successful in its goal of increasing readership.

The same picture of the ultimate purpose of media practices emerged from studies by other Business historians. Stephen Davis, in "'A Matter of Sensational Interest': The *Century* 'Battles and Leaders' Series" (1981), argued that the magazine's series of Civil War articles began in 1884 not for scholarly reasons, but as a way to increase readership and profits.[12] In the early 1880s, *Century* and *Harper's Weekly* competed hotly for subscribers, and the "Battles and Leaders" series was calculated to give *Century* the edge. Davis said that the idea for the series came from the success of one *Century* Civil War article in 1883. The series was carefully planned so as to maximize the benefits of the articles. A year after the series began, the circulation of the magazine had nearly doubled. The series was so successful that the editors decided to exploit that success by issuing a four-volume collection of the articles. The editors attributed the success of the series to "peculiar circumstances," but Davis argued it was shrewd business management of the magazine that made the series so popular.

The Cultural School

While Business historians studied the effects of business practices on the performance of the media, Cultural historians studied the performance of the newspaper industry in relationship to the broader environment in which it operated. They believed that surroundings played a key role in explaining the nature of the media; and they therefore examined the sociological, economic, political, technological, and psychological atmosphere in which an event occurred.

The Cultural view on the impact of surroundings formed the basis for Morton Keller's study of the cartoonist Thomas Nast. In *The Art and Politics of Thomas Nast* (1968), Keller's central thesis was that Nast's work was influenced by his upbringing, the political and social climate in the United States, and the status of the art world. His work became popular and influential because he played off of the expectations and attitudes, the disappointments and frustrations of the American public, especially the Radical Republicans, during Reconstruction. These matters fueled Nast's work. Keller contended that when Radical Republicanism died out, so did the power of Nast's work.

Nast is particularly remembered for his efforts against the corrupt Tweed Ring in New York City. Keller argued that Nast was

---

[12]Stephen Davis, "'A Matter of Sensational Interest': The *Century* 'Battles and Leaders' Series," *Civil War History* 27 (1981): 338-349.

disturbed by more than the corruption. The predominance of Irish-Catholics in the ring outraged his Protestant sensibilities; the ring was Democratic, and Nast was Republican; and his views that politics should be moral and used for the betterment of society opposed the views of the ring, which was interested only in preserving itself. These conditions shaped Nast's attack on the corrupt political ring and eventually helped bring it to ruin.

How three other environmental factors—the audience, technology, and interpersonal dynamics—interacted to explain how the media operated can be seen in Everette E. Dennis and Christopher Allen's study, "*Puck*, the Comic Weekly" (1979). Their goal was to discover the factors that accounted for the success of America's first widely popular humor magazine. *Puck*, they found, appeared at a fortuitous time in American history. The growing affluence of middle- and upper-class Americans afforded them more leisure time—time that could be spent with *Puck*. Although cartoons, especially those of Thomas Nast, had already become popular in magazines and newspapers, they were often "mean, personal attacks laced with vitriol and geared to a high bound morality." In contrast, *Puck's* cartoons "had a kindly air—even in ridicule they were more likely to bring a hearty belly-laugh than snarls of contempt."[13]

The development of lithography allowed the artistic style of *Puck's* cartoons to be much smoother than the cross-hatched woodcuts of Nast. In addition, the lithographic process allowed the use of color in the cartoons, making them stand out from black-and-white competitors.

Dennis and Allen contended that the "collaborative style" of the staff at the magazine also made it different and attractive to readers. The editorial staff discussed which ideas should be presented to the public and how those ideas would be presented. "The collaborative sessions had a happy outcome—experience and judgment interacted with creative sparks and the result was a lively, fine-tuned magazine."[14] These factors, combined, allowed the magazine to become successful.

Discussion

Historians in recent years, like most other historians, tend to be influenced by the conditions of their own time. Recent trends toward concentrated media ownership have encouraged historians to examine the economic aspects of the media of the past. As a result, the press of the Industrial Age has attracted growing attention from historians who believe they can perceive during that time the real

---

[13]Everette E. Dennis and Christopher Allen, "*Puck*, the Comic Weekly," *Journalism History* 6 (1979): 4.

[14]Ibid., p. 5.

beginnings of the rapid growth of newspapers as big business. In their quest to understand the fundamentals of media operations, they have posed a number of questions deserving of attention; and yet a number of critical questions remain unanswered.

1. How did media business practices affect success in the period after the Civil War?

2. How did the growth of newspapers as businesses affect their relationship to "big business" and the wealthy?

3. How did big-city newspapers influence small-town papers?

4. Developmental historians have posed a variety of questions relating to the origin and practice of journalism techniques during the period. How did the interview begin, for example, and which journalist was most instrumental in developing practices such as more appealing newspaper appearance? Who were the most important figures in Industrial Journalism? How did they contribute to the evolution of the profession?

5. In attempting to answer such questions as the previous one, one must ask whether historians are influenced too much by conditions of today. Might historians be so concerned with changes of the past few years that their view of earlier times is clouded?

6. Once such fundamental questions about historical study are answered, one still is left with the major questions about the nature of the Industrial Press that historians have propounded. How did journalists think of themselves—as journalists, mere employees, or as reformers? Were their main considerations journalistic, ideological, or economic? Were they generally reform-minded or reactionary?

7. What factors influenced the media? Were they mainly journalistic ones, or were they environmental?

8. What impact did individual journalists have on the nature of the media? How did their impact compare to that of impersonal cultural forces?

Readings

Romantic School

Bisland, Elizabeth, Ch. 4, "The Last Stage," pp. 136-162, *The Life and Letters of Lafcadio Hearn*, 2 vols. Boston: Houghton Mifflin, 1906.

O'Connor, Richard, "Preface," pp. 5-9, *The Scandalous Mr. Bennett*. New York: Doubleday, 1962.

Ogden, Rollo, ed., Ch. 3, pp. 21-108, *Life and Letters of Edwin Lawrence Godkin,* 2 vols. New York: Macmillan, 1907.

Paine, Albert Bigelow, Ch. 23, "After the Battle," pp. 202-205, *Thomas Nast,*

His Period and His Pictures. New York: Macmillan, 1904.

Stone, Candace, Ch. 25, "The *Sun* Shines for All," pp. 380-404, *Dana and the Sun*. New York: Dodd, Mead, 1938.

Developmental School

Clayton, Charles G., Ch. 5, "The New Journalism" pp. 85-108, *Little Mack: Joseph B. McCullagh of the St. Louis Globe-Democrat*. Carbondale: Southern Illinois University Press, 1969.

Marcosson, Isaac, Ch. 4, "The Old Lady at the Corner," pp. 80-117, *Marse Henry: A Biography of Henry Watterson*. New York: Dodd, Mead, 1951.

Rogers, Charles E., "William Rockhill Nelson and His Editors of the *Star*," *Journalism Quarterly* 26 (1949): 15-19, 60.

Sim, John Cameron, "19th Century Applications of Suburban Newspaper Concepts," *Journalism Quarterly* 52 (1975): 627-631.

Progressive School

Bryan, Carter R., "Carl Schurz: Journalist and Liberal Propagandist," *Journalism Quarterly* 40 (1963): 207-212.

Fuess, Claude M., "Prelude," pp. 1-4, *Carl Schurz, Reformer (1820-1906)*. New York: Dodd, Mead, 1932.

Harrison, John M., Ch. 20, "In Conclusion" pp. 318-324, *The Man Who Made Nasby, David Ross Locke*. Chapel Hill: University of North Carolina Press, 1969.

Schaaf, Barbara C., "Afterward," pp. 375-379, *Mr. Dooley's Chicago*. New York: Anchor Press/ Doubleday, 1977.

Business School

Davis, Stephen, "'A Matter of Sensational Interest': The *Century* 'Battles and Leaders' Series." *Civil War History* 27 (1981): 338-349.

Rammelkamp, Julian S., Ch. 11, "To the National Stage," pp. 284-303, *Pulitzer's Post-Dispatch, 1878-1833*. Princeton, NJ: Princeton University Press, 1967.

Smythe, Ted Curtis, "The Advertisers' War to Verify Newspaper Circulation, 1870-1814," *American Journalism* 3 (1986): 167-180.

Cultural School

Bard, David R., and William J. Baker, "The American Newspaper Response to the Jamaican Riots of 1865," *Journalism Quarterly* 51 (1974): 659-653, 709.

Dennis, Everette E., and Christopher Allen, *"Puck*, the Comic Weekly," *Journalism History* 6 (1979): 2-7, 13.

Hart, Jack R., "Horatio Alger in the Newsroom: Social Origins of American Editors," *Journalism Quarterly* 53 (1976): 14-20.

Keller, Morton, Ch. 1, "The Art of Thomas Nast," pp. 3-9, *The Art and Politics of Thomas Nast*. New York: Oxford University Press, 1968.

Kielbowicz, Richard, "Origins of the Second-Class Mail Category and the Business of Policymaking, 1863-1879," *Journalism Monographs* 96 (1986).

Knights, Peter R., "The Press Association War of 1866-1867," *Journalism Monographs* 6 (1967).

Kreiling, Albert, "The Rise of the Black Press in Chicago," *Journalism History* 4 (1977): 132-136.

Thorn, William J., "Hudson's History of Journalism Criticized by His Contemporaries," *Journalism Quarterly* 57 (1980): 99-106.

14

New Journalism, 1883-1900:
Social Reform or Professional Progress?

In 1883 Joseph Pulitzer bought the New York *World*. The changes
that he brought to the paper, and its resultant success, revolutionized
American journalism. Named "New Journalism," his approach
was imitated by scores of other newspaper publishers. Foremost
among them was William Randolph Hearst, who engaged in an
intense journalistic combat with Pulitzer after buying the New York
Journal in 1895. The fierce competition between the two shortly developed into the sensational "yellow journalism" at the end of the
19th century and included jingoistic promotion of the United States'
war with Spain in 1898.

Pulitzer's formula for success included several distinctive features. Most important were the following:

First and foremost, good coverage of serious news made up the
framework on which the rest of the paper was built. To an extent previously unmatched, however, the *World* and its imitators emphasized sensational news. Reporters searched for scandals, crimes,
and disasters that they could embellish and make more interesting
to readers. Previously unknown citizens found themselves, quite
unexpectedly, the center of public scandal. Stories about crimes and
disasters recorded as much detail as possible in order to appeal to the
curiosity of the public.

Pulitzer gave paramount importance to the editorial function of
the *World* and made crusading for reform a primary function.
Crusades and stunts proliferated. Crusades curried favor with
readers because they fought corruption in government or tried to end
some social wrong. Oftentimes, the newspaper crusades themselves
were sensationalized. Stunts appeared in various forms. Some were
as simple as opinion polls or drives to raise money, such as the
World's campaign for the pedestal of the Statue of Liberty. Others,
like Nellie Bly's race against time in her trip around the world,

By Jana Hyde
University of Alabama

were much more complex.

The *World* also attracted readers for its value. Its number of pages increased, while its price of two cents remained competitive with other papers. Illustration proved an excellent selling point, as well. Diagrams of crime scenes, portraits, and cartoons decorated the pages of the *World*.

Although the concepts of New Journalism dominated the period, other changes occurred as well. Newspapers made use of recent inventions such as the linotype. Reporters continued to rise in importance. They formed professional organizations and published professional journals. They began to receive more credit for their work. Use of the byline increased, as did reporters' salaries. Women became more common on newspaper staffs. Illustrations, which previously had been used sparingly, appeared more often. New processes of engraving made the printing of illustrations easier, and some papers founded during the period depended heavily on pictures for their popularity. Coverage of sports increased so much that most of the large metropolitan papers now had "sporting editors" who commanded their own staffs of reporters trained in sports reporting.

Historians studying the era of New Journalism have been especially concerned over the question of the motives of journalists. Were journalists and newspapers trying to improve social conditions with their crusades and sensational news items, or were they simply trying to capitalize on the morbid side of human nature? Or, those questions aside, did New Journalism provide one of those instances in history when great contributions were made in a brief period of time to originating and advancing the practices of journalism? Historians differ considerably in their viewpoints on the answers to these questions.

Historians writing on the age of New Journalism can be divided into several schools of interpretation. Romantic historians viewed the innovations of this period as the results of the work of great individuals in the press. Consequently, they wrote almost exclusively about the most well-known individuals. Developmental historians considered the changes in the press to be part of the progress toward modern-day journalism, and they found a large number of instances of such progress, as few other periods had witnessed. To these historians, publishers such as Pulitzer and Hearst had provided the foundation for the principles of professional and successful journalism that was to be practiced in the 20th century. Progressive historians, on the other hand, were interested in the new journalistic practices mainly as they related to social and political issues. Concerned about the great influence that corrupt industrialists exercised and about the social problems that industrial conditions presented, Progressive historians focused their attention on the economic, political, and social motivations of publishers. Rather than concerning themselves with ideology, a final school of historians, those writing from the Cultural perspective, focused more generally on the broad environmental context in which the press operated.

The Romantic School

Historians writing about New Journalism from the Romantic perspective began publishing their works at the end of the 19th and the beginning of the 20th centuries. Most were not trained historians, but rather were educated individuals who had a personal acquaintance with the journalists about whom they wrote. They believed that media history could be told through biographies of these prominent journalists, and they were generally complimentary of them, rationalizing character faults as the price paid for genius. Romantic historians wrote not for a scholarly audience but for the lay public. Therefore—assuming that it was the personal side of prominent individuals that interested readers—they gave attention to personal aspects of their subjects, although they recognized that it was the professional talents that accounted for their success.

The first works on the life of Pulitzer following his death in 1911 concentrated on his greatness as an individual and as a maker of journalism. Alleyne Ireland, who had served Pulitzer as his secretary during his declining years, produced the first two admiring biographies in 1914. They concentrated almost entirely on Pulitzer's personal characteristics. The two books, *Joseph Pulitzer: Reminiscences of a Secretary* and *An Adventure With A Genius: Recollections of Joseph Pulitzer*, were primarily character sketches. Although Ireland did not agree with some of Pulitzer's policies, his admiration of Pulitzer was evident. After describing the rigorous training he underwent in order to become one of Pulitzer's secretaries, Ireland observed, "When I recall the capaciousness of his understanding, the breadth of his experience, the range of his information, and set them side by side with the cruel limitations imposed upon him by his blindness and by his shattered constitution, I forget the severity of his discipline, I marvel only that his self-control should have served him so well in the tedious business of breaking a new man to his service."[1] In a similar tone, Ireland described Pulitzer as "one of the most vigorous, picturesque, and original personalities that ever played a part in the interesting drama of American public life. . . . [He was a man of] deep affection, keen intelligence, wide sympathy, tireless energy, delicate sensitive-

---

[1]Alleyne Ireland, *An Adventure with a Genius: Recollections of Joseph Pulitzer* (New York: Mitchell Kennerly, 1914; repr., New York: Dutton, 1920), 141.

ness, tearing impatience, cold tyranny and flaming scorn."[2] Ireland regretted the fact that Pulitzer would not write about his own life. In typical Romantic fashion, he expressed this regret: "It is a thousand pities that he adhered to this resolution [not to write his biography], for his career, as well in point of interest as in achievement and picturesqueness, would have stood the test of comparison with that of any man whose life-story has been preserved in literature."[3]

Even though Ireland's accounts were almost as much about himself as about Pulitzer's life, they do give the reader an excellent idea of what life with the publisher was like. Ireland provided details that could be furnished only by one who lived in close proximity to the man. Ireland used anecdotes about Pulitzer's insatiable desire for information, his need for total silence due to his shattered nerves, and his demand for complete loyalty from his servants and secretaries to give understanding to the man behind the powerful *World*.

The Developmental School

Although Developmental historians continued, as the Romantic historians had done, to write about important individuals in a glowing fashion, they were primarily interested in the progress of the profession of journalism during the age of New Journalism. Rather than concentrating on an individual's personal characteristics, Developmental biographies focused more on how individuals furthered the profession of journalism. Developmental historians concerned themselves mainly with journalism's progress toward its present state or how it was performed well—or sometimes poorly—according to what historians considered the proper standards. They tended to judge the events of the past by the value of their contributions to the present state of journalism, and to evaluate journalists by how well they performed journalistic practices. They told the story of New Journalism in terms of an evolutionary process to modern journalism.

One of the first Developmental biographies of Pulitzer was written, like those of Ireland, Pulitzer's Romantic biographer, by a close personal acquaintance. And also like Ireland's work, it told a similarly favorable story. Written 10 years later, however, not by a secretary but by a member of the New York *World's* news staff, Don C. Seitz's *Joseph Pulitzer: His Life and Letters* (1924) concentrated primarily on Pulitzer's professional accomplishments. He viewed Pulitzer, his enterprising employer and close friend, as the originator of the most successful modern concepts of journalism, concepts

---

[2]Alleyne Ireland, *Joseph Pulitzer: Reminiscences of a Secretary* (New York: Kennerly/Dutton, 1914).

[3]Ireland, *An Adventure. . .* , 175.

that had been so effective as to bring about a revolution in newspapering. He was, as the book's subtitle claimed, the "Liberator of Journalism."

Seitz gave much attention to Pulitzer's acquisition of the New York *World* and its subsequent success with sensationalized news. Rather than criticizing Pulitzer's sensationalism, he excused it by praising the high moral quality of Pulitzer's editorials. "His editorial views," Seitz wrote, "were then and always of the soundest and highest character in the interest of a free government and the public welfare."[4]

In his later years, Pulitzer left New York in order to soothe his frayed nervous system, but he retained control of his papers. Frequent letters from his yacht, or from wherever he might be staying in Europe, commented upon, censured, praised, and commanded the editors and reporters writing for his papers. In describing Pulitzer's journalistic methods and control over the New York *World* and the St. Louis *Post-Dispatch* in his absence, Seitz used letters that illustrated Pulitzer's "driving impulse." Although those letters frequently criticized the editors, Seitz glossed over them, describing them as "delightfully pungent." Having been involved so closely with Pulitzer's journalistic innovations, Seitz naturally looked at them as progress and admired Pulitzer's contributions to improving journalism. In that view, he seemed typically Developmental.

Seitz combined, however, the strictly professional Developmental view of Pulitzer with an ideological view closely resembling that of Progressive historians. Influenced by the reform spirit of the times and Pulitzer's own emphasis on improving society, Seitz explained Pulitzer favorably as a dedicated social reformer. Both men believed that "an intelligent newspaper must be independent, but not indifferent or neutral on any question involving public interest. Its rock of faith must be true Democracy. . . . The *World* promised . . . to maintain such a Democratic character; to oppose organized monopolists, who, coveting and possessing exclusive rights under the aegis of public charters, were undermining a political freedom won more than a hundred years before."[5]

These Developmental and ideological views combined into Seitz's description of Pulitzer's aloof character in glowing terms: "He believed in Liberty, Equality and Opportunity. Fraternity was not in his code. He lived most of his days apart from other men, having a feeling that this was the fate of the true journalist, that he must immolate himself upon the altar of his profession, devote his inter-

---

[4]Don C. Seitz, *Joseph Pulitzer: His Life and Letters* (New York: Simon and Schuster, 1924), 151.

[5]Ibid., p. 137.

est to his paper and have none other!"[6]

Although Pulitzer made his greatest mark on journalism through the New York *World*, Developmental historians could trace the origins of his contributions to his earlier newspaper career in St. Louis. Eight years after Seitz published his biography of Pulitzer, George S. Johns wrote a series of articles for the *Missouri Historical Review* which traced Pulitzer's life and work during his western years. In "Joseph Pulitzer: Early Life in St. Louis and his Founding and Conduct of the *Post-Dispatch* up to 1883" (1932), Johns outlined the changes Pulitzer made in the paper which propelled it to prosperity and on toward modern-day journalism. "The merger of the *Post* and *Dispatch* under the domination of Joseph Pulitzer marked the birth of a new force in journalism," he wrote. "It was a blend of new ideas, new methods, new purposes."[7]

By the time Pulitzer bought the New York *World*, he had developed a formula for creating a successful, prosperous newspaper. This formula, according to Johns, included accurate and truthful reporting, crusading against corruption, and using the paper as a "powerful moral force for the public welfare."[8] Pulitzer transferred these policies to the *World* to create one of the most powerful and influential papers in the world.

Similarly, Homer W. King traced the origins of modern journalism to Pulitzer's St. Louis *Post-Dispatch*, but he argued that the true genesis of the "New Journalism" could be found not so much in Pulitzer's ideas as in the contributions of a real working journalist, John Cockerill. In *Pulitzer's Prize Editor: A Biography of John A. Cockerill, 1845-1896* (1965), King outlined Cockerill's influence on the profession of journalism. He argued that Pulitzer received too much credit for the success of both the *Post-Dispatch* and the *World*. He relied first on his managing editor at the *Post-Dispatch* and, after purchasing the *World* in 1883, took him to New York City to institute the journalistic practices that had proved so successful in St. Louis. Pulitzer, who was away from New York most of the time, could not possibly have run the paper's day-to-day operations. Instead, Cockerill's daily management steered the *World* to the top of the New York press heap. "Someone had to be there, in the flesh, to make fast and astute decisions, to dream up new crusades and story ideas, 'to mind the store,'" wrote King. Without Cockerill's skillful direction of the newsroom, the paper might not have lasted past the early years of Pulitzer's ownership. King considered Cockerill a "pioneer in newspaper techniques and responsibilities" who

---

[6]Ibid., p. 3.

[7]George S. Johns, "Joseph Pulitzer: Early Life in St. Louis and his Founding and Conduct of the Post-Dispatch up to 1883," *Missouri Historical Review* 26 (October 1931-July 1932): 54.

[8]Ibid., pp. 279-281.

"encouraged new methods and techniques in handling news and pictures."[9] Although Cockerill participated in, and was quite skilled at, the sensationalism that Pulitzer used to increase circulation, King believed Cockerill to be a responsible journalist. Cockerill's later criticism of the paper indicated a rejection of sensationalism and an admirable change of heart.

The Progressive School

Although Progressive historians studied the progress of media practices, they also examined the media in terms of how they supported the struggle of the masses against the wealthy and powerful minority. They felt that the duty of the media was to fight against "big business" and to keep an eye on the government. Some Progressive historians believed that crusades for the betterment of society were more important than the reporting of news. As instruments for social change, they argued, the media should act as a voice for the common man, demanding democracy and equality.

Historians writing from the Progressive perspective projected a diverse picture of journalism in the late 1800s. Those who selected crusading journalists as their subjects painted a highly favorable portrait of New Journalists as compassionate and courageous fighters for the cure of society's ills, whereas historians who studied conservative newspapers revealed a group of reactionary ideologues and self-interested profit seekers. On the one hand, the picture that emerges from Progressive studies is a generally favorable one of newspapers crusading against social ills and fighting for social reform, and of crusading individual journalists fighting to solve the ills of society despite the fact that many newspapers were run mainly as businesses by conservative owners. On the other is a description of publishers who had no interest in solving the problems confronting an urban society, or in some instances actually opposing solutions, because they found that the status quo protected their financial interests.

The disparity in those two assessments can be seen in the differing biographies of the two great figures of the period, Pulitzer and Hearst. In the comparison of the two, the latter consistently came out looking the worse. Most biographies of Pulitzer praised his liberal social positions, whereas Progressive biographies of Hearst, such as Ferdinand Lundberg's *Imperial Hearst: A Social Biography* (1936), treated him as an unscrupulous publisher whose financial interests provided the foundation for his journalism practices and editorial stands. Some Progressive historians, such as Roy Littlefield in *William Randolph Hearst: His Role in American Progressivism*

---

[9]Homer W. King, *Pulitzer's Prize Editor: A Biography of John A. Cockerill, 1845-1896* (Durham, NC: Duke University Press, 1965), 194, viii, xvii.

(1980), took a dissenting view and presented Hearst as an advocate of the "underprivileged and the discontented,"[10] but such an assessment was rare.

Although concerned about the media and domestic social issues, Progressive historians had a special interest also in the role of the American media in international affairs. The late 1800s offered a fertile time for studies of such a subject, for it was at the end of the period that the United States was involved in the Spanish-American War. Progressive historians, as a general rule, saw the war as an imperialistic venture spurred on by yellow newspapers, most prominently Pulitzer's *World* and William Randolph Hearst's New York *Journal*. Motivated by the typical big-business desire to make money, they resorted to jingoism mainly to increase circulation and profits.

Two of the earliest studies dealing with the press and the Spanish-American War took almost identical approaches. The first, Walter Millis' *The Martial Spirit; A Study of Our War with Spain* (1931), provided a critical, ideological examination of the reasons that led the United States jingoistically to go to war with Spain. The reasons that Millis gave, despite the fact that his study did not focus primarily on the press, included the imperialistic, propagandistic efforts of Pulitzer and Hearst.

Whereas Millis included a discussion of the role of the yellow press as only one factor in the decision to go to war, Joseph E. Wisan's *The Cuban Crisis as Reflected in the New York Press* (1934) focused on that subject. Regarding the press, he came to the same conclusion as Millis had. He claimed that the war was largely a product of warmongering by sensational newspapers. The public clamored for the war, he argued, but the press created, to a great degree, that desire for war. Not all of the New York papers agreed on the handling of the relations between Spain and America. The papers most widely circulated, the *World* and the *Journal*, however, "employed every sensational device to foster pro-Cuban sympathy, to provoke contempt and hatred for Spain and her people, and to prevail upon the United States Government to assume a partisan role in the struggle."[11] Wisan concluded that the war could have been avoided if Hearst and Pulitzer had not waged their own circulation war. The Cuban revolution gave those members of the press so inclined a prime opportunity to sensationalize upon the events on the island, and therefore an opportunity to sell more papers. Readers fell prey to the subjective stories that appeared in the papers. Their

---

[10]Roy Everette Littlefield, III, *William Randolph Hearst: His Role in American Progressivism* (Boston: University Press of America, 1980), ix.

[11]Joseph E. Wisan, *The Cuban Crisis as Reflected in the New York Press* (New York: Columbia University Press, 1934), i.

resounding cry forced the United States into the war with Spain.

The Cultural School

Cultural historians did not support the argument that ideological beliefs underlay the growth of the press during this era. These historians, instead, interpreted the operation of the press as a result of its interaction with the environment in which it existed. They defined the press as a product of the technological, sociological, economic, political, and psychological atmosphere. Society shaped the press even more than did the powerful publishers who tried to bend it to their ideals.

Biographies presented from the Cultural viewpoint often stressed the environment in which the subject grew up or his or her psychological makeup. These forces shaped the individual, who in turn influenced the journalistic process. In *Hearst, Lord of San Simeon* (1936), a psychoanalytical portrait, Oliver Carlson and Ernest Sutherland Bates argued that several factors influenced Hearst's career: his mother and father's differing values, "his privileged upbringing, his California background of raucous wealth, crude force, and noisy demagoguery," and his experience with Eastern snobbery.[12] Carlson and Bates claimed that, although no work could tell everything about Hearst, theirs was, at least, true Hearst.

Their concluding chapter, for example, discussed the peculiar fact that Hearst would not allow the subject of death to be discussed in his presence. "The hard-headed realistic journalist who for half a century has featured in his papers the most horrible crimes of murder, the blatant super-patriot who has tried again and again on the slightest pretext to force his country into war and send millions of her sons to slaughter—this man dares not face the thought that the common fate of humanity will some day touch him, too."[13] Carlson and Bates attributed that idiosyncrasy to Hearst's belief that he was somehow different from common men, that his wealth insulated him from the rules that governed them. They argued that Hearst's attitude developed as a result of his past experiences with wealth and power.

Carlson and Bates were unusual among Cultural historians, for they focused their study on an individual. Most Cultural historians gave little attention to individuals, for they assumed that the great impersonal forces in the environment were paramount, and the individual in that context was inconsequential. The only historian to provide a general survey history of the age of New Journalism used

---

[12] Oliver Carlson and Ernest Bates, *Hearst, Lord of San Simeon* (New York: Viking Press, 1936), xiv.

[13] Ibid., p. 311.

just that thesis. He was Sidney Kobre, who, through a number of works written from what he called a "Sociological" approach, became the most prominent advocate of applying sociological principles and methods to the study of media history. Trained as a sociologist, he concentrated his attention on sociological forces rather than on the actions of individuals. He subjected New Journalism to his sociological examination in *The Yellow Press and Gilded Age Journalism* (1964).

As in his other studies of media history, in *The Yellow Press* Kobre began with the assumption that to understand the media one has to concentrate on the broad factors that were shaping society. In the late 19th century the most important of these factors was industrialization. In the post-Civil War period, the United States was undergoing a transition from an agricultural to an industrial, urban society. The press naturally was caught up in the transformation. It not only reported on those changes, but it mirrored them also. Since newspapers were part of society, they became a part of the changes, so that the transformation taking place in the larger society also altered newspapers along the same lines. Thus, American newspapers, which had been marked by personal journalism at the end of the Civil War, by the end of the 19th century had changed to industries with the characteristics—mechanization, centralization, and standardization—distinctive of industrialization.

Cultural historians dealt less clearly with the relationship of the press to the Spanish-American War. Most who addressed the subject concentrated on the influence of Yellow Journalism in bringing about the war. On that point, the majority of historians concluded that the newspapers were less influential than contemporary critics or earlier historians had assumed. The question of *why* publishers took the stands they did in regard to the war was not as easy to answer. Although Cultural historians presented no uniform answer to that question, the efforts of researchers in one study will help illustrate the broad approach of the Cultural school to the subject of New Journalism.

In "The Rhetoric of War Preparation: The New York Press in 1898" (1968), Meredith Berg and David Berg proposed that different factors motivated the publishers of the New York *World, Journal,* and *Times.* To a large extent, though, those factors involved economics, readership, public opinion, and interests of the business community, all of which involved the publishers' self-interest. Hearst's *Journal,* the authors said, "geared its appeal to the jingoists and superpatriots, realizing that this group comprised a substantial body, if not a majority, of the newspaper-buying public." This group of people would be worth attracting, even if it did alienate the readers who disagreed. Pulitzer's *World,* on the other hand, initially argued for moderation, but gave in to public opinion and demanded action. Pulitzer was against war so long as the majority of the public was against war, "but when popular opinion changed, his paper made the proper adjustment." The *Times*, unlike the *Journal* and the *World*, tried to remain objective. Its conservative reporting of the events contrasted sharply with the inflammatory stories of the other two papers. The Bergs contended that "the *Times* policy of calm consideration and thoughtful action directly served the interest of big business which, for the most part, was hostile to any action which might tend to disrupt business activity."[14]

Discussion

The era of New Journalism has received substantial historical treatment, primarily because of the prominence of Pulitzer and Hearst and because of the excesses of Yellow Journalism. Historical interest has been increased by what appears to be a clear tie between those subjects and the Spanish-American War.

1. It is that interrelationship that gives rise to some of the most important questions that historians have asked about the period. What, for example, was the relationship between the press and the war? Were the yellow journals responsible, as some historians have claimed, for causing the war; or were they comparatively unimportant in the whole milieu of causes?

2. Although the question of press influence has been much debated, it is reasonably clear that the yellow journals promoted war. What was their motivation for doing so? Was it to free Cuba from the repressive rule of Spain, as some early historians argued, or was it simply to promote newspaper circulation, as others have claimed?

3. On domestic issues, what were the motivations? Were publishers such as Pulitzer and Hearst truly concerned about solving social problems, or were they unscrupulously using the problems for their own self-promotion and circulation building? Were they, as Progressive historians would state the question, true social reformers or reactionary, profit-oriented businessmen?

4. Should the primary historical consideration of New Journalism be on such social issues that Progressive historians emphasized, or should historical study focus instead on the contributions that New Journalism made to advancing journalistic practices?

5. Is New Journalism best understood, as Developmental historians have argued, as the origin of modern journalism?

6. If so, who or what forces provided the impetus for changes?

7. On the matter of newspaper practices, was sensationalized news really what the public wanted, or was that desire created by the press itself?

---

[14]Meredith Berg and David Berg, "The Rhetoric of War Preparation: The New York Press in 1898," *Journalism Quarterly* 45 (1968): 654, 655.

8. Did journalism progress with the use of sensationalism, or did sensationalism set journalism back?

9. Was sensationalism a natural outgrowth of new urban conditions, or the shrewd approach of insightful journalists such as Pulitzer who used it to increase circulation and eventually enlarge the body of the American public who became serious newspaper readers?

10. Were the practices of New Journalism really an attempt to clean up society, or were they merely a means of increasing circulation?

11. What is the legacy of New Journalism?

Readings

Romantic School

Davis, Richard Harding, Ch. 5, "First Travel Articles," pp. 67-91, Charles Belmont Davis, ed., *Adventures and Letters of Richard Harding Davis*. New York: Scribner's, 1917.

Ireland, Alleyne, Ch. 4, "Yachting in the Mediterranean," pp. 103-141, *An Adventure With a Genius: Recollections of Joseph Pulitzer*. New York: Dutton, 1914.

Developmental School

Brooker-Gross, Susan R., "Timeliness: Interpretations from a Sample of 19th Century Newspapers," *Journalism Quarterly* 58 (1981): 594-598.

Brown, Charles H., Ch. 19, "The Final Dispatches," pp. 428-449, *The Correspondents' War*. New York: Scribner's, 1967.

Creelman, James, "Joseph Pulitzer—Master Journalist," *Pearson's Magazine* 21 (March 1909): 229-256.

Johns, George S., "Joseph Pulitzer: His Early Life in St. Louis and His Founding and Conduct of the Post-Dispatch up to 1883," *Missouri Historical Review* 26 (October 1931-July 1932): 54-67.

Juergens, George, "Preface," pp. vii-xv, *Joseph Pulitzer and the New York World*. Princeton, NJ: Princeton University Press, 1966.

King, Homer W., Ch. 16, "For the Good of the World, Mostly," pp. 171-181, *Pulitzer's Prize Editor: A Biography of John A. Cockerill, 1845-1896*. Durham, NC: Duke University Press, 1965.

Mander, Mary, "Pen and Sword: Problems of Reporting the Spanish-American War," *Journalism History* 9 (1982): 2-9, 28.

Seitz, Don. C., Ch. 6, "The 'New World'—1883-1885," pp. 129-154, *Joseph Pulitzer: His Life and Letters*. New York: Simon and Schuster, 1924.

Progressive School

Barrett, James W., "Foreword," pp. xi-xvi, *Joseph Pulitzer and His World*. New York: Vanguard, 1941.

Cline, H. F., "Flower and the *Arena*: Purpose and Content," *Journalism Quarterly* 17 (1940): 247-257.

Emery, Edwin, "William Randolph Hearst: A Tentative Appraisal," *Journalism Quarterly* 28 (1951): 429-439.

Littlefield, Roy Everette, III, Ch. 1, "The Rise of a Patrician Reformer," pp. 1-27, *William Randolph Hearst: His Role in American Progressivism*. Boston: University Press of America, 1980.

Lundberg, Ferdinand, Ch. 2, pp. 23-48, *Imperial Hearst: A Social Biography*. New York: Equinox Cooperative Press, 1936.

Perry, Clay, "John P. Mitchell, Virginia's Journalist of Reform," *Journalism History* 4 (1977): 142-147, 156.

Swanberg, W.A., "Eye on the White House," pp. 173-194, *Citizen Hearst*. New York: Scribner's, 1961.

Tebbel, John, Ch. 6, "The Man Who Would Be President," pp.165-197, *The Life and Good Times of William Randolph Hearst*. New York: Dutton, 1952; Paperback Library Edition, 1962.

Vanderburg, Ray, "The Paradox That Was Arthur Brisbane," *Journalism Quarterly* 47 (1970): 281-286.

Wisan, Joseph E., "Conclusion," pp. 455-460, *The Cuban Crisis as Reflected in the New York Press*. New York: Columbia University Press, 1934.

Cultural School

Berg, Meredith, and David Berg, "The Rhetoric of War Preparation: The New York Press in 1898," *Journalism Quarterly* 45 (1968): 653-660.

Carlson, Oliver, and Ernest Sutherland Bates, "Introduction," pp. ix-xv, *Hearst, Lord of San Simeon*. New York: Viking Press, 1936.

Everett, George, Ch. 10, "The Age of New Journalism, 1883-1900," pp. 217-241, Wm. David Sloan, James G. Stovall, and James D. Startt, eds., *The Media in America*. Worthington, OH: Publishing Horizons, 1989.

Henry, Susan, "'Dear Companion, Every-Ready Co-Worker': A Woman's Role in a Media Dynasty," *Journalism Quarterly* 64 (1987): 18-25.

Nord, David Paul, "Conclusion," pp. 127-130, *Newspapers and New Politics: Midwestern Municipal Reform, 1890-1900*. Ann Arbor, MI: UMI Research Press, 1981.

Olasky, Marvin, "Late 19th-Century Texas Sensationalism: Hypocrisy or Biblical Morality?" *Journalism History* 12 (1985): 96-100.

Ponder, Stephen E., "Conservation, Community Economics, and Newspapering: The Seattle Press and the Forest Reserves Controversy of 1897," *American Journalism* 3 (1986): 50-60.

Smythe, Ted Curtis, "The Reporter, 1880-1900. Working Conditions and Their Influence on News," *Journalism History* 7 (1980): 1-10.

Wilkerson, Marcus M., "The Press and the Spanish-American War," *Journalism Quarterly* 9 (1932): 129-148.

15

Modern Journalism, 1900-1945:
Working Profession or Big Business?

The 20th century witnessed two trends that dominated the American press: the growth of the news media as business institutions and the increased professionalization of working journalists. Although both had their roots in the 1800s, it was not until the turn of the century that the two became the most significant forces in determining the nature of American journalism. Whereas journalists of the 18th and 19th centuries seem to have been motivated substantially by partisanship and the desire to affect social conditions, owners in the 1900s seemed more and more to view the media as profit-making properties, whereas working journalists saw themselves more and more intensely as members of a profession.

The two most prominent figures in this shift were Adolph Ochs of the New York *Times* and E. W. Scripps, the chain newspaper owner. After Ochs assumed the job of publisher of the struggling *Times* in 1896, he focused his attention mainly on the paper's business rather than its editorial operations. Combining an emphasis on sound business principles with an emphasis on news over editorial opinion, he quickly turned around the *Times'* financial picture. By 1925, the paper's annual profits totaled at least $2,000,000. Other publishers, seeing the *Times'* success, began to adopt Ochs' approach.

That approach provided one part of the business picture of the newspaper field. Another was provided by the trend toward mergers, local monopolies, and chain ownership. All accelerated during the first half of the 20th century. In 1900, for example, eight newspaper chains controlled 27 newspapers representing 10% of the total daily circulation in the nation. By 1935 there were 63 chains which operated 328 newspapers representing 41% of the circulation. One of the most visible people contributing to that trend was E. W. Scripps. His chain, the Scripps-Howard newspapers, killed 15 newspapers in merger efforts between 1923 and 1934.

Going hand-in-hand with the increasing emphasis on newspapers as business was the professionalization of working journalists. Stabilized by its business underpinnings, the journalism field began to attract larger numbers of editors and reporters who believed it offered long-term career opportunities. Education and training of journalists, in turn, increased; and editors and reporters themselves began to put more efforts into developing such features as professional organizations.

Historians writing about the press of the first half of the 20th century tended to explain it primarily in terms of one of the two trends, although their explanations reflected diverse points of view. They offered varying pictures of the members of the press, both working journalists and owners. Were working journalists to be seen as crusaders for reform or as detached, responsible professionals? Were owners conservative profiteers who used the media for their own personal gain or energetic, innovative businessmen who made the American mass media into the best in the world? Or were they all, journalists and owners alike, simply actors influenced by the conditions of the American environment? A majority of historians, in answering these questions, tended to agree in their criticism of the business-related developments in American journalism while looking with favor on professional growth. Yet while recognizing the sharp dichotomy that existed, they made little attempt to show the relationship between the two dominant characteristics.

Four schools dominated historical interpretation, and in general a liberal political and social viewpoint marked most works. Progressive historians of the 1920s-1940s presented the most liberal view, a view marked by political partisanship and based on a concept of conflict between America's business and working classes. These historians placed particular emphasis on the crusading function of the press and were strongly biased against the trend toward increased emphasis on profit by media owners.

Developmental historians, who also were writing as early as the 1920s, also had a liberal perspective, but they primarily were concerned with the professional development of journalism standards. They equated liberalism just as much with professionalism as with political ideology. They considered liberalism and crusades, in other words, simply as inherent and appropriate journalistic practices, rather than as partisan ideology and methods. Treated most favorably by these historians were those journalists and events that contributed to journalistic progress. Although some Developmental historians held critical opinions of the growing business orientation of the press, they based their objections on fears of its influence on professional practices rather than on a business-labor class division, as the Progressive historians did.

The view of Progressive historians was altered even more by the work of Business historians, most of whom wrote within a Neo-Conservative perspective. Business historians challenged the

Progressive view that big business was the villain in American history. They believed media owners had provided creative and constructive approaches to major and difficult economic situations and in the process had helped make America's mass media system superior to any other in the world.

Cultural historians, whose approach resembled that of the Business/Neo-Conservative school in its acceptance of the work of media owners, differed from Business historians by emphasizing environmental factors rather than the motives and achievements of owners. They believed factors in the social, economic, and political environment determined the nature of the media. The first works on American journalism by the Cultural school appeared in the early 1900s, but Cultural historians did not apply their concepts to the 20th-century press until the 1930s. Writing against a background of the industrialization of the United States and the growth of big business in the American economy, Cultural historians considered the increase in the importance of the press as a business institution a natural development. Rather than viewing it critically as Progressive historians had done, they approached the trend toward big business in journalism with a neutral attitude and simply assumed that it was to be expected as the normal result of economic conditions.

The Progressive School

The Progressive historians, who thought of journalism in ideological terms, believed the primary purpose of the press was to crusade for liberal social and economic causes, to fight on the side of the masses of common, working people against the entrenched interests in American business and government. The heroes in their histories were journalists such as Heywood Broun, a leader of efforts to unionize other journalists in the 1930s; Marshall Field III, liberal owner of *PM* in the 1940s; William Allen White, who turned from his early Republican conservatism to become a mainstream leader of liberal causes; and E. W. Scripps, whose newspaper chain crusaded for improvement of various social conditions. John L. Heaton's early study *Cobb of "The World": A Leader in Liberalism* (1924) typified the biographers' works. Heaton viewed Frank Cobb, Joseph Pulitzer's successor as editor of the New York *World*, as a pure liberal, honest and sincere, who made the *World* American journalism's leading advocate of liberal causes aimed at improving political, judicial, economic, and social conditions.

One of the leading advocates of the Progressive interpretation was George Seldes. In two major works in the 1930s, he attacked the self-serving uses to which wealthy owners put their newspapers. In *Freedom of the Press* (1935), he argued that big business' control of the press was destroying press freedom. The American press, he argued, was "subject to the control of an oligarchy of big money and big business which is trying to destroy the foundations upon which free government is built." No section of journalism went untouched. Advertisers, public utilities, big business in general, and propagandists colored and suppressed the news and corrupted both the press and the public. The Associated Press, Seldes declared, always sided with authority, no matter how corrupt, whereas the conservative New York *Times* spoke for the status quo, and William Randolph Hearst was a friend of privilege and possessed no social conscience. In the areas of social reforms, Seldes denounced the press for opposition to the rights of labor, support of child labor for "purely financial reasons," scandal and invasion of privacy, interference with trial by jury, and critical treatment of the American Newspaper Guild. "When you have," he concluded, "a majority of the American press publishing . . . propaganda . . . because they are paid to do so rather than giving the truth on both sides," it is impossible to have a freedom of the press "where truth is not concealed." Seldes followed his first work with *Lords of the Press* in 1938. Employing the same theme of the pernicious effect of "wealthy money-makers'" ownership of newspapers, he argued that the press typically was ultraconservative and failed to ensure fair news treatment of labor or social and economic reforms.

One of the foremost villains in this Progressive approach was Frank Munsey, the consolidator of newspapers. In a work preceding Seldes', Robert Duffus claimed that Munsey's papers had no "general or permanent significance. They merely reflect Mr. Munsey, and when he is dead they will reflect someone else. He has acquired no following in daily journalism. He has demonstrated that newspapers are not institutions, like schools and churches, but commodities, like motor cars. . . . Perhaps this consoles him for his inability to own and edit one thousand 'independent, fearless and honest' American newspapers."[1] In a fuller 1935 biography, *Forty Years, Forty Millions*, George Britt painted Munsey as a man who executed papers and made journalism into a business with a primary concern for money. In most instances, Britt said, Munsey's editorial stands were determined by their potential to make him profit or increase his personal standing.

Such works by journalism professors as Raymond B. Nixon's "Concentration and Absenteeism in Daily Newspaper Ownership" (1945)[2] and Edwin Emery's *History of the American Newspaper Publishers Association* (1950) presented similar views on the business ownership of the press. Nixon especially lamented the potential loss of editorial vitality which the decrease in the number of compet-

---

[1] Robert Duffus, "Mr. Munsey," *American Mercury* (July 1924).

[2] Raymond B. Nixon, "Concentration and Absenteeism in Daily Newspaper Ownership," *Journalism Quarterly* 22 (1945): 97-114.

ing daily newspapers posed; whereas Emery, who was especially concerned with the professional development of the press and its advocacy of liberal causes, claimed that as newspapers became big businesses, publishers revealed self-serving attitudes and were primarily concerned with protecting their own interests.

Whereas these historians deplored newspaper owners' emphasis on profit, Oswald Garrison Villard and other Progressive historians focused on the decline of liberalism in journalism. Villard, equal to George Seldes as a Progressive critic of conservatism, deplored what he called the "crass materialism of the bulk of the American press" which resulted in the loss of a liberal, crusading spirit. Considering the best newspapers to be those that led the fight for improved social conditions, he believed that newspapers too often deserted their leadership role in molding public opinion and instead appealed to public tastes in scandal, racial hatred, and social animosities—all because owners thought they could make the most money by appealing to public passions. Villard pictured Adolph Ochs' New York *Times*, for example, as racist and a promoter of discriminatory separation between Blacks and Whites. In *Some Newspapers and Newspapermen* (1923) he concluded that newspapers treasured profit more than principle. In *The Disappearing Daily: Chapters in American Newspaper Evolution* (1944), a revision of his earlier work, Villard argued that fighting crusades was more important than providing news, and he scorned the trend toward pictures, features, and a generally soft approach to news. Believing that the role of the press was to keep a wary eye on the government in order to protect the public, he argued that the newspaper that did not champion enough causes was the "disappearing daily."

Jonathan Daniels reflected a similar view in a work published two decades later, *They Will Be Heard: America's Crusading Newspaper Editors* (1965). Although Daniels was not so concerned with business ownership, he did consider crusading to be the primary purpose of newspapers; and he viewed the best crusades as the ones that took the side of the average person against the wealthy, egalitarianism against elitism, and the rights of the people against a repressive class structure and the power of money. In a series of brief biographies, he praised journalists who had stood for liberal causes. Typical was his favorable treatment of William Allen White as an editor transformed from a reactionary Republican in the 1890s to a respectable social liberal with a tame vision of revolution by the 1930s.

In basing their evaluations of journalism on the ideology of the press, Progressive historians thus were severe in their criticism of attitudes and ideas that did not measure up to their liberal ideal. Two biographies of Walter Lippmann by David Weingast and John Luskin typified works on these intellectual aspects of journalism.

Many non-Progressive historians considered Lippmann to be the leading philosophical, liberal luminary that 20th-century journalism produced. Weingast and Luskin pointed out his shortcomings. In the 1949 biography *Walter Lippmann*, Weingast found much to be admired in the journalist's writing style, but he criticized Lippmann for relying on "important figures in politics, diplomacy and business" for his ideas and for failing to draw enough of his views from "labor and farm people, and from leaders of minority groups." Although Weingast looked favorably on Lippmann's "support of liberal theories of social reform," he concluded that Lippmann's "frequent disapproval of actual legislation" intended to implement reform largely offset such support.[3] Similarly, Luskin's biography *Lippmann, Liberty and the Press* (1972) pictured Lippmann not as a great champion of freedom of the press but an indecisive observer who wavered on freedom. "Civility" rather than liberalism was the unifying feature of Lippmann's philosophy, Luskin concluded, and Lippmann himself was an elitist who had little trust in the common people.

The Developmental School
Developmental historians, whose works comprised the largest number among the schools of interpretation, were concerned—just as the Progressive historians had been—with a crusading spirit among journalists. Developmental historians, however, viewed journalism of the early 20th century not in partisan or ideological terms. They believed, instead, that journalism history could best be explained in terms of the progress of professionalism. Thus, in effect, they adopted crusading and liberalism as professional standards; or, it might be said, they institutionalized the practices that Progressive historians had viewed in partisan, ideological terms.

Developmental historians tended to select for study those journalists and practices that contributed to the advance of the profession, and thus their works tended to be laudatory, rather than condemnatory. Whereas, for example, Progressive historians had criticized Adolph Ochs for the conservative policies of the New York *Times*, Developmental historians attributed to him a major positive influence on such professional improvements as an emphasis on news and the triumph of objectivity in news coverage.

Such was the approach defining the biographical studies by most Developmental historians. Thus, the theme of the individual as a talented journalist underlay the studies of reporters, columnists, and editors such as Carr Van Anda and Arthur Sulzberger of the New York *Times*, the New York *World's* foreign correspondent Irv-

---

[3]David Weingast, *Walter Lippmann* (New Brunswick, NJ: Rutgers University Press, 1949), 118.

ing S. Cobb, Harold Ross and A. J. Liebling of the *New Yorker*, Bernarr MacFadden of the New York *Graphic*, and the political reporter Dorothea Thompson. In this "talented journalists" line of biographies, one of the most highly acclaimed works was Ronald Steele's *Walter Lippmann and the American Century* (1980). Winner of the Kappa Tau Alpha research award, the book described Lippmann as one of the most influential journalists of all time, a writer whom America's presidents and other world leaders sought out, and the greatest journalist of his era.

Whereas the Developmental biographies of "great men" told one aspect of the story of the progress of journalism, studies of the development of techniques provided another. Developmental historians selected for treatment such topics as technology, foreign correspondence, sports coverage, news wire services, ethics, objectivity, freedom of the press, criticism of the press, and education. Such studies were framed in terms of the development of professional standards and the improvement of professional practices. Developmental historians considered the growth of journalism education, for example, implicitly as evidence of the fact that journalism as a profession had gained respect. This concept provided the basis of biographies of such educators as Walter Williams and Frank Luther Mott of the University of Missouri and of histories of organizations such as the American Society of Journalism School Administrators. Simon Hochberger's short narrative "Fifty Years of Journalism Education" (1958) stated this view cogently. Journalism education, Hochberger wrote, contributed to the profession of journalism by turning out graduates to work in the field and by producing research and criticism. "In a half-century," he said, "journalism education in this country has grown from the fumblings of infancy and the uncertainties of childhood into an adolescence marked by a surprised recognition of increasing power. Now it is entering a period of maturity, a maturity notable, thus far, for introspective self-criticism and self-conscious striving toward improvement."[4] The improvement in journalism education, in Hochberger's view, thus mirrored the development of the journalism profession itself.

As Developmental historians constructed the story of the professional progress of journalism, most incorporated crusading as a standard practice. Usually, a tinge of liberalism colored their view. In Developmental history, however, crusading was considered not in partisan terms, as it had been by Progressive historians. Instead, Developmental historians implicitly considered the press as an institution whose purpose was to scrutinize the activities of other institutions such as government and big business in order to protect the

---

[4]Simon Hochberger, "Fifty Years of Journalism Education," *Journalism Educator* 13:2 (1958): 2-5, 24.

public. In contrast to the Progressive historians, who believed that
the role of the press was to serve as a political instrument, they perceived the press as a watchdog over government and other institutions in general. Thus, Developmental historians viewed the crusading function of the press not as a partisan and ideological tool but
as part of its professional role.

The crusading interpretation of the Developmental school was
presented most forcefully in a 1939 work by Silas Bent, *Newspaper
Crusaders: A Neglected Story.* In the professional progress of the
press, Bent argued, the chief element was crusading. The press, he
said, is "our most powerful single agency of information, opinion,
and reform"; and "since its beginning in this country," the press
had made crusading one of its "immensely important," if not its
most important, functions. Newspapers always had exercised a vital influence, Bent declared, "as champions of reforms, as defenders of individuals." The quality of newspapers, he believed, could be
determined by their crusading spirit, whether in the cause of traffic
safety, civic betterment, freedom of expression, judicial practices,
or any of a number of areas in the public interest. Likewise, newspaper editors and publishers could be considered deserters of the
high professional calling of the press if they opposed causes such as
the rights of labor or if they based their practices not on principle but
on profit. Roy Howard, for example, who was E. W. Scripps' successor as manager of the Scripps-Howard chain, received little but
scorn from Bent, for Howard "disavowed and repudiated" Scripps'
policy of fighting for the rights of the public. Howard "lopped off less
profitable [newspaper] properties here and there: and in some instances it was clear that these newspapers had lost ground because
they had ceased to be good crusaders. . . . Howard's illiberalism and
his bootlicking of the advertiser were making money in some
quarters, but they were curtailing the circulation, the prestige, and
the influence of the Scripps papers."[5]

Such an approach typified a score of biographies and newspaper
histories. Developmental historians lauded such journalists as
Scripps, Dallas *News* owner G. B. Dealey, New York *World* editor
Herbert Bayard Swope, York (Pa.) *Gazette* publisher J. W. Gitt, and
chain owner James W. Cox for crusades to improve civic, political,
and social conditions. They praised newspapers ranging from the
Kansas City *Star* and the Milwaukee *Journal* to small weeklies for
the same reason.

Typical of such works was George Turnbull's 1955 biography,
An Oregon Crusader, a story of the editorial courage of George Putnam of the Salem *Capital Journal* in the 1920s. Putnam was an editor of principle and character who was unafraid to take on Oregon's

---

[5]Silas Bent, *Newspaper Crusaders* (Freeport, NY: 1939), 80.

powerful political groups and its reactionary forces. Even in the face of a timid, or at best indifferent, electorate and while most other editors looked the other way, Putnam did not hesitate to fight legal, political, and judicial corruption and racial and religious bigotry. He believed in uncensored news and in the need for an editorial page that attacked evils. As a result of his sticking to such high professional principles, he became an influential force in helping bring to fruition the causes that were right.

Putnam's efforts in the area of freedom of the press evoked special admiration. As most Developmental historians did, Turnbull placed considerable importance on journalists' taking libertarian stands on press freedom.[6] A number of historians noted advances in an expanding freedom of the press during the first half of the 20th century, praising those journalists who aided the advance and condemning those who hindered it. In, for example, *Minnesota Rag: The Dramatic Story of the Landmark Supreme Court Case That Gave New Meaning to Freedom of the Press* (1981) Fred Friendly gave a favorable evaluation of the decision in the 1931 case *Near v. Minnesota* even though he believed the newspaper involved was a tasteless, antisemitic scandal sheet. Friendly, a national television network news executive, placed primary emphasis on the fact that the decision expanded the principle of the liberty of the press. At issue in the case were authorities' attempts to silence Minneapolis' *Saturday Press* under the Minnesota Public Nuisance Law of 1925. Most respectable newspapers in the state did not oppose the legislation, and Friendly concluded that a large number of the state's journalists were not crusading idealists. Instead, newspapers may have been taking bribes and extorting advertising in exchange for running favorable stories or squelching exposés. Friendly, however, did praise Robert McCormick, owner of the Chicago *Tribune*, who took up the *Saturday Press* issue, championed the concept of freedom of the press in practice, and became the main figure in the case.

Although Developmental historians such as Friendly thus normally attempted to detail the progress made in freedom of the press, they were especially critical when journalists did not support a broad libertarian approach to the First Amendment. Such an interpretation was presented most succinctly by John Lofton in *The Press as Guardian of the First Amendment* (1980). Although detailing the history of press freedom since the American Revolution, Lofton devoted most attention to developments after the 1917 case *Schenck v. United States*. Rather than finding, however, that the 20th-century press had staunchly advocated freedom, he concluded that "except when their own freedom was discernibly at stake, established gen-

---

[6]See George Turnbull, *An Oregon Editor's Battle for Freedom of the Press* (Portland: Binford and Mort, 1952).

eral circulation newspapers have tended to go along with efforts to suppress deviations from the prevailing political and social orthodoxies of their time and place rather than to support the right to dissent."

The Business School

A departure from the liberal interpretation of Progressive and Developmental historians came from the Business/Neo-Conservative school of historians beginning in the 1920s. Their reinterpretation was most evident in a number of biographies of media owners. Progressive historians had portrayed owners as selfish, conservative profiteers. Business historians found that owners often had made lasting, constructive contributions to mass communication, and that they symbolized some of the fundamental positive aspects of the American character. Whereas Progressive historians had viewed most owners with suspicion, Business historians described them as individuals of high principle.

Although the appellation "Neo-Conservative" may be applied appropriately to this school, its perspective is most appropriately thought of as "business history." Following the leadership of scholars in the prestigious Harvard Graduate School of Business Administration in the 1920s, Business historians developed their own approaches to explain American industrial history.

Those historians who studied the media argued that owners were not predatory profit seekers but farsighted, thoughtful entrepreneurs who made considerable contributions to American mass communication. Owners' goals were not simply to accumulate money but to bring new efficient methods of management to the media industries and in the process to serve better the information needs of the American public. Business historians also rejected the Progressive critique of media owners as enemies of democracy and freedom. They argued instead that owners, by providing efficiency and larger operations, gave America the best news media system in the world and actually contributed to greater democracy and freedom.

Such an approach provided the basis for one of the earliest studies of Adolph Ochs, a 1926 article by Benjamin Stolberg entitled "The Man Behind the Times." Stolberg described Ochs as a daring, courageous, honorable American who made the *Times* successful through faith in the "ordinary virtues," hard work, common sense, self-reliance, and honesty. The *Times'* owner, believing journalism's first obligation was to inform the public, refused to be influenced by advertisers and maintained a low editorial profile. In emphasizing news, rather than opinion, he adapted the *Times* to conditions of his era, while he also "caught the idea of mass production at just the right time in the New York newspaper field." Stolberg thus viewed Ochs not as a reactionary businessman, as Progressives had painted him, but as a leader in journalistic improvements and as a newspaper owner of highest ideals.[7]

In the fullest biography of Ochs, *An Honorable Titan* (1946), Gerald Johnson described him in almost identical terms, while incorporating a strong Developmental flavor into the interpretation. Ochs, Johnson said, was one of the financial titans of the late 1800s who had so much to do with making industrial America what it is. Unlike many of the industrialists who were materialists and rogues, however, Ochs was an honorable businessman committed to the ideal of the newspaper as a public institution: impersonal, reliable, responsible, and devoted primarily to serving the public with news. Ochs' journalistic career exemplified principle, and the history of the New York *Times* under his direction provided a story of advancing journalism. Ochs broke with the personal journalism of the past, while shunning the sensational techniques of Pulitzer and Hearst. He thus laid the essentials of the foundation of modern journalism, and as the *Times* quickly acquired a reputation for excellence, its owner gained a reputation for honor, character, and integrity.

Negley Cochran's *E.W. Scripps* (1933) typified the Business school's view, presenting the newspaper chain owner as "a great journalist, profound philosopher, and at once a great master and a great public servant." Even though Scripps was concerned with the business operation of his newspapers, he was just as interested in their content; and he deserved credit, according to Cochran, for America's development of a politically independent press.

While even Progressive historians had viewed Scripps favorably as a liberal newspaper owner, Samuel Williamson's biography *Imprint of a Publisher: The Story of Frank Gannett and His Newspapers* (1948) painted a favorable picture of a conservative businessman who had high standards for the news and editorial operations of his papers. Nothing, according to Williamson, so inspired Gannett as a business opportunity, and the story of his career was one of how he bought, merged, and controlled newspapers. Yet for all his conservatism and his attention to the business operation of his 21 newspapers, Gannett prided himself on not dictating editorial policies, and he created a model for editorial independence and quality journalism on chain-owned newspapers.

Traditionally, historians had portrayed business owners as selfish, conservative profiteers. The counter-argument that owners often had made lasting, constructive contributions to journalism was central to the Business school's interpretation. Contrary to the view of the Progressive school, Business historians denied that

---

[7]Benjamin Stolberg, "The Man Behind the Times," *Atlantic Monthly* (December 1926): 721-731.

owners were reactionary simply because their newspapers made money. This change in attitude toward the role of the press as a business investment was manifest in biographies of two leading newspaper publishers, Ira Copley and Gardner Cowles. In *The Thin Gold Watch, A Personal History of the Newspaper Copleys* (1964) Walter Swanson painted a favorable picture of Copley as one of the first 20th-century businessmen to see that the newspaper was a business that could make a profit. Rather than condemning Copley, Swanson pointed out frankly and without apology that before Copley started building his newspaper chain he had been quite successful at making money in gas and electricity utilities.

In the 1978 biography *Harvey Ingham and Gardner Cowles, Sr.: Things Don't Just Happen*, George Mills took a similar approach to analyzing the financial success of Ingham and Cowles with the Des Moines (Iowa) *Register*. The news and editorial quality for which the *Register* "has become known," wrote Mills, "was the consequence of foresighted business practices begun by the elder Cowles and continued by his sons John and Gardner Jr." Cowles, for example, "shrewdly used Iowa's railroad network to achieve the *Register's* statewide circulation and championed highway improvement programs with that same circulation problem in mind." At the same time, by using imaginative circulation techniques and wooing advertisers, he built up the paper's advertising and circulation revenues. Although noting that Cowles' principles sometimes influenced his business practices, Mills did not suggest that any incongruity existed between good journalism and profitable newspapers. Indeed, he reasoned that the two worked hand-in-hand.

Implicit in the Business/Neo-Conservative interpretation was the belief that the liberal Progressive view of American political history was inappropriate. Few Business historians, however, attempted to provide a direct refutation of liberal ideology. One who did try to do so was Finis Farr. In *Fair Enough: The Life of Westbrook Pegler* (1975), Farr praised Pegler, a conservative national columnist after World War I, for the quality of his writing style and argued that the only reason Pegler had not been given the acclaim accorded such liberal columnists as Heywood Broun was his conservatism. Had Pegler written on the political and social left rather than the right, Farr argued, historians would have regarded him more highly.

The Cultural School

A fourth approach to interpreting American media in the first half of the 20th century came from the Cultural school of historians beginning in the 1930s. Although many of these historians incorporated into their writings concepts of both professional development and ideology, their studies were characterized more obviously by a concern for the influence of social, political, and economic conditions on the media. Their most evident reinterpretation of the media of the early 20th century was their approach to the increased emphasis on the media as business institutions. Rather than criticizing the spread of the profit motive and the concept of the press as a business (as Progressive and many Developmental historians had done) or attributing them to the high character and business acumen of owners (as Business historians had done), Cultural historians considered the changes as a fact of economic life in an industrialized, commercialized nation. They viewed the changes as a natural result of the social and economic environment.

Works in the early 1930s by two prominent journalism educators, Ralph D. Casey and Willard G. Bleyer, presaged the change in historical attitudes. In surveying literature on journalism being published, Casey concluded in a 1931 study that more and more articles were being devoted to business management, whereas the number of articles on "editorial methods" was not increasing.[8] Bleyer, in surveying the journalism profession in 1933, concluded that the year had demonstrated "the fact that the fortunes of newspapers as private business enterprises are inextricably bound up with the success or failure of modern capitalism."[9] The important historiographical point to note is that neither Casey nor Bleyer criticized the change toward the growth of newspapers as profit-oriented businesses.

During the next 25 years, a number of books and articles appeared detailing several media characteristics directly related to business developments: newspaper feature syndicates, daily newspaper chains, monopoly in the newspaper field, and circulation figures of daily papers, for example. Cultural historians explained these characteristics by such factors as normal practices in business operations, competitive conditions of the marketplace, growth of cities, geographical influences, economic depression, war conditions, and personal income of individual Americans.

The most extensive attempt to provide a cultural explanation of the 20th-century press was made by Sidney Kobre in his 1959 work *Modern American Journalism*. Emphasizing the development of the modern press in terms of press interaction with its environment, Kobre (who used the word *sociological*, rather than the broader *cultural*, to describe his historical approach) believed that "gigantic forces" including population changes and growth, industrialization, labor organization, and a spirit of social reform transformed

---

[8]Ralph D. Casey, "The Present Status of Journalistic Literature," *Journalism Quarterly* 8 (1931): 125-136.

[9]Willard G. Bleyer, "Journalism in the United States: 1933," *Journalism Quarterly* 10 (1933): 296-301.

America in the first half of the 20th century and thus drastically altered the nation's press. As the press mirrored the changes in economics and society, it changed to conform to new conditions. Accordingly, there developed a greater emphasis on interpretive journalism and column writing to explain a complex society to readers. Journalism schools and associations of journalists grew in importance, he reasoned, as the profession grew more sophisticated. Technological developments in radio and television altered traditional journalistic practices. Because of rising costs of labor and newsprint, publishers employed newspaper consolidations and chain ownership to save money and to buy production material on a large scale, mirroring similar developments in such other businesses as grocery store chains. Unlike most Progressive and liberal Developmental historians, Kobre thus explained the business growth of the press as going hand in hand with the tremendous changes in industrial, social, and economic conditions of the 20th century. Although the business growth frequently was accomplished in very dynamic ways, Kobre concluded that changes in the press resulted naturally from the press' social and economic environment.

On a more limited scale, various Cultural historians examined a range of content characteristics of the media in relation to the changes in the national environment during the first half of the 20th century. They usually assumed that journalistic practices and decisions were determined by cultural factors and that press content simply mirrored the interests of the reading public. Sherilyn Cox Bennion, for example, explained the decline of muckraking, reform-oriented material in mass-circulation magazines of the 1920s from such an outlook. The magazines did not emphasize reform because their readers did not want to hear about reform. With World War I, changes in society had occurred and magazines after the war simply reflected the interests of the public—whereas the muckraking journalists prior to the war had been instrumental in molding opinion.[10]

Similarly, John Brazil explained the content of tabloid newspapers in 1920s as a result of changes in Americans' attitudes. It was such a change that accounted for the tabloids' attempt to appeal to the masses and to compete with cheap literature and movies by emphasizing sensational murders and murder trials. Brazil believed that the attention the press gave to such events reflected specifically a change in American beliefs about individualism.[11]

---

[10]Sherilyn Cox Bennion, "Reform Agitation in the American Periodical Press, 1920-1929," *Journalism Quarterly* 48 (1971): 652-659, 713.

[11]John Brazil, "Murder Trials, Murder, and Twenties America," *American Quarterly* 33, 2 (1981): 163-184.

Discussion

For historians of the early 20th century press, the paramount question has been what determined the nature of the media. Progressive historians believed a class conflict between the rich and the masses was the essential factor, with wealthy owners too often subverting the press for their own benefit. Business historians argued to the contrary: that owners were men of high principle who had made major contributions to the quality of the press. Developmental historians tended to view changes in the press as a part of the natural progress of journalism, whereas Cultural historians reasoned that the nature of the media at any particular time was determined primarily by their environment.

1. How can the media of the period best be evaluated? (a) Did they lay the foundation for our modern concepts of journalism? (b) Were they primarily ideological instruments, controlled by conservative owners for their own benefit? (c) Or were the changes that took place primarily the result of powerful economic forces that transformed American society in general?

2. What role did individuals—as contrasted with great forces— play?

3. Were the owners themselves reactionary and interested only in profit, as Progressive historians argued, or were they also concerned about making the news media more efficient and, as a result, better at performing the job of informing the public?

4. If the distinctive characteristic of the period was the increasing transformation of the media into big business, how does one account for the increasing professionalization and—some would say—liberalism of working journalists? How could both conservatism and liberalism exist in the same field at the same time?

Readings

Progressive School

Britt, George, Ch. 11, "1912," pp. 158-184, *Forty Years, Forty Millions: The Career of Frank A. Munsey.* New York: Farrar and Rinehart, 1935.

Daniels, Jonathan, Ch. 16, "The Death of *The World,*" pp. 277-295, *They Will Be Heard: America's Crusading Newspaper Editors.* New York: McGraw-Hill, 1965.

Harlan, Louis R., "Booker T. Washington and the Voice of the Negro, 1904-1907," *Journal of Southern History* 45 (February 1979): 45-62.

Seldes, George, Ch. 6, "Lord Howard and His Empire," pp. 76-86, *Lords of the Press.* New York: Julian Messner, 1938.

Villard, Oswald Garrison, Ch. 8, "The New York Times and Adolph S. Ochs," pp. 78-92, *The Disappearing Daily: Chapters in American Newspaper Evolution*. New York: Knopf, 1944.

Weingast, David E., Ch. 3, "Lippmann's Economic Views," pp. 33-46, *Walter Lippmann: A Study in Personal Journalism*. New Brunswick, NJ: Rutgers University Press, 1949.

Developmental School

Bent, Silas, Ch. 4, "Scripps: Bare-Knuckle Fighter," pp. 60-80, *Newspaper Crusaders: A Neglected Story*. Freeport, NY: Books for Libraries Press, 1939.

Fine, Barnett, Ch. 8, "Van Anda's Contributions to Journalism," pp. 65-78, *A Giant of the Press*. New York: Editor & Publisher Library, 1933.

Lofton, John, Ch. 8, "A Presidential Big Stick Against Press Freedom," pp. 146-168, *The Press as Guardian of the First Amendment*. Columbia: University of South Carolina, 1980.

Morris, Joe Alex, Ch. 1 (untitled), pp. 17-31, and Ch. 34 (untitled), pp. 337-339, *Deadline Every Minute: The Story of the United Press*. Garden City, NY: Doubleday, 1957.

Steele, Ronald, Ch. 5, "A Little Iconoclasm," pp. 45-57, *Walter Lippmann and the American Century*. Boston: Little, Brown, 1980.

Towers, Wayne M., "World Series Coverage in New York City in the 1920s," *Journalism Monographs* 73 (August 1981).

Business and Neo-Conservative Schools

Cochran, Negley, Ch. 30, "Scripps Principles and Methods," pp. 231-243, *E. W. Scripps*. New York: Harcourt Brace Jovanovich, 1933.

Fleener, Nickieann, "'Breaking Down Buyer Resistance': Marketing the 1935 Pittsburgh *Courier* to Mississippi Blacks," *Journalism History* 13 (1976): 78-85.

Johnson, Gerald W. Prologue: "A Discourse on Titans," pp. 1-12, *An Honorable Titan*. New York: Harper and Row, 1946.

Olasky, Marvin N., "When World Views Collide: Journalists and the Great Monkey Trial," *American Journalism* 4 (1987): 133-146.

Swanson, Walter S. J., Ch. 16 (untitled), pp. 199-215, *The Thin Gold Watch, A Personal History of the Newspaper Copleys*. New York: Macmillan, 1964.

Williamson, Samuel T., Ch. 14, "'I Have Never Dictated,'" pp. 143-154, *Imprint of a Publisher: The Story of Frank Gannett and His Independent Newspapers*.

New York: McBride, 1948.

Cultural School

Bennion, Sherilyn Cox, "Reform Agitation in the American Periodical Press, 1920-1929," *Journalism Quarterly* 48 (1971): 652-659, 713.

Brazil, John, "Murder Trials, Murder, and Twenties America," *American Quarterly* (1981): 163-184.

Neurath, Paul, "One-Publisher Communities: Factors Influencing Trend," *Journalism Quarterly* 21 (1944): 230-242.

Stenerson, Douglas C., Ch. 1, "Mencken and *The American Mercury*," pp. 3-33, *H. L. Mencken: Iconoclast from Baltimore*. Chicago: University of Chicago Press, 1971.

Waldrop, Frank C., Ch. 7 (untitled), pp. 86-102, *McCormick of Chicago*. Englewood Cliffs, NJ: Prentice Hall, 1966.

16

Public Relations, 1900-1950:
Tool for Profit or for Social Reform?

The first half of the 20th century saw an American industrial revolution, World War I along with the wealth and prosperity that resulted from it, the worst economic disaster ever known to the United States, and a second World War that saw business and government working toward the same goal. During these tumultuous times, public relations served many needs and slowly became an accepted, professional field. American industry developed a more organized communications effort; and as a result of this effort, public relations became a prominent method by which business attempted to solve its problems. Although public relations efforts were not entirely successful, they did provide a foundation for the building of future social and political strength.

Many questions surround the history of corporate public relations in the United States. For the most part, historians agree that big business reacted to forces such as public dissatisfaction and politics. However, these reactions, which were often in the form of public relations, raise the question of whether big business was *forced* to improve policies that both directly and indirectly affected the public. Did big business actually undergo a reformation, or did it simply respond to unavoidable circumstances? Was public opposition the origin of public relations, or did big business react to government with public relations in order to acquire political power?

Modern public relations began with the Progressive reform movement in the early 1900s. At that time, a small number of "publicity" men existed; and the idea of professional, corporate public relations had evolved. By the beginning of the 20th century, the United States had seen an explosive growth in its business environment. Consequently, individuals such as William Vanderbilt, J. P. Morgan, and John D. Rockefeller established fame, fortune, and a firm hold on the majority of big American businesses. These

By Vanessa Murphree
University of Alabama

men and others who had suddenly gained control of the system treated the public with such disregard that some historians referred to the period as "the public be damned" era. Unethical practices, which included the prevention of public disclosure regarding big business, created controversy and fostered public dissatisfaction. As a result, during the years between 1901 and 1917, a journalistic movement known as muckraking gained increasing popularity. Muckrakers published explicit articles describing the ills of big business. Although short-lived, this movement spurred public concerns regarding America's corrupt business practices. Business leaders, who were accustomed to conducting their affairs in complete privacy, were now being forced to acknowledge and answer public questions.

In order to respond to criticism, big business turned to public communication, and "publicity" men were becoming common among industrial hierarchies. Moreover, agencies also were established to assist big business with public communication. One of these was Parker & Lee. Although the organization lasted only a few years, Ivy Lee, the junior partner, made innumerable contributions to the public relations field in the following years. When the Pennsylvania Railroad hired Lee as a director of information, he urged the company to supply complete and accurate facts regarding accidents—even those accidents that the railroad caused. Such honesty and frankness were the foundation of much of Lee's work and led to increased awareness and acceptance that enabled the railroads to maintain a private enterprise. Lee also worked with such notable individuals as John D. Rockefeller and advised them regarding employee and public relations. For example, at Lee's suggestion, the American Tobacco Company initiated a profit-sharing plan. Often called the "father of public relations," Lee is credited with introducing the concept of sincere, honest public communication efforts to the American business system.

During the 1920s, practitioners were still thought to be, and most still were, publicity agents. However, professionalism increased. Edward L. Bernays, one of the most important figures in public relations history, emerged as a leading figure and helped in bringing more respect to the field.

The poor economic conditions of the nation during the Great Depression brought about much growth in public relations. Big business leaders were often blamed for causing the conditions of the 1930s. As a result, they turned toward public relations to tell their side of the story. Additionally, big business had to build a stance against the New Deal regulatory policies that President Franklin Roosevelt and his administration designed to correct the economic condition of the country. As the Depression deepened, determining whether business operations actually caused the Depression did not seem to be as important as what the public thought. Once business had recognized a need to change, the change was facilitated by strong external forces such as government regulation and public opinion—forces so powerful that business had to acknowledge and correct its faults with immediacy.

The 1930s served as an era for an immense growth in public relations. By the end of the decade, most large corporations had public relations departments that practiced "two-way street" methods. That is, they not only sent messages, but they also listened to the public and asked for opinions and ideas. Publicity was still a major part of the practice, but public relations directors were gaining seniority in corporate environments and often were involved in management decisions. Additionally, employee and community relations had become important aspects of business operations as industries worked to regain lost respect. By the time the Depression came to a close, the business world had recognized public relations as a necessary function of its activities. Though big business was still often thought of as dishonest, criticism had declined. Actions had been taken to improve business' negative image, and in most cases these actions had a positive effect. Business leaders frequently appeared unorganized and reactive to problems concerning public relations; but they had succeeded in their efforts to improve their image, and they had gained public and political support.

As the 1940s approached, big-business leaders had created the foundation for public relations and were continually expanding their efforts. Moreover, the years surrounding World War II brought about a consolidated effort throughout the country—an effort that included business, government, and the public. As a result, big business was once again a respected entity; and rather than working against one another, business and government were working toward the common goal of winning the war. Internal employee relations played a large part in public relations. Because of the war effort, big businesses encouraged workers to produce more in less time. Furthermore, higher prices had prompted workers to demand increased wages, and labor unions were gaining members and power. Business was again forced to respond. It had to maintain employee loyalty despite efforts to organize around employee self-interest. For the most part, business efforts were successful. Employment and income increased, and after mid-1943 strikes were rare.

The war also created an increased demand for consumer goods that were becoming more and more scarce. Business was doing well financially; but, because products were not available, it was not in a position to market them through advertising. But big business needed to spend profits in order to avoid higher taxes. Consequently, business turned to institutional advertising as a method to acquire public support and to spend new-found profits.

With the war's end and as 1950 approached, most of the direct criticism of big business had declined. Business leaders, however, were still turning to public relations as a central part of their management plan. In many ways, growth during this period indicated that public relations had finally come to be understood as a necessary, on-going function. It was no longer a reactive solution to unplanned crises. Big business had acknowledged and responded to the idea that it needed to operate in accordance with public opinion.

Historians described the development of public relations in different ways. Although nearly all stressed a Progressive-style idea of big business versus the middle-class citizen, the great majority of historians were primarily concerned with the professional development of public relations or with the economic factors involved in the practice. Among those historians focusing on the development of the profession, there was considerable emphasis on the role that had been played by prominent individuals. A number of Developmental historians wrote about their personal experiences as they interpreted past practices, whereas others placed their studies within biographical frameworks, detailing how particular individuals influenced the field. Historians from the Economic school, on the other hand, were more interested in the influences of business practices and financial conditions on public relations.

The essential differences in interpretations were over the question of whether public relations was a tool for social reform or if public relations was a tool for profit. Did public relations evolve because business leaders had become more socially minded during economic hardships, or because these leaders were attempting to gain political power to defend themselves against regulatory policies?

The Developmental School
Developmental historians were primarily interested in the origin, practice, and advance of the field of public relations. They were mainly concerned with documenting the progress of public relations, and they attempted to explain and evaluate public relations in the past by exploring its contribution to present professional standards. They tended to focus on determining the origins of corporate communications practices and on the individuals who made substantial contributions to public relations progress. Most also viewed corporate public relations as developing out of and operating within a conflict between business and the middle class.

Some Developmental historians gave particular attention to the role of influential individuals and sometimes portrayed them as essential to the development of public relations. Such historians generally were favorable toward public relations. The practice of examining a particular person and relating his life to public relations development was common among historians and biographers who lived during the early 1900s and participated in the practice of public relations. Frequently, these historians used their personal recollections as the only source. This practice gave personal insight, but it lacked objectivity and left unanswered questions. Others wrote biographical descriptions of a particular person in an attempt to explain public relations history. In many cases, these autobiographies and biographies are the most detailed and comprehensive analyses available about a particular period in public relations history. Historians who did not take an autobiographical or biographical approach tended to be more critical.

The most famous public relations practitioner, Edward L. Bernays, recorded many of his experiences in several articles and books, and the Developmental perspective is clearly visible in his work. In addition to contributing information about public relations history, Bernays is thought to have had a major influence on its development. His book *Crystallizing Public Opinion* (1923) served as a beginning for the various areas of public opinion research and methods of persuasion used in public relations practice. It was in this book that the techniques of public relations were first explored.

In *Public Relations* (1952), Bernays described each period in the field's development. He proposed that the period between 1600 and 1800 served as the origin of public relations. Public relations was not yet identified, but it was practiced. The following years, from 1800 until 1865, were a time when the field experienced growth but still had not adjusted into a precise function. During the years between 1865 and 1900, the last concern of big business was public opinion. Bernays called this "the public be damned" period. By 1900 business opened up and entered the "public be informed" period, which lasted until 1929. The Great Depression served as an era of "coming of age" for public relations as the field became a "two-way street." Not only did business leaders inform, but they also listened. Bernays designated the years since 1941 as a "time of integration."

In his 1965 book *Biography of an Idea: Memoirs of Public Relations Counsel Edward L. Bernays* (1965), Bernays gave a detailed account of his years as a public relations practitioner. He discussed his life, family, and education and offered descriptions of many of his campaigns as well as several discussions about his relationships with famous people, including his uncle, Sigmund Freud. He also provided first-hand descriptions of the development of public relations with explanations of the formation of professional organizations such as the National Association of Accredited Publicity Directors.

Much later, Bernays looked back at the growing professionalism of business in a 1971 article entitled "Emergence of the Public Relations Counsel: Principles and Recollections." Here, he discussed the importance of public relations to a democratic society as well as the relationship between the two. "In a democratic society," he stated, "almost every activity depends on public understanding and support."[1]

Bernays shared his title as the founder of public relations with another important figure, Ivy Lee. The historian Ray Eldon Hiebert compiled a detailed account of Lee's life and influence on public relations. Hiebert's 1966 biography provided a comprehensive look at public relations development and credited Lee with much of the profession's growth. *Courier to the Crowd: The Story of Ivy Lee and the Development of Public Relations* investigated social, political, and economic factors when describing the state of public relations. Combining the biography of Lee with an examination of outside factors helped complete the account. Hiebert praised Lee's efforts to promote and maintain democracy. Despite the fact that Hiebert included a final chapter directly addressing criticism, he left the suggestion that Lee had the power to change America's destiny—and that perhaps he did. The Chrysler Corporation, for example, Hiebert declared, pulled free of the Depression under the direction of Lee. Furthermore, Lee possibly could have prevented the Depression single-handedly had he not been out of the country. "In the middle of the pile [of cablegrams]," Hiebert observed, "was one that told about Black Friday. It was of course too late for Lee to do anything."[2]

Public relations practitioners did not have to be as prominent as Lee and Bernays, however, to gain attention from Developmental historians. The role of the individual was emphasized in other studies of lesser known figures. Noel L. Greise described such an individual in "James D. Ellsworth, 1863-1940: PR Pioneer" (1970). Ellsworth played an important role in the development of AT&T's public relations department, and in many cases it was this organization that set the standards for other corporate departments. Ellsworth was an assistant vice-president in charge of public relations during the late 1920s and 1930. Greise looked at Ellsworth's contributions as a writer for the Publicity Bureau before he was hired at AT&T. While there, he initiated new internal communication devices and made numerous achievements in establishing an appropriate corporate image. These activities assisted AT&T during the Depression and enabled the company to minimize paycuts and layoffs. After Ellsworth's retirement in 1930, he was replaced by Arthur Page, who continued to enhance the growth of pub-

---

[1]Edward L. Bernays, "Emergence of the Public Relations Counsel: Principles and Recollections," *Business History Review* 45 (Autumn 1971): 277.

[2]Ray Eldon Hiebert, *Courier to the Crowd: The Story of Ivy Lee and the Development of Public Relations* (Ames: University of Iowa Press, 1966), 215, 200.

lic relations.[3]

In a similar study, Greise described the life and career of Page. In "He Walked in the Shadows: Public Relations Counsel Arthur W. Page" (1976), Greise referred to Page as "one of the most powerful public relations men America has ever produced."[4] Page was appointed vice-president of public relations at AT&T in 1927. He replaced Ellsworth, who became an assistant to the company president. While holding this position, Page created a special staff for attitudinal surveying, and he played a large role as his company fought the adverse effects of the Depression.

Along with individual practitioners, Developmental historians looked at other factors in the origins and practice of public relations. In *Public Relations and Business, 1900-1920* (1968), Alan R. Raucher attempted to examine the development of public relations by concentrating on specific entities such as the railroads and public utilities. He restricted his study to individuals actually using the term *public relations* and, therefore, omitted many important circumstances. According to Raucher, big business leaders responded to the "economic realities" of their society and consequently encouraged the use of publicity men. He provided discussions of such influential men as Bernays, Lee, and Harry Bruno, another public relations pioneer.

One of Raucher's main objectives was to determine the reasons for public relations development and its significance. In doing this, he often was critical of the profession. He implied that Lee, Bernays, and others in the field were not as intelligent as they portrayed themselves to be. Their goal was to detect and control public opinion, and in their efforts to accomplish this goal, they created public relations. However, Raucher maintained that this so-called "two-way street" communication had little influence on actual business practices. That is, big business may have asked the public for its opinion, but it did not consider that opinion when making profit-oriented decisions.

In examining other features of early public relations practices, Raucher was just as critical. He observed, for example, that considerable conflict occurred between public relations practitioners and the muckrakers. Upton Sinclair, he noted, called Lee "Poison Ivy" because of his dealing with the Rockefeller family. Moreover, Raucher claimed that World War I did little to facilitate the growth of public relations and that the wartime techniques that were used had been used in previous crises. During the 1920s, he said, press

---

[3]Noel L. Greise, "James D. Ellsworth, 1863-1940: PR Pioneer," *Public Relations Review* (Fall 1970): 16-20.

[4]Noel L. Greise, "He Walked in the Shadows: Public Relations Counsel Arthur W. Page," *Public Relations Review* (Fall 1976): 36-41.

agentry and public relations were synonymous.

Because of the success of their textbook, *Effective Public Relations* (1978), Scott Cutlip and Allen Center may be two of the best-known Developmental public relations historians. Their book's chapter on "The Origins of Public Relations: How it all began" attempted to detail the conditions from which modern public relations sprang. "[T]he twentieth-century developments in this field," they argued, "are directly tied to the power struggles evoked by the political reform movements. . . ." The "evolution of maturity" took place in five stages. First was the era of Muckraking Journalism when corporations reacted with defensive publicity. Second was the World War I era. This period brought about a cumulative patriotism among the American population. Third, the Roaring Twenties era saw the practices of publicity that had been employed during the war used to promote products and other corporate expenditures. The Roosevelt era followed and "advanced the art and extended the practice of public relations." Finally, 1945 to present was the Post-industrial era in which there were numerous and substantial movements toward professionalism. The authors credited World War II with much of public relation's development during this time. They wrote: "In industry, public relations was used primarily to spur war production by promoting productivity and combating absenteeism. But there were other, equally challenging tasks that could best be met by specialists, such as the lack of goods to sell and the need to keep the company name before the public, and these spurred the organization of new departments and the wider use of institutional advertising."[5]

As Developmental biographers traditionally had done, Cutlip and Center also examined the role of Lee, Bernays, Carl Byoir, and others who were instrumental in the establishment of public relations.

The Economic School

An economic perspective stands out in much of public relations history. Even Developmental historians often used economic factors as a secondary theme. Whereas Developmental historians, however, concentrated on what might be considered "professional" features of public relations' progress, Economic historians described the practice of corporate public relations as it related to economic and business influences. Whenever the economy faltered, according to these historians so did the public image of big business. Therefore, big business turned to public relations efforts. And these efforts created a more socially responsible and publicly acceptable business world.

---

[5]Scott Cutlip and Allen Center, "The Origins of Public Relations: how it all began," in *Effective Public Relations* (Englewood Cliffs, NJ: Prentice Hall, 1978), 65-94, 90.

Throughout the Economic explanations of public relations, historians pointed out that public relations was created to protect big business and its profits from public and political attacks. These conflicts provided the basis for Richard S. Tedlow's *Keeping the Corporate Image: Public Relations and Business, 1900-1950* (1979). Tedlow maintained that public relations was not a response to a certain crisis, but was a corporate strategy to create customer and community rapport. Despite the fact that this strategy lacked the desired "two-way street" approach, it still improved big business' sensitivity to public issues and had an impact upon everyday business practices.

Tedlow described the muckrakers, because of economic concerns, as an important factor in public relations' development. "They heated up the atmosphere," he observed. The American work force was unable and the American government unwilling to challenge corporate power during the 1920s, a time when "deep currents of unease persisted in the business community," Tedlow stated.[6]

During the Depression, big business attempted to maintain power as the New Deal gained public support and as labor movements grew. In order to fight for their position, business leaders began working together as a group in the National Association of Manufacturers. In 1933, N.A.M. leaders saw their problem as public misunderstanding and began to explain and distinguish their side of the story. According to Tedlow, "The aim of the N.A.M. in 1920 was solely propaganda, but during the New Deal, the Association also sought in a modest way to reform and educate employers."[7]

In his discussion of the 1940s, Tedlow placed special importance on the improving relationship between government and business. "When Roosevelt effected his celebrated switch from 'Dr. New Deal' to 'Dr. Win the War,'" Tedlow argued, "he automatically earned the support of many nationalistic corporate leaders who had previously opposed him, at least for the duration." Tedlow described the difficulties created by the war as "problems of success."[8] Demand for products was greater than the supply, and the federal government was the main consumer. Consequently, employee and community relations multiplied, and big business leaders accepted public relations as an on-going profession.

Presenting a similar assessment of corporate public relations from the Economic perspective was Marvin N. Olasky's *Corporate Public Relations: A New Historical Perspective* (1987), an account of major public relations activities throughout the early 20th cen-

---

[6]Richard S. Tedlow, *Keeping the Corporate Image: Public Relations and Business, 1900-1950* (Greenwich, CT: JAI Press, 1979), 14-16.

[7]Ibid., 59-79.

[8]Ibid., 114, 117.

tury. Through examples such as the railroads and public utilities, Olasky described how business executives and public relations counselors attempted to solicit public opinion. He portrayed the evolution of public relations as a response to poor economic or social conditions. The railroad industry, he stated, "plunged into public relations when the public was no longer voluntarily greeting new track with enthusiasm. Utilities embraced public relations when they were criticized as swollen monopolies. As long as industry executives generally believed that the public naturally would accept their leadership, there would be little willingness to develop massive public relations budgets and staffs."[9]

Despite the concern for economic motivation, Olasky was not entirely critical of public relations. He noted various contributions made by such prominent figures as Bernays and Lee, along with other lesser-known, but still important individuals such as Theodore Vail and Samuel Insull. These men, Olasky said, were leaders in developing public relations practices within public utilities.

On the whole, however, Olasky pointed to the problems that financial concerns presented for public relations. In examining public relations practices during the Great Depression, he argued that it was business—rather than government regulation, as businessmen had argued—that was the main cause of hardships for business. Business' failure to comply with the National Recovery Act requirements created a dishonest image, not the stock market crash or reports of misconduct.

Discussion
The topic of public relations has concerned writers and thinkers since the early 1920s. Yet relatively little historical research has been conducted on the subject. Furthermore, the field has only recently been accepted as a professional area of study.

Despite the lack of research, or perhaps because of it, historians disagree on several fundamental questions. While attempting to examine the origins of public relations, some historians maintain that the beginnings were during the period of the Roman Empire, and that the American Revolution led to public relations practitioners such as Samuel Adams, Patrick Henry, and Thomas Jefferson. Others state that the railroad industry in the early 1900s laid the foundation. Still other historians suggest that the field was not defined until the 1920s and did not become an organized, widespread profession until the 1930s.

The confusion appears to arise from a lack of definition over the

---

[9]Marvin N. Olasky, *Corporate Public Relations: A New Historical Perspective* (Hillsdale, NJ: Lawrence Erlabaum Associates, 1987), 80.

term *public relations*. Therefore, historians have shown considerable disagreement in their definitions of the term and in their interpretations. They confront a number of questions.

1. The first question they face is, What is meant by the phrase *public relations*? Did public relations in some form or fashion exist during the Roman Empire? Or, if the field is defined as a professional science, did it originate before the 1900s?

2. Furthermore, how can the historian properly delineate the areas covered by such an extensive subject as "public relations"? Such a broad subject is difficult to centralize and often overlaps into other areas such as politics and business management and into related areas such as press agentry, publicity, and advertising. Is it possible for the historian to separate the subject of "public relations" from those areas? Should areas such as publicity and business management properly be a part of historical studies in public relations? Can such functions as distributing press releases and organizing special events be included as a part of professional public relations, or are these activities merely publicity attempts?

3. What was the essential difference between public relations and publicity?

4. Can the evolution of public relations be credited, as some Developmental historians claimed, to particular individuals such as Bernays and Lee, or should it be attributed to the entire cultural environment?

5. In particular, what role did economic considerations play?

6. In attempting to answer that question, how can the historian determine the intent of American business leaders? Did they honestly see the value of social responsibility, or did they adopt public relations simply as a profit-making tactic?

Readings

Developmental School

Bernays, Edward L., "The Era of Integration, 1941-1951," pp. 115-125, *Public Relations*. Norman: University of Oklahoma Press, 1952.

Cutlip, Scott, and Allen Center, "The Origins of Public Relations: how it all began," pp. 65-94, *Effective Public Relations*. Englewood Cliffs, NJ: Prentice Hall, 1978.

Greise, Noel L., "James D. Ellsworth, 1863-1940: PR Pioneer," *Public Relations Review* (Fall 1970): 16-20.

Harlow, Rex, "A Public Relations Historian Recalls the First Days," *Public Relations Review* (Summer 1981): 33-42.

Hiebert, Ray Eldon, Ch. 10, "Public Relations for Public Utilities," pp. 86-93,

Courier to the Crowd: The Story of Ivy Lee and the Development of Public Relations. Ames: Iowa State University Press, 1966.

Raucher, Alan R., Ch. 5, "'Turning Point' for PR?" pp. 65-74, *Public Relations and Business 1900-1929.* Baltimore: Johns Hopkins Press, 1968.

Economic School

Olasky, Marvin N., "Come the Depression: Corporate Public Relations and the National Recovery Administration," pp. 67-77, *Corporate Public Relations: A New Historical Perspective.* Hillsdale, NJ: Lawrence Erlbaum Associates, 1987.

Tedlow, Richard S., Ch. 2, "Up from Press Agentry," pp. 25-57, *Keeping the Corporate Image: Public Relations and Business, 1900-1950.* Greenwich, CT: JAI Press, 1979.

17

Advertising, 1900-Present: Capitalist Tool or Economic Necessity?

Advertising volume began to increase tremendously in the early 20th century, and along with the increase came greater efforts to make advertising more effective. As a result of Albert Lasker's pioneering efforts, advertising became persuasive and pervasive. In the 1920s, advertisers found a new medium, radio, and began to spend substantial portions of their budget on it. The decade of the '20s also saw the introduction of new approaches, most notably the "image-building" concept. That approach to advertising emphasized not how a product would serve its user, but what the buyer could become through it.

Yet while Lasker's protegés were creating new approaches, the number of critics of advertising were increasing. From a free-wheeling, devil-take-the-hindmost, raucous combination of greed and innovation, advertising began to clean its own house. The dates usually associated with the first reform movement in advertising were from about 1905 until the beginning of World War I. Reformers from outside the industry remained dissatisfied, however, with internal efforts to clean up advertising, and the criticisms grew and became more shrill with the founding of the consumer movement during the Great Depression.

Following the war-filled decade of the 1940s, the key feature in the history of advertising in the 1950s was again, like the earlier advent of radio, the appearance of a new medium. This time, it was television. The increase in its use was rapid and immense. From $10 million spent on television advertising in 1950, the total reached $22.6 billion in 1986, accounting for approximately 22% of all expenditures on advertising in the United States that year.

Along with television and the large amounts spent each year on advertising, the other critical aspect of advertising in recent history has been the growing dominance of the field by corporate agencies.

By Donald R. Avery
Samford University

No longer is it the creative individual who plays the key role in designing advertising. The job is done by a team of specialists who handle not only the creative idea but marketing research and other features that go into the complex job of producing an ad.

Much of the history written about advertising has supported one side or another in the dispute over the effects of advertising on consumers. Whereas much of the early historical work on advertising was produced as a kind of defense of advertising, much of the later work has been active in its opposition to advertising. Those who wrote as insiders tended to praise the process, whereas those on the outside were prone to attack advertising as the bane of society.

The compositional structure of writing in advertising history also shows considerable diversity. The early work tended to be broadly descriptive and the biographies and autobiographies anecdotal. Much of advertising's history was produced in bits and pieces by writers and scholars interested in the history of advertising only peripherally. The later writing has been cultural and social and has tended to say more about American culture and social mores than about advertising *per se*.

The scholarship falls into several historical schools. First, the Developmental approach, almost always descriptive, sought its answers to the study of the past by incremental accounting of ever-advancing technique. A second approach—that of Business historians—held a similarly favorable view of advertising but was primarily concerned about the dynamics of the advertising industry and the positive role that it played in the American economic system. The Cultural school, however, was almost always denigrating. It saw advertising as a mirror of society, either being influenced by its surroundings or having an influence on them. Ideological historians, on the other hand, viewed advertising in a narrower context, that of socio-political issues. They made up two groups, Progressive historians and Marxist historians. The Progressive school explained advertising as it related to democratic principles and to the clash between the masses and the wealthy class. The Marxist school, generally condemning all approaches but its own, saw advertising history in terms of a classic class struggle and efforts aimed at reforming advertising as an exercise in futility, because true reform needed to undermine existing political, economic, and social systems. Finally, the Economic school, almost always positive and thus in direct contrast to the Ideological schools, explained history in terms of what advertising did for the economic well-being of society.

Developmental School

The earliest historians were from the Developmental school and saw much that was praiseworthy in advertising. They were much concerned with change, with improvements in how advertising practitioners did advertising. This preoccupation with technique led to a series of histories that read very much alike, featured the same advertising pioneers, discussed the same developments, and were almost universally high in their praise of advertising as a promoter of the American Way. If the techniques, such as developments in copywriting, media, and agency growth, have less salience when viewed in retrospect, it may be because the modern observer sees either the past from a greater distance or the world with clearer glasses.

The earliest important history of advertising was written in 1929 by Frank Presbrey. In *The History and Development of Advertising*, he presented a positive view of the origin and progress of advertising. His presentation revolved around two fundamental claims regarding the importance of advertising. First, he argued that advertising historically had been the engine that drove economic development. Second, he considered advertising to be one of the most important social forces in history. Advertising, he argued, was the vehicle that led America and, indeed, most of the world to prosperity. "That advertising," he said, "has been a substantial factor in the upbuilding of prosperity and in widening the horizon and increasing the happiness of the masses is beyond discussion.... Its development has kept pace with the growth of intelligence. It has led in the expansion of trade throughout the world. A nation is just as enterprising and prosperous as is its advertising. Because of this, advertising is a barometric indicator of a nation's commercial progress."[1] His claims, however, gave little weight to other variables in the marketing mix.

He saw advertising as part of a cost-to-income relationship created by the existence of advertising. Without advertising, goods would cost too much, production and distribution costs would increase, and income would be reduced. The costs and losses in income would be greater than the costs of advertising.

As a socializing and civilizing force, advertising was virtually without peer, Presbrey argued. "There appears to be," he wrote, "a growing realization among those who trace for the rest of us the factors which bring about profound changes that advertising is a civilizing influence comparable in its cultural effects to those of other great epoch-making developments in history. Some future 'History of Civilization' perhaps will give advertising credit as the power that in the nineteenth century began to make a large part of the world so speedily a more comfortable sphere for the human family to

---

[1]Frank Presbrey, *The History and Development of Advertising* (Garden City, NY: Doubleday, Doran, 1929), v.

be on."[2]

Presbrey believed that advertising was the source of a cornucopia of cultural, educational, and social advances. There was little that was good in American life that had not been created by advertising. Indeed, advertising was responsible for the spread of love of music, art, dress, manners, improved diet, sanitation, and so forth. "Advertising," he declared, "probably is our greatest agency for spreading an understanding and love of beauty in all things."[3]

Presbrey considered advertising a major tool of education, arguing that it had barely touched the surface in its development and that its persuasive techniques could easily find their way into other fields. He believed that through education alone mankind could achieve nearly universal happiness. "[W]hen it comes to that big, all-comprehensive job of achieving an ideal social state," he concluded, "the potent force of advertising will at least be one of the agencies through which it will be accomplished."[4]

The Business School

Sharing the positive view of the Developmental school were historians from the Business school. Especially concerned about the critical view of American business that had been popular among historians from the time of the Progressive reform era to the Great Depression of the 1930s, they offered a revised assessment that emphasized the talents and achievements of business people. The foundation for the Business perspective was laid by the Harvard Graduate School of Business Administration, along with a number of favorable biographies that were written to counteract the stereotype of American industrialists as predatory profit seekers. Business historians insisted that industrialists were talented, innovative entrepreneurs who contributed immensely to the success of the American economic system. The benefits extended not only to business but to all Americans, who as a result enjoyed the highest standard of living in the world.

Ralph M. Hower's *The History of an Advertising Agency* (1949) epitomized the Business approach. A part of the Harvard Studies in Business History, the book was an in-house history that was commissioned by the subject. As a result, it suffered some of the shortcomings common to such works. The editor's introduction to the first edition was revealing. He talked about approaches to writing histories of organizations. First, such histories can be written by an outsider using whatever public records exist. A second approach is to write history from the inside using someone from the organization

---

[2]Ibid., p. 608.
[3]Ibid., p. 611.
[4]Ibid., p. 608.

utilizing in-house records. Third, a history of an organization can be written by an outsider using in-house records and discussions with employees. Hower used this final approach, and he ultimately had serious difficulties with his benefactors. The reader is left to guess which parts of the book are tainted.

Despite the editor's claims that Hower had been given virtual free-rein in his study of the agency, his work displeased the president of N. W. Ayer & Son. The company had the final say on the book's publication and contents. "When the history was first [1935] submitted," the editor explained, "Fry [the president of N.W. Ayer & Son] opposed publication, partly because the text raised insoluble questions of business policy and also, I feel, partly because the exposition was more critical and less personal than was expected." Fry's death permitted negotiations on some of the areas of disagreement, and the book was finally published but not before the editor got in one final shot: "In studies of existing firms which are owned by single entrepreneurs or by partners . . . we may expect to fall somewhat short of full information on the financial side."[5]

Despite the disagreements between Hower and Ayer, the book was essentially a paean in praise of Ayer for the development of the advertising agency and the contribution of advertising and business to the rise and growth of America. Like other modern corporations, N. W. Ayer employed an operating structure in which specialized functions were assigned to various departments, which then were integrated into a cohesive, smoothly working whole.

Hower condemned his fellow historians for their failure to give business its proper due and for their penchant for pointing too often to the negative side of business. He was particularly scathing in his criticism of those who would attack profit-making and individualism. His call for a more "dispassionate frame of mind" in the study of business was ironic in view of his own passion in the praise of business.

Hower concluded his bulky volume with a Business-school credo. "The success of N. W. Ayer & Son transcends in significance the realm of business alone," he wrote. "This firm and others like it have helped to build the American nation. . . . We have had a continent to settle, great resources to exploit, cities and factories to build, and trade and industry to develop. These ends were accomplished by individual effort, hard work, and intelligence. There was no other way. Given the actual circumstances—our historical background, the multiplicity of interests and opportunities, the growing complexity of economic life, the irrational nature of man, and other unpredictable elements—we could not possibly have

---

[5]Ralph M. Hower, *The History of an Advertising Agency* (Cambridge, MA: Harvard University Press, 1949), xxxi-xxxii, xxxiii.

achieved what we wanted in any other way. . . . Whatever views one may have about the future, it is clear that individual firms like N. W. Ayer & Son have done the bulk of our work in the past."[6]

Cultural School

In the Cultural approach to history, historians viewed the media in general and advertising in particular as mirrors of society, on the one hand influencing culture and society and on the other being influenced and shaped by those same variables. To explain advertising, they believed, one needed to look at its sociological environment.

Advertising's influence on society and the American character was the primary concern of David Potter. In *People of Plenty: Economic Abundance and the American Character* (1954), he argued that the most distinctive feature of the modern American character was materialism, which resulted from affluence and from an abundance of goods produced by the economic system. The role of advertising was central in such a system. "If abundance can legitimately be regarded as a great historical force," Potter asked rhetorically, "what institution is especially identified with it?" He answered directly: "If we seek an institution that was brought into being by abundance, without previous existence in any form, and, moreover, an institution which is peculiarly identified with American abundance than with abundance throughout Western civilization, we will find it, I believe, in modern American advertising."[7]

Advertising's role was to stimulate consumers to purchase goods. In doing that, it had been immensely successful. "[A]dvertising," Potter wrote, "is not badly needed in an economy of scarcity, because total demand is usually equal to or in excess of total supply, and every producer can normally sell as much as he produces. It is when potential supply outstrips demand—that is, when abundance prevails—that advertising begins to fulfil a really essential economic function."[8] Thus, in the early 1900s, as the United States' economy became capable of producing more goods than necessary for people's needs, producers used advertising to encourage the public to shift its thinking from needs to desires, so that the emphasis was on consumption. That change, Potter declared, altered the American character.

In his study of the relationship of advertising to consumption, *Advertising, The Uneasy Persuasion* (1984), Michael Schudson argued that advertising had helped shape American culture but often

---

[6]Ibid., p. 585-586.

[7]David M. Potter, *People of Plenty: Economic Abundance and the American Character* (Chicago: University of Chicago Press, 1954), 166, 167.

[8]Ibid., p. 172.

in ways that were detrimental. Although he was more interested in contemporary analysis of advertising than in history, his view of the cultural role of advertising epitomized the approach of historians who emphasized "symbolic meaning" as the essence of mass communication. "No one," he wrote, "has been so crude as to imagine that advertising created 'consumer culture' single-handedly, but few critics of advertising have thought very hard about *what else*, besides advertising, has brought us to the kind of consumer culture we have today." He looked, he explained, "at advertising as a system of symbols and [stood] as an analyst, outside, interpreting the Cultural form of the advertisement in its social context."[9]

But he was less interested in symbols than he might appear, seeing his work as an exercise in the study of "the sociology of culture." Disavowing symbols as they related to content, Schudson believed it was crucial to look at "the social situation of the symbol makers and to the responses of the audiences or clients for the symbols. . . . The complexity and variety of audience response is probably better documented here than in any other field of Cultural studies. But there is danger in audience studies, too. It lies in the seductiveness of pluralism: when one discovers that different kinds of people assimilate very different meanings from the same mass culture, it is too easy to conclude that the symbols of mass culture have little authority in the face of human diversity."[10]

Schudson wrote about American values and daily life being fashioned by advertising, often bad or false. He saw much of advertising as a kind of exercise in misleading. "National consumer product advertising," he claimed, "is the art form of bad faith: it features messages that both its creators and its audience know to be false and it honors values they know to be empty.

"This, it seems to me, is the primary fact to understand about advertising. The question, What work does advertising do in the culture? quickly becomes the question, How can it do any work if people are so inattentive to it? and when attentive, so critical, so able at recognizing its propagandistic intent and techniques? Apologists are wrong that advertising is simply information that makes the market work more efficiently—but so too are the critics of advertising who believe in its overwhelming power to deceive and to deflect human minds to its ends. Evaluating its impact is more difficult than these simplicities of apology and critique will acknowledge."[11]

Taking the long-term view of advertising, Schudson alter-

---

[9]Michael Schudson, *Advertising, The Uneasy Persuasion* (New York: Basic Books, 1984), 13.

[10]Ibid., p. 12.

[11]Ibid., p. 11.

nately praised advertising for its informational role in society and attacked it for its bad faith, bad products, and bad values. Still, he concluded that advertising was only one of many factors which shaped human values.

Whereas Potter and Schudson focused sharply on the cultural role of advertising, a number of historians in the Cultural school mixed that perspective with definite Developmental views. In essence, they told the history of advertising as the story of the progress that the field had made within the context of its role in American culture. That combination was evident in two works published in the mid-1980s, Stephen Fox's *The Mirror Makers* and Roland Marchand's *Advertising the American Dream*.

Fox's work, published in 1984, used personalities as its vehicle, a kind of recital of the craft's great men and women. Fox admitted to having had a change of heart during the course of his writing, as he explained: "[B]roadly, I have tried to understand the relationship between advertising and American culture. I started this book, as an observer of contemporary America, with the impression that advertising wields substantial independent power to create and shape mass tastes and behavior. Now, after changing my mind a couple of times while writing this book, I have concluded that advertising gathered power early in this century, reached a peak of influence in the 1920s, and since then—despite consistent gains in volume and omnipresence—has steadily lost influence over American life." He argued that advertising became an easy target for critics, a "scapegoat for our times," and then chastised naysayers for failing to take a more Cultural approach to advertising history.[12]

Fox's emphasis on biographical sketches made the work read like a Developmental history. Each great man or woman brought his or her own contribution to the craft of advertising, and many were concerned about reform and social development. Fox gave considerable attention to the advances in the business including advances in strategic and tactical techniques, reform concerning women, Blacks, and White ethnics, and the evolution of advertising interest groups and associations.

Still it was with culture that Fox was primarily concerned. Advertising, he believed, served as a cultural mirror. "Thus," he explained, "the favorite metaphor of the industry: advertising as a mirror that merely reflects society back on itself. Granted that this mirror too often shows our least lovely qualities of materialism, sexual insecurity, jealousy, vanity, and greed. This image in the advertising mirror has seldom revealed the best aspects of American life. But advertising must take human nature as it is found. We all would like to think we act from admirable motives. The obdu-

---

[12]Stephen Fox, *The Mirror Makers* (New York: William Morrow, 1984), 8.

rate, damning fact is that most of us, most of the time, are moved by more selfish, practical considerations. Advertising inevitably tries to tap these stronger, darker strains."[13]

However, Fox took issue with earlier critics of advertising. Although conceding that those critics who found American culture hopeless because of self-centeredness and greed, and hopelessly wedded to progress had a strong case, Fox pointed out that observers found these characteristics among Americans from the early days of the republic, long before advertising developed. "To blame advertising . . . for these most basic tendencies in American history is to miss the point. It is too obvious, too easy, a matter of killing the messenger instead of dealing with the bad news. The people who . . . created modern advertising [were] not hidden persuaders pushing our buttons in the service of some malevolent purpose. They [were] just producing an especially visible manifestation, good and bad, of the American way of life."[14]

Like Fox, Marchand in *Advertising the American Dream* (1985) approached advertisements "as reflections of American culture." However, unlike most historians, he believed the focus of historical scholarship should be limited to the 1920s and 1930s. "I have concluded," he wrote, "that the 1920s and 1930s provide the optimum era for exploring this approach to historical interpretation. American advertising took on a new scope and maturity during these years. Not only did the number of advertisements, the variety of products advertised, and the media available to advertising expand dramatically; in addition, advertisements increasingly gave predominant attention to the consumer rather than the product. In their efforts to win over consumers by inducing them to live through experiences in which the product (or its absence) played a part, advertisers offered detailed vignettes of social life. This evolution toward an emphasis on consumer anxieties and satisfactions, which culminated by the 1930s, was what made American advertising 'modern.'"[15]

Although fundamentally Cultural in approach, Marchand's work incorporated a strong Developmental perspective. His occasional regressions to Developmental history were employed, however, mainly as a means of exploring the Cultural impact of advertising. "By examining the social backgrounds of those who shaped the advertisements and by listening to their shoptalk about themselves, their audiences, and their working conditions, I have tried to assess their biases and the accuracy of their perception of social re-

---

[13]Ibid., pp. 329-330.

[14]Ibid., p. 330.

[15]Roland Marchand, *Advertising the American Dream* (Berkeley, CA: University of California Press, 1985), xxi-xxii.

alities. In interpreting advertising content, I have tried to work backward to the underlying social realities by correcting advertising's depiction of American society for the refractions introduced by such biases, motives, and assumptions."[16]

He was especially alert to the use of advertisements in the study of history. Although he saw extensive distortions in advertising, he believed many of them were merely artifacts of advertising as a process and thus problems they create can be worked around in the study of history. "Advertisements," he wrote, "present problems that differ more in degree than in kind from those involved in interpreting social reality from more conventional historical sources. We may not be able to prove the specific effect of an advertisement on its readers, but neither can we prove the effects of religious tracts, social manifestos, commemorative addresses, and political campaign speeches on their audiences. Much popular communication, he argued, cannot be taken as gospel; and advertising often shared the attributes "of many other suspect forms of evidence about popular attitude: we do not know exactly why they were popular or successful; we do not know if audiences shared or adopted the ideas presented; and we have reasons to suspect that the authors had motives and biases that did not completely coincide with those of the audience." Still, as historical records, advertisements, Marchand claimed, have much to offer the historian.[17]

Ideological Schools

Whereas Cultural historians believed advertising played a key role in American values, ideological historians were convinced that it was a critical factor in socio-political issues. Among themselves, however, they disagreed about the nature of the effects of advertising. Their differing views grew out of the fundamental differences between Progressive and Marxist perspectives. Whereas Progressive historians believed constructive reforms would bring about the needed changes in American society, Marxists believed that the changes could be achieved only through radical alterations of the existing system. Within these perspectives, some historians viewed advertising positively as a means of helping the middle and working classes to attain higher standards of living, whereas others condemned it as a tool of capitalists to subjugate the masses.

Advertising originated from the very class, the wealthy, that liberal and radical historians normally viewed as the antithesis of the ideological ideal. Ideological historians explained advertising history within a conflict between the conservative business class, which was bad, and the masses, who were good. At the root of this

---

[16]Ibid., p. xx.
[17]Ibid., p. xviii.

conflict was the struggle between the individual and the forces of oppression. The force for good that advertising potentially represented had to be used in the name of liberty and reform.

For James Playsted Wood's Progressive *The Story of Advertising* (1958), the locus was democratic theory, the idea that an institution existed in its relationship with democratic principles. Advertising was a powerful force, Wood argued, for it "is a primary expression of the entire democratic concept of freedom of enterprise and consumer freedom of choice. In this way, advertising has stature and importance beyond its proven ability to distribute merchandise. Advertising is also one of the most powerful forces contributing to produce a sheeplike conformity in entire populations, helping create the compulsions to which the community responds."[18]

Wood considered advertising an institution of high political importance because it was the instrument of democracy. It was, he said, a necessary part of an "industrial democracy." He argued that democracy provided the underpinning for the American economic system and that private enterprise could not exist without democracy. Advertising provided freedom of choice for the consumer, and it was that freedom of choice that provided the counterpoint to the entrenched social and economic classes that were the object of the Progressives' attention. Indeed, democracy was necessary for the development of advertising in America, and democracy was necessary for advertising to survive.

Like other Progressive historians, Wood identified with the masses, and he wrote of advertising history as "the story of people." He saw advertising as a mirror that reflected "their desires, tastes, habits, weaknesses, hopes, and pretensions. In advertising can be seen the actuality of what people have been like in their day-to-day living through the centuries and what we are like now."[19] There was, he said, no better or more accurate picture of people and their time than that shown by their advertising.

Typical of Progressive historians, he also considered economics to be a central feature of history. Advertising, he said, was the necessary component of marketing to the masses and the driving force behind sales: "This process becomes even more important economically as production and productive capacity expand and as wealth spreads. Recent studies have emphasized the greater reliance of the economy upon advertising and provided further economic justification even of advertising appeals directed at snobbery and self-indulgence."[20]

---

[18]James Playsted Wood, *The Story of Advertising* (New York: Ronald Press, 1958), vi.

[19]Ibid., pp. v-vi.

[20]Ibid., p. 493.

Wood was critical not only of the motives of advertisers and the nature of the appeals in advertising, but of advertising's effect on people's values. Although advertising had been a positive force in improving the material conditions of the great mass of people, it had, at the same time, changed their values from the ideal to the material. As he described historical developments in advertisements, they had changed from announcements of the early years, to more brazen forms at the turn of the century, and finally to the psychological appeals to emotion used by his contemporaries. Despite such techniques, advertising had contributed to making America a society of plenty. "People," Wood wrote, "have more food, clothing, and shelter than many of them can use." Ultimately, however, even the result of material well-being was damaging. "[T]he same culture that has given [people] manifold possessions has," he lamented, "in the mass deprived them of other good things, pride and pleasure in work, creative joy, and the simplicities, said to bring serenity."[21] Wood added that advertising had had a leveling influence over society in that it had made available to the masses what was previously only the province of the wealthy.

There is a certain wistfulness to Wood's discussion of advertising reform in the early decades of this century. Unrestricted competition at the turn of the century permitted a vigorous pursuit of material gain and a boldness in advertising not seen since: "The idea prevailed without serious question that it was legitimate and laudable to make money, as much as possible, in business, and certainly in advertising. Advertising was vigorous, and it was fun. The men who plied it plied it lustily."[22]

The world of modern advertising, he concluded, is barely a shadow of itself. "It is more subtle, less spectacular, sometimes a little dull. It is more insidious, and it is more powerful, yet in gaining outward dignity and respectability it has suffered some of the same loss of individuality that it has itself inflicted on so much else in modern life."[23]

Marxist historians went even further than Wood and his fellow Progressive historians. With a beginning assumption that capitalism was the core cause of society's problems and that materialism corrupted basically good human nature, Marxists argued that advertising had simply served as a means by which the capitalist class exerted control over the masses. The work of Stewart Ewen epitomized their approach. In *Captains of Consciousness: Advertising and the Social Roots of the Consumer Culture* (1976), he argued that the capitalist class attempted to control the masses by persuad-

---

[21]Ibid., p. 494.
[22]Ibid., p. 500.
[23]Ibid., p. 502.

ing them to think in terms of consumption and by substituting an economic truth for real truth. A key instrument in that attempt, he said, was advertising. Capitalists used it to sell more goods and extend their control over laborers. Describing "a political ideology of consumption," by which the business class intended to prevent unrest in the laboring class, Ewen argued that advertisements "created a vision of social amelioration that depended on adherence to the authority of capitalistic enterprise. . . . Within the schema of the businessmen," he wrote, "the very notion of truth emanated not from any social values or ethics external to their business, but was a product of their business."

Thus, efforts to clean up advertising had been simply "part of a public relations campaign which attempted to legitimize the ad industry's own conception of honesty." The attempts of Progressive reformers in the early 1900s were superficial. Similarly, the advertising industry's own attempts to assure "truth in advertising" were really aimed at circumventing consumers' complaints and at inculcating the business class' own artificial truth. "Purportedly a device of consumer protection," Ewen wrote, "the installation of truth into advertising's ideological pantheon was one more form of attempted domination—not unfamiliar to students of the 'big lie' which was emerging elsewhere [in the 1920s]." The advertisers' ultimate purpose was to forge consumerism as the fundamental American character and "to shape a culture which responded to and communicated through advertising."[24]

Economic School
Ideological historians' concerns for the role of economics in advertising history were shared by Economic historians. Whereas, however, ideological historians explained economics in socio-political terms, Economic historians looked at economics in terms of human and institutional dynamics. They tended to be deterministic, assuming that economics was the engine that drove all earthly pursuits. Most events, trends, and manifestations of society and culture could be explained as being driven by business. Simply put, in the case of advertising, it existed as a handmaiden of business and had no other purpose than promoting sales. The study of advertising history from an Economic perspective was hampered, however, by the general absence of historical concerns by those writing about the place of advertising within economics.

Daniel Pope's Economic history of advertising, *The Making of Modern Advertising* (1983), grew out of a fundamental argument

---

[24]Stewart Ewen, *Captains of Consciousness: Advertising and the Social Roots of the Consumer Culture* (New York: McGraw-Hill, 1976), 109, 70-71, 72, 74.

that advertising functioned in response to business needs. No matter what other justifications, praise, or criticism was handed advertising, Pope believed its only reason for existence was to promote business and generate sales. "We may or may not get the kind of advertising we deserve; we most certainly get the kind of advertising corporations require," he argued. "Businesses do not spend more than fifty billion dollars a year to create works of art or to undertake psychological experiments or to bring the deep structures of our psyches to the surface."[25]

Admitting that his approach to advertising history grew out of Economic determinism, Pope maintained that economic matters were the major reason for advertising. However, he hedged a bit by admitting that economics had not always been the only stimulus for practitioners. "External pressure for reform, legal regulation, their own social backgrounds, and their ethical and esthetic beliefs all left marks on the work they did." Still, he believed the development of advertising should be explained most basically in the business needs it met.

Pope's work differed from that of several other historians in that he maintained that much of the important formative developments in advertising were completed by the 1920s. He argued that the structure of advertising, its values, and its internal development were basically complete by 1920 and that there have been no fundamental changes within the institution since then. "Moreover, many of the themes that scholars have noted in advertising in the 1920s—a quest for professional respect, ambivalence toward government regulation, an expansive faith in advertising's power, and a desire to use it for social control—can also be discerned in the Progressive Era early in the century."[26]

In discussing the early years of this century, Pope pointed out that advertising practitioners were not much interested in the consequences of their activities. When they did think about the cultural impact of advertising, they saw it as a democratizing force, what Pope called "the herald of that democracy." Abundance, he said, "allows us to choose what kind of person we want to be; advertising displays the alternatives before us and imbues them with meanings. Advertising proclaims our liberation from the dictates of scarcity and invites us to enter into 'consumption communities.'"[27] It was freedom of choice that permitted consumers to participate in such consumption, not where they lived, who they were, what job they held.

[25]Daniel Pope, *The Making of Modern Advertising* (New York: Basic Books, 1983), 7.

[26]Ibid., p. 8.

[27]Ibid., p. 11.

With their desire to sample the new, consumers later loosened their bonds to the past, according to Pope. Still, the Progressive Era was not yet ready to deliver on the "promises of democratic mass consumption." Manufacturing and labor needed to alter their relationships because mass consumption depended upon a stable economic environment in order to flourish. Advertising might be a leveling influence on business, but mass production required control with its attendant loss of individual freedom. "In the final analysis," Pope said, "advertising negated its own democratizing pretensions. The growth of the advertising industry implicitly challenged the models of human thought and behavior underlying nineteenth-century democratic individualism."[28]

Discussion

A large part of advertising history has been written by historians with a business, social, cultural, or political axe to grind—and often while the historians were on the way to doing something else. As a result, many traditional concerns of history have not been addressed; and a number of fundamental questions remain unanswered.

1. The most basic question is this: Is the history of advertising the history of business and economics, or is it the story of culture and society or some combination of the two?

2. Is advertising the history of an institution that has steadily improved or that has been constantly in need of reform? Or, as Marxists have argued, is it the political, social, and economic systems that must be reformed?

3. Can the history of the United States be told, as Economic and Business historians have suggested, in terms of business activities with an occasional hand from advertising?

4. Questions about historians' perspectives raise questions about how methodological approaches have affected the writing of advertising history. Has the Developmental approach relied too heavily on superficial and often minor changes in the advertising process to the exclusion of environmental factors?

5. Has the use of a "Great Man" approach granted too much importance to decision makers and not enough to evolution within the process?

6. Have historians in general and Cultural historians in particular credited too much power to advertising to manipulate the public? What evidence would be adequate to demonstrate such influence?

7. Have historians spent too much time in either defending or attacking advertising, and too little in examining the process of ad-

---

[28]Ibid., p. 13.

vertising and its place in society?

Readings

Developmental School

Cone, Fairfax M., Part 1, "The View from the Tower," pp. 1-10, *With All Its Faults*. Boston: Little, Brown, 1969.

Ogilvy, David, Ch. 18, "Lasker, Resor, Rubicam, Burnett, Hopkins and Bernbach," pp. 189-205, *Ogilvy on Advertising*. New York: Vintage Books, 1963.

Presbrey, Frank, Ch. 56, "The 'Cleaning Up' of Advertising and Good Effect Thereof," pp. 531-540, *The History and Development of Advertising*. Garden City, NY: Doubleday, Doran, 1929.

Rowsome, Frank Jr., Ch. 2, "Windows on the Past," pp. 2-19, *They Laughed When I Sat Down*. New York: Bonanza Books, 1959.

Business School

Hower, Ralph, Ch. 17, "Development of Organization and Management," pp. 460-496, *The History of an Advertising Agency*. Cambridge: Harvard University Press, 1949.

Cultural School

Fox, Stephen R., Ch. 3, "High Tide and Green Grass: The Twenties," pp. 78-117, *The Mirror Makers*. New York: William Morrow, 1984.

Marchand, Roland, Ch. 1, "Apostles of Modernity," pp. 1-24, *Advertising The American Dream*. Berkeley: University of California Press, 1985.

Potter, David M., Ch. 8, "The Institution of Abundance: Advertising," pp. 166-188, *People of Plenty: Economic Abundance and the American Character*. Chicago: University of Chicago Press, 1954.

Schudson, Michael, Ch. 1, "The Advertiser's Perspective," pp. 3-43, *Advertising, The Uneasy Persuasion*. New York: Basic Books, 1984.

Ideological Schools

Ewen, Stewart, Ch. 3, "Advertising's *Truth*," pp. 69-76, *Captains of Consciousness: Advertising and the Social Roots of the Consumer Culture*. New York: McGraw-Hill, 1976.

Wood, James Playsted, Ch. 1, "What is Advertising?" pp. 3-17, *The Story of*

Advertising. New York: Ronald Press, 1958.

Economic School

Pope, Daniel, "Introduction: The Age of Advertising," pp. 3-17, *The Making of Modern Advertising.* New York: Basic Books, 1983.

18

Mass Magazines, 1900-Present: Serious Journalism or Mass Entertainment?

From the first colonial magazines of 1741 to the modern specialties which cover every conceivable subject, magazines traditionally have provided for the exchange of information between writers and their audiences. Mass magazine history has been marked by a capricious cycle of industry changes, with many fortunes gained and reversed during the 18th, 19th, and 20th centuries. At the fulcrum of these changes has been advertising, the magazine industry's strong, but forceful, silent partner.

As from the very beginning magazines have mirrored the tastes of their reading publics, the task of defining and servicing their needs has been compounded and confounded by events throughout history. From the late 1700s, a plethora of magazines served varied and sophisticated audiences but nothing on the scale of those started during the industrial revolution of the late 1800s. Industrialization offered newer and cheaper production technologies, and magazines could be reproduced quickly and efficiently in large numbers. Developments in photoengraving techniques guaranteed the inexpensive reproduction of illustrative matter as well. The stage was set for magazines to appeal to wider audiences. Publishers of such industry notables as *McClure's, Ladies' Home Journal,* and *Munsey's Magazine* boasted large circulations, had general appeal, and were national in scope.

The mass magazine industry managed to stay intact during World War I and afterward maintained a peaceful coexistence with the new media challenger of the 1920s, radio. After World War II, the industry flourished. Mass magazine circulation giants emerged, and so did fierce competition for advertising dollars. Magazine publishers aggressively promoted their magazine formats, editorial styles, the size and quality of their audiences, and anything else to influence advertisers. The competition was to be-

By Bea Julian
University of Alabama

come even more intense in the 1950s with the increasing popularity of a powerful new competitor, television.

Initially the impact of television on subscriptions was not great, but advertisers flocked to the new medium. The lure of having their products made accessible to the widest audience ever was attractive and convincing. Combined with other industry problems such as rising publishing costs, the coming of television signaled the decline and eventual collapse of many general-audience magazines.

In their place arose the new challengers, specialized magazines aimed at the general consumer. Specialized magazines had always existed, but during the 1970s and 1980s they came into their own. Yet, even some of the best of these magazines outlived their usefulness, always attended by replacements aimed toward meeting the capricious demands of the masses while contending with advertising's now more prominent influence.

Although historians have taken different approaches to the study of magazines, the central historiographical issue revolves around their role as a medium of popular communication. That role has involved a number of issues on which historians have disagreed. Some have assumed that magazines provided serious, useful information, whereas others have argued that they simply offered mass entertainment. They also have disagreed on what the relationship between public opinion and magazines has been. The central disagreement has been on the question of whether magazines provided commentary on the real world, or created a reality for the world to follow. Aside from the practical work of tracing years and variations in the long list of magazine publications, most historical attention has centered on the factors that influenced the answers to such questions.

Three interpretive approaches have dominated historical works on American magazines. Cultural historians emphasized the importance of societal forces in shaping the progress and development of magazines. They viewed such factors as the public temperament, contemporary manners and tastes, levels of education, the status of the economy, and the political climate as highly significant. They also looked closely at the successes of individual magazines and how they appealed to mass audiences.

A second group of historians who examined mass magazines from the point of view of their influence on American literature made up the Literary school. They looked at the characteristics of magazines as compared to other print media in an attempt to determine their unique qualities, describe the different forms and genres, critically assess the social and literary value, and examine the many ways in which the literature of mass magazines appealed to vast and diverse audiences. These historians focused upon the histories of the individual magazines, the organizations and leaders who produced them, and editorial quality.

Economic historians, making up the third school, tried to explain the development of magazines in terms of their dual role as products of commercial venture and as organs of amusement and education. They tended to view the impact of business in favorable terms and placed a greater importance on the influence of economic factors than Cultural or Literary historians did.[1]

The Cultural School

Historians in the Cultural school explained magazine history in social terms. From their point of view, factors in the media environment had a significant effect upon shaping the nature of mass magazines. Some of these historians viewed the evolution of the mass magazine concept in the larger context of the complex industrial and commercial changes that accompanied the growth of American technology in the latter part of the 19th century. Increases in mass production meant more goods and services, better business, and improved financial health for all enterprises, including magazine publishing. Mass production also led to more leisure reading time for working class society, which meant magazine editors had to contemplate the information and recreational reading needs of a different type of audience; old publications had to change, or new publications had to be generated in order to serve them.

Other Cultural historians viewed the changes in publisher and editor attitudes toward their audiences as more significant. In doing so, they chronicled the successes of great magazines and innovative publishers. Some of their studies involved an assessment of trends in magazine readership in terms of demographics (regional versus national publishing), in categorical terms (appeal of magazines to different groups based on gender, social class, or age), and in political terms (effects of the reform movements, wars, and governmental policies).

Some historians documented the contributions of mass magazines toward such things as the promotion of free enterprise, the fostering of democratic ideals, improving public welfare, or raising the educational or consciousness levels in society.

Finally, other historians viewed all of the preceding factors as part of the media environment that influenced the growth of magazines.

Although Algernon Tassin did not consider *The Magazine in America* (1916), his informal history of magazine publishing in the

---

[1]One of the cornerstones upon which the history of mass magazines is built is the reform movement of the early 1900s. In explaining such an important period in magazine history, historians have largely adopted a Progressive interpretation. This ideological approach is discussed in Chapter 19.

United States from 1741 until 1900, to be the work of a "genuine historian," the book introduced central issues that would be addressed in studies by later historians.

His attempt to bring together the diverse and complex elements that made up 150 years of American periodical publishing into a running account of the intellectual and literary movements their content expressed was based upon published works which included reminiscences of publishers and editors, as well as survey histories from scholarly books and journals. Tassin asserted that his book was more representative as an interesting record than an interpretation of absolute fact. Further, he admitted to having made no attempt to resolve contradictions in detail or consequences in his work, a position that resulted in critics assailing the book as inaccurate. Yet Tassin's prefatory remarks suggested that his disregard for contradictions resulted in an accuracy of a different sort: "the maker of this mosaic frankly confesses that his interest lies rather in hearing what people have thought of themselves and of each other than in the absolute facts at the bottom of their opinions; and ventures to think that in so indulging himself he gets a clearer idea, as well as a more colorful one, of the fundamental truth."[2]

The Magazine in America dealt with a period in society when the groundwork was being laid for the advent of mass magazines. One of the mass magazine characteristics established early in the 19th century was the tendency toward proliferation, on which Tassin remarked, "[M]agazines indicated at the outset their eternal disposition to multiply faster than the traffic will stand."[3] A second trend was the growing belief that magazines should appeal to popular tastes.

Tassin was especially interested in the environmental influences upon the generation, publication, and distribution of magazines during this period. He described the influences as geographic (much of the early publishing activity was centered in Boston, Philadelphia, and later New York); economic (production costs were related to the financial health of industry in general); and social (recreational reading was associated with the well-educated, upper classes, thus affecting magazine content).

By the end of the 19th century, magazines such as *Munsey's*, *Ladies' Home Journal, Cosmopolitan*, and *Everybody's* heralded the beginning of modern mass magazines. Tassin concluded that factors within the industry—such as cheaper-per-issue costs; the trend toward topical, concise human-interest-centered journalism inspired particularly by *McClure's*; changes in editors' attitudes that

---

[2]Algernon Tassin, *The Magazine in America* (New York: Dodd, Mead, 1916), Preface.

[3]Ibid., p. 2.

would bring them closer to their audiences; the introduction of advertising as a remedy for the problem of rising production costs; the rising popularity of pulp literature; and, finally, continued professional growth of writers as a result of their prestigious exposure through magazines—would sustain the newer magazines and set them apart from their predecessors.

Social and economic changes in the late 18th, 19th, and 20th centuries played, according to Cultural historians, an immense role in shaping the character of mass magazines. Nowhere are the results more evident than in Frank Luther Mott's *A History of American Magazines*. The author's work on this comprehensive, critically annotated bibliography of magazine journalism was awarded the Bancroft and Pulitzer prizes for history. Although characteristically a Developmental historian when dealing with newspaper history, Mott adopted a Cultural approach to magazines, with which he expected to trace the "growth in the value of magazines as popular informers and interpreters." Social history—the times, the people, the major events—provided the framework for Mott's treatment of the dramatic increase in quantity and the gradual development in quality of the mass magazine.

Each volume in Mott's series presented an overall assessment of a period followed by brief histories and critical analyses of the major magazines. Published in 1930, Volume I, covering the period from 1741 (the year in which the first American magazines were published) to 1794, introduced Mott's perspective on the historical significance of magazines. He viewed them as responsible for three valuable contributions to American society: a democratic form of literature which was reflective of public tastes; a reader-supported industry which allowed for economic support and recognition of publishing in general, and authors in particular; and a valuable source of social history providing a contemporaneous record of the times.

Volume IV, *A History of American Magazines 1885-1905*, published in 1957, covered the era that set the stage for the development of the mass magazine industry, as well as for the dramatic social and intellectual changes that took place. In the Introduction to Volume IV, Mott commented on the period as a time when "[n]ewspapers flourished, books at low prices multiplied, the platform [providing speakers with opportunities to express their opinions] was active; but of all the agencies of popular information, none experienced a more spectacular enlargement and increase in effectiveness than magazines."[4] In his estimation, the advent of the cheap, well illustrated, weekly magazine had a powerful effect on society and lasting sig-

---

[4]Frank Luther Mott, *A History of American Magazines*, Vol. IV (Cambridge, MA: Belknap Press of Harvard University Press, 1957), 2.

nificance for magazine history.

Plans for publication of Volume V, which covered the succeeding years 1905 to 1930, were interrupted by the author's death in 1964. The initial work on 21 of the 31 magazine sketches slated for the volume was completed by Mott's daughter with assistance from his former associates in the profession and was published in 1968.

James Playsted Wood continued the approach of Mott in a broad survey of the social and economic influence of magazines from 1741 until 1949, *Magazines in the United States.* Originally published in 1949 and later updated with two revised editions, this informal history represented Wood's attempt to bring together in a single work critical analyses of major general-audience magazines, along with an examination of the effects of these magazines upon media audiences as a group and upon the individual reader. His overall evaluation of the contributions of mass magazines to American life and literature was positive, especially in terms of their roles as "national educators" and "strong proponents of democracy."[5]

In the first edition of *Magazines in the United States* (1949), Wood identified three controlling influences on public opinion in the early 20th century: magazines, newspapers, and radio. Allowing for the more popular appeal of radio, he suggested that magazines were a strong influence as creators of public opinion. Radio tended to refer listeners to printed sources for more detail on broadcast subjects. Newspapers could respond with timely, concise, simplified, usually visual, coverage on subjects. Magazines offered timely coverage as well, but in a more deliberated, skillfully edited, and physically attractive version, with a format that encouraged retention for future reference. As to magazines' societal roles as creators of public information, Wood noted that "magazine influence in the United States is pervasive. It is a continuous pressure, continually molding the ideas of many millions, both the leaders of public opinion and the followers. Although this influence is difficult to isolate and to prove, cause and effect are discernible in given instances."[6] Among the examples that followed, Wood cited how *Harper's Magazine* and the *Saturday Evening Post* played an important role in introducing the concept of atomic power, and its scientific and social significance, to the American public.

In their capacity as educators and informers, Wood concluded, magazines were perishable products, subject to pressures from competitors, from public demand for fairness and accuracy, and from advertisers who provided financial support for their businesses. De-

---

[5]In that assessment, one sees hints of Wood's Progressive perspective that was evident in work that he did on advertising history. (See Chapter 16 of this book.)

[6]James P. Wood, *Magazines in the United States* (New York: Ronald Press, 1949), 281.

spite these circumstances and after more than 200 years of growth, magazines represented "one of the most characteristic products of American democracy" as well as serving as one of its strongest supporters.

Besides the addition of new chapters to accommodate the new trends and magazines, in the third edition of *Magazines in the United States* (1971) Wood looked at the tremendous social and economic changes that had affected the magazine publishing industry. His neutral assessment explained the impact of television as a competitive new medium, the growth in complexity of the pursuit for advertisers' dollars, the dominant trend toward specialization in magazines, and how all of these led to a general decline in the quantity and editorial quality of mass magazines.

In spite of these changes and the inevitable death of the mass magazine concept, history and experience indicated that magazines, imperfect as they were, were useful and important enough to guarantee their place in the scheme of total public communications. Wood believed that magazines provided both serious journalism and mass entertainment and therefore would persist in some form for a long time to come.

The Literary School

Frank Luther Mott and a number of other historians credited the magazine movement with introducing some of America's finest literary talent to mainstream audiences via the pages of magazines. In the earlier days, when magazine content was decidedly more literary, mass magazines featured such distinguished authors as William James, Louisa May Alcott, William Dean Howells, and Henry Wadsworth Longfellow. During the Progressive reform movement of the early 1900s, a trend toward more factual coverage in magazine content signaled the decline of mass magazines with a strong literary format. Around this same time, the concept of the little magazine—a periodical whose main purpose was the publication of artistic work over commercial interests—emerged to foster the publication of fiction and poetry, particularly the work of beginning writers.

Historians in the Literary school approached the study of magazine history in terms of the contributions of artistic movements or trends, such as the proliferation of little magazines, to the whole of American literature. Generally these historians were journalists, literary scholars, critics, or specialty writers, and they examined the quality and type of literature as well as the value of certain contributors and their contributions. Literary historians published a wide range of works, from survey histories to bibliographical compilations on specialized topics, to critical analyses of popular genres or enduring themes.

In "American Magazines," a survey covering a 30-year period beginning in 1898, Agnes Repplier concluded that general audience magazines were journalistically accurate, responsive to audience needs, admirable in breadth of coverage, but "less than praiseworthy" in terms of literary value. Her evaluation of the content of these early magazines revealed that authors were subject to measures of moral censure or social propriety—as "general audience" meant that the magazine was directed toward the amusement and instruction of the entire family.[7]

Other noticeable trends in content that led to Repplier's estimation that mass magazines were less than distinguished included a preponderance of stories blatantly stolen from British magazines (a practice that was shamefully engaged in by publishers in Britain and the United States), a preference among important American magazines to purchase the work of well-known British writers, excessive use of serial fiction, and an excess of nature studies and animal stories.

Later studies by historians continued to look at topical areas of magazine history and, especially as the years progressed, noted those important areas that had received little attention. One of these areas was magazines for children. Though the growth and development of children's magazines closely paralleled the trends in the adult publishing industry, there were unique differences as described in R. Gordon Kelly's impressive compilation *Children's Periodicals of the United States* (1984). The first children's magazines were similar to those for adults in format and, according to Kelly, featured miniscule type, were overly didactic, dry in tone, and featured no illustrations. *Our Young Folks*, founded in 1865, was the first children's magazine with a childlike format and content that was relevant to a child's world. Kelly attributed most of the success of children's magazines in the late 19th century to their alliance with prestigious publishing houses. These firms were able to obtain writers who wanted to do more than entertain children with their writing, but sought to acculturate them to a world view that would one day enable them to play a part in fulfilling the nation's destiny. Children's magazines followed the trend toward specialization of their adult counterparts in the 1970s; but contemporary magazines, with their focus on non-fiction and activities, have never, in Kelly's view, reached the literary acclaim enjoyed by their 18th-century predecessors.

Little magazines may be considered as part of American mass magazine history because *en masse* they make up quite a mass. Through a collection of essay-memoirs of representative literary

---

[7]Agnes Repplier, "American Magazines," *Yale Review* 16 (1926-1927): 261-274.

magazine editors from 1950 through 1978, *The Little Magazine in America* (1978), editors Elliott Anderson and Mary Kinzie illustrated how the various types of little magazines communicated with their audiences. As part of assessing their meaning and value, editor and poet Michael Anania concluded in the introductory essay, "Of Living Belfry and Rampart," that any historical interpretation of little magazines since 1950 required that the literary historian look beyond literature into the realms of psychology and political science. Anania's essay was built around an incident in which a Russian magazine editor on tour of America happened to visit a small-press publisher's warehouse in Chicago. After surveying the great quantity of titles and learning of the average circulation figures for literary magazines, the editor posed the question: Why so many? This prefatory essay and the essays following form an attempt to respond to this question, one which could apply to any specialized magazine. Why so many literary magazines for so few readers? In response Anania referred back to the beginning of the century when little magazines were gaining in number and importance. The reasons in 1900 were the same as in 1978: "Because that's how it is for literature committed to change. . . . [Little magazines] give a place to writing for which no other place has been made."[8]

The Economic School
Economic historians explained magazine history with an eye trained on the financial aspects of publishing. Some, writing from a business perspective, especially praised the magazine industry for its contributions to America's free-enterprise system, as well as the impact of magazine advertising on increasing the American standard of living to the highest in the world. Unlike the works of ideological historians writing on other topics in mass communication history, the works of Economic historians were usually neutral or positive in their assessment of the effects of economic and financial interests on the magazine publishing industry, and in their analysis of the relationship between magazines and advertising. Quantitative analyses of trends in readership, ownership, and circulation figures, as well as works on successful publishers and magazine management practices, also were popular with historians in this school.

The exploration of commercial aspects in mass magazine publishing received detailed treatment in Theodore Peterson's *Magazines in the Twentieth Century*, published in 1957 and followed with subsequent revisions. Peterson's historical approach, documented in the book with circulation figures, profit and loss statements, and

---

[8]Elliott Anderson and Mary Kinzie, eds., *The Little Magazine in America: A Modern Documentary History* (Stamford CT: Pushcart/Frieman, 1978), 22.

critical analyses of editorial formulas, suggested that the "accomplishments of magazines resulted from their twofold nature as an editorial medium and as an adjunct of the marketing system."[9] Even though this relationship had the positive effect of improving the lives of consumers, Peterson, unlike several other Economic historians, criticized the influence that advertising exercised in shaping editorial opinion and magazine content. In some cases, commercial magazines created and promoted mainstream values and ideologies in response to the conservative ideals of their advertisers. However, these strengths and weaknesses considered, Peterson was convinced of the social and educational value of mass magazines, both as entertainment media and as vehicles for the dissemination of ideas and opinion that guarantee the important free flow of information in a democracy.

A. J. van Zuilen assessed the impact of technology on the decline and demise of important mass magazines in *The Life Cycle of Magazines* (1977). He looked at magazines between 1946 and 1972 and determined that the American mass magazine was a well-liked, well-known, and trusted institution that could create and inform national audiences. Yet, the nature of the mass magazine made it vulnerable to certain patterns of economic influence in its life cycle. Borrowing from the life cycle theories of other historians such as Arnold Toynbee in *A Study of History* (1946), van Zuilen proposed that the life cycles of magazines contained five stages: development, growth, maturity, saturation, and decline and death. His cyclical theory emphasized that the developmental stage, when a great deal of money must be spent toward marketing and promotion, as the most critical for a magazine. After studying the publishing careers of four quality mass magazines, *Collier's*, *Saturday Evening Post*, *Look*, and *Life*, in terms of his life-cycle criteria, van Zuilen concluded that it was possible for even the best magazines to outlive their usefulness.

Discussion

The study of magazine history, a relative new field compared with some other areas of mass communication history, faces some of the handicaps of a young area. There is a need, for instance, for a comprehensive bibliography; more interpretive studies, especially those that explain the social mediating power of mass magazines; and more research into areas such as the development of religious and foreign-language periodicals. Despite the fact, however, that much work waits to be done, historians have raised a number of intriguing questions about the nature of magazines and the various influ-

---

[9]Theodore Peterson, *Magazines in the Twentieth Century*, 2nd ed. (Urbana: University of Illinois Press, 1964), 441.

ences operating on them. Other questions need to be asked.

1. What was the relationship between advertising and magazines?

2. What accounted for the development of mass-circulation women's magazines?

3. How did advertising shape the character of American women's magazines? Did advertising dollars assure the health of these and other specialized magazines?

4. How did the appearance of radio, and later television, affect the mass magazine's entertainment potential from the points of view of both publishers and advertisers?

5. Were certain magazines institutions of acculturation, or were they products of business enterprise?

6. With these questions, the key one in magazine history—as with other areas of mass communication history—deals with the essential nature of magazines. What was that nature? Were magazines essentially products of culture, literary vehicles, or economic products?

7. Whatever the nature was, what were the primary reasons that magazines possessed it?

Readings

Cultural School

Mott, Frank Luther, Ch. 1, "The End of a Century," pp. 1-14, *A History of American Magazines 1885-1905*, Vol. IV. Cambridge, MA: Belknap Press of Harvard University Press, 1957.

Schmidt, Dorothy, "Magazines, Technology, and American Culture," *Journal of American Culture* 3 (Spring 1980): 3-16.

Tassin, Algernon, Ch. 14, "The End of the Century," pp. 340-359, *The Magazine in America*. New York: Dodd, Mead, 1916.

Wood, James Playsted, Ch. 33, "Conclusion," pp. 452-468, *Magazines in the United States*. New York: Ronald Press, 1971.

Literary School

Anania, Michael, "Of Living Belfry and Rampart: On American Literary Magazines Since 1950," pp. 6-23, *The Little Magazine in America: A Modern Documentary History*, Elliott Anderson and Mary Kinzie, eds.. Stamford, CT: Pushcart/Ray Frieman, 1978.

Felker, Clay S., "Life Cycles in the Age of Magazines," *Antioch Review* 29 (Spring 1969): 7-24.

Fleming, Herbert E., "Magazines of a Market-Metropolis: Being a History of the Literary Periodicals and Literary Interests of Chicago," Part 1, *American Journal of Sociology* 11 (1905-1906): 377-408.

Kelly, R. Gordon, ed., "Introduction," pp 19-29, *Children's Periodicals of the United States*. Westport, CT: Greenwood Press, 1984.

Repplier, Agnes, "American Magazines," *Yale Review* 16 (1926-1927): 261-274.

Economic School

Peterson, Theodore, Ch. 15, "Magazines 1900-64: An Assessment," pp. 441-451, *Magazines in the Twentieth Century*, 2nd ed. Urbana: University of Illinois Press, 1964.

Taft, William H., Ch. 8, "Mass Magazines: *Life* to *People*," pp. 143-156, *American Magazines for the 1980s*. New York: Hastings House, 1982.

Tebbel, John, Ch. 3, "The Rise of the Magazine Business 1850-1905," pp. 195-202, *The American Magazine: A Compact History*. New York: Hawthorn, 1969.

van Zuilen, A. J., Ch. 5, "The Life Cycles of Magazines," pp. 268-311, *The Life Cycle of Magazines: A Historical Study of the Decline and Fall of the General Interest Mass Audience Magazine in the United States During the Period 1946-1972*. The Netherlands: Graduate Press-Unithoorn, 1977.

19

The Muckrakers, 1901-1917:
Defenders of Conservatism or Liberal Reformers?

The domination that industry came to exert over American life in the late 19th century resulted in a movement for broad reform. The movement reached its peak between 1901 and 1912 and generally is considered to have ended with the United States' entry into World War I in 1917. The reforms that were advocated covered a wide range of problems and not all reformers agreed on all reforms, but their reform programs in general came to be known as the Progressive movement. Although the movement had adherents throughout the country, it was centered in the growing cities; and its backbone was composed of middle-class, white-collar professionals such as businessmen, lawyers, and publishers.

The Progressive movement grew out of the criticism and discontent over conditions related to industrialism. Above all, people feared the power of the huge corporations then emerging as the dominant factor in American economic life. Big business, banks, and industry exercised overwhelming power not only over the economy; but as businessmen achieved greater wealth, they turned to government to protect their interests. Soon, they gained control of the government. Progressivism therefore became a movement aimed primarily at attempting to take control from business and return it to the middle class.

In this reform movement, the print media played a pivotal role. The primary technique the reformers used was exposure, and it was the press that exposed the problems that needed correction. The exposé was the most prominent feature of journalism of the period, and the technique so famous that it was given a name: *muckraking*. President Theodore Roosevelt applied the term, claiming the investigative journalists were like the man with the muck-rake in John Bunyan's *Pilgrim's Progress* who, continually looking down, saw only the filth and not the celestial crown offered him. The journalist muckraker, Roosevelt implied, focused only on the bad and overlooked the positive aspects of American life.

The most important muckraking works appeared in magazines. Among them, *McClure's* led the field. Although its owner, S. S. McClure, may have thought of muckraking as a popular and convenient way to increase profits, he gave writers adequate time and money to investigate topics in depth. Other prominent muckraking magazines were *Collier's, Cosmopolitan, Ladies' Home Journal, Everybody's*, and *Arena*. Of the more than 2,000 muckraking articles that appeared in magazines, the following typified those that stood out: Lincoln Steffens' "Shame of the Cities" (*McClure's*), Ida Tarbell's "History of the Standard Oil Company" (*McClure's*), Ray Stannard Baker's "Railroads on Trial" (*McClure's*), and David Graham Phillips' "Treason of the Senate" (*Cosmopolitan*). Book authors Upton Sinclair (*The Jungle*) and Frank Norris (*The Octopus* and *The Pit*) also gained fame.

Despite its very visible successes, muckraking declined rapidly. By 1912 many poorly researched articles had made readers question the credibility of the muckrakers, and the government had remedied many of the ills through passage of laws and establishment of regulatory agencies. The public therefore could see little need for the muckraking magazines, and readership dropped. Advertisers whose companies had been attacked sometimes withdrew advertising. World War I erupted, and in 1917 the United States entered it, diverting concern from domestic problems to the battlefield. Although some newspapers and magazines continued to crusade, many editors had lost faith in crusading as a remedy for social ills, whereas some believed it was at best only a means of building circulation.

Despite its short life, Progressivism had made some substantial achievements. Much of the credit must be given to the muckrakers. The work of Progressivism had rested on the journalism of exposure. Muckrakers therefore had been important instruments in encouraging legislation to correct social ills. In the long run, they may have helped move American opinion away from an emphasis on material success to an emphasis on social responsibility, helping restore the balance between powerful business interests and the middle class.

Most historians considered muckraking within the context of the Progressive movement. Although a handful studied the press in terms of the development of professional techniques such as interviewing and writing, in general historians analyzed it as an aspect of the reform impulse of 1901-1917. The essential difference in interpretations was over the question of whether muckrakers were liberal social reformers or conservative advocates of middle-class values and interests.

The Progressive School
There was little disagreement among historians about either the

Progressive movement or muckraking until after World War II. Most historians were writing within the Progressive school of interpretation and placed the reformers within a positive liberal American tradition. In their view, muckrakers clearly were on the side of the "people" in an attempt to challenge the dominant and corrupting position of big business and a privileged class in American life. Progressive historians reasoned that reformers were attempting to restore both political and economic democracy to the nation.

Such was the approach employed in the pioneering study of muckraking, Cornelius Regier's *The Era of the Muckrakers*, published in 1932. Told in terms of how the muckrakers exposed numerous social, economic, and political evils, Regier's work examined the conditions that stimulated muckraking, the rise of popular-priced magazines which provided a medium for exposés, the subjects the muckrakers exposed, the success of muckraking, and the reasons for its decline. Muckraking, Regier wrote, was "the inevitable result of decades of indifference to the illegalities and immoralities attendant upon the industrial development of America." Americans were in a crusading mood, recognizing that the chief culprits were the selfish and privileged business interests.

Regier's only reservations about muckraking were over the motives of some publishers and the effectiveness of the techniques. Magazine owners found muckraking to be "a paying business" and sometimes promoted sensationalism solely for commercial purposes. Regier also concluded that muckraking was "essentially a superficial attack upon fundamental problems," as he exhibited the liberal view that more was needed than mere exposé to alleviate the wealthy class' threat to America.

Still, Regier argued that "the liberal movement" had triumphed in the numerous reforms between 1900 and 1915, virtually all made possible by the muckrakers. "It is impossible," he concluded, "to prove that business methods were bettered in such and such a way by such and such an attack, but it is quite possible to argue that the whole tone of business in the United States was raised because of the persistent exposures of corruption and injustice."

The class-conflict explanation of the Progressive school was presented even more forthrightly by Louis Filler, one of the most prolific historians of the Progressive era and muckraking. In the 1939 study *The Muckrakers: Crusaders for American Liberalism*, a book sometimes considered the standard work on the muckrakers, Filler presented a classic liberal, conflict, and anti-big-business interpretation. Although he held views similar to Regier's, he credited the muckrakers with a greater influence on bringing about reform. Muckraking, he said, was the natural response that was expected to the abuse the industrialization of America presented. In the introduction to the 1976 edition of *The Muckrakers*, Filler observed that the journalists were "neither radical nor conservative" but provided "the several social sectors of society with knowledge and understanding." Dealing with "facts and not theory," they were tough-minded, non-ideological investigators who "wrote because there was a demand for their work, and because they wanted more reform and more democracy." After the publication of Phillips' "Treason of the Senate" series in 1906, which marked muckraking's highpoint, the journalists shifted their emphasis away from exposure to reforms—reforms that were "so broad, so interrelated, that they predicted a full change in American life and thought." The muckrakers were so effective that big business considered them dangerous and finally "deliberately planned and accomplished" the destruction of muckraking magazines by an advertising boycott. Despite the fact that the industrial class opposed them so intensely, the muckrakers accomplished considerable change and progress. Although "these crusaders," Filler said, "did not transform the nation, they modernized it. No other band of social workers in any country or time ever accomplished more."[1]

The Marxist School

The opposition to the Progressive interpretation came from several historical schools spanning the range from radical to liberal to conservative. In the same year that Regier published his Progressive study of the muckrakers, the Marxist historian John Chamberlain published his critical analysis *Farewell to Reform* (1932), a full-scale attack on American reform in general. He criticized Progressivism because of its superficial approach to solving deep-seated problems when radical solutions were needed. The Progressive movement was a horrendous failure, he said, because its followers really desired to return America to a golden past of virtue, when no such return was possible. Capitalists were motivated by self-interest rather than virtue and could be loosed of their grip on America only by wrenching changes in the social, political, and economic structure of the nation.

In general, however, Chamberlain was not quite so harsh on muckrakers as on other reformers. Although some, such as Phillips and William Randolph Hearst, were in exposé journalism simply for money, others were sincere, "doing some harm, but an incalculable amount of good in the way of educating the American people to realities." Indeed, muckraking "provided the basis for the entire movement toward social democracy that came to its head" during the first administration of President Woodrow Wilson. Despite

---

[1]Louis Filler, *The Muckrakers: Crusaders for American Liberalism*, rev. ed. (University Park: Pennsylvania State University Press, 1976), viii, 5, 217, 260, 170.

such accomplishments, however, muckrakers in the end were relatively powerless to solve the underlying problems of the system, such as the rising cost of living and the nature of business. "They could do nothing, ultimately," Chamberlain argued, "to right any of the fundamental wrongs."[2]

Despite such a critique of Progressivism, not all radical historians so negatively condemned the movement. They sometimes praised individual muckrakers, with the most highly acclaimed being Lincoln Steffens, whom they described as a radical himself. In the 1974 work *Lincoln Steffens: A Biography*, for example, Justin Kaplan reasoned that Steffens was intent on revealing the sins of a corrupt system and that he believed ownership and distribution of property were of critical importance in creating corruption and other shortcomings of the American democracy.

The Liberal School

The fullest critique of the Progressive movement came, however, not from radical historians but from both Liberal and Neo-Conservative ones after World War II. Oddly enough, the criticism of the historians of the two schools seemed similar in many respects. Both believed that the Progressive school's class-conflict interpretation of American history was simplistic. Neo-Conservative historians argued that there were no extraordinary disagreements among various factions in America's past. Instead, Americans generally had agreed on the broad Enlightenment tenets of natural rights, popular sovereignty, individualism, private property, and political liberalism. Because these beliefs, according to Neo-Conservative historians, were so universally accepted, they accounted for a conservative tradition. Therefore, they argued, American history took place within a context of consensus rather than conflict about basic principles.

Many Liberal historians reasoned, on the other hand, that although there had been class conflict, the muckrakers and other adherents of the Progressive movement actually were conservatives themselves—rather than liberals, as Progressive historians had described them—and were more interested in their own positions than in the welfare of the masses.

Both schools therefore discredited muckrakers as moral crusaders on behalf of the "people" against special privilege. The question left for the re-interpretation of muckraking became a basic one: What did muckrakers and other Progressives stand for if not for equality and democratic reform?

The most provocative answer was given by Richard Hofstadter,

---

[2]John Chamberlain, *Farewell to Reform* (New York: John Day, 1932), 127, 128, 142.

an eminent historian who in a number of books attempted to dissect the inadequacies of American liberalism. A liberal himself, he believed that liberalism had failed because it was founded on a system of beliefs that emphasized individual interests rather than the welfare of society as a whole. Progressivism therefore had failed to face up to the problems that an industrialized nation presented. In *The Age of Reform: From Bryan to F.D.R.* (1955) Hofstadter argued that the Progressive movement was not aimed at liberal reform and adjusting society to a new industrial age. Instead, Progressives acted as they did because of their anxiety over their social, political, and economic status; that is, they viewed with alarm the role big business had gained and were attempting to obtain for themselves a secure position in society. Thus, the Progressive movement really was an attempt by middle-class individuals of character to restore traditional values and systems which they believed had existed before the industrialization of America in the late 1800s.

Muckrakers fit squarely into the Progressive frame of mind. Publishers used muckraking primarily as a way to make their magazines profitable, and most of the journalists "were simply writers or reporters working on commission and eager to do well what was asked of them." In all, they were "moderate men who intended to propose no radical remedies," and their "chief appeal was not to desperate social needs but to mass sentiments of responsibility, indignation, and guilt," typical concerns which traditionally had influenced American thought. Thus, Progressivism, which possessed a narrow and undemocratic ideology, was not a liberal movement at all, but one intended to recapture America for a middle class alienated and dispossessed by rapid industrial changes. For Hofstadter, the class struggle Progressive historians had described never had taken place, and the Progressive era left no liberal legacy.[3]

One of the leading advocates of the interpretation of Progressives as members of a middle class attempting to halt its decline and reestablish its leadership in society was George Mowry. In a number of works on Progressivism and muckraking,[4] he argued that middle-class and older aristocratic Americans, victims in the social upheaval brought on by industrialism, led movements for re-

---

[3]Richard Hofstadter, *The Age of Reform* (New York: Knopf, 1955), 194, 196.

[4]George E. Mowry, *Theodore Roosevelt and the Progressive Movement* (Madison, WI: 1946); Mowry, "The California Progressive and His Rationale: A Study in Middle Class Politics," *Mississippi Valley Historical Review* 31 (1949): 239-250; Mowry, *The Progressive Era, 1900-1920: The Reform Persuasion* (Washington: American History Assoc., 1972); and Mowry and Judson E. Grenier, "Introduction," in Mowry and Grenier, eds., *The Treason of the Senate* (Chicago: Quandrangle Books, 1964).

forms in politics, government, and business in order to take power from the new industrial capitalists and restore their own social position. In their attempts, however, they were not truly liberal, for they proposed no fundamental economic changes or drastic alterations in the structure of American society.

The Hofstadter-Mowry thesis as applied specifically to journalism can be seen most clearly in Robert Bannister's biography of one of the leading magazine muckrakers, *Ray Stannard Baker: The Mind and Thought of a Progressive* (1966). Intended as a history of the intellect of an influential journalist, Bannister's study explained Baker as a reformer with deep concern for social problems, but also as one who preferred moderate reform measures to radical ones. Typical of Progressives, he was concerned about problems of the 20th century but had a 19th-century philosophy about what ideal conditions should be. Because of his dated outlook, determined by his rural, middle-class, Protestant background, he could do little more than react with anguish to the urban problems confronting America.

Taking similar approaches, other historians found that, among other things, muckrakers reacted negatively to a movement for women's rights and some magazines were more interested in economic survival than social and journalistic integrity.

The Neo-Conservative School
Neo-Conservative historians, however, found such conservatism on the part of Progressives a source of positive achievements. Muckrakers, they argued, comprised a constructive force precisely because they did advocate traditional moral and political principles and shunned radical changes in a structure that essentially was good.

The two major works this school produced came, coincidentally, in the same year, 1974. In the biography *Ida M. Tarbell*, Mary Tomkins declared that the author of the Standard Oil exposé was primarily in her philosophical outlook a defender of traditional, Puritan New England values. Her attack on Standard Oil and its owner, John D. Rockefeller, resulted from her concern for morals, democracy, justice, and individual independence. Rockefeller, Tarbell believed, lacked concern for morality and had no compunction against using ruthless methods to drive his competitors out of business, as had happened to her own father and other middle-class oil producers.

Similarly, in the biography *Lincoln Steffens*, Russell Horton explained that Steffens, who some historians had considered as the most radical of the muckrakers, was not so extreme in his beliefs as he was concerned with improving social conditions in the best of American values and traditions. "Steffens's success as a muckraker," Horton wrote, "indeed the success of muckrakers in general, was based on a direct appeal to the moral and civic pride of the mass middle class rather than any intellectual challenge. With a few notable exceptions, the exposé journalists of the Progressive era scrupulously avoided even the suggestion of any radical changes in the basic arrangement of society. Rather, they emphasized the need for a rejuvenation of traditional Protestant values."[5]

At the same time, the reputation of muckraking suffered in the hands of another, although small group of Neo-Conservative historians. Some business-oriented historians denied that business as a whole was bad and instead argued that it frequently had improved the overall conditions of American life. Although sometimes acknowledging that muckrakers had served admirably in bringing about some much-needed reforms, these historians claimed that muckrakers frequently were amateurish in their understanding of problems and business conditions and at times aimed their darts at targets that did not deserve attack. James Cassedy, for example, in studying Samuel Hopkins Adams, who had exposed the patent medicine industry, argued that although Adams was more positive than most muckrakers and had served an important function by educating the public, he was not very knowledgeable about medicine. From muckraker he progressed to medical writer, but in the 1920s he finally got out of the field because he could not keep up with the advances in medicine and because more knowledgeable writers were available.[6] Similarly, Paul Uselding, a historian of industry and economics, argued that in their attacks on the mortality rate in industry the muckrakers exaggerated the dangers. Without possessing an adequate understanding of the death rate or of comparative statistics for mortality in other areas, they misled the public and unfairly attacked industry.[7]

The Neo-Progressive School

Not all historians joined the attack on the liberal interpretation of the Progressive historians. A number took issue with the Hofstadter and Mowry interpretations and attempted to reassess the liberal nature of muckraking. These historians considered Progressivism and muckraking to have been sincere attempts to deal with social problems. They tried to defend the muckrakers against a number of criticisms, such as their use of sensationalism and that publishers such as McClure published muckraking articles simply because it

---

[5]Russell M. Horton, *Lincoln Steffens* (New York: Twayne, 1974), 69.

[6]James H. Cassedy, "Muckraking and Medicine, Samuel Hopkins Adams," *American Quarterly* 16 (1964): 85-99.

[7]Paul Uselding, "In Dispraise of Muckrakers: United States Occupational Mortality, 1890-1910," in *Research in Economic History* I (Greenwich, CT: 1976).

was financially astute to do so. They instead viewed muckrakers as advocates of democracy, optimistic believers in the possibility for progress, dedicated social reformers, and compassionate crusaders.

The most thorough elaboration of this Neo-Progressive interpretation was provided by David Chalmers in *The Social and Political Ideas of the Muckrakers* (1964). The study was intended as a refutation of the "status anxiety" and the critical Neo-Conservative interpretations. Contrary to claims critical historians made, the muckrakers, Chalmers argued, did attempt to gain worthy achievements and perform worthwhile services. They were interested in more than commercial sensationalism, and they offered more than moral indignation over the problems of society. They proposed specific solutions. After analyzing the economic philosophies of 13 muckrakers, Chalmers concluded that their views covered a wide range from socialist to moderate. Generally, however, they believed that society's problems were caused by the failure of businessmen to accept their social responsibility.

The Communication-Effects School

Although the ideology of muckrakers was the primary concern of historians, another area of interest was the effectiveness of muckrakers in bringing about reform. Generally, the Progressive and Liberal historians assumed that muckrakers had been influential. Even most historians critical of muckrakers, such as Chamberlain and Hofstadter, credited the writers with successful exposure, which they believed was the greatest achievement of the Progressive movement. Although the question of effectiveness was implicit in a number of studies, it was of primary concern in a few others. Those historians who pointedly argued in favor of the effectiveness of muckrakers did so as part of their attempt to rescue the reputation of muckrakers from Hofstadter and other critical historians. On the other hand, most of the attack on the muckrakers' effectiveness came from historians who were not so much concerned with ideology as with persuasiveness theories of mass communication. These historians primarily took objection to the long-held assumption among media historians that the press exercised great influence on public opinion.

David Chalmers presented the most salient argument in favor of the view that muckrakers were effective. In "The Muckrakers and the Growth of Corporate Power: A Study in Constructive Journalism" (1959) he attempted to analyze why the muckrakers were important and concluded that it was because of their critical attitude toward big business. Admitting, as some historians had claimed, that muckrakers occasionally used questionable tactics such as sensationalism, Chalmers nevertheless argued that the reason some historians had underestimated the influence of muckrakers was that the muckrakers were journalists, not philosophers. Historians, he said, had tended to overlook writing that may have seemed temporal in favor of the more lasting works of individuals such as social thinkers and political leaders. The muckrakers' work, however, "was adapted to the nature of the popular magazines," and even though "few writers began with a broad analysis of the national ills"—since their work "tended to develop in installment fashion"—they still wound up realizing that the small chapters they wrote were part of a greater national problem. By informing the public, furthermore, they laid "the popular groundwork of public concern which resulted in many reforms of the next half century." The fact, Chalmers reasoned, that muckrakers "presented no innovations to the world of social theory and that their functions were often crude and unsophisticated does not detract from the importance of the role that they played as educators of the public. If the picture they painted was rough and a little overdrawn, it was because they were describing a new business dynamo at the period of its greatest and most unabashed power. The significance of the muckrakers is that they had positive views to express and were able to do so over a decade in the popular magazines of the nation. These journalists made the public aware of the degree to which corruption had become general in the national life."[8]

Richard B. Kielbowicz presented a diametrically opposing point of view in "The Limits of the Press as an Agent of Reform: Minneapolis, 1900-1905" (1982), a study aimed specifically at the impact newspapers had in ameliorating corruption in city government. After analyzing a case involving the Minneapolis press, Kielbowicz concluded that newspapers were not as successful in bringing about reform as historians believe, and he argued that historians should be cautious in ascribing influence to the press. Historians, he said, tend to exaggerate the effect that press exposure has on bringing about reform because of two reasons: (a) historians tend to "select obtrusive incidents of change for their study," and (b) they do not adequately specify their standards for measuring change. As a result, instances in which obviously the press never brought any changes are neglected, and historians tend to claim in other instances that the press was responsible for change anytime change occurred.[9]

---

[8]David M. Chalmers, "The Muckrakers and the Growth of Corporate Power: A Study in Constructive Journalism," *American Journal of Economics and Sociology* 18 (1959): 299, 310-311.

[9]Richard B. Kielbowicz, "The Limits of the Press as an Agent of Reform: Minneapolis, 1900-1905," *Journalism Quarterly* 59 (1982): 21.

Discussion

Among the various topics in media history, muckraking has attracted the interest of more historians from outside mass communication than any other topic has. As a result, few topics have shown as much historiographical vitality as muckraking, and a number of questions central to the nature of muckraking remain the subjects of lively debate.

1. Were muckrakers, as the Progressive historians originally claimed, true liberal reformers with the correction of social ills foremost in their motives?

2. Is the view of Progressive historians overly romanticized because they agreed with the goals of the muckrakers?

3. Were muckrakers, as both Marxist and some Neo-Conservative historians argued, superficial in their understanding of problems and their proposals for solutions?

4. Is a Marxist critique valid in the face of the fact that the class struggle as proposed by Marxists never marked American history?

5. Were muckrakers really concerned, as Liberal historians such as Hofstadter and Mowry suggested, not primarily with solving problems but with re-establishing their position in society?

6. Is it possible for historians to apply psychoanalysis, which is the basis of the "status anxiety" theory, to historical subjects? If such analysis faces unreasonable difficulty, is there any basis for the status-anxiety explanation?

7. Were muckrakers—if they did base their motives and approaches on traditional values, as Liberal historians claimed—asserting principles, as some Neo-Conservative historians argued, that in the long run were the only truly effective means of bringing about reform?

Readings

Progressive and Neo-Progressive Schools

Chalmers, David M., Ch. 10, "The Celestial Crown," pp. 104-116, *The Social and Political Ideas of the Muckrakers*. New York: Citadel Press, 1964.

Filler, Louis, Ch. 18, "The Search for Democracy," pp. 234-244, *The Muckrakers: Crusaders for American Liberalism*, rev. ed. University Park: Pennsylvania State University Press, 1976.

Lyon, Peter, Part 3, "The Magazine [parts 13 and 14]," pp. 210-230, *Success Story: The Life and Times of S. S. McClure*. New York: Scribner's, 1963.

Regier, C.C., Ch. 10, "The Muckrakers and the Underdog," pp. 147-157, *The Era of the Muckrakers*. Chapel Hill: University of North Carolina Press, 1932.

Marxist School

Chamberlain, John, Ch. 4, "The Muck-rake Pack," pp. 119-143, *Farewell to Reform*. New York: John Day, 1932.

Kaplan, Justin, Ch. 8, "The Man with the Muckrake," pp. 134-152, *Lincoln Steffens: A Biography*. New York: Simon and Schuster, 1974.

Liberal School

Bannister, Robert, Ch. 5, "Muckraking," pp. 86-107, *Ray Stannard Baker: The Mind and Thought of a Progressive*. New Haven, CT: Yale University Press, 1966.

Hofstadter, Richard, Part 5, Ch. 2, "Muckraking: The Revolution in Journalism," pp. 186-198, *The Age of Reform: From Bryan to F.D. R..* New York: Knopf, 1955.

Hynes, Terry, "Magazine Portrayals of Women, 1911-1930," *Journalism Monographs* 72 (1981).

Mowry, George E., and Judson E. Grenier, eds., "Introduction," pp. 9-46, *The Treason of the Senate*. Chicago: Quadrangle Books, 1964.

Reynolds, Robert D., "The 1906 Campaign to Sway Muckraking Periodicals," *Journalism Quarterly* 56 (1979): 513-520, 589.

Wilson, Harold, Ch. 8, "The Second Decade: The Problem," pp. 148-167, *McClure's Magazine and the Muckrakers*. Princeton, NJ: Princeton University Press, 1970.

Neo-Conservative School

Cassedy, James H., "Muckraking and Medicine, Samuel Hopkins Adams," *American Quarterly* 16 (1964): 85-99.

Evensen, Bruce, "The Evangelical Origins of the Muckrakers," *American Journalism* 6 (1989): 5-29.

Tomkins, Mary E., Ch. 4, "The History of the Standard Oil Company," pp. 59-77, *Ida M. Tarbell*. New York: Twayne, 1974.

Uselding, Paul, "In Dispraise of Muckrakers: United States Occupational Mortality, 1890-1910," in *Research in Economic History I* (1976): 334-371.

20

The Media in Trying Times, 1917-1945: Propagandists, Patriots, or Professionals?

In the 20th century, the United States moved into one of the most extended critical times in its history. A global war was followed by a decade of economic depression, followed by a second world war. In such crucial and devastating events, the American media naturally were caught up.

In addition to covering the nation's involvement in World War I, journalists had to decide what their reaction to America's participation should be. As the debilitating depression of the 1930s set in, journalists found themselves facing another national crisis and had to decide how they stood on major social, economic, and political issues. How were they to view sweeping changes in government's role in social and economic programs? What should be their role in regard to racial injustice? How were they to stand on the question of the position organized labor should have in American industry and politics? Should the media support the causes of labor and minorities, or should they accept the beneficent influence that business had in both American society as a whole and the media in particular? Similar questions confronted the media during the second world war. Should the media support American military participation in wars? Should they accept censorship of information that comes with wartime? Should the media oppose war on the grounds of the damage it does to liberal reform and libertarian ideals? Or should the media simply not get involved in any such questions and remain instead professionally detached?

These same questions confronted historians of the American media in the critical period of 1917-1945. The answers they gave depended to a large extent on the conceptions of the nature of media and American society which they brought to the study of media history.

In general, historians' conceptions defined three divergent approaches to explaining and evaluating the media during times of national crisis. The first approach was characterized by a Progressive or liberal viewpoint and embodied a conflict view of history.

Progressive historians believed differences among sections of American society were the underlying causes of change in history. They usually supported the rights of labor and of unionized journalists, opposed the malignant influence that big-business media owners had on journalistic practices, opposed or only reluctantly supported American involvement in war because they believed war halted liberal reform and killed responsible reporting, and supported libertarian views of freedom of expression and liberal views on social justice.

In a contrasting approach, Consensus historians played down the differences among Americans and emphasized the ideas and beliefs they shared in common. These historians generally were nationalistic in outlook and favored media philosophies and activities that they believed worked for the good of the nation as a whole. Most argued that the nation's good was served by its participation in both world wars and that the media served well by supporting the nation during wartime, accepted the need for limited wartime censorship, argued that the media did an adequate job of informing the public during times of major crisis, and argued that radicalism among journalists was not effective.

The third school of historians employed a Developmental approach to media history and assumed that the proper stance of the media should be neither liberal nor conservative, that instead the media should be apolitical. The history of the media in the 20th century, they believed, was not primarily the story of how the media stood on issues, but of how they performed their professional role as informer of the public, supporter of press freedom, and watchdog over government. These historians, therefore, attempted to analyze the media of 1917-1945 in terms of how they advanced in their performance of strictly journalistic practices.

Historical evaluation of the media in these trying times depended on historians' views on the role the media should play in society in general and during crises in particular. Progressive historians believed the media should help bring about greater social and political equality among segments of society, whereas Consensus historians believed the media should attempt to unify the various groups in America. Developmental historians reasoned that the role of the media was a professional one that should be unrelated to ideological arguments.

The Progressive School
The most aggressive historians in arguing their point of view were those who comprised the Progressive school. Approaching history with an outlook that favored liberal reform and their particular brand of humanitarianism, they opposed American participation in World War I because they believed that it did little to improve condi-

tions at home, that America got involved in the war because of British and chauvinistic propaganda, and that war resulted in dangerous censorship and irresponsible, jingoistic journalism. Although they were not as hostile about U. S. involvement in World War II, they still were concerned about nativism and jingoism in the media and about the war's effect on journalism. On the issue of the media's role during the Great Depression and the government's attempts to alleviate many of the problems the depression caused, Progressive historians generally were extremely critical of the purely financial motivations of media owners and their failure to support President Franklin Roosevelt's New Deal policies. At the same time, historians were complimentary of journalists who worked for social reform and of specialized publications such as labor newspapers that supported workers and the underprivileged.

The view Progressive historians were to take was argued forcefully by media critics of the 1930s, who believed that newspaper owners had sold their souls to capitalism and the wealthy class. Typical of the criticism was the presidential address Kenneth E. Olson delivered to the 1935 national meeting of the American Association of Teachers of Journalism. Entitling his speech "The Newspaper in Times of Social Changes," Olson argued that media owners should be using their profits to help the less fortunate members of society, that the media should be "a champion of their rights." Approaching the social role of the media with a Progressive, pro-New Deal point of view, he criticized newspapers for becoming "the voice of an institution representing stockholders interested in profits." Increasingly, he declared, "as it has demonstrated its effectiveness as an advertising medium, the newspaper has become the aide of business until today it is one of the foremost agencies in our American scheme of distribution. . . . I cannot avoid realizing the social significance of this development. As the newspaper has become dependent upon advertising it has become less dependent upon its readers and less concerned with their welfare."[1]

The most fully elaborated and one of the most trenchant Progressive attacks on the conservative media came from another New Deal supporter, Harold L. Ickes, Secretary of the Interior under Roosevelt and director of the Public Works Administration. In the 1939 book *America's House of Lords*, a caustic criticism of newspaper publishers who opposed the New Deal, Ickes argued that the shortcomings of the press were the result of modern publishers being businessmen who were more interested in running their newspapers as business enterprises than journals of news. Publishers, he said, imparted to their newspapers an "upper stratum interest and

---

[1]Kenneth E. Olson, "The Newspaper in Times of Social Changes," *Journalism Quarterly* 12 (1935): 9-19.

outlook." They considered newspapers primarily to be private profit-seeking businesses rather than public-spirited agencies concerned about social good. As a result, the emphasis on business endangered the free press required by democracy and led to lack of fairness in newspaper pages, unreliability, suppression of information, and fabrication of news. Other critics echoed these charges, claiming that the emphasis on obtaining advertising dollars and making more and more profits finally distorted the concept of "freedom of the press" into "freedom of the press to make money."

Such arguments against the conservative, money-oriented media typified numerous studies by Progressive historians. They painted conservative journalists as reactionaries of the far right and argued that newspapers were nativist, that they sometimes had used inaccurate and distorted news reporting in attempts to court advertisers, that selfish motives on the part of publishers determined newspapers' editorial and news treatment of major public issues, and that conservative publishers opposed Roosevelt's policies primarily because of personal financial interests.

On the issue of the media's role and performance during the two global wars, most Progressive historians argued that war was either unnecessary or damaging to the nation's ideals and that it had a detrimental effect on the media and journalistic standards. They were concerned especially about the increase in censorship that war brought on, the deleterious effect and misuse of propaganda, the tendency for the media's reporting of war to be biased and inaccurate, and how the media fostered aggressive and discriminatory attitudes. The beginning of World War II served as a catalyst for historical work on the first world war, as historians showed a growing concern about the effect war has on the media and about how the media perform during wartime. In general, Progressive historians pointed out problems and failures of the press in World War I in the hope that such shortcomings would not be repeated with World War II.

In a study of the influence of propaganda in bringing about America's entry into World War I, published just two years before the nation entered the second war, H. C. Peterson decried the gullibility and the deplorable performance of journalists in serving as mouthpieces for British propaganda efforts. Such propaganda, he argued, was a major factor in getting America to enter the war. Peterson's book, *Propaganda for War: The Campaign Against Neutrality 1914-1917* (1939), which was written from a non-interventionist or isolationist viewpoint, was based on the argument that Americans went to war against Germany because they were gulled by British propaganda, that America's journalists were all too willing to promote the propaganda, and that British influence permeated the American media.

In the event America should enter World War II, Progressive historians attempted to find lessons from history to prevent the nation from repeating mistakes from earlier wars. One lesson was to be found in the history of censorship employed during World War I. Published only a few months before Japan attacked Pearl Harbor in December 1941, James R. Mock's *Censorship, 1917* typified liberal concern and provided the most prominent arguments against censorship that the Progressive school of historians wrote. Mock's intent was to examine America's experience with censorship in World War I and to draw from it some guidance for World War II. Although he found that absurdities occasionally marked the censorship of 1917, such instances were few, and rarely was censorship used to protect dishonest or incompetent officials. However, although reasoning that censorship during the first war had served a useful purpose, he believed that the real danger from wartime censorship lay in the threat to democratic government that resulted from carrying over into peacetime an oppressive attitude that war engendered. Thus, Mock argued, the system of censorship used during World War I led perniciously into peacetime repression after the war had ended. The censorship that followed the war—such as state and municipal ordinances limiting freedom of speech, and state and federal criminal syndicalism laws—was aimed primarily at preventing unpopular ideas from being expressed rather than at suppressing truly subversive action.

Of similar concern to later historians was the detrimental effect war had on media news coverage and journalists' tendencies to become advocates of their nations' actions rather than seekers and reporters of truth. The most pointed critique of the performance of the media during war was made by leftist historian Philip Knightly in *The First Casualty* (1975), a study of news coverage of conflicts from the Crimean War of 1853-1856 to the Vietnam War. The "first casualty" during war was truth, Knightly declared, for the war correspondent consistently trampled on truth and served more often as "hero, propagandist and mythmaker" than as journalist.

Rather than placing the blame on government and difficult wartime conditions, as some historians had done, Knightly concluded that the fault for bad reporting lay squarely on reporters. In wartime, correspondents forgot they were journalists and became instead part liar, part hero, part soldier, and part diplomat. Most were less concerned with truth than with scoops and glory, Knightly claimed, and acted as irresponsible adventurers, always ready to believe their own country's censors and propagandists. Because reporters were influenced by patriotism and ideology and had a team attitude with their fellow countrymen, they forsook truth, giving only warped accounts of reality. The end result was that they greatly damaged people's understanding. In World War I, for example, the

Allied media led people to believe simplistically that the war was one between two forces—one of pure good and the other of evil—and thus, in their devotion to nationalism rather than truth, had helped lead the world into war. For such failures, correspondents' misguided attitudes about their role as patriots and propagandists rather than as journalists were more culpable than the conditions—such as censorship, transportation difficulties, and hazardous situations—under which they operated.

Rather than trying to be glamorous adventurers and heroes for their countries, Knightly argued, war correspondents, like other good reporters, should attempt to find and tell the truth no matter what the consequences. In time of war, journalists' main allegiance should be to truth, he said; and journalism itself should be independent, critical, and analytical of the political, social, and economic causes and effects of war, rather than loyal to its nation. If the press had reported truthfully, Knightly claimed, the course of history would have been different, for the press for generations had been influential in determining whether wars were to begin.

Although many Progressive historians—or in the case of Knightly, radical—were critical of the mainstream of journalism, some found much to praise among particular journalists and incidents. Finding favor with these historians were Progressive journalists, labor-oriented newspapers, freedom of expression, anti-imperialism, and similar topics.

One of the most favored journalists was the New York *Evening Post's* liberal publisher, Oswald Garrison Villard. He was the grandson of the abolitionist William Lloyd Garrison and son of Henry Villard, the liberal owner of both the *Evening Post* and *The Nation* in the late 1800s. Progressive historians considered Oswald Villard the epitome of the media mogul who used his journal for the proper and grandest media cause, support of liberal reform and ideals. The liberal reputation of Villard was advocated most fully in D. Joy Humes' biography *Oswald Garrison Villard: Liberal of the 1920s* (1960). Reacting to the Consensus interpretation of American history which attempted to downplay sharp ideological differences in the nation's past, Humes argued that even in the conservative 1920s there were many liberal causes and that Villard was a true liberal and leader of many of the causes. Along with being a pacifist, he battled for human rights and dignity and for the extension of democracy to more groups of Americans. Because his philosophy was a modern liberalism, he always was willing to listen to ideas and experiment with new methods that might protect the underprivileged.

On the deepest level, Humes wrote, he was concerned with a "free flow of ideas." Liberty, Villard said, "means above all else tolerance," even of "bad taste and folly in public utterances." The role of the government therefore was not to attempt to repress expression but to protect the right to freedom of expression even in times of war.

Villard also believed strongly in a "kind of noblesse oblige—an effort on the part of the privileged class to have their privileges extended to others." This required support for such groups as immigrants and Black Americans. On the other hand, he opposed business' domination of politics and society and the favoritism that government showed business in such matters as a protective tariff.

Villard faced his greatest dilemma, however, with the two world wars. A pacifist, he could not favor war; but, according to Humes, neither was he an extremist who would hinder his nation in its quest for victory. Still, although he had no desire for the enemy to win, ultimately he believed that war never solved international problems and that there must be a better solution.

Other Progressive studies extolled the virtues of pacifist journalists; accused conservative publishers of being reactionary, distorting foreign reporting, and blindly arguing that Roosevelt wanted America to join the Allied cause in World War II so that the President could achieve his dreams of complete dictatorship; argued that the labor press succeeded in bringing news to the American public that other papers would not print; praised publications that supported the right of expression by people who objected to serving in the military; and praised the efforts of American journalists who exposed America's imperialistic intentions.

The Consensus School
Although the Progressive interpretation of history had a lengthy tradition, the fact itself that from 1917-1945 America faced major crises encouraged a diametrically opposing interpretation. With the nation confronting external threats and domestic problems, a large number of historians sought to present a picture of America and its media that was characterized by basic agreement and unity. These Consensus historians reasoned that America's past was marked more by general agreement than by conflict and that Americans, rather than being sundered by class differences, tended to be more united than divided. Although Americans from time to time might disagree on certain issues, their disagreements took place within a larger framework—such as a belief in democracy, human freedom, and constitutional government—that overshadowed their differences. Generally, Consensus historians claimed that American history was not marked by extreme differences among groups; and in their hands the Progressives' villains such as industrialists, businessmen, and big media owners were molded into less evil people who made constructive contributions to America, whereas Progressives' heroes such as reformers and the labor press were painted

as less idealistic and more egocentered. Forsaking the critical attitudes that had characterized much Progressive writing, Consensus historians tended to emphasize the achievements of America and its media, with the intent of showing a national unity among Americans.

The Consensus outlook had a major impact on the interpretation of numerous aspects of media history. Consensus historians explained the media's role in America's entry into the two world wars in terms of the general agreement among Americans that involvement was necessary. They viewed the media's performance during the wars positively, crediting the media and government information agencies for providing adequate information, while accepting the censorship that was practiced as necessary and fairly administered. They evaluated media treatment of social issues and problems during the 1920s and 1930s positively, while criticizing extremism in labor and radical publications for its narrow perspective and ineffectiveness. In general, Consensus historians approached media history of 1917-1945 from the viewpoint that the media should work with the public and government to solve problems rather than create divisions by emphasizing conflicts.

The Consensus viewpoint tended to be especially strong at those times during which the United States faced grave dangers. A large number of studies of the press during World War I, for example, appeared in the years surrounding World War II. The Consensus attitude indeed reflected that of many observers during the crises themselves. In a 1933 essay entitled "Newspaper Leadership in Times of Depression,"[2] Thomas F. Barnhart argued that as newspapers and society faced severe economic problems, "the editor has been faced with new demands which have forced the newspaper to occupy a position of leadership, a position it may not have taken in times of well-being and prosperity." Presenting case studies of how specific newspapers had served as community leaders during the Great Depression years of 1930-1932, Barnhart pointed out that the economic situation had "turned the editorial office into a headquarters to mobilize relief, welfare, and socializing enterprises." Similarly, in an essay in 1942 entitled "Editorial Pages in Wartime—Their Techniques and Ideology," William Wesley Waymack, Pulitzer Prize-winning editorial editor of the Des Moines (Iowa) *Register and Tribune,* relied on the Consensus argument. The job of the newspaper editorial page, Waymack reasoned, was more than simply to reflect or react to what was occurring on a day-to-day basis. With military threats confronting the world, he said, the press' purpose was instead to encourage democratic progress in both the world

---

[2]Thomas F. Barnhart, "Newspaper Leadership in Times of Depression," *Journalism Quarterly* 10 (1933): 1-13.

and the nation by making "more of our citizens better informed about grave issues of great complexity and better qualified therefore to influence the making of profoundly wise decisions through workable democratic processes."[3]

Consensus historians shared such concern for the media's aiding in defeating the threat and solving the problems facing the nation. To them, the past revealed that the media had performed best when they had contributed to national unity. They believed that the media's attitude toward America's entry into both World War I and World War II was responsible and reflected the consensus of the American people, that the proper role of the media during the wars was to support the aims of the nation, that freedom of the press during wartime must conform to the overriding needs of the nation, and that government information efforts during the wars were exercised acceptably.

Against the Progressive argument that propagandists, profiteers, and reactionary publishers misled the public and led America into wars, Consensus historians declared that the position of the media mirrored the opinions of the majority of the American public and that the enormity of the threat from America's and democracy's enemies justified media support of the war effort. As Axis powers engulfed the world in war in the 1930s, Edwin Costrell examined American and press attitudes toward the United States' entry into World War I. In "Newspaper Attitudes Toward War in Maine 1914-17" (1939), he examined the views of six Maine newspapers in an attempt to answer the Progressive question of whether American leaders plunged the nation into World War I contrary to popular desires. He concluded that newspaper content indicated that the press and the public had favored America's entry. By 1917, he wrote, "gone was all opposition to jingoism, all desire for neutrality, all talk of isolation. Although then, as many writers contend, public opinion may not have been the primary cause of America's involvement in the World War and its citizens may not even have desired to engage in hostilities, the people of Maine may safely be said to have definitely committed themselves in favor of a belligerent course. War headline after war headline over a period of more than two years at last had infected Yankee blood, aided by Germany's renewed disregard for the rights of American nationals; and a restless belligerency which had been held in abeyance by stronger peace forces broke all bonds. War sentiment had grown slowly; it had not come to full flower during the crisis, nor during the crisis which shortly followed; but by February of 1917 it had undoubtedly come into its own, not reversing itself once in the two months which intervened

---

[3]William Wesley Waymack, "Editorial Pages in Wartime—Their Techniques and Ideology," *Journalism Quarterly* 19 (1942): 34-39.

before war actually was declared. Whatever the rest of the nation may have thought, Maine advanced to battle when it most fervently desired to go."[4]

In a similar study conducted during World War II and intended to determine whether journalists elsewhere shared the pro-war attitude of Maine newspapers, Andrew C. Cogswell concluded that Montana newspapers were pro-Ally by July 1914. "Through the pre-war Montana newspapers of 1913 and 1914," Cogswell wrote, "ran discernible threads of traditional American concepts of right and wrong. Upon these concepts Montana newspapers judged the Central Powers. It is hard to believe that these concepts were those of newspapers alone."[5]

In other studies, Consensus historians came to similar conclusions, finding that newspapers and magazines supported American war efforts because they mirrored the views of the American public; that whereas most discussions of the government-media relationship center on the watchdog role of the media, the activities of publications during the world wars should remind the media that they can serve the public by working with the government in distributing information; and that Black editors believed that Black Americans should support the war efforts because such support would result in equal treatment of Blacks after the wars and that a world crisis was no time to demand a complete change in discriminatory racial practices.

Consensus historians also broke sharply with the views of Progressive historians on the issue of the concept of freedom of the media and government control over information. Whereas Progressive historians generally argued that freedom of the press should be absolute and that cooperation of the conservative media with government posed the danger of compromising honest, liberal journalism, Consensus historians believed absolute freedom and independence of the media could result in a journalism that was irresponsible and that ultimately could endanger the nation and the democratic system that made press freedom possible. To merit freedom, Consensus historians argued, the media must perform responsibly in relation to the rest of society, with the welfare of the nation as a whole rather than of the media alone of primary importance. This view led Consensus historians to the natural conclusion that restrictions on press freedom during wartime may be acceptable and that such restrictions—because of the circumstances under which they are implemented—do not abandon the concept of freedom in a demo-

---

[4]Edwin Costrell, "Newspaper Attitudes Toward War in Maine 1914-17," *Journalism Quarterly* 16 (1939): 334-344.

[5]Andrew C. Cogswell, "The Montana Press and War: 1914 to 1917," *Journalism Quarterly* 21 (1944): 137-147.

cratic philosophy. As the United States faced wartime conditions in the 1930s and 1940s, Consensus historians attempted to look to press operations during World War I to provide guidance in World War II and generally concluded that limited censorship and government information agencies had served the nation well with minimal damage to the media.

One of the foremost media historians on World War I, Reginald Coggeshall, argued against the view of some journalists of the 1930s that American officials had practiced impermissible censorship at the Paris peace conference following World War I. A journalist himself, Coggeshall had been a member of the staff of the Paris edition of the New York *Herald*. In a 1939 article, "Was There Censorship at the Paris Conference?"[6] he assumed implicitly that censorship during wartime is acceptable and concluded that American military officers at the peace conference considered the conference to be part of a continuing war, thus justifying control of information. Any censorship of news that did occur was usually unintentional and therefore justifiable.

In the fullest study of censorship during World War II, Theodore F. Koop reached a conclusion similar to Coggeshall's. Koop's *Weapon of Silence* (1946) analyzed the job performed by the United States' civilian censorship organization, the Office of Censorship under Byron Price, and concluded that even though at times censorship exceeded what was necessary, all in all it served a very useful purpose and prohibited little innocuous material from being distributed. Price acted responsibly in establishing policies and carrying them out, Koop reasoned, and exhibited a true concern about both informing the public and working for the national welfare.

Along with censoring information during the wars, the American government also carried on operations to provide information to the American public and present the Allied point of view. Consensus historians generally argued that such efforts were performed in a reasonable manner and were necessary as part of the larger effort to win military victory. In "Mysterious Silence, Lyrical Scream: Government Information in World War II"[7] (1971), Robert L. Bishop and LaMar S. Mackay outlined what they considered the "main problems in setting up U.S. information agencies" and in protecting "the historic right of the people to know about the policies and programs of their government while maintaining the security of the nation." Detailing the history of the Office of War Informa-

---

[6]Reginald Coggeshall, "Was There Censorship at the Paris Conference?" *Journalism Quarterly* 16 (1939): 125-135.

[7]Robert L. Bishop and LaMar S. Mackay, "Mysterious Silence, Lyrical Scream: Government Information in World War II," *Journalism Monographs* 19 (1971).

tion, they concluded that because of the complexity of the American government and the immensity of national propaganda operations, a government information agent no longer can be the leader in forming policy—as the OWI did—but must work with both government and the mass media and in effect serve as an auxiliary weapon for the nation.

In a larger study of the OWI, *The Politics of Propaganda: The Office of War Information* (1978), Allan M. Winkler also accepted the legitimacy of government information programs and concluded that the OWI performed an important role in America's efforts to win the war. In chronicling the struggles within the OWI itself to determine what procedures it should use, Winkler found that some libertarians such as Archibald MacLeish and Robert Sherwood preferred a straightforward approach in propaganda rather than scare tactics, basing their decision on their belief in the fundamental rationality of Americans and citizens of other countries. Elmer Davis, more pragmatic and less idealistic, was not as confident of the desire of the people for rational truth; and, as OWI director, he redirected the agency toward military-oriented propaganda rather than propaganda primarily promoting democracy, as liberals had hoped. The liberals' ideas, however, Winkler concluded, were either inappropriate or unworkable in the wartime conditions, and the OWI's primary purpose of winning the war was the most proper one, as even the liberals themselves eventually came to realize.

As with wartime issues involving the media, Consensus historians believed that the media during difficult domestic times should contribute to the solution of social problems, and they tended to argue that the most workable and equitable solutions could be found in mainstream institutions and ideas. They therefore were critical of radical journalists and press movements—which they concluded frequently performed poorly—and argued that journalists who advocated causes could be most effective by working within the established system. The labor press, for example, fared poorly with these historians. Earl W. Simmons, in "The Labor Dailies" (1928), a study of various labor newspapers from 1886 to 1924, pointed out that most such papers had short lives and concluded that "the American labor movement has not made much progress in the field of daily journalism" and that the labor press had no national influence. The causes of its problems lay with both its editors and the newspaper audience. "With few exceptions," Simmons wrote, "the American editors have been first-rate fighters, but they have lacked the cultural breadth necessary for a clear perspective on national and international problems." Furthermore, the working reader was more interested in sensationalism and entertainment in his newspaper than in labor issues. "The average American working man," Simmons reasoned, "is not class conscious enough to support a labor press.

The New York *Daily News* and the Chicago *Herald-Examiner* contain what he likes to read."[8]

In a 1937 study focused more narrowly on the newspapers published by the Nonpartisan League, an agrarian political movement, from 1915 to 1920, Joseph H. Mader argued that even though the League had some success using propaganda, its newspapers failed because of factional fighting and incompetent management. The League experienced rapid growth because of its leaders' "mastery of propaganda techniques," and it had early success with its attempts at journalism, but ultimately, careless financial management and political bickering among League leaders marred its newspapers, resulting in their demise after only a short publishing period.[9]

Consensus historians viewed the minority press in a similar fashion. In *No Crystal Stair: Black Life and the Messenger, 1917-1928* (1975) Theodore Kornweibel Jr. argued that the magazine became a successful advocate of the cause of Black Americans only after it gave up its early radical stance and moved toward the center of national politics. In the 1920s, Blacks received no help from government, the political right or left, industry, or labor. A. Phillip Randolph helped found the *Messenger* as a forthright Socialist magazine and tied its fate for the first five years to the American Socialist party. Once Randolph realized, however, that the party offered no real hope for Blacks, he gradually changed the magazine's stance toward a pro-business one. Randolph's pragmatism—contrasted with an idealism which Progressive historians admired in American reformers but which Consensus historians argued was ineffectual in bringing about change—provided one of the prime factors in the magazine's surviving as long as it did. By the time the *Messenger* died in 1928, Randolph had moved it into the mainstream of American politics, where it sought accommodation with the Republican and Democratic parties and even with the mainline labor groups hated by Socialists.

The Developmental School
The third major approach to the media of 1917-1945 was provided by Developmental historians. Unlike the ideological viewpoints of the Progressive and Consensus historians, the interpretation of Developmental historians normally displayed little concern for partisanship. Most Developmental historians attempted to explain the performance of the media in terms of professional journalistic practices rather than ideology. Thus, in examining the media in

---

[8]Earl W. Simmons, "The Labor Dailies," *American Mercury* 15 (September 1928): 85-93.

[9]Joseph H. Mader, "The North Dakota Press and the Non-partisan League," *Journalism Quarterly* 14 (1937): 321-322.

regard to the two world wars and the Great Depression, they placed primary emphasis on how the media operated according to journalistic standards with little regard for ideological conflict. Although a number of Developmental historians did believe the media should be advocates of truth, crusaders for justice, protectors of the underprivileged, guardians of fairness, or performers of some other such role, they did not consider these roles to be ideological in nature. Instead, they thought of them simply as professional aspects of journalism.

A typical Developmental study of the media in such terms was Daniel W. Pfaff's "The Press and Scottsboro Rape Cases, 1931-32" (1974). The cases were brought against several Black males in the South, providing "an interesting challenge to the press to exercise its functions as interpreter in the struggle between truth and falsehood and as watchdog in the interests of fair and equal justice. They served to demonstrate the vicissitudes of dealing evenhandedly in print with a story that involved both inflammatory racial attitudes and international ideological controversy."[10] The press failed to perform according to proper journalistic standards during the cases, Pfaff concluded, for it was prejudiced, and the information and editorial opinion it carried failed to provide the public with fair or accurate accounts.

With a similar concern for journalistic practices, Developmental historians conducted a number of studies of media performance and advances, including among others relations between the U.S. Presidents and the press, presidential press conferences, presidential press secretaries, media access to information, journalistic nonpartisanship, the media's "watchdog" role over government, press freedom during wartime, interpretive and investigative reporting, newspapers' emphasis on news, the rise of female journalists, editorial integrity and independence, the growth of the American Newspaper Guild, advertising, and magazines.

The subject of most interest to Developmental historians, however, was war reporting. With the period 1917-1945 witnessing two wars of great magnitude during which reporting seemed to improve, it was only natural that the subject of war reporting should attract a large number of historians. They published numerous biographies of war correspondents and histories of war reporting.

Developmental historians believed that truly professional war reporting developed in the 20th century and that war reporters were fully committed to the job of providing accurate and complete information to their readers. War correspondents faced great hazards, and Developmental historians gave considerable attention to

---

[10]Daniel W. Pfaff, "The Press and the Scottsboro Rape Cases, 1931-32," *Journalism History* 1 (1974): 72-76.

their derring-do and heroic adventures. Whereas historians often had pictured reporters of the 19th century as mere adventurers and famous journalistic stars, Developmental historians described the modern correspondents as more serious about their task and role. They were concerned about their preparation, their qualifications, and their performance as competent journalists. The most successful war correspondents, Developmental historians believed, were those who were most determined to do their job despite obstacles—both military and political—and who were concerned with gaining access to information, with accuracy, and with speed in transmitting news. Lee G. Miller's *The Story of Ernie Pyle* (1950) was typical. Pyle, Miller wrote, did not succeed as a war reporter by accident. He had university training and had worked as a reporter and copy editor. He exhibited the hallmarks of the superior professional journalist. Most notably, he was concerned about preparing for his career, about human interest, and about accuracy. All in all, historians concluded, although reporting often was colored and incomplete, the primary motivation of journalists was the desire to provide immediate and valuable information to the public, and war correspondents as a whole performed admirably.

Discussion

How, in the final analysis, are the media during the national crises of 1917-1945 to be judged: as advocates of social reform and liberalism, as irresponsible and jingoistic propaganda tools, as a constructive force for combatting immense international threats to democracy, as servants of entrenched conservative interests, or as practitioners of high journalistic standards? That is the central question that has confronted historians. How should it be answered? Once that question is addressed, one needs to consider a number of other questions that grow out of it.

1. Considering the enormity of the problems confronting the United States and the rest of the world during this period, how much consideration should be given to them when assessing the performance of the media?

2. Is it reasonable, as Developmental historians have done, to evaluate the media by detached professional standards during such critical times? Or must historians assess media performance within the context of the time?

3. Similarly, is it proper for historians to critique media performance, as Progressive historians have done, on the basis of liberal social ideology when such ideology was not the overriding consideration for the media of the time?

4. When did the media during this modern critical period serve best—when they supported such ideology; when, as Consensus historians argued, they joined the national effort to combat the problems

the nation faced; or when, as Developmental historians assumed, they acted according to detached, professional news standards?

5. How should media practitioners from 1917 to 1945 be judged—as dangerous propagandists, as constructive patriots, or as responsible professionals?

Readings

Progressive School

Humes, D. Joy, Ch. 5, "Toward More Political Democracy," pp. 105-125, *Oswald Garrison Villard: Liberal of the 1920s*. Syracuse, NY: Syracuse University Press, 1960.

Knightly, Philip, Ch. 6, "Enter America 1917-1918," pp. 113-136, *The First Casualty*. New York: Harcourt, Brace, Jovanovich, 1975.

Peterson, H. C., Ch. 15, "Decision for War," pp. 306-325, *Propaganda for War: The Campaign Against Neutrality 1914-1917*. Norman: University of Oklahoma Press, 1939.

Richstad, Jim Andrew, "The Press Under Martial Law: The Hawaiian Experience," *Journalism Monographs* 17 (1970).

Consensus School

Bishop, Robert L., and LaMar S. Mackay, "Mysterious Silence, Lyrical Scream: Government Information in World War II," *Journalism Monographs* 19 (1971).

Coggeshall, Reginald, "Was There Censorship at the Paris Conference?" *Journalism Quarterly* 16 (1939): 125-135.

Costrell, Edwin, "Newspaper Attitudes Toward War in Maine 1914-17," *Journalism Quarterly* 16 (1939): 334-344.

Jones, Lester, "The Editorial Policy of Negro Newspapers of 1917-1918 as Compared with That of 1941-1942," *Journal of Negro History* 29 (January 1944): 24-31.

Larson, Cedric, "Censorship of Army News During the World War, 1917-1918," *Journalism Quarterly* 17 (1940): 313-323.

Moffett, E. Albert, "Hometown Radio in 1942: The Role of Local Stations During the First Year of Total War," *American Journalism* 3 (1986): 87-98.

Seller, Maxine S., "Defining Socialist Womanhood: The Women's Page of the *Jewish Daily Forward* in 1919," *American Jewish History* 76 (1987): 416-438.

Developmental School

Crozier, Emmet, Ch. 18, "Big Bertha and Little Cantigny," pp. 198-211, *American Reporters on the Western Front, 1914-1918*. New York: Oxford University Press, 1959.

Mander, Mary S., "American Correspondence During World War II: Common Sense as a View of the World," *American Journalism* 1, 1 (1983): 17-30.

Mathews, Joseph J., Ch. 11, "World War II," pp. 174-196, *Reporting the Wars*. Minneapolis: University of Minnesota Press, 1957.

Pratte, Alf, "The Honolulu Star-Bulletin and the 'Day of Infamy,'" *American Journalism* 5 (1988): 5-13.

21

American Radio, 1920-1948: Traditional Journalism or Revolutionary Technology?

The history of American radio has been given comparatively limited consideration within the discipline of mass media research: first, because it is a relative newcomer to the field; and second, because the luster of television and the other competitive media has overshadowed radio—which was really the first medium to make, as one observer said, a "whispering gallery of the skies."

Radio's roots are easily chronicled within the historical eras of the 20th century: the industrial, expansionist, Roaring '20s, the Depression, and World War II. During the industrial era, radio was but one of the many new innovations. At the turn of the century it was primarily a laboratory toy. In 1864 James Clerk Maxwell had theorized on the nature and properties of the electromagnetic spectrum. Heinrick Hertz took Maxwell's theories and demonstrated them. Hertz was the first to transmit and receive radio waves. The Italian Guglielmo Marconi developed a commercially successful enterprise. At the turn of the century Reginald A. Fessenden and Lee de Forest added their contributions which facilitated the broadcast of voice and music.

There was a slow transition among the experimental developments of the industrial era, the era of American Expansionism, and the Roaring '20s. As America began to look abroad, radio took on an important role in ship-to-shore communication. The progress of this function was apparent with the beginning of radio legislation passed in 1910 and 1912. The new radio laws placed governing control under the supervision of the Secretary of Commerce. The advent of ship-to-shore, of course, did not close experimentation. Many of America's growing industries became involved: General Electric, the Radio Corporation of America, American Telephone and Telegraph, and others. Each corporation and individual experimenter took out patents on its particular contribution to radio communica-

By Wm. David Sloan, *University of Alabama*
and Donald G. Godfrey, *Arizona State University*

tion. However, when World War I began, these competing patents were pooled for the purposes of the war effort and radio was placed temporarily under the control of the United States Navy.

Following World War I, President Woodrow Wilson declared his intentions to return America to "normalcy." Radio was very much a part of the revolution of the Roaring '20s. As Fredrick Lewis Allen declared, radio was the "youngest rider" on this "prosperity bandwagon." The 1920s had three significant impacts on the history of radio. First was the adoption of the 1927 Radio Act. This act provided the foundation of regulatory concepts that continue today. Second, many of the commercial organizations that were developed in the late 1920s and 1930s are still with us. Each of the networks has its roots in this era, as do the practices of syndication and the patterns of organization and financial support. Finally, the social issues of the time had an effect. For example, the issues of censorship, the ownership of the airwaves, and the political utilization of media all have their roots in the issues of the 1920s, and these issues have worked their way into today's governing standards.

During the 1930s, radio was one of the few American industries not adversely affected by the Great Depression. The federal government enacted a new communications law (the 1934 Communications Act), and although it extended the responsibilities of the Federal Communications Commission, it reinstated the fundamental hypotheses of the 1927 Radio Act. Perhaps more important than the legislation in the 1930s, however, were the social impact and utility of radio. Radio was used by the politicians to debate the issues and to inspire a discouraged electorate, entertained an audience looking for hope, and informed an audience fearful of an oncoming war.

It was the approach of World War II that led to the development of network news. During the war, radio played a propaganda role for the German leadership as well as a news, informational, and propaganda role for the Allies. Edward R. Murrow, the first correspondent sent to Europe to arrange events for broadcast on the Columbia network, soon was well known, and his words "This is London" echoed across America. Radio brought the war in Europe home to an American audience.

Following World War II, radio underwent great change. The change has yet to end. Radio was forced to adapt to the introduction of television, and the music disc jockey filled the void left when radio listeners switched to television for their weekly drama and comedy programs. AM radio station owners fought the advent of FM and then got the licenses for most of the frequencies. The static of the AM stations gave way to the high fidelity of the FM signal and the advent of digital audio that we have today.

Histories of broadcasting had been written as early as the 1920s, although the greatest output began in the 1960s. A major stimulus to research was the founding of the *Journal of Broadcasting* in 1956 and the growth of a broadcast curriculum within universities. Historians have focused their attention on a wide variety of topics defined by the nature of the medium. The most popular subjects have included radio technology, programming, broadcast journalists, stations, national networks, government regulation of broadcasting, the interrelationship between broadcasting and its audience, and the economics of broadcasting. Within these broad areas, the major differences in historical interpretation were over whether the topic should be approached in terms of professional development, in ideological terms, or in terms of radio's technological characteristics.

Most historians approached broadcast journalism from one of three points of view: the Developmental school, the Progressive school, or the Cultural school. The Developmental approach was based on the concept of the professional development of radio, viewing the history of broadcast journalism as the continuing evolution of practices and standards. Progressive historians believed the primary purpose of broadcasters should have been to crusade for liberal social and economic causes, and to fight on the side of the working people against the entrenched interests in American business and government. Cultural historians were more interested in the factors that accounted for the founding of radio broadcasting and under what conditions it operated.

The predominant school of interpretation has been a Developmental one, accounting for substantially more than one-half the works. Most Developmental historians exhibited a favorable attitude toward broadcast journalism, and were concerned primarily with the progress made toward higher standards. Their attention focused on such topics as outstanding broadcast journalists, news programming, and commentary. At the same time, a more critical group of Developmental historians, although most interested in the advance of broadcast journalism as a profession, institutionalized an anti-establishment attitude as a professional standard.

Unlike the mainstream Developmental historians, Progressive historians were critical of conservative trends in journalism and of what they perceived as failures of conservative journalism. In some respects they resembled the anti-establishment Developmental historians. They cast their criticism of conservative journalism, however, in primarily ideological terms. These historians took an approach that strongly favored "democracy," a view that argued that government and the media should support social progress for the masses of American people. In general, they were concerned with how economic factors affected broadcasting's ability to serve the public and how big business—through its ownership of radio and its alliance with government—controlled broadcasting to the detriment of the public interest.

Cultural historians, on the other hand, showed little ideological concern for the performance of broadcasting. They were primarily interested in society's effect on broadcasting, cultural factors important in the development of broadcasting, and broadcasting's influence on American society and attitudes.

The Developmental School

The earliest histories of American radio came from the Developmental school. Beginning in the 1920s, Developmental historians dominated the field, at least in the number of works they produced. They approached history primarily as the story of how the field advanced. Inherent in their approach was a belief that history could explain how conditions evolved and how the quality of practices in the historian's own time usually surpassed that of earlier periods. Thus, they wrote of broadcast history as the unfolding of progress. They focused their attention primarily on the episodes that contributed to the advance of broadcasting. Popular topics with these historians were early experiments with broadcasting technology, the origins of such practices as the broadcasting of presidential news conferences and election returns, the question of "firsts," the development of news programming, the contributions of "pioneers" and "great" broadcasters such as Raymond Swing, Lowell Thomas, and Edward R. Murrow, the role of women and minorities in broadcast journalism, the progression of broadcasting as a legitimate form of journalism, the beginnings of commentary and news analysis, the origins and advances in noncommercial broadcasting, the development of and improvements in broadcast education at the university level, and the emergence of broadcasting as an important factor in mass communication and in American society in general.

Most Developmental historians were favorably disposed toward the performance of broadcast journalism. Therefore they differed markedly from Progressive historians. Whereas the latter tended to be critical of the economic aspects of broadcasting and often of government regulation of broadcasting, Developmental historians usually were inclined to point out the contributions to broadcasting progress made possible by broadcast media ownership. Likewise, they normally viewed government regulation in a positive or, at worst, neutral manner.

Incorporating these attitudes were some of the earliest works on broadcasting technology and governmental regulation. Orrin E. Dunlap's 1927 study *The Story of Radio*, for example, provided a history of the important technical developments in radio; and a year later, Paul Shubert included discussions of developments in technology, economic factors, and governmental policies in his book

The Electric Word: The Rise of Radio. Such interest in the relationship of radio networks and the federal government, and especially the licensing of radio, has remained strong with historians since. They generally have argued that early regulations such as the Radio Act of 1927 set the standards and rules for broadcasting which are still followed today.[1]

Similarly in other areas of radio broadcasting, Developmental historians searched for the roots of professional practices and attempted to trace their progress with time. The search for origins provided the theme for one of the first scholarly research articles on radio history, Chester Giraud's "The Press-Radio War: 1933-35" (1949). It chronicled the conflict between newspapers and radio and the restrictions the newspaper press placed on radio news. The press-radio war, Giraud concluded, forced the radio networks to develop their own in-house news services.[2]

Emphasizing Developmental historians' increasing identification of broadcasting as a serious area of journalism was the appearance of Harold E. Fellows' article "The Expanding Sphere of Journalism" (1956) in the *Journal of Broadcasting* (during that publication's first year). Many parallels, Fellows wrote, "existed between the development of newspaper journalism and broadcast journalism, and one may determine the progress of broadcasting to some extent by looking at newspapers." Among the similarities he found were the development of technology, early government regulation, and support by advertising. Fellows argued that broadcasting should be taken seriously and thought of and treated just as print journalism was.[3]

In a similar attempt to point out that radio broadcasting had come of age, Leslie Smith in a 1964 article in the *Journal of Broadcasting* traced the growth of broadcast education in American universities as an adjunct of the broadcast profession. Education, he argued, "has generally managed to follow the trends and needs of the industry. The first radio course was offered within a decade of the beginning of that industry, and as the infant radio broadcasting industry grew to great and influential proportions, Radio Speech grew into a major in Radio. When commercial broadcasters criticized the products sent them by the colleges, the colleges responded by gradually upgrading their level of instruction, quality of equipment, and competence of instructors. As the network broadcasting industry concentrated on television and the nature of radio changed

---

[1]See, for example, Darrell Host, "The Origin of the Public Interest in Broadcasting," *Educational Broadcasting Review* 1 (October, 1967): 15-19.

[2]Chester Giraud, "The Press-Radio War: 1933-35," *Public Opinion Quarterly* 13 (Summer 1949): 252-264.

[3]Harold E. Fellows, "The Expanding Sphere of Journalism," *Journal of Broadcasting* 1 (1956): 211-219.

markedly, the major became Radio and Television or simply Broadcasting. Education and industry now work together. . . . The future of the major and its curriculum can, therefore, best be predicted in terms of the future of the broadcasting industry."[4]

In attempting to describe the origin and progress of broadcasting, Developmental historians also produced a number of works dealing with the question of "firsts" in broadcasting. In "'Oldest Station in the Nation'?"[5] (1959), R. Franklin Smith established the analytical criteria for analysis and issued the implied challenge of discovery—the study of firsts being a historical curiosity to determine the chronology of things. Other historians followed with attempts not only to describe technological growth, but to provide methodological definition of "firsts." The number of attempts to apply such methods and to discover firsts illustrate a fascination with origins and development that is distinctive among radio historians.

Along with the origins of radio and various broadcast practices, Developmental historians were interested in tracing the progress and maturation of those practices. Three articles published in the 1960s served as a body of chronologies on the subject. In the first, "The Radio Election of 1924" (1964), Lewis E. Weeks argued that radio "grew up" during the 1924 presidential campaign. The campaign, he said, "was of significance because it introduced new techniques in political campaigning, and because it served as a proving ground for the interconnection of radio stations by wire and short wave for the purpose of nationwide broadcasting. By 1928, when the Hoover-Smith contest took place, the major parties had accepted radio as a major campaign tool. AT&T and Westinghouse made use of the broadcasting of political talks of the 1924 campaign to perfect techniques for coast-to-coast radio transmission. AT&T did outstanding work in the interconnection of stations by long distance telephone wires; Westinghouse linked the east to the Pacific coast by short wave. Certainly these accomplishments would have come about in time, but the stimulus of using radio as a medium of political campaigning in 1924 probably brought about the advances sooner than could have been expected without the radio election."[6] With the Developmental outlook on the advance of broadcasting as a profession, Weeks concluded that the 1924 campaign probably benefited radio more than it did politics.

In the second article, published a year after Weeks' work and

[4]Leslie Smith, "Education for Broadcasting: 1929-1963," *Journal of Broadcasting* 8 (1964): 394-395.

[5]R. Franklin Smith, "'Oldest Station in the Nation'?" *Journal of Broadcasting* 4 (Winter 1959-1960): 40-55.

[6]Lewis E. Weeks, "The Radio Election of 1924," *Journal of Broadcasting* 8 (1964): 242-243.

written from a similar outlook, Robert R. Smith focused on the development of radio network commentary as the foundation of radio journalism. In "Origins of Radio Network News Commentary" (1965) he pointed out that commentary was not only the forerunner of news as we know it, but was in many ways "related to the social and political developments of the 1930s."[7] It was during the 1930s, as Smith pointed out, that the number of commentators grew from six to twenty. To support them, both the CBS and NBC networks established their first guidelines for news.

The third study, Thomas W. Bohn's "Broadcasting National Election Returns: 1916-1948" (1968), examined the development of radio reporting of returns for each presidential election from 1916 to 1948. Bohn found that election night coverage provided a testing ground for many major developments in broadcasting, covering such areas as studio facilities and equipment, personnel, program formats, and program audiences. Coverage developed slowly because of the inability of broadcasting to collect and assemble data and because broadcasters thought the audience would not enjoy intense information and news coverage from broadcasting. As full-time coverage occurred, however, stations and networks improved their techniques. Finding they could not fill the entire broadcast time with statistics, they gave more attention to analysis and interpretation, and exhaustive coverage of presidential election night became a staple of American broadcasting.[8]

As Developmental historians attempted to chronicle the progress of broadcasting as journalism, their attention naturally focused on the pioneers in the field. Their intent normally was to paint a favorable picture of broadcasters as talented newspeople with high standards, with the natural result that broadcast practices had to be counted as serious journalism.

Such a framework provided the basis, for example, of Eugene Lyons' *David Sarnoff: A Biography* (1958), in which the president of the Radio Corporation of America (RCA) was pictured as having the highest expectations and requirements for quality in broadcast programming. Similarly, R. Franklin Smith's biography *Edward R. Murrow—The War Years* (1972) argued that the CBS newsman was primarily interested in the content of broadcast news and documentary and had a natural journalistic instinct for news.

Recent Developmental biographers, although interested in personalities, were also concerned with technological, governmental, and environmental circumstances relative to radio's progress.

---

[7]Robert R. Smith, "Origins of Radio Network Commentary," *Journal of Broadcasting* 9 (Spring 1965): 113-122.

[8]Thomas W. Bohn "Broadcasting National Election Returns: 1916-1948," *Journal of Broadcasting* 12 (1968): 267-286.

They believed that the developmental situation was a complex "series of persons, events, objects and relations presenting an exigency which can be removed by the process of historical discovery." Works written with this perspective dealt with such topics as Herbert Hoover's contributions to the American system of broadcasting, the political personalities involved in the 1920s legislative process, and broadcast figures H. V. Kaltenborn and Philo T. Farnsworth.[9]

Several radio pioneers—William S. Paley, Paul White, William L. Shirer, and Edward R. Murrow, among others— recorded their personal accounts of radio news and its development. These works not only chronicled advances, but outlined them from the perspective of the participants. Several of these pioneers argued that radio news grew up with World War II, an event that some of them covered. Radio, they believed, provided the basis of mass communication as we know it today.

A second group of Developmental historians, while also placing primary emphasis on the progress of broadcasting, incorporated into their interpretation an attitude favoring critical or liberal anti-establishment journalism. These historians took as their heroes radio journalists who stood up for "professional" practices even when those practices might not coincide with popular values or even with what was popularly considered to be national interests. The villains frequently showed up as advertisers who would prefer to support entertainment rather than serious journalism and as broadcasting executives who made their programming decisions with an eye primarily on audience ratings rather than on what was best for the audience. Roger Burlingame's *Don't Let Them Scare You: The Life and Times of Elmer Davis* (1961), a biography of the CBS radio commentator, typified this approach. Burlingame painted Davis as a talented and courageous journalist who stood up for liberal ideas. Davis, Burlingame believed, possessed a brave spirit and greatness as a journalist and was able to see clearly the truth and transmit it to others.

Although liberal Developmental historians found much to be admired in the character and performance of such radio figures, they frequently were critical of mainstream practices and conditions in the radio industry that prevented broadcast journalists from doing an adequate job. The question of how broadcast journalism might perform better was addressed directly by Ernest D. Rose in an arti-

---

[9]Daniel E. Garvey, "Secretary Hoover and the Quest for Broadcast Regulation," *Journalism History* 3 (1976): 66-70; Donald G. Godfrey and Val E. Linburg, "The Rogue Elephant of Radio Legislation: Senator William E. Borah," *Journalism Quarterly* 67 (1990): 214-224; David G. Clark, "H. V. Kaltenborn and His Sponsors...," *Journal of Broadcasting* 12 (1968): 309-321; and Stephen F. Hofer, "Phil Farnsworth: Television's Pioneer," *Journal of Broadcasting* 23 (1979): 153-165.

cle which appeared the same year as Burlingame's book. In "How the U.S. Heard about Pearl Harbor" (1961), Rose attempted to determine "what kinds of things happened to our news communication under conditions of extreme surprise, complete emotional involvement, and little first hand information." Believing that accurate reporting of events is more important than molding national morale, he concluded that radio reporting of the Japanese attack on Pearl Harbor in 1941 often was inaccurate, there was confusion about what information should be withheld for the common good, information was misinterpreted and even deliberately falsified, and there was a preference for "what could be" over the reality of "what is." Rose then argued that for a better job of reporting under difficult circumstances there needed to be more "responsibility" and more "wisdom," for "how to update the democratic handling of communications in a modern world is an inseparable part of our battle for survival."[10]

The critical Developmental interpretation was elaborated more fully in Alexander Kendrick's *Prime Time: The Life of Edward R. Murrow* (1969). Kendrick argued that even though the CBS newsman was a great journalist, he could have made broadcast journalism even better had it not been for pressure from advertisers and CBS' management. Murrow had been an outstanding correspondent during World War II and then made even more significant contributions to broadcasting by building up CBS' stable of correspondents and serving as a model for other network journalists to follow. By the 1950s, however, Murrow—like Kendrick, a CBS newsman from the 1940s to the 1970s—had become disillusioned with the commercialization of broadcasting and its emphasis on meaningless entertainment rather than news. In an indictment of contemporary television, Kendrick claimed that the medium Murrow had worked so hard to make great was dying to the ratings race, and even the news documentary, in contrast to Murrow's works, was losing its boldness.

The Progressive School
Sharing the concern for the failures of broadcast journalism were Progressive historians. They based their criticism, however, not on the journalistic shortcomings of radio but on radio's failure to promote the interests of the American public. The problem, Progressive historians argued, was caused by economic factors. It lay in the control that big business exerted on both broadcasting and the government. Government was allied with big business, they argued; so it placed the welfare of business above the public interest. The effects

---

[10]Ernest D. Rose, "How the U.S. Heard about Pearl Harbor," *Journal of Broadcasting* 5 (1961): 285, 298.

were pervasive. One result was that government regulation worked primarily to serve the interest of radio owners rather than to protect the public, with the Federal Communication Commission vulnerable to political and economic pressure. Advertisers' desires, rather than radio journalists' beliefs and the public's needs, determined the nature of programming. Broadcasting thus failed, Progressive historians argued, in its responsibility to provide full information and necessary interpretation. Broadcasting was used too frequently as an imperialistic and propaganda tool of the American government and business interests, and censorship of critics' use of the airwaves was used as an ideological weapon. In general, Progressive historians declared, broadcasting failed to promote either social or international justice.

The first works by Progressive historians were produced in the 1930s, a time when the Great Depression had created numerous social and economic problems and when government reform programs under President Franklin Roosevelt often met head-on opposition from big business. Influenced by such conditions, reform historians argued that American history was essentially the story of the battle between the wealthy class, which desired primarily to ensure its privileges and to continue its control over social and government policy, and the masses of the American people, who wished to increase political democracy and social justice. Within this context, the fundamental nature of radio could be explained by economic factors and the wealthy class' attempts to control radio for its own benefit.

Written from that perspective, the work of Gleason L. Archer became the standard in the field of broadcast history. Archer's classic two-volume study was one of the first comprehensive histories of American broadcasting. His first volume, *History of Radio to 1926*, published in 1938, provided primarily a chronological discussion of such topics as technology, the founding of RCA, governmental regulations, "firsts," and networks. It was in the second volume of the work that Archer developed a Progressive interpretation of history. Revealingly entitled *Big Business and Radio* (1939) and written from an economic approach, the book provided a history of business' war for control of radio from 1922 to 1939. Businessmen-owners of radio stations and networks, Archer argued, used cut-throat practices to gain command of the industry. Among the episodes in the conquest of radio, which was led by RCA president David Sarnoff, were the FTC's investigation of RCA, the antitrust suit against the Radio Group, the rise of NBC, CBS, and Mutual Broadcasting System, and the development of television. In all their efforts during such episodes, the business interests employed unscrupulous tactics, leading to threats by outside critics. Then, sensing the danger posed by the possibility of government's establishing rules and regulations to require the industry to operate in the public's interest, the more brilliant broadcasting leaders, with Sarnoff at the forefront, relied on arbitration, mediation, discussion, and litigation finally to obtain a set of government regulations that promoted the broadcasters' interest.

The two major strands of historical interest provided by Archer and other early Progressive historians—the dominance of economic factors in broadcasting and the failure of government regulation to protect the public interest—provided the model for most Progressive historians who followed. They believed that big business wanted control of the broadcast media not only for the huge profits involved but also to dictate the content and tone of programming, thus attempting to manipulate and create an entire ideological system in America. Big business was aided by government through regulations that masqueraded as being in the public interest but which actually worked primarily for the benefit of media owners.

Three historians were most prominent among this later Progressive school: David G. Clark, Erik Barnouw, and J. Fred MacDonald. Clark argued that the entrenched and conservative powers that controlled radio generally opposed controversial or liberal ideas and often were openly belligerent against individuals committed to high principles. In "H. V. Kaltenborn's First Year on the Air" (1965), one of several Progressive articles on controversial programming, Clark provided the story of Kaltenborn's difficulties with WEAF radio station in 1923 because of his views. Kaltenborn's opinion on several issues angered many individuals and groups, and WEAF declined to renew his contract, revealing its "weakness by succumbing to fear of possible consequences." Kaltenborn, however, had enough "personal courage" to refuse to "yield to pressure." In his losing battle with WEAF, he became "a pathfinder for freedom of expression on the air, and his controversies show that personal and institutional courage were prerequisites for the journey."[11]

In the most extensive and one of the most significant histories of American broadcasting, Erik Barnouw argued that by the 1950s America's military-industrial complex, big business, and the "eastern establishment" had taken control of the media in not only the United States but the world as well. His work consisted of three volumes. The first, *A Tower in Babel* (1966), covered the history of radio to 1933, including such topics as early experimenters, the establishment of and eventual domination by networks, government regulations, the impact of advertising and business, and educational broadcasting. The second volume, *The Golden Web* (1968),

---

[11]David G. Clark, "H. V. Kaltenborn's First Year on the Air," *Journalism Quarterly* 42 (1965): 373.

extended the study to 1953. It narrated such episodes as the press-radio conflict of the 1930s, Franklin Roosevelt's "fireside chats," broadcasting in World War II, and the contributions of Kaltenborn, Murrow, and Davis, while criticizing the influence of advertising on programming and detailing government's investigation of monopoly and ownership of radio and television. His three-volume history concluded with *The Image Empire* (1970). It was in that volume that he developed his criticism most fully. Although the book dealt primarily with television from 1953 to 1970, its criticism could be extended generally to the history of radio. It argued that by 1953 American television had permeated other countries and served to impose American military, industrial, capitalistic, and cultural ideas throughout the world. American broadcasting became an imperialistic tool of government and industry, and management of events and news became common, with the Voice of America, Radio Free Europe, and television network news inculcating the American government's attitudes on other nations.

J. Fred MacDonald, on the other hand, although critical of the manipulation of radio by both the government and big business, also argued that American radio had served as a great democratizing instrument and that as a result it had made significant contributions to social progress and justice. In *Don't Touch That Dial: Radio Programming in American Life from 1920 to 1960* (1979) and a number of articles published in the 1970s, MacDonald pointed out that though American broadcasting had many shortcomings, it also helped improve many conditions. One failure was broadcasting's inundating the American public in the early 1950s with propagandistic images urging it to support without question the politics and policies of the government. Programs gave Americans the impression that communists threatened the American way of life but that United States espionage agencies and the military gave able protection. The result of such programming was "a nation of patriotic, trusting citizens left under-informed and fearful." Furthermore, broadcasting during its "Golden Age" stereotyped Black people and discriminated against them, generally doing little to fight racial injustice.

In general, however, radio as it grew reflected a "commercial democracy and the character of the people who made it work," both mirroring and creating popular values and attitudes. Network radio "bound together the American people as had no single commercial medium since the printing press" and became one of the most critical factors in modern American democracy and freedom. Although radio often had shortcomings because of its commercial needs and subservience to business, it only reflected its economic environment, and "the development of American radio as a commercialized medium was inevitable." Even though most programs

were aimed at entertainment and the lowest common tastes, Mac-
Donald argued, such was understandable in a society dominated by
the middle class and democratic ideals, and the nature of popular
culture in general in American society is such that "it functions to
improve and stabilize society, not to undermine its operative value
system." Thus, although MacDonald believed that American radio
often had functioned to serve the interests of government and big
business, he argued that in the long run it had served to democratize
America.

Generally more critical were those Progressive historians who
studied government regulation of broadcasting. Their criticism
was that regulations usually were at best a facade, appearing to be
for the protection of the public while in reality benefiting media
ownership. They argued, for example, that the Radio Act of 1927 was
not supported by the radio industry until it guaranteed the interests
of owners, even though without the legislation broadcasting might
have died during its infancy; that the FCC consistently showed favoritism toward media owners; and that broadcasters virtually
were free to pursue their own private interest rather than serving
public interests and had little reason to fear government regulation.

This Progressive concept was elaborated most fully in Robert
Sears McMahon's *Federal Regulation of the Radio and Television
Broadcast Industry in the United States, 1927-1959* (1979). The FCC
in its first 25 years, McMahon argued, failed to become an effective
guardian of the public's interest, as it was charged to do by requiring
radio and television to operate in the public interest, convenience,
and necessity. The reasons were two-fold. One problem was that after the U.S. Congress initially gave the FCC broad powers, Congress
consistently refused to give the FCC adequate support in setting
more specific standards. On the other hand, the FCC itself did not
wish to battle the powerful broadcast owners and therefore failed to
oversee the industry adequately.

The Cultural School

Such ideological considerations held little interest, on the other
hand, for Cultural historians. These historians believed that radio
could not be explained without consideration of the surrounding
cultural, social, economic, and political conditions. They reasoned
that the importance of radio lay in the interrelationship of broadcasting and the environment in which it operated. Their studies
therefore focused broadly on two areas: the impact that society and
cultural factors had on radio and the impact, in turn, that radio had
on American society and culture.

Although Cultural historians emphasized the influence of outside factors, they often also had a developmental outlook, attempting
to explain how various agents had effected the changes and ad-

vances in broadcasting. The development of radio, they reasoned, could not be understood without reference to such factors as technology, advertising, audience, personalities, politics, economics, government regulation, competition among media, and world and national news events.

One of the more fully developed studies of cultural influences was J. Fred MacDonald's 1979 Progressive work *Don't Touch That Dial*. Apart from his ideological arguments, MacDonald reasoned that aspects of American culture such as popular democracy, public tastes and interests, and a capitalistic economy determined the nature of radio programming during the period from 1920 to 1960.

This concept of influences on broadcasting was typified by studies on advertising by John W. Spaulding and on ethnic radio by Jorge Reina Schement and Richardo Flores. In "1928: Radio Become a Mass Advertising Medium" (1963),[12] Spaulding said that in the late 1920s conditions in broadcasting facilities, audiences, programs, and the attitudes of station owners were right for the national advertiser to enter radio sponsorship in a serious way, although radio itself had not done much to service advertisers. To serve effectively as an advertising medium, radio needed to have the technical facilities for broadcasting and receiving, it needed an audience of considerable size, broadcasters had to accept advertisers as partners in producing programs, and radio stations had to provide programs that would give appropriate formats for advertising. It was not until all these factors converged that radio could become a national advertising medium, and that convergence occurred in 1928.

Schement and Flores believed advertising and a number of other factors determined the development and growth of ethnic radio. In "The Origins of Spanish-Language Radio: The Case of San Antonio, Texas" (1977),[13] they concluded that the factors were diverse and showed up originally as problems that had to be overcome. These problems included the reluctance of advertisers to invest in Spanish advertising because they weren't convinced Chicanos had enough income, difficulties in providing effective programming for the potential audience, the lack of trained station personnel, and inadequacies in the news-gathering process. When these problems were solved—in the case of news gathering by taking material from the local newspaper—Spanish-language radio succeeded.

Among the more substantial works based on the Cultural interpretation of the influence of the milieu on radio was Philip T.

---

[12]John W. Spaulding, "1928: Radio Becomes a Mass Advertising Medium," *Journal of Broadcasting* 8 (1963-1964): 31-45.

[13]Jose Reina Schement and Richardo Flores, "The Origins of Spanish-Language Radio: The Case of San Antonio, Texas," *Journalism History* 4 (1977): 56-58.

Rosen's *The Modern Stentors: Radio Broadcasters and the Federal Government, 1920-1934* (1980). Rosen argued that "but for the particular interplay during the crucial years 1920 to 1934 among businessmen in the nascent industry, the prospective market, politics and bureaucrats . . ." radio could have developed into something completely different in the United States. "The contours of the American broadcasting industry were established fifty years ago," Rosen argued, "and have never changed fundamentally."

Other Cultural historians, impressed by the pervasiveness of radio in American society, believed that one of the most important aspects of radio history was the medium's impact on America. These historians therefore focused their attention on the influence radio had exercised in determining the nature of American culture and in bringing about changes in the nation's institutions. A large number were interested specifically in the effect radio and television had on politics and public affairs.

One of the most persuasive studies of a specific aspect of radio and the American political system was Pat Cranston's "Political Convention Broadcasts: Their History and Influence" (1960). Cranston attempted to show the changes that radio and television had wrought in the national party conventions. After examining radio reporting of conventions from 1924 and television coverage from 1940, she concluded that the electronic media helped shape the way in which convention sessions were conducted and influenced the behavior of delegates. "From the history of political convention broadcasting," she wrote, "it is evident that the presence of the electronic media had induced changes in the national conventions. The convention time schedule and location, use of visual material in the hall, the behavior of delegates and the pacing of proceedings all now bear the mark of planning for electronic coverage. To brighten the package in hopes of pleasing the audience, convention planners have added entertainers. . . ." Broadcasting's effect also could be found, Cranston said, in the print media, which "re-evaluated their convention reporting role. A new depth in convention reporting in print seems evident."[14]

As interest in the influence of the broadcast media increased in the 1970s, historians produced a number of more elaborate studies. Two of the most fully developed were David Halbrook Culbert's *News for Everyman: Radio and Foreign Affairs in Thirties America* (1976) and Irving Fang's *Those Radio Commentators!* (1978). Both examined the roles radio commentators played in affecting American attitudes on public affairs during the Great Depression and World War II. Both concluded that the commentators' impact

---

[14]Pat Cranston, "Political Convention Broadcasts: Their History and Influence," *Journalism Quarterly* 37 (1960): 186-194.

had been substantial.

Culbert analyzed the development of commentary in the late 1930s and the relationship between radio's coverage of foreign affairs and the making of foreign policy by the Roosevelt Administration. Focusing on the style and impact of Kaltenborn, Swing, Davis, Murrow, Boake Carter, and Fulton Lewis Jr., Culbert concluded that radio news created a mass audience interest in foreign affairs in the pre-World War II period. Commentators in the wake of the Munich crisis, although differing widely in their political beliefs, generally opposed Germany fervently and changed American public opinion from isolationist to interventionist, thus greatly influencing the foreign affairs process. Pioneers in a new field, the commentators developed large personal followings and helped radio news become "an integrating force in America by helping to create a national foreign policy consensus."[15]

Fang examined the careers of 15 commentators, including those treated by Culbert, during the period from 1929 to 1948 and concluded that, "for whatever reason, Americans came to trust radio commentators more than they did newspapers" and that the influence the commentators wielded came from that trust. "These were troubled times," Fang observed. "The commentators brought explanation, sometimes along with delivering the day's news. . . . The radio commentators helped to clarify it all, letting others see matters as they saw matters, talking to their fellow Americans. . . . Our favorite radio commentator was there to sort it all out."[16]

Other Cultural historians believed that outside politics the influence of radio extended to such areas as crime, race relations, and economic and social attitudes. Typical of the studies of these historians was Reynold M. Wik's "The Radio in Rural America during the 1920s" (1981). Wik argued that radio had a major impact on rural culture by providing useful information to farmers and a window on the outside world in a new and dramatic way. "Rural Americans," he reasoned, "may have benefitted the most from radio because they were the most isolated and had the most to gain from an improved communication system. . . . The radio was of profound importance . . . because it opened their ears to the sounds of the world and provided a medium which became an instrument for social change." Radio directly affected farmers by giving then practical information with heretofore unknown immediacy. Stations first began broadcasting weather reports and commodity market reports and in the 1920s began running advertising. The farmer's main

---

[15]David Halbrook Culbert, *News for Everyman* (Westport, CT: Greenwood Press, 1976).

[16]Irving Fang, *Those Radio Commentators!* (Ames: Iowa State University Press, 1978), 3-4.

interest was in such practical matters. "He wanted," Wik wrote, "the daily weather forecasts to help protect his property and to help in the management of his affairs. Before radio, rural people relied on newspapers and local telephone lines for weather reports, and although this information was helpful it tended to be too vague in nature and too slow in delivery."[17]

Discussion

The history of American radio is still being written. In its comparatively short lifespan, it nevertheless has established itself as a legitimate and growing field of inquiry. As a result, new topics, methods, and interpretations have surfaced rapidly; and historians have raised a number of significant questions. The major questions focus on the essential nature of broadcasting and the development of the field.

1. Should broadcasting history be viewed, as Developmental historians assumed, as the study of the origin, day-to-day practice, and progress of standard professional procedures and techniques? If not, how should it be viewed?

2. How appropriate is the Developmental tendency to approach broadcasting as just another form of journalism?

3. Since the Developmental approach gives special attention to the great individuals who contributed to such practices, how would another interpretive perspective (such as the Cultural or Progressive view) affect the assessment of those individuals?

4. How accurate were Progressive historians in emphasizing economics as the primary factor in broadcasting history? How valid is it in any explanation of history to attribute exclusive importance to any single factor?

5. How valid was the Progressive historians' explaining such areas as broadcast ownership and regulation in terms of ideology? How did their own ideological viewpoints affect their explanation?

6. Aside from ideology and economics, how accurate was Cultural historians' view that the key to understanding radio was the relationship between radio and the surrounding environment?

7. How reasonable was their assumption that radio played a major influence in affecting the public's attitudes and lifestyles? What type of evidence would be necessary for a historian to make such claims? Have Cultural historians done an adequate job of presenting the necessary evidence?

8. Along with such interpretive questions, historical study of radio also has raised a number of questions about the nature of historical research methods. How can the historian analyze oral and vi-

---

[17]Reynold M. Wik, "The Radio in Rural America during the 1920s," *Agricultural History* (October 1981): 340-341.

sual sources as primary documents? Is it possible to apply the methodology of print, rhetorical criticism, literary criticism, art, drama, or traditional history to the broadcast situation?

9. If the analysis of broadcast programming faces exceptional difficulties, what methods could be used?

10. If huge portions of broadcast material have been lost—as they have—how reasonable is it to expect that any historical study of radio will provide an accurate, credible explanation?

Readings

Developmental School

Bilby, Kenneth, Ch. 6, "The Television Era Begins," pp. 111-138, *The General: David Sarnoff and the Rise of the Communications Industry*. New York: Harper and Row, 1986.

Bohn, Thomas W., "Broadcasting National Election Returns: 1916-1948," *Journal of Broadcasting* 12 (1968): 267-286.

Hofer, Stephen F., "Phil Farnsworth: Television's Pioneer," *Journal of Broadcasting* 23 (1979): 153-165.

McChesney, Robert W., "Roosevelt and the Communications Act of 1934," *American Journalism* 5 (1988): 204-229.

Smith, R. Franklin, "'Oldest Station in the Nation'?" *Journal of Broadcasting* 4 (Winter 1959-1960): 40-55.

Progressive School

Archer, Gleason L., Ch. 23, "David Sarnoff Looks Ahead," pp. 468-478, *Big Business and Radio*. New York: American Historical Society, 1939.

Barnouw, Eric, "Web," pp. 189-234, *The Golden Web: A History of Broadcasting in the United States, 1933-1953*. New York: Oxford University Press, 1968.

MacDonald, J. Fred, "The Maturation of Programming, 1932-1939," pp. 39-76, *Don't Touch That Dial: Radio Programming in American Life, 1920-1960*. Chicago: Nelson-Hall, 1979.

Sterling, Christopher H., and John M. Kittross, "Challenge and Competition," pp. 446-546, *Stay Tuned: A Concise History of American Journalism*. Belmont, CA: Wadsworth, 1990.

Williams, Robert J., "The Politics of American Broadcasting: Public Purposes and Private Interests," *Journal of American Studies* 10 (December 1976): 329-340.

Cultural School

Fang, Irving, Ch. 1, "The 'Excess Prophets,'" pp. 3-14, *Those Radio Commentators!* Ames: Iowa State University Press, 1978.

Ostroff, David H., "Equal Time: Origins of Section 18 of the Radio Act of 1927," *Journal of Broadcasting* 24 (1980): 367-380.

Rosen, Philip T., "Introduction," pp. 3-14, *The Modern Stentors: Radio Broadcasters and the Federal Government, 1920-1934*. Westport, CT: Greenwood Press, 1980.

Spaulding, John W., "1928: Radio Becomes a Mass Advertising Medium," *Journal of Broadcasting* 8 (1963-1964): 31-45.

Wik, Reynold M., "The Radio in Rural America during the 1920s," *Agricultural History* (October 1981): 339-350.

22

The Contemporary Press, 1945-Present: Profiteering Business or Professional Journalism?

American journalism since World War II has been in one of the most dynamic stages in its entire history. Changes in journalists' attitudes and professionalism, in the economic structure of the mass media, in technology, and in other aspects of media operations have taken place at a time when external conditions and influences also were undergoing major alterations. The result was that the press that emerged from the war had been significantly altered by the 1990s. The change was apparent in areas ranging from freedom of the press and government-press relations to an increase in the value of media properties and a decline in the number of locally owned newspapers.

The most obvious change was the accelerated growth of the media as businesses. Chain ownership of newspapers increased substantially after 1945. In 1935, 63 chains owned 328 daily newspapers (approximately 17% of all dailies), whereas in 1960 a total of 114 chains owned 563 dailies (32% of all dailies), and in 1977 chains owned 1,061 dailies (60% of the total). A related trend was the elimination of competing newspapers in the same city. Whereas 117 cities had competing dailies in 1945, only 45 had them in 1980. The post-1945 period also witnessed an increase in the value of media properties. Newspapers had operating profit margins that were attractive to investing companies, and the sale prices of newspapers soared dramatically as an awareness of their profitability increased. As corporations bought up newspapers, local ownership decreased, a trend that concerned critics.

As the press increasingly took on characteristics of a business, it also developed as a profession. Activities oriented to professional journalism—such as college training, professional journals, and organizations of working journalists—flourished as they never had before. These factors and others contributed to an increasing recognition of journalism as a well-defined field with its own training, practices, sets of ethics, and other features denoting an occupation as a profession. One of the paramount professional concerns of journalists was freedom of the press. Overall, they were quite successful in their attempts to broaden freedom. Especially notable was the 1964 U.S. Supreme Court decision in *New York Times v. Sullivan* giving journalists a safe operating area in the field of libel as they rarely had imagined possible.

Perhaps the most marked changes brought about by the increased professionalization was the press' relationship with government. Whereas the press prior to World War II generally was neutral toward or supportive of government, the period after the war saw a swing toward a neutral-to-antagonistic attitude. Although many critics claimed such an attitude indicated that the press had a liberal bias, it appears just as likely that the attitude also represented journalists' institutionalized, professionalized view of themselves as the "watchdogs" of government. Thus, at the same time that some critics claimed that big business' control of newspapers made them conservative, working journalists seemed to be both liberal and critical toward government and other institutions such as business and religion. Such attitudes, historians noted, grew out of episodes such as Sen. Joseph McCarthy's attacks on communism in the early 1950s, the civil rights movement of the mid-1950s to mid-1960s, the Vietnam War, and the Watergate political scandal. In all of these episodes, the "press" found itself critical of the government power structure.

Historians tended to react strongly to the changes that took place in journalism after 1945. Writing about issues and trends of their own times, they often produced studies about events and episodes on which they held strong opinions. Thus, historical study of American journalism after 1945 tended to be marked by vigorous viewpoints and to present one of the more energetic interpretive pictures that media historiography has given. Reflecting their perspectives on such matters as the role of journalism in society and the motivations of journalists, historians tended to present evaluations of recent journalism that were either intensely positive or negative.

In general, their assessments depended on how well they assumed journalists had served either their profession or society as a whole. The final evaluations tended to extremes, with some historians concluding that journalism in the second half of the 20th century progressed markedly toward becoming an important and socially responsible part of American society, whereas other historians argued critically that journalism had failed seriously in a number of ways because of either its underlying economic structure or its internal methods of operation. The underlying question historians confronted thus tended to be whether the fundamental characteristic of American journalism after 1945 was responsible professionalism in both journalistic and social roles or irresponsibility motivated by media owners' desire for profits. The answers historians gave to that question tended to determine their ultimate interpretation of modern journalism history.

Historians had difficulty in objectively explaining press history in the post-war period if for no other reason than the fact that they had lived through the period and lacked a detached perspective. Confronted with so many events and issues which their own generation had experienced, they found it hard to place isolated incidents into an overall picture. One effect was that they produced no history of the period as a whole, attempting to put into perspective the age of the contemporary American press. Although the field has numerous works on individual journalists, newspapers, and issues, no historian apparently has been bold enough to attempt to provide an integrated story of the last half century. The bewildering volume of material presenting itself for study seems a morass waiting to entangle and then trap the historian who would venture there. Historians faced an additional problem in the unavailability of many sources of information that simply had not been opened to examination by scholars.

Despite such handicaps—or perhaps because of them—historians tended to write of journalism of the period in fairly opinionated and sharply defined terms. To an unusual degree, studies tended to offer strongly positive or negative pictures of journalism, with only a relatively small group of historians taking a neutral ground about events and changes, attempting neither to applaud nor to condemn. Those historians who treated journalism favorably wrote almost wholly within the Developmental framework, albeit frequently incorporating liberal social and political attitudes into their approach. On the other hand, journalism found itself suffering harsh criticism from several groups of historians. Although they differed in their criticisms, most based their attacks in some way on economic factors. The most sustained criticism came from what might be described as Progressive or Liberal Economic historians, whose fundamental argument was that the profit motive of owners prevented the news media from performing in socially responsible ways. Whereas similar attacks were leveled by Neo-Marxist historians, other criticisms came from both Neo-Conservative historians and some Developmental historians. Neo-Conservative historians placed the blame for problems in journalism on such factors as unfair demands by labor unions, whereas Developmental historians believed a number of internal circumstances made it difficult for the press to perform adequately according to established professional standards.

In the middle ground separating the ardently negative and positive evaluations of the press were a handful of historians who took a neutral view. To a large extent, these historians wrote within the Cultural school and focused on trends and changes in journalism, the press' responses to issues of the period, and the reasons that the press exercised an influence on society.

The Cultural School

Cultural historians tended to assume that journalistic changes were inevitable results of changes in society, public attitudes, economic systems, and institutional dynamics of the press itself. Whereas, for example, many liberal historians considered the growth of chains to be the result of the avarice of big business, Cultural historians explained the growth as the normal development from prevailing circumstances of economics and the marketplace. They did not view such changes as the result of some supposed sinister plot. Instead, they accepted them as a realistic fact of economic life, and they pointed out other factors that mitigated any damages that might occur because of increasing chain ownership or other trends in publishing. They viewed cross-media ownership—that is, chains linking newspapers with radio and television stations—with little alarm, for it presented, Cultural historians said, a negligible threat, if any threat at all, to the number of outlets for points of view on public issues. Likewise, they accepted suspensions of both weekly and daily newspapers as posing little danger. They attributed newspaper disappearances to poor local and national economies, increasing production costs, internal management problems, and in many instances the absence of a need for the papers. In cities with two daily papers, for example, the public showed little concern over the merger of competitors simply because one paper could serve their interests just as well.

The work of this group of historians was exemplified by the studies of Raymond Nixon, who produced a number of articles in the 1950s and 1960s on trends in media ownership. He argued that the publishing industry after World War II had attained the highest degree of stability in its history and that fears of a monopoly on the expression of ideas caused by the decline in newspaper competition were unfounded. The total number of newspapers, he pointed out, was increasing in proportion to increases in the nation's population, as was newspaper circulation. "[T]he last 16 years," he wrote in 1961, "have brought us very close to the realization of . . . the possibility that competition from the broadcast media would increase to such an extent that fears as to the consequences of local newspaper 'monopoly' would subside. For newspaper ownership in the United States now has stabilized according to a pattern of only one publisher to community in all except the larger cities, and the public obviously has accepted the situation with equanimity." Despite anxiety among critics over declining newspaper competition, Nixon declared that daily newspapers were continuing to prosper, that the competition between broadcast and print media provided the public with a method of checking each, that more media voices were competing for attention than ever before, and that the continued growth of daily newspapers at a time of a vast increase in broadcasting competition indicated that each medium had distinctive functions to perform. "In those cities," he pointed out, "where each medium performs well the distinctive functions that it is best suited to perform, the media seem to supplement and complement each other even more than they compete."[1]

Concerned especially about the relationship between the press and society, Cultural historians conducted a number of studies on the nature of the press' influence and on the responses the press made to occurrences and issues in its surrounding culture. Representative of these studies were such works as Eric Veblen's *The Manchester Union Leader in New Hampshire Elections* (1975), which concluded that the paper influenced statewide elections because political candidates made decisions based on their belief that the paper influenced voters, and Harold H. Osmer's *U.S. Religious Journalism and the Korean War* (1981), which analyzed the religious press' views on the war in its relation to communism.

The Developmental School

Developmental historians, who made up the largest single group, tended to view journalism after 1945 in a highly favorable light. Their attention focused on how journalism had changed and concluded that the press by the 1990s was improved in various areas over the press that had emerged from World War II. In general, they emphasized advances in professional practices and the journalists and media organizations that had contributed to the progress. Whereas some Developmental historians incorporated a liberal social view into their interpretation, others concerned themselves almost solely with journalistic methods and practitioners.

Typical studies dealt with techniques and practices such as coverage of presidential campaigns and press conferences, coverage of major events and issues such as ecology and energy use, coverage of business, column writing, and investigative reporting. Individual journalists ranging from publishers to columnists and reporters—such as "Washington-Merry-Go-Round" columnist Drew Pearson, and John S. Knight, editorial writer and president of the Knight newspaper chain—were singled out for individual attention, as were leading news organizations such as the New York *Times*, Detroit *Free Press*, Baltimore *Sun*, Chicago *Tribune* and *Sun-Times*, San Francisco *Chronicle*, and the Hearst corporation. Although Developmental historians frequently mentioned shortcom-

---

[1]Raymond B. Nixon and Jean Ward, "Trends in Newspaper Ownership and Inter-Media Competition," *Journalism Quarterly* 38 (1961): 3-14.

ings, they tended to treat such people and institutions as superior practitioners of journalism.

Representative of such works was Howard Bray's *The Pillars of the Post: The Making of a News Empire in Washington* (1980), which provided a highly favorable treatment of Katharine Graham and Ben Bradlee, publisher and editor of the Washington *Post*, both of whom, Bray declared, believed in journalistic excellence and helped make the *Post* exceptional during such episodes as the Vietnam War, the civil rights movement, and Watergate. Other studies analyzed such topics as professional attitudes among news and editorial staff members, the progress women had made in journalism, the growth of press criticism as part of the journalism profession, development of the suburban press, successes of weekly newspapers, expansion and financial prosperity of the press, successful techniques in publishing, press influence on public affairs, and the growth of the press as a stable and powerful institution.

Serious scholarly studies, such as several works by James Pollard on relations between U.S. presidents and the press, made up the bulk of the work by Developmental historians, but the two works that received most attention were by practicing journalists, Gay Talese and David Halberstam. Both had been members of the New York *Times* staff, and both brought a professional background and perspective to their histories. Talese's history of the *Times*, revealingly titled *The Kingdom and the Power* and subtitled *The Story of the Men Who Influence the Institution That Influences the World—The New York Times*, was published in 1969 and made the non-fiction best-seller list. It provided an inside view of *Times* reporters, executives, editors, and publishers, and it dwelled on the struggle among them to determine the nature of the paper and the direction it would take. Although the account of the people who ran the *Times* revealed personal ambition and interpersonal rivalries, it also placed the story against the panorama of the *Times* institution itself, for the newspaper was so vast and great that it had a life and continuing daily operation of its own. After each internal conflict, the characters in the drama worked together again, carried along in the relentless movement of the *Times* itself and aware once again that the most important factor in the influence and stature of the newspaper was the paper itself.

The influence of the news media provided the theme also for Halberstam's *The Powers That Be* (1979), a book that gained wide popular readership. Although Halberstam can be classified as a modern Romantic historian, he also held a favorable Developmental outlook on the news media. Taking as his subjects the Washington *Post*, Los Angeles *Times*, CBS, and *Time* Inc. and the men and women who helped build them into media empires, he examined their rise to power and argued that the huge media dominated Amer-

ican national government and often shaped politics and society, acquiring in the process status and magnificent profits. The people
who ran the organizations frequently were ambitious and at times
irresponsible, but in the end and as a whole they used their power
wisely for the good of society. Although the Los Angeles *Times*, for
example, had a history of bias against groups and people who opposed its financial and political interests, the media in general responded responsibly to their prestige and the power they wielded.
The *Times* under Otis Chandler became an excellent news organization which opened its columns to conservatives and liberals
alike, and the Washington *Post* under Katharine Graham used its
considerable profits to improve its news coverage.

As a rule, Developmental historians accepted press opposition to
established institutions as a professional standards. Many viewed
it as such a legitimate aspect of journalism that it formed the basis
for their historical studies. Most writers of Developmental history
were either practicing journalists or were college teachers of journalism with a background in professional journalism. Thus, they
usually accepted the tenets of professional practice. Many tended to
believe that support of the underdog was a role of the press and that
the proper role of the press was to serve as a watchdog or adversary of
government and other established institutions such as big business.
In general, these historians tended to view the history of recent
journalism in terms of the press fighting evil in American politics
and society. The heroes of their histories often were journalists crusading to correct the ills and problems of their communities and the
nation, and the opposition was composed of authorities or groups that
espoused repression and injustice, the wealthy class in American
society, demagogues, or government. Some Developmental historians went so far as to declare that one of the government's paramount
designs was to control information, silence the press, and deceive
the public.

For Developmental historians, some of the most heroic figures
were Southern journalists who stood up bravely for justice and human rights during the civil rights movement of the 1950s and 1960s.
The archetype of the crusading journalist was Ralph McGill, editor
of the Atlanta *Constitution*. The subject of numerous works, he was
painted as a courageous and fearless advocate of equal rights for
Black Americans. A classic liberal and moral person, he favored
freedom and rightness, identified with the poor and underprivileged, and opposed violence and injustice. Developmental historians described other journalists such as Hodding Carter and Hazel
Brannon Smith of Mississippi as courageous figures who fought
corrupt government and powerful racists despite physical threats,
economic boycotts, and bombings of their homes and newspaper offices. Their goals ultimately were to help those people against whom

the power of established groups seemed to be arrayed and to make their communities and the nation better places to live.

Opposing the press in many situations, some Developmental historians argued, was the government, which often was reactionary and repressive. One of the government's primary aims, they claimed, was to muzzle the press. Officials realized that the press presented a barrier to their accomplishing their objectives, for it always was attempting to bring to public view what officials were trying to conceal. In such a situation, these historians declared, the press was required to act as an adversary and a watchdog of the government, aggressively protect its rights under the First Amendment, improve its investigative practices in order to uncover official wrongdoing, fight for civil liberties, and remain constantly vigilant, ready to sound the alarm should government demagogues take any action to endanger American liberty.

The concept of an antagonistic relationship between government and the news media was presented cogently by the journalism educator William Rivers in a work entitled *The Adversaries: Politics and the Press* (1970). Although the book was a critical commentary on contemporary practices rather than an historical work, it epitomized the view taken by many Developmental historians. Whereas the press previously had served ably as a critic of government, Rivers argued, by the 1960s it had given up its adversary role against what he called the governmental-industrial-military-educational complex. In doing so, the press had deserted its necessary and desirable function, for the only proper relationship between the press and government should be an adversarial one. "The only way for a reporter to look at an official," Rivers wrote, "is skeptically."[2] Although he disclaimed that the press' attitude should be a hostile one, he argued that there should be tension and contention between journalists and officials such as exists between opposing lawyers, rather than an amiable relationship. Believing that the governmental-industrial-military-educational complex was responsible for most of society's ills, Rivers claimed that government tried to control information through both dissemination and suppression for its own self-interest and the benefit of the establishment. It was therefore up to journalists to provide balance to the situation and thereby make the American democratic society work.

A similar theme underlay William E. Porter's *Assault on the Media: The Nixon Years* (1976), which expressed the prevailing view among liberal Developmental historians about President Nixon's attitude toward the press. Nixon, according to Porter, viewed the press with hostility and waged a deliberate campaign to "intimidate, harass, regulate and damage" the news media. Al-

---

[2]William Rivers, *The Adversaries: Politics and the Press* (Boston: 1970), 273.

though the press approached Nixon with similar antagonism, in the long run Nixon's continuing battle with the media posed a great threat to freedom of the press and eventually damaged it. As a result of widespread criticism of the press encouraged by Nixon's attacks, newspapers began running more conservative material, the media grew more willing to correct errors, local television stations began to stand up to the liberal networks, local government bodies and officials became more prone to be secretive in their meetings and records, and the watchdog role of the press came to be viewed more suspiciously. All these changes, Porter said, helped point out the "frailty" of press freedom when it is subjected to a full-scale attack by a strong public official, even when that official is corrupt and has little true concern for the public interest.

A final critique of modern journalism came from a group of Developmental historians who based their judgments not on ideological grounds but on standards of professional journalistic practices. They argued that problems in journalism were caused primarily by internal structural characteristics and operating procedures of the media and by dominant journalistic attitudes. The most devastating attack from this school of historians came from Peter Braestrup in *Big Story: How the American Press and Television Reported and Interpreted the Crisis of Tet 1968 in Vietnam and Washington* (1977). A voluminous and minutely documented attack on press coverage of the Tet military offensive during the Vietnam War, the study argued that logistical and structural problems in press operations and the press' negative reaction to President Lyndon Johnson's tactics resulted in distorted news and interpretations and outright falsification. The Tet offensive was a military defeat for the North Vietnamese and Viet Cong forces, but the media wrongly concluded that it was a victory. This misrepresentation of the campaign to the American public eventually caused Johnson to change his commitment to the American war effort and led to the withdrawal of American troops and the defeat of South Vietnam.

The press, according to Braestrup, misrepresented most aspects of Tet, which failed to achieve most of North Vietnam's and the Viet Cong's objectives. The press, however, pictured it as a major disaster for United States policy and as an indication that North Vietnam and the Viet Cong could mount a major offensive. The misinterpretation was based on and led to factual errors. The media emphasized, usually inaccurately, the futility of United States policy, the supposed shortcomings of the American military, and the enemies' strength. While the press pictured American forces as facing continual and certain defeat and stereotyped South Vietnamese forces as inefficient and brutal, it claimed falsely that the North Vietnamese and Viet Cong were superior in ethics, military discipline, humane treatment of the populace, support from the people, and will to win. Although Braestrup concluded that—with exceptions such as the New York *Times*—the press' misrepresentation was not based on ideology, he drew a picture of a press that presented selective and distorted information because of its adversary role toward the government.

The Ideological Schools

Although Developmental historians sometimes pointed out the failures of the press, they normally concluded that the failures were temporary and that in the end the press had performed well. Such was not the case with a number of ideological historians. Although their beginning assumptions varied, these historians argued that press performance was inadequate and often reprehensible. Some historians, primarily from Liberal or Neo-Marxist schools, viewed the root of the problem in economic terms, as press owners subverted social responsibility because of their overriding desire for profits. Directly opposing such an interpretation were a number of Neo-Conservative historians who argued that the primary problem presented to modern journalism came from liberal organizations such as labor unions which presented selfish and unreasonable demands on the news media and their management.

The bulk of the critical historians wrote from a liberal economic perspective. Generally employing a Progressive point of view, they pointed to a number of shortcomings within the press and placed the blame on the underlying economic motivations of media owners. Among the problems were the emphasis on journalism primarily as a business, the growth of chain ownership, a decline in editorial vitality, a decline in newspaper competition, and reduced newspaper expenditures for news services. Among the failures created by these problems were the resultant press advocacy of its own interests and ideological conservatism, the press' reluctance to speak out on issues, a threat posed to freedom of the press by economic considerations, a control exercised over information through journalism's close ties to government, a middle-class definition of news, American informational "imperialism," and media owners' insatiable quest for money and conservative power.

These historians subjected the press to highly critical attacks in a number of major works. The tone of the attack was set by Carl E. Lindstrom in *The Fading American Newspaper*, a book published in 1960 and intended primarily as a contemporary criticism of the press. The newspaper was disappearing, Lindstrom argued, because it had failed to compete effectively with television and had become primarily a business enterprise. He complained that the press was too concerned with deadlines and scoops rather than significant news and issues, that chain ownership was rationalized as an economic necessity when in reality it was strangling the vitality from journalism, and that publishers did not have the courage to take stands on issues.

The danger that economic motives presented to freedom of the press was detailed in a subsequent study by Bryce Rucker, a historian specializing in press law. In *The First Freedom* (1968), he argued that overwhelming economic concentration had transformed the news media into gigantic interconnected conglomerates which approached every aspect of the news process as a business. Focusing on the economic-industrial structure of the media, the growth of the economic control of the press by chains and corporations, and their attempts to eliminate competition, he concluded that a grave new threat was posed to press freedom and American democracy.

In a biting analysis two years later, James Aronson argued that the press had lost its honor, that it had helped lead the nation into a dangerous political reactionarianism, and that it needed reforming. Government, he wrote in *The Press and the Cold War* (1970), consistently had attempted to manage the flow of information and frequently had succeeded because the press had acted as an accomplice. In league with giant economic interests, government attempted to promote the status quo, and the people who owned the press shared the same interests as government and big business. The press therefore gave up its role of independent analysis and criticism. Examining how American newspapers had treated episodes in some of America's most critical periods since the Russian revolution, Aronson argued that growing military, private, and government bureaucracies had inserted themselves into the information transmission process. The press played a major role in a number of episodes—such as McCarthyism; U.S. imperialism; domestic attacks on socialists, liberals, and Marxists; the debacle of the attempted invasion of Cuba at the Bay of Pigs; illegal activities of the Central Intelligence Agency; and America's immoral participation in the Vietnam War—because it supported or initiated government actions by either accepting them or promoting them without any serious questioning. The only hope lay in a press not controlled by big business. "The press," Aronson reasoned, "helped to lead the nation into accepting a quarter century of the Cold War, with the awfulness that ensued. An alternative press can help dismantle the Cold War and lead the nation into accepting its place in the family of man."[3]

In another study of the international aspects of American journalism, William H. Read focused on the "expansion of American mass media abroad." In *America's Mass Media Merchants* (1976), he examined how since World War II U.S. "transnational" media

---

[3]James Aronson, *The Press and the Cold War* (Indianapolis: Bobbs-Merrill, 1970), 288.

organizations—such as the Associated Press, United Press International, the New York Times News Service, *Time* magazine, and *Reader's Digest*—had extended their operations far beyond the borders of America and had gained worldwide distribution, sizable financial investments abroad, and a major international impact. Profits, Read argued, lay at the base of their operations, efforts, and content. The results of such a global extension of American media were a danger to "information sovereignty" for each nation, a restriction on the free international flow of information, and American cultural impact abroad.

The Liberal interpretation of modern American journalism also frequently offered a critical estimation of leading journalists such as those whom Developmental historians had praised. Gaeton Fonzi, for example, in *Annenberg: A Biography of Power* (1970), described Walter Annenberg, owner of the Philadelphia *Inquirer* and *Bulletin* and a number of other publications, as vindictive and interested primarily in making money. Annenberg believed that money rather than integrity provided the route to respectability and influence. As a result, ultimately he had failed—even though his publications were successful, he contributed generously to charities and institutions, and he was appointed U.S. ambassador to England—because he never showed any concern for truth, the highest calling of journalism. He had no scruples against twisting the truth to benefit his conservative friends, such as President Nixon and Ronald Reagan, then governor of California; and, according to Fonzi, it was widely known that Annenberg used his newspapers to "get even" with opponents and make money unscrupulously—so widely known that one of Annenberg's top reporters was able to extort money from criminals because they assumed the reporter had the support of Annenberg.

Even more critical of the conservatism and profit orientation of the modern press was a small group of Neo-Marxist historians. Like Progressive historians, they viewed history in the context of a conflict between groups, although Neo-Marxists viewed the conflict in more extreme terms. To them, it seemed that the capitalist class, which included not only media owners but mainstream American journalism in general, used its wealth and power to suppress the working class and impose its conservative ideas on society. The fullest elaboration of the Neo-Marxist interpretation was offered by Todd Gittlin in *The Whole World is Watching: Mass Media in the Making and Unmaking of the New Left* (1980). A former member of the radical group Students for a Democratic Society, Gittlin argued that American society and the press were characterized by "hegemony," that is, domination by a ruling class. Examining the relationship between the mass media and the New Left in the 1960s, he reasoned that mainstream journalism tended to stereotype challenges to the established order and to attempt to make leftist groups look ridiculous. With such an outlook, the media had contributed to the perpetuation of the ruling class by characterizing the New Left as violent, deviant, and silly.

In direct contrast to the Neo-Marxist interpretation, another small group of Neo-Conservative historians laid the blame for the problems in modern journalism on liberal groups, especially organized labor. The most prominent work by this school was Joseph Sage's *Three to Zero: The Story of the Birth and Death of the World Journal Tribune* (1967), a history from management's point of view of the brief life and the death in 1967 of the three combined New York newspapers. Commissioned by the American Newspaper Publishers' Association to do the study, Sage argued that the newspaper failed because unions were reckless in their demands. Spurred by their personally ambitious leader, printers' and other craft unions played New York's newspapers against each other. They also attempted to assume many of management's prerogatives, such as deciding whether to adopt measures to cut costs and devices to save time and labor. As one result, the *World Journal Tribune* was forced to keep on its payroll 500 employees for whom there was no job at a time when the newspaper budget required reduced expenditures if the paper were to survive. The failure of management and of the ANPA was in not presenting a united front against the unions, Sage said, as some newspapers took advantage of the situation to work out labor agreements that benefited only themselves in the short run rather than journalism in the long run.

Discussion

Historians continue to have an intense interest in recent journalism history. That interest appears, in many instances, to be primarily because of an interest in contemporary conditions rather than purely an interest in history. As a result, historians have had difficulty separating the recent past from their concerns about contemporary events. Interpretations of the recent past, therefore, have shown the effects of historians' passions more than interpretations of most other periods have. That situation raises a number of questions not only about the post-1945 period but about the nature of historical study as well.

1. As to the actual substance of the period, one must begin by asking what the essential nature of the press was. Is the press best explained in terms of professional journalism practices and progress, as Developmental historians have argued?

2. If so, when did it perform best—when it operated in a balanced, detached manner or when journalists viewed their role as adversaries of other established institutions such as government or business? Should the press have been an adversary? From where did

that concept arise—from the press or from other institutions?

3. In a democratic society, what should have been the preferred role?

4. If one believes it is an adversary role, what is the basis for determining that a professionalized press serves the interests of the public better than elective government representatives do?

5. As one considers the nature of historical study, scholarship on the post-1945 period presents a number of intriguing questions. If one accepts an ideological role as appropriate for the press, as liberal Developmental, Progressive, and Marxist historians did, on what basis does one determine what the preferred ideology should be? Is there any reason to believe that a liberal ideology, the type advocated by the majority of historians, should be preferred over a moderate or conservative one?

6. Should historians bring an ideological perspective to their study of the past? Is it possible for them not to do so?

7. What effect has historians' interest or involvement in recent events had on their ability to explain the recent past?

8. Is it appropriate for historians to be more deeply motivated by their interest in the present than in the past? Can the past be studied fairly if the historians' primary interest springs from the present? If historians are influenced by their own times, is it possible to provide accurate assessments of events until a length of time has passed?

9. What must be done for historians to provide meaningful assessments of events that occurred during their own lifetime and in which they may have been deeply involved?

Readings

Cultural School

Nixon, Raymond B., "Trends in Daily Newspaper Ownership Since 1945," *Journalism Quarterly* 31 (1954): 3-14.

Osmer, Harold H., Ch. 2, "1950: Year of Intensifying Conflict," pp. 27-59, *U.S. Religious Journalism and the Korean War.* Washington, DC: University Press of America, 1980.

Shmanske, Stephen, "News as a Public Good: Cooperative Ownership, Price Commitments, and the Success of the Associated Press," *Business History Review* 60 (Spring 1986): 55-80.

Sterling, Christopher H., "Trends in Daily Newspaper and Broadcast Ownership, 1922-70," *Journalism Quarterly* 52 (1975): 247-256, 320.

Developmental School

Braestrap, Peter, Ch. 15, "An Extreme Case," pp. 705-728, *Big Story: How the American Press and Television Reported and Interpreted the Crisis of Tet 1968 in Vietnam and Washington.* Boulder, CO: Westview, 1977.

Bray, Howard, Ch. 3, "Mrs. Graham Takes Charge," pp. 58-87, *The Pillars of the Post: The Making of a News Empire in Washington.* New York: Norton, 1980.

Halberstam, David, Ch. 19, "The Washington *Post*," pp. 515-549, *The Powers That Be.* New York: Knopf, 1979.

Marsh, Harry, Ch. 18, "The Contemporary Press, 1945-present," pp. 397-417, Wm. David Sloan, James G. Stovall, and James D. Startt, eds., *The Media in America.* Worthington, OH: Publishing Horizons, 1989.

Porter, William. E., Ch. 1, "Background for the Nixon Attitude," pp. 1-36, *Assault on the Media: The Nixon Years.* Ann Arbor: University of Michigan Press, 1976.

Scharff, Edward E., Ch. 15, "Creative Tension," pp. 271-292, *Worldly Power: The Making of the Wall Street Journal.* New York: Beaufort Books, 1986.

Talese, Gay, Ch. 20 (untitled), pp. 572-627, *The Kingdom and the Power.* New York: World, 1969.

Ideological Schools

Aronson, James, Ch. 17, "Journalism of the Absurd," pp. 231-245, *The Press and the Cold War.* Indianapolis: Bobbs-Merrill, 1970.

Dan, Uri, Ch. 4, "The Turning Point," pp. 173-208, *Blood Libel: The Inside Story of General Ariel Sharon's History-Making Suit Against Time Magazine.* New York: Simon and Schuster, 1987.

Fonzi, Gaeton, "The Press Lord," pp. 147-168, *Annenberg: A Biography of Power.* New York: Weybright & Talley, 1970.

Kreigh, Andrew, Ch. 11, "The Spike," pp. 110-123, *Spiked: How Chain Management Corrupted America's Oldest Newspaper.* Old Saybrook, CT: Peregrine, 1987.

Sage, Joseph, Part 4, "233 Days to Disaster," pp. 55-74, *Three to Zero: The Story of the Birth and Death of the World Journal Tribune.* New York: American Newspaper Publishers Association, 1967.

23

Television, 1948-Present:
Entertainment or Information?

The years following World War II witnessed a television revolution in the United States. Close to nonexistent just after the war, TV was found in 9 of 10 U.S. homes just 15 years later. No medium had ever seen such rapid acceptance in so short a period. The difference between television and other media was TV's ability to transmit both sound and pictures, a technological advancement which dramatically widened information horizons. Yet to historians, television's bigger impact was in deepening a perennial "What is news?" question because it was TV entertainment, not information, that explained the medium's enormous popularity. It is no surprise that the competing dimensions of entertainment and information have inspired television's primary historical questions.

A mixture of information and entertainment can be traced to the beginning of television. When CBS introduced the first regular evening newscast in 1948, it chose former actor Douglas Edwards as its anchor. The first anchors at NBC and ABC, John Cameron Swayze and John Daly, appeared on popular quiz shows during the years they hosted news programs in the 1950s. Although TV journalism became more self-contained early in the 1960s, the field never fully shed a show-business stripe. Historians were reminded of it in the immensely popular and entertaining CBS program "60 Minutes" beginning in the 1960s, the rise of research-consultants and their news formulas in the 1970s, and the appearance of the "tabloid" genre of television news in the 1980s.

Three dominant schools of historical interpretation emerged in television, each distinguished by the way it measured the influence of entertainment in TV's information process. A Neo-Romantic school saw harmony between entertainment and information, that the two evolved mostly independent from one another and provided compatible chapters in a grand television story. In contrast, a De-

By Craig Allen
University of Alabama

velopmental school conceived no compatibility with entertainment and information and established instead an enduring competition between the two in which entertainment was a cruel "Goliath" and information a well-meaning "David." Because TV swelled as an entertainment medium, its historical turning points came when journalists fought for social responsibility, their many failures only advancing a positive, redeeming legacy. A Progressive school, also seeing TV sloped in an entertainment direction and equally concerned about that characteristic as Developmental historians were, found little redemption in the past. Progressive historians argued that good journalists, as responsible as they might have been, were never in a position to keep entertainment and information from growing hopelessly intertwined. The Progressive depiction was essentially an argument for reform, often directed at government figures, the academic community, and citizens who, it was felt, might intervene and should, at the least, be very concerned.

Neo-Romantic School
Although the Neo-Romantic perspective in television history does not contain the artistry, fancy, and emotion associated with the Romantic movement in the 19th century, many authors wrote of television in passionate, adventurous, and idealistic terms. Television had a natural romantic appeal for many reasons. When it began in the late 1940s, it was promoted by the industry and contemporary observers in bigger-than-life-terms. They saw Americans spellbound by the sporting events, motion pictures, and other fare suddenly available in their living rooms. The Neo-Romantic school did not materialize, though, until after the novelty of TV had passed in the 1960s and 1970s. If Neo-Romantic historians were critical of any aspect of television, it was the tendency of the public to take television for granted. Indifference was cured by appreciation of the big, the colorful, and the dramatic.

The Neo-Romantic school relied on linear chronology and detailed description that usually identified major news broadcasts and prominent news people as guideposts to the field's various stages. Usually, they were found to be powerful, sometimes controversial, and always interesting. Much of Neo-Romantic history elevated Marshall McLuhan's 1960s "global village" concept that saw the people of the world drawn together by common TV viewing opportunities. Although few Neo-Romantic historians discussed McLuhan in so many words, they clung to the notion that television was pervasive and influential.

David Halberstam's widely-acclaimed *The Powers That Be* (1979) contained an encyclopedic construction common in the Neo-Romantic school. Like many Neo-Romantic historians, Halberstam was impressed with the monumental size of the television industry and how it resembled journalistic empires in the print field. He integrated a history of CBS with those of Time Inc., two newspapers (the Washington *Post* and Los Angeles *Times*), and the stories of the men and women who helped build them into media empires. He focused on their rise to power and argued that the huge media dominated American national government and often shaped politics and society, acquiring in the process status and magnificent profits. The people who ran the organizations frequently were ambitious and at times irresponsible, but in the end and as a whole they used their power wisely for the good of society. Although William Paley of CBS, for example, let highly profitable entertainment programming supersede news, the media in general responded responsibly to their prestige and the power they wielded. Similarly, they made responsible use of their profits. Money, Halberstam reasoned, was necessary for the press to perform its job well, the most notable instance being the media's coverage of Watergate. "It was a curious irony of capitalism," he wrote, "that among the only outlets rich enough and powerful enough to stand up to an overblown, occasionally reckless, otherwise unchallenged central government were journalistic institutions that had very, very secure financial bases."

As a journalist himself and a popular writer—and one who observed first-hand TV coverage of major events—Halberstam was typical of numerous broadcast historians in all schools. *The Powers That Be* was particularly representative of several Neo-Romantic histories of television journalism that appeared beginning in the post-Watergate 1970s, when authors had the enticing events of that decade and the 1960s to consider.

A Neo-Romantic trademark apparent in Halberstam was a firm line between television's news and entertainment functions and how they lived in an uneasy yet co-equal partnership. This balance was traced at CBS through people in its news division, almost always the network's most-visible and recognizable on-camera personalities. The careers of these individuals often turned when important news events broke. Halberstam found a cradle of the field's history in the 1952 political conventions when the networks for the first time had to remove tedium from extended live coverage. Edward R. Murrow and his "Murrow men"—Eric Sevareid, Howard Smith, Charles Collingwood, William Shirer, and David Schoenbrun—had difficulty. They were "notoriously cerebral and had been picked for that reason" when radio was king. They lacked the appeal and durability that TV now needed of its "stars." That year Walter Cronkite demonstrated the required traits and became the model TV journalist for a generation. In Cronkite, CBS executives "knew they had a winner and a new dimension of importance for television."[1]

The remainder of the 1950s and the next two decades saw occasional tests of strength at CBS between news managers and entertainment programmers, such as the removal of Murrow's "See It Now" documentary series because of low ratings. Yet news stood solidly because it, like entertainment fare, was tremendously profitable, proven at NBC where ratings "soared" under the Chet Huntley-David Brinkley anchor team. CBS gained economic parity with NBC soon after the engaging Cronkite was made anchor in 1962 and a newer breed of dedicated professionals, including Roger Mudd, Bill Moyers, and Dan Rather, were added to its ranks. Although a profit mentality prevailed, Halberstam cited successive journalistic achievements as evidence that entertainment values did not impede news coverage. Cronkite's reporting in Vietnam marked the "first time in American history a war had been declared over by an anchorman." Only when Cronkite gave his "stamp of approval" did doors open publicly to the Watergate investigation.[2]

Halberstam's conclusions showed the way in which Neo-Romantic historians conceived a certainty-of-performance in television journalism which made it natural they spotlight news events and news people. This viewpoint was also seen in most survey histories of television, a standard work being Christopher Sterling and John Kittross' *Stay Tuned* (1978), which highlighted TV coverage of President Kennedy's assassination in 1963, the violent Democratic convention in 1968, the Apollo 11 moon landing in 1969, and the Watergate scandal of 1972-1974.

Aside from TV's ability to cover these events, the news itself was a major reason the field was easily romanticized. To a large extent, this was because almost the entire history of TV coincided with the Cold War and its numerous spectacles. *Stay Tuned*, like many Neo-Romantic interpretations, read like a Cold War chronology and suggested that television influenced the conflict. Senator Joseph McCarthy's 1950s anticommunist crusade was brought down by a critical Murrow "See It Now" broadcast and ABC's live coverage of the Army-McCarthy hearings. The authors also stressed the Vietnam War and "its unanswered question whether coverage of wartime violence deadened Americans to reality or whether the reporting showed the forest behind the trees and changed American thinking."[3] Whereas Halberstam used a narrative approach based on primary sources, Sterling and Kittross finished with a reference book account of television history that was a product of secondary

---

[1]David Halberstam, *The Powers That Be* (New York: Knopf, 1979), 242-243.

[2]Ibid., pp. 422, 651-663.

[3]Christopher Sterling and John Kittross, *Stay Tuned* (Belmont, CA: Wadsworth, 1978), 348-352, 407-417.

sources.

Developmental School
Developmental historians, not accepting the Neo-Romantic view that television was a compilation of breathtaking events that viewers watched on home screens, saw an historical fulcrum within the walls of the television industry. They were critical of television, and their primary concern was entertainment's intrusion into TV journalism. Yet the Developmental interpretation was positive at its roots. Despite vehement assaults on entertainment profit motives, Developmental historians were satisfied with the existing free-enterprise TV system and saw the past as a series of positive internal attempts to wrest the medium from entertainment domination.

Resistance to entertainment values, for example, expedited journalistic elements specific to television, such as the balanced "package" story and the neutral anchor. New technology reared new show business possibilities that had to be confronted. Such was the case with electronic news gathering, which was used routinely in live coverage of riots and violence in the 1960s and 1970s until it was discovered that such savagery was often staged for TV cameras. But more important than technique was the evolution of TV news standards, also a fight against entertainment influences. Because of these standards, Developmental historians considered TV information, despite limitations, as the medium's eternal flame. Efforts to keep it burning boded well for the future.

Because it affirmed the free enterprise status quo, the Developmental interpretation was essentially conservative. That was ironic because Developmental history appeared in two major periods, both responses to neo-conservative political trends that made Developmentalism appear liberal by comparison. The first came in the late 1960s when television journalists, apart from their corporate supervisors, were assailed by the Johnson and Nixon administrations for alleged liberal tendencies that furthered domestic unrest and hampered execution of the Vietnam War. The second period came in the late 1980s when Reagan-era deregulation increased competition in the broadcast arena and impelled mergers and retrenchment that reduced radio news operations and led to major layoffs in the news divisions at CBS and NBC.

Although the fires of Developmentalism have tended to be fanned by conservative winds, more noteworthy was that its political perspectives were usually benignly tucked away. The reason was that much Developmental history was advanced by practitioners, people grounded in workaday journalism who were not conditioned to stray from a neutral mainstream and who were disinclined to invite political alternatives such as governmental intervention. It was the effect of the prevailing corporate system on journalistic integrity, not its political meaning, that drove most Developmental historians.

A pattern in Developmental history was the arrangement of battles between a protagonist group of beneficent TV journalists and their antagonistic, more conservative corporate managers who had more clout. The balance the Neo-Romantic school accepted between news and entertainment never existed, according to Developmental historians. Instead, because TV was placed in private hands and owners had to locate lowest common denominators in mass taste, news was an intruder on a show business stage. The development of television was spun by the relentless efforts of journalists. They were guardians of the public interest who made TV news more than what entertainer Oscar Levant once chided as "a parade of catastrophes that ends with a fashion show."

Components of the Developmental interpretation were defined in Fred Friendly's *Due to Circumstances Beyond Our Control* (1967), the first major critical history of television journalism. Although the essence of the book was a personal memoir, Friendly's perspective was extremely significant. Friendly was Murrow's closest associate in the 1950s and president of CBS News the following decade. He countered the Neo-Romantic interpretation by emphasizing that techniques and accomplishments in television did not "just happen," but were the result of substantial tug-of-war behind the scenes. His major contribution was in showing historians it was safe to depict television as an entertainment-first industry. The spectacles of TV's past, while captivating millions, were actually internal struggles that gave the field its form and vigor.

Friendly, for example, was not interested in whether the 1954 "See It Now" broadcast on McCarthy was the "decisive blow" against the Senator. The program was important because it was mounted without the wholehearted support of its sponsor and the network. Moreover, a "heartbreaking casualty" was CBS newsman Don Hollenbeck, who, amid harassment for continuing to examine McCarthy on television, committed suicide.[4] More internal struggle preceded the litany of dramatic event coverage of the 1960s. "Higher judgment did not have to be consulted" after the Kennedy assassination, but other achievements, such as live reporting of space missions, resulted in a "stalemate of command" between news and programming that was usually "bad for news coverage."[5] The unwavering journalistic spirit that had confronted these obstacles for so long accounted for Friendly's departure from CBS News in 1966 when the network aired a rerun of "I Love Lucy" instead of hearings

---

[4]Fred Friendly, *Due to Circumstances Beyond Our Control* (New York: Random House, 1967), 23-67.

[5]Ibid., pp. 164-165.

on the Vietnam War. Offering his resignation as a victory for social responsibility, Friendly was his own martyr to the cause of good television. "If I can't tend the big switch," he wrote, "perhaps I can... stoke a fire."[6]

It was through the Developmental school that the most studied single region in television journalism history was mapped. The subject was Edward R. Murrow, who in both the 1960s and 1980s waves of Developmental interpretation was presented as television's quintessential positive figure. Friendly's book from the 1960s did much to initiate Murrow history by playing up the contribution of all "the professionals at CBS News" but casting Murrow as "the hero" who gave the network its "heart."[7] Also from the 1960s phase of Developmental historiography came the first major Murrow biography: *Prime Time* (1969) by Alexander Kendrick, another CBS veteran. Articles traced Murrow's early career and provided texture to the historical thread that connected radio journalism to television. In the 1980s, however, when deregulation was changing the economics of TV and CBS felt the most severe shockwaves, historians focused more on Murrow's television period. They declared that Murrow was an innovator, that he was sensitive to TV's pervasiveness, and that he rose in indignation when entertainment forces threatened social responsibility.

These themes were well represented in A. M. Sperber's *Murrow: His Life and Times* (1986), the most comprehensive biography of the CBS newsman. It characterized Murrow as a "heretic" undaunted by those in the CBS executive suites who would burn him at the stake. Murrow's 1954 McCarthy broadcast was a "virtuoso performance," but what made more difference was the 1955 debut of the quiz show "The $64,000 Question" that ended up "swamping not only 'See It Now' but all of television." The "$64,000 Question" became the most popular show on TV. Because it preceded "See It Now" and its meager audience on the Tuesday night schedule, Murrow was left a "pauper in the penthouse." Sperber also traced Murrow's complex but ultimately arms-length relationship with CBS chairman William Paley, two people who "knew how to hurt each other."[8]

Even though Murrow ended his career as director of the United States Information Agency under President Kennedy, and not in television, Sperber contended that he departed with a crusading flourish. Highlighted was a 1958 speech in which he blasted the Federal Communications Commission, the television industry, and CBS. "One of the basic troubles," said Murrow, is "an incompatible

---

[6]Ibid., p. 265.

[7]Ibid., p. xxiii.

[8]A. M. Sperber, *Murrow: His Life and Times* (New York: Freundlich Books, 1986), 449, 484, 542.

combination of show business, advertising and news. . . . And when you get all three under one roof, the dust never settles." Later when working at the USIA and former colleague Howard K. Smith was fired by CBS for editorializing, Murrow told him, "Why don't you sue the bastards?"[9]

Because of its depth and primary source construction, Sperber's book, like Friendly's, was extremely influential. Sperber's work galvanized an important "CBS subschool" of Developmental history in the late 1980s that included, among others, Bill Leonard's *In the Storm of the Eye* (1987), Edward Joyce's *Prime Time, Bad Times* (1988), and a third Murrow biography in Joseph Persico's *Edward R. Murrow: An American Original* (1988). Although each author presented some criticism of the nation's commercial broadcast system, none wanted it changed. For these Developmental historians, the past, at its worst, was an inventory of mistakes to be avoided; at its best, it was a showcase of individuals whose ideas and struggles lit the future.

Progressive School

Progressive historians shared much with Developmental historians. Both had critical interpretations, and both maintained that only persistent study of factors inside the TV industry could resolve the field's salient questions. Both schools, at roughly equivalent levels, also tended to link the ills of television to economics and argued that cash flow was governed by entertainment values *vis-à-vis* the ratings system.

Nevertheless, the differences between the Progressive and Developmental interpretations were dramatic. Unlike the Developmental historians, Progressives maintained that the daily struggle for journalistic standards neither contained redeeming social value nor had any realistic prospect for success in a commercial television system. As if to echo fictional news anchor Howard Beale in the 1976 movie *Network*, Progressive historians were "mad" and did not want "to take it any more," believing society's stake in television information was monumental. TV history suggested reform. Nevertheless, Progressives regarded the entertainment-information nexus as so formidable that they never displayed great confidence that change would come to pass.

The Progressive interpretation appeared in the mid-1970s, much of it a rejoinder to the first wave of Developmental history in the late 1960s. Whereas Developmental historians were annoyed by conservative politicians and controversies over the management of TV journalism, Progressives took even more liberal stances and proposed that the system itself was flawed. Still, Progressive sentiment

---

[9]Ibid., pp. xvi, 641.

had a serious inconsistency that in no small way limited reform concepts. Basically, Progressive historians saw social harm in a monolithic, free enterprise institution that influenced the mass public. At the same time, though, Progressives widely acknowledged the hands-off, free-press libertarianism of the First Amendment, which, in practice, preserved the conservative status quo. Few went the distance to hold that America's system of broadcast news would have been better off had the government managed it, as was the case in many other countries. Progressive history featured a shotgun array of reform ideas and lacked true reform muscle. It had value, though, in pressing questions about the evolution of TV that were untended in the other schools.

For example, prior to Ron Powers' *The Newscasters: The News Business as Show Business* (1977), local television journalism was a blind spot in the field's literature. Powers both corrected this and initiated new critical reasoning in television study that helped ground the Progressive interpretation. Whereas Neo-Romantic and Developmental historians were intrigued with major on-air spectaculars, Powers drew inspiration from the most mundane: UFO sightings, "manhunts" with meaningless consequences, capsized canoes, and multiple-part series on sexual fantasies. Such treatment underpinned a Progressive definition that these banal moments—not the Herculean achievements—most represented television journalism and the forces at work in it. Accordingly, Progressives reached the conclusion that TV news was not really journalism but rather something, in Powers' words, embedded with an "entertainment bias."[10]

Powers agreed with the Developmental historians that TV news, at least through the 1950s and 1960s, held ground against entertainment encroachment. Powers, though, took little stock of the journalistic crusade the Developmental historians promoted, suggesting they missed a turning point in the 1970s when local news attracted an infusion of corporate investment and public interest. Instead of remaining a journalistic domain, "the salesmen...took [local news] away from the journalists, slowly, patiently, gradually, and with such finesse that nobody noticed until it was too late."[11] This *fait accompli* culminated with the entrenchment of gigantic nationwide research-consulting firms that marketed an entertainment "blueprint" for television news. A rush toward entertainment values in news was irresistible and unstoppable.

Although Powers readily faulted the existing system, he typified the noncommittal nature of Progressive thinking in proposing solu-

---

[10]Ron Powers, *The Newscasters* (New York: St. Martin's Press, 1978), 33-34, 68-77, 286.

[11]Ibid., p. 1.

tions. On one hand, he encouraged government action. Congress, he maintained, never assumed responsibility for investigating reportorial practices in TV news. Neither did the Federal Communications Commission, despite obvious conditions that were "in direct opposition to the provisions of the Communications Act of 1934." Powers even pleaded for the ultimate reform lever, that of challenging station licenses, necessary because the industry engaged in a "pollution of ideas" that required options equivalent to those of any polluter: "clean up the mess or pay the consequences."[12] In the end, though, Powers, whose background was in print journalism, recognized that broadcasters, too, had First Amendment rights that constitutionally protected the "mess."

Because they were leery of outlining a specific governmental reform strategy, many Progressives, including Powers, focused on the American public for solutions. Powers' so-called entertainment blueprint was drawn from immense scientific market research that clearly indicated that viewers preferred what he regarded as "pollution." That tens of millions of viewers may have joined the station executives and news consultants in wearing a black hat was a major Progressive issue.

By focusing more directly on the audience question, John Robinson and Mark Levy in *The Main Source* (1986) proposed a different approach to reform. Although this book did not use primary historical sources and was mainly a social scientific study, it was rich in Progressive historical insights. It addressed the relatively unfulfilled development of television news scholarship and theory, which "have posed important questions about the merits of TV news but . . . have not provided definitive answers to them."[13] The main barrier to understanding television was its journalistic technique. In opposition to the positive Developmental portrayal of TV news processes, Robinson and Levy insisted that dominant techniques evolved to attract audiences, not serve them. They rounded out this argument with empirical research indicating that time-honored news traditions had left audience members appallingly uninformed.

Robinson and Levy considered the competitive marketplace, not the government, a source of this grave problem. They proposed that scholars, professionals, and others join in a new normative theory for television, along the lines of the 1947 Hutchins Commission and its market-attuned Social Responsibility notion, allegedly too abstract and vague in the TV age. The new theory was less a set of guidelines and more a bulwark of concerns that would hold profes-

---

[12]Ibid., pp. 236-238.

[13]John Robinson and Mark Levy, *The Main Source* (Beverly Hills, CA: Sage, 1986), 30-31.

sionals responsible for increasing public participation in society's affairs.[14] Robinson and Levy conceded this reform looked better on paper than in actual practice, but they offered some evidence that a unified scholarly-professional impulse was possible.

Still, the scholarly community was reticent about reform, in large measure because it accepted the more popular and less caustic Developmental interpretation. The stress the Developmental historians placed on journalistic purpose, progress, and idolatry made it difficult for Progressives to convey their belief that TV journalism, in the end, was entertainment. Many tried, however. Barbara Matusow in *The Evening Stars* (1983) was one of the first to recognize the latent conservatism in the Developmental perspective and, thus, question its positive outlook. She put the nation's most prominent TV journalists in the same category as their corporate bosses: self-serving egotists interested mainly in consolidating their power and inflating their multimillion dollar personal salaries.[15]

Progressives have even confronted the Murrow legend, the steel chain in the Developmental interpretation. Jeff Merron in "Murrow on TV" (1988) granted that Murrow vouched for television standards but showed as well that much of Murrow's life was selectively constructed by other historians. Merron maintained that Murrow basked in the prestige of "See It Now" and was personally bitter when the show was cancelled. That fact, as much as any feeling of social responsibility, accounted for Murrow's assault on the television industry. Yet "the monkey wrench of Ed Murrow's career" was his long association with the popular "Person to Person," a CBS program that "played a major part in the emergence of television news as entertainment." Murrow, concluded Merron, "was the reason the show existed," and it "accounted for a substantial chunk of his income." Merron's goal was not primarily to denigrate Murrow but rather to underscore the Progressive restlessness with those who conceive television journalism as something not enveloped by profit-making entertainment values: "Many judged Murrow as somehow separate from the structure of the television medium and culture that he was part of. It is unrealistic—and unfair—to hold Murrow to standards that simply did not fit the cultural arena and business he worked in."[16]

The Progressives would argue that if Murrow could not escape the harmful entertainment imperatives in television, it is likely, given its existing state, no one could or will.

---

[14]Ibid., pp. 52-54.

[15]Barbara Matusow, *The Evening Stars* (Boston: Houghton Mifflin, 1983), 251-279.

[16]Jeff Merron, "Murrow on TV," *Journalism Monographs* 106 (1988): 3, 22, 24, 28-29.

Discussion

The advent of television was a landmark event in the history of mass communication. Not only was TV rapidly accepted by all sectors of the American population. According to public opinion polls, television immediately surpassed newspapers, radio, magazines, and all other media as the nation's most-used and most-believed source of information—even though the American system of television rested primarily on entertainment programming. The nature of television has raised a number of difficult questions for historians. A barrier in dealing with them is television's relative news-ness and its limited historical perspective. In a short time, historians have taken strides in linking the well-being of American society to the television medium and showing TV to be conducive to both information and entertainment. What historians have not found is a single common ground that accepts television's great expectations in information, as well as the natural tendencies of an intensely popular mass medium in a free-market system. If historians can locate such a common ground, the essence of American television will assume a much sharper view. In the meantime, here are some of the major questions with which they must deal.

1. Did television, as Neo-Romantic historians suggested, wear "two hats," in which news and entertainment were on an equal footing and TV journalists had a wherewithal to influence world events?

2. Was television, as Developmental historians contended, so attuned to the profit-making potential of entertainment fare that newsrooms, rather than promoting social change, had to be internal fortresses for journalistic responsibility?

3. Had television, as the Progressives pleaded, made information and entertainment indistinguishable? If so, was reform necessary?

4. Did audiences perceive any significant difference between traditional newscasts and the much criticized tabloid formats, high-appeal interview programs, and docudramas?

5. If not, as the Progressives argued, can historians continue to interpret television journalism without defining precisely what it is?

Readings

Neo-Romantic School

Garay, Ron, "Television and the 1951 Senate Crime Committee Hearings," *Journal of Broadcasting* 22 (1978): 469-490.

Halberstam, David, Ch. 16, "CBS," pp. 407-444, *The Powers That Be*. New York: Knopf, 1979.

Sharp, Harry, Jr., "Live From Washington: The Telecasting of President Kennedy's News Conferences," *Journal of Broadcasting* 13 (1968-1969): 23-32.

Yaeger, Murray R., "The Evolution of See It Now," *Journal of Broadcasting* 1 (1956): 337-344.

Developmental School

Friendly, Fred, "Introduction," pp. xi-xxvi, *Due to Circumstances Beyond Our Control*. New York: Random House, 1967.

Leonard, Bill, Ch. 5, "CBS Reports—With Murrow and Friendly," pp. 73-89, *In the Storm of the Eye*. New York: Putnam, 1987.

Murray, Michael D., Ch. 17, "The Television Revolution, 1945-present," pp. 367-395, Wm. David Sloan, James G. Stovall, and James D. Startt, eds., *The Media in America*. Worthington, OH: Publishing Horizons, 1989.

Persico, Joseph E., Ch. 1, "The Peak or the Precipice," pp. 1-14, *Edward R. Murrow: An American Original*. New York: McGraw-Hill, 1988.

Sperber, A. M., "Prologue," pp. xiii-xx, and Ch. 1, "The Heretic," pp. 1-9, *Murrow: His Life and Times*. New York: Freundlich Books, 1986.

Progressive School

Matusow, Barbara, Ch. 9, "The Triumph of the Anchor," pp. 251-279, *The Evening Stars*. Boston: Houghton-Mifflin, 1983.

Merron, Jeff, "Murrow on TV," *Journalism Monographs* 106 (1988).

Powers, Ron, Ch. 1, "Faces and Places," pp. 1-7, *The Newscasters*. New York: St. Martin's Press, 1978.

Robinson, John, and Mark Levy, Ch. 2, "Information Flow in Society," pp. 13-28, *The Main Source*. Beverly Hills, CA: Sage, 1986.

24

The Entertainment Media, 1900-Present: Diffusers of Culture or Seekers of Profit?

The introduction of electronic entertainment into the home created a permanent change in the lifestyle of the American public. In the late 19th and early 20th centuries, the talking machine, or phonograph, became popular. It allowed recorded music and comedy to be transported outside the music hall. Through recordings, entertainment in the home became more accessible to the general public. No longer was it reserved for the wealthy alone, who could afford to pay for music lessons or to hire their own entertainment. The phonograph made both popular and classical music available to almost everyone. Around the turn of the century, with prices of machines ranging from $3 to about $25, they were affordable and became commonplace in home parlors. Though classical music recordings were numerous, popular music quickly gained in strength and by the 1940s was the mainstay of the recording industry. As equipment and recordings improved in quality, sales increased dramatically and recorded music became a multimillion dollar industry.

The second important form of electronic home entertainment was professional radio broadcasting, introduced in 1920. Since World War I, the "wireless" had been a popular evening pursuit for amateur operators. These enthusiasts spent hours hunched over bought or homemade sets, twisting the dial, hoping to capture even the faintest sound of music or the human voice from experimental stations. Programming varied widely, often including recorded music, sports scores, and news. The exact date of the first professional broadcast is a matter of debate, but many histories credit Pittsburgh's KDKA with inaugurating regularly scheduled broadcasting with the election returns of the presidential election between Harding and Cox on November 2, 1920.

Commercially sponsored programming began two years later amid much debate about how radio stations should be supported fi-

By Jana Hyde
University of Alabama

nancially. Until then most stations were owned by educational institutions, many of which could not afford to keep them operating; by manufacturers and distributors of radio sets; and by newspapers, which used them for promotion. When WEAF of New York City successfully debuted a program sponsored by a local real estate agency, the question of ownership seemed to be decided. Broadcasting in America would be primarily a commercial enterprise.

In 1922, AT&T began using telephone lines to connect stations and transmit programming around the country. Music, sports, and presidential speeches were typical fare on early network programming. Soon, other forms of entertainment flooded the airwaves: comedy, variety, quiz shows, and drama. This "free" entertainment changed the way Americans spent their evenings. Instead of going out as often, they stayed in to listen to their favorite programs. Many vaudeville and film stars who adapted their acts for the medium became even more famous. Fans of many of the early radio shows were loyal to their favorite programs. When "Amos 'N' Andy" aired, movie theaters would stop their film and pipe in the program so their patrons wouldn't miss a single episode. Many programs lasted for decades, even surviving the transition to television.

By the time television became widely available after World War II, the networks were firmly established as the main providers of entertainment programming. Since networks had experimented with radio programming, television did not require much experimentation. The networks merely adopted the format that radio had been using for two decades and moved it to the small screen. In many cases, the programs continued with the same title and characters. Many familiar names in radio also became stars of the popular new medium.

As the price of television receivers dropped and the quality of the picture rose, television became the medium of choice for evening entertainment at home. Radio's ratings suffered, and many doomsayers predicted its death. Radio, however, did not die. It simply changed its format. Instead of relying on programming from the national networks, it became more of a locally oriented medium. Music and news became its staples.

Historians have addressed the electronic entertainment industries in a variety of ways. Owing to the relative newness of radio and television and the fact that many early participants are still alive, some historians have been able to collect interviews with them. Others have based their explanations of the media on detailed examinations of the program content, whereas still others have analyzed the entertainment from an industry point of view.

Whatever the approach, historical work has centered around the question of what role the electronic entertainment media played in

American life. Some historians believe the media created and spread American culture to the masses. Others believe they simply were vehicles for making money for large companies in the entertainment industry.

The Developmental School

Developmental historians viewed the history of entertainment in terms of how it evolved to its state at the time the historians were writing. They were interested primarily in how the entertainment media grew from relatively primitive forms into more sophisticated ones. Adherents to this perspective looked at the development of electronic entertainment in terms of how it progressed as a profession. For example, decisions in programming, improvements in quality of equipment and writing, and regulatory or policy changes were made with the advancement of the industry in mind, according to Developmental historians.

Concerned with the transition radio programming had made since its beginning, Peter Fornatale and Joshua Mills in *Radio in the Television Age* (1980) described the evolution of radio from the network-dominated medium of the 1920s-1950s to the locally programmed, specialized station of the latter part of this century. They interpreted the rise of the disc jockey, the development of "format radio," and the localization of stations as steps the industry took toward its present-day structure. Their evaluation of those changes was generally favorable.

Fornatale and Mills used landmark occurrences to highlight the radio industry's progress in reasserting itself as an important entertainment medium after the popularity of television grew to such great heights. They detailed the importance of court cases, individuals, and stations which made a significant change or started a trend in radio programming. They presented Alan Freed as an individual who had made a large contribution toward the development of rock 'n' roll teen radio. He was the first disk jockey to systematically promote and build a White audience for rhythm and blues music, which traditionally had an all-Black audience.

Fornatale and Mills provided an extended account of the payola scandals of the late 1950s, denoted the major players, and outlined the changes the industry made as a result of those charges, including amendments to the Federal Communications Act which were intended to prevent incidents of payola from recurring. These amendments prohibited recording companies and artists from paying or offering gifts to disk jockeys in return for playing their music on the air. Under these new laws, radio stations themselves were held responsible for employees who accepted illegal gifts.

With these amendments holding stations responsible, management continued a movement to centralize control of the disk jockey shows. Instead of each deejay playing different versions of a song, the play-list was standardized and relied more and more on charts from trade magazines such as *Billboard* and *Cashbox*. This move solidified the Top 40 format, which continued to popularize rock 'n' roll music, and in turn became a widespread, profitable format for radio stations.

As Fornatale and Mills had done with music programming, other Developmental historians detailed the advances made in other types of content. Quintin J. Schultze traced the transition and rise to popularity of one particular type of religious broadcasting in "Evangelical Radio and the Rise of the Electronic Church, 1921-1948"[1] (1986). He covered the beginnings of evangelical broadcasting by early station owners and gave an account of the fundamentalist radio preachers' struggle to remain on the air despite policies of the networks and the FCC which severely restricted such broadcasting, even though many programs enjoyed a popularity that rivaled the better known prime time comedy shows.

As a result of those policies, religious broadcasters made changes in their programs in order to stay on the air. These changes shaped the growth and structure of future religious broadcasting to make it more than just religion over the airwaves. Religious broadcasting became more of a business, wielding great influence both spiritually and economically. By the time television became popular, the institution of religious broadcasting was so well developed that the electronic church followed close behind.

The Cultural School

Although all histories of electronic entertainment traced the development of the subject to a certain extent, Cultural historians placed their emphasis on the study of influences on the medium. The conditions surrounding an event or a medium, Cultural historians believed, were of paramount interest because they affected it. Media did not exist in a vacuum, according to this interpretation, but were influenced by the environment in which they existed. Sociological, economic, political, technological, and psychological elements all played a part in the development of a particular genre of programming or provided the impetus for a specific event.

Arthur Frank Wertheim studied the environment in which early radio comedy grew and developed into popular, mass appeal programs. His Cultural interpretation of comedy in radio programming, *Radio Comedy* (1979), examined comedy shows from

---

[1]Quintin J. Schultz, "Evangelical Radio and the Rise of the Electronic Church, 1921-1948," *Journal of Broadcasting and Electronic Media* 32 (1986): 289-306.

the 1920s through the 1950s, when television began to have an effect. He argued that early American humor, as well as vaudeville and stage traditions, contributed to the popular programming genre, especially in the beginning. But just as important as influences on radio comedy were American society and values.

Wertheim demonstrated how new forms of comedy, especially suited to radio's needs, were created through the work of innovators such as Freeman Gosden and Charles Correll ("Amos 'N' Andy"), Jack Benny, and Fred Allen. Through excerpts from scripts and descriptions of programs, he argued that during the period spanning the Great Depression through World War II radio comedy became popular because it commented on and reflected American life in ways that the listening public could understand and accept. It allowed people to laugh at themselves and their predicaments.

Wertheim examined events surrounding a talented comedian's lack of mass appeal in another study, "'The Bad Boy of Radio': Henry Morgan and Censorship" (1978). Morgan had earned this title through his flippant attitude toward sponsors and station management. His humor was off-beat, often ad libbed, and frequently directed toward the sponsors of his programs. More often than not, he angered sponsors to the extent that they were unwilling to continue supporting his program. As a result, he moved from station to station and from network to network during his broadcasting career. His popularity, to be sure, was never as great as that of more famous comedians such as Bob Hope or Jack Benny. However, he had a loyal cult following who admired his irreverence toward established institutions and values. Wertheim attributed his reputation as a "bad boy" and his narrow appeal to the fact that the medium in which he worked was "controlled by the pressures of commercialism and censorship."[2]

The economic environment was a large factor in precipitating a ban on recording which Mary Austin examined in "Petrillo's War" (1978).[3] Austin stated that in order to understand why the American Federation of Musicians (AFM) could and did impose a successful ban on music recording for over two years, one must look at the events leading up to the ban, as well as the man who ordered it. She outlined the conditions that led to James Petrillo's rise to control of the AFM. His personality, combined with hard work and luck, won him the national presidency of the union.

Austin also delineated several environmental conditions which precipitated the ban and aided its success. The Great Depression, the

---

[2]Arthur Frank Wertheim, "'The Bad Boy of Radio': Henry Morgan and Censorship," *Journal of Popular Culture* 12 (Fall 1979): 351.

[3]Mary Austin, "Petrillo's War," *Journal of Popular Culture* 12 (Summer 1978): 11-18.

jukebox, declining popularity of vaudeville performances, and, finally, radio's growing use of recorded music had greatly reduced the number of employed musicians. To make matters worse, musicians did not earn royalty payments from the recordings they made. The ban was not enacted in order to coerce the entertainment industry to hire musicians, but to force recording companies to pay royalties to the artists, in addition to the composers, authors, and publishers, who were already receiving royalties. The ban eventually, after 27 months' duration, was effective in obtaining this goal.

The factors in the settlement of the ban, according to Austin, were several. Public pressure, discontent among those artists who had had popular recordings, court cases, and the capitulation of several smaller recording companies were some of the reasons an agreement between the union and the recording industry was finally reached.

The Progressive School

Progressive historians studied the development of the electronic entertainment media and the factors surrounding that development, but they were concerned primarily with how "big business" and government affected the development. They criticized the government and "big business" for using their power to manipulate the media. This manipulation provided not only for the profits that could be squeezed from enormously popular forms of entertainment, but also for the control of the American mind through program content and music. Businessmen came under fire from Progressives for their policies which restricted forms of entertainment and payment rights that might lessen their control of the industry. Progressive historians censured the government because it enacted legislation and handed down regulations that were usually favorable to the big media powers and that failed to protect the public's interests. Historians writing from this perspective found the entertainment industry rife with incidents to examine, as well as numerous parties to blame for the perceived failure of the industry to serve the public.

One of the most prolific Progressive historians, J. Fred MacDonald, covered early radio programming, government sponsored programming, and the role of Blacks in television programming. In "Government Propaganda In Commercial Radio—The Case of Treasury Star Parade, 1942-1943" (1979), he argued that the government-produced program not only promoted the sale of war bonds, but also sold Americans, the majority of whom had been isolationists until Pearl Harbor, on the idea of World War II. Condemning the government for manipulating "a supposedly-free and responsible mass medium," he outlined several approaches the radio series used to persuade Americans to turn their spare cash into war bonds. He warned that "Treasury Star Parade" set a dangerous precedent and that "a free system of broadcasting should not tolerate such direct governmental propagandizing."[4] When the government uses broadcasting in this way, he said, then broadcasting is no longer a source for objective truth and entertainment; it is merely an extension of the government.

In a criticism of business practices in broadcasting, MacDonald described the condition of Black employment in the early years of television programming in "Black Perimeters—Paul Robeson, Nat King Cole and the Role of Blacks in American TV" (1979). He blamed the broadcasting industry's lack of courage for Robeson's banishment from television. Robeson's outspoken political activism made him unpopular with the conservative majority of the American citizenry. In this instance, it was not a particular policy of a company to ban Robeson; rather, it was that company's fear of angering viewers that prevented his acceptance on programs. This policy extended to other Black performers who expressed racial "resentment and frustration," which were not acceptable on television.[5]

In the case of the "Nat King Cole Show," MacDonald laid the blame for the lack of sponsors at the feet of Madison Avenue and the large advertising companies. He agreed with Cole's assertion that advertising agencies were hesitant for their clients to sponsor the program because it presented a positive image of Blacks, which they felt would infuriate Southerners, causing a boycott of products. Admitting that in later years of television programming, Blacks did make more appearances, MacDonald criticized the industry for portraying the characters as stereotypes, albeit updated, of Blacks.

Peter Lewis and Corinne Pearlman criticized both government and media moguls in *Media and Power: From Marconi to Murdoch* (1986). They charged powerful companies and governments with controlling the development of media systems and, therefore, programming. They claimed that from the beginning, the path of development of the radio and television industries was largely decided by governments and the huge media companies. They warned that newer means of communication have eluded customary systems of censorship and cultural control, thereby allowing large media companies to control mass communication all over the world. As a result, governments in the future will have less control over what communication type and content will cross their borders. In

---

[4]J. Fred MacDonald, "Government Propaganda in Commercial Radio: The Case of Treasury Star Parade, 1942-1943," *Journal of Popular Culture* 12 (Fall 1979): 304, 287.

[5]J. Fred MacDonald, "Black Perimeters—Paul Robeson, Nat King Cole and the Role of Blacks in American TV," *Journal of Popular Film and Television* 7, 3 (1979): 246-264.

Third World countries, the disparity of power distribution has been most evident. More foreign, often commercialized, communication has passed into these countries than out of them. Lewis and Pearlman said that many of these countries have been getting a "raw deal" because of the situation.

Several developments in the broadcasting industry, Lewis and Pearlman argued, resulted from governmental or business influence, or a combination of both. For example, the "Sesame Street" series, they said, was created partially as a commercial for American values aimed at Americans and the rest of the world during a time when there were a great many serious social problems in this country. They attributed cable's slow rate of penetration into large metropolitan areas to the broadcasting industry's fears of loss of revenue to the growing new medium. The combined forces of government and powerful business shaped broadcast entertainment's structure and content in order to benefit themselves.

The Economic School

Whereas Progressive historians studied the effects of government and "big business" on electronic entertainment, Economic historians studied the business practices of the industry and how they affected the development of the electronic media. Economic historians generally viewed the media companies and owners in a favorable light, feeling that they made contributions to the industry. Generally, they believed that the evolution of the entertainment industry was accomplished through intelligent business decisions. The prime motivation for the decisions was to make a profit—a large one. But Economic historians, unlike their Progressive counterparts, did not argue that the profit-making motive was evil. Instead, they viewed it as a normal part of the American "free enterprise" system. The development of the commercial broadcasting system that is in place today in the United States arose mainly from the desire of the infant broadcasting companies to make money. Programming decisions, artist promotion, and advertising decisions were all prompted by the profit motive. Instead of seeing this purpose as bad, Economic historians viewed it simply as part of the grand American work ethic and the aspiration for success.

Recognizing this spirit of free enterprise, Marc Hugunin described the formation and competition of music licensing organizations in "ASCAP, BMI and the Democratization of American Popular Music" (1979). The American Society for Composers, Authors and Publishers (ASCAP), he said, held a grudge against radio broadcasters although the organization benefited directly from the royalties earned from the airplay its music received on broadcasting stations. Sheet music sales, from which most of ASCAP's income was derived, had declined. ASCAP attributed that to the fact that more people were listening to the songs on radio rather than playing them on their pianos. Also, some rural stations were avoiding royalty payments to ASCAP by playing "hillbilly" music that was not licensed by ASCAP. The organization generally did not approve that type of music, as members felt it "degraded" the musical taste of Americans. Seeing that it was losing power and money, ASCAP began to demand higher fees from radio stations for using its music.

The National Association of Broadcasters (NAB), which had been outraged at having, in effect, to pay to advertise ASCAP's music, formed its own rival organization, Broadcast Music, Inc. (BMI). The NAB put into effect a ban of ASCAP music (in which most radio stations participated) and substituted BMI music, reasoning that the public did not know or care where the music came from. During the ban, BMI also built up its catalogue of titles. Eventually, ASCAP capitulated and lowered its royalty demands, and the ban ended. This ban effectively broke the monopoly ASCAP had held, giving BMI a large share of the market, and made for a more diverse marketplace for new types of music that were beginning to develop.

Hugunin claimed there were no "villains" in this episode in music business history. He found fault with both sides of the battle on some points and defended both on others. Both sides used conventional American business practices and, most importantly, "contributed to the emergence of a new order, a way of doing business that . . . prevails to this day."[6]

Not all Economic historians viewed business practices of the entertainment industry in such a favorable light. Some held a more critical opinion of the profit motive that drove decisions. In *From Print to Plastic: Publishing and Promoting America's Popular Music (1900-1980)* (1983), Russell Sanjek began with the publication of sheet music and the development of the Tin Pan Alley song pluggers, who traveled to radio stations to play their publishers' songs, helping to make the music popular. He then outlined the development of the recording industry, which was loosely based on the song plugging system, and the economic history of the growing use of recordings for radio. The battles between licensing organizations, musicians' unions, and broadcasters were based on economics as well. Although Sanjek remained relatively impartial through most of the work, he criticized the industry for providing inferior products in the last several years, and for its inability to deal with the problems changing technology imposed on the industry.

---

[6]Marc Hugunin, "ASCAP, BMI and the Democratization of American Popular Music," *Popular Music and Society* 7 (1979): 14.

Discussion

As we draw farther away from the beginnings of the American recording and broadcasting industries, more historical work is being done on these areas of mass culture that have so affected the way people spend their leisure time today. Yet, many historians are still awed by the magic of music making and broadcasting, and they tend to hold a romanticized view of the industry. Others who were part of the industry, either in management, production, or as performers, write on their area of expertise, but with a hidden agenda: to vindicate themselves, to expose others, to brag about their accomplishments, or simply to bring up fond memories. Many works about this industry have been written for the popular press. That is understandable, owing to the fascination the public has for behind-the-scenes looks at entertainment. More critical looks at the formulation of the electronic entertainment industry are needed.

Many events and personalities still need to be examined in detail. Many of the larger works cover long periods of time and, as a result, must gloss over important events or genres of entertainment. Historical work on the recording industry is particularly prone to superficial study. Several works on the development of popular music include the recording industry in them, tying together the two developments. Although they certainly influenced and helped shape each other, they can and need to be examined separately. The study that has been done leaves a number of questions still in need of answers.

1. The biggest question about the electronic entertainment industry, one which has plagued it since its beginning, is whether the industry existed to provide and promote culture or whether it existed to make money. What was its central purpose?

2. If it existed to promote culture, then who decided what that culture was to consist of? Was the deciding force talent, originality, charisma, or money-making ability?

3. If it existed to make money, then who decided which forms of entertainment would make money?

4. What role did public opinion play in such decisions?

5. Did the leaders of the industry and the government abuse the public's trust, giving it what they thought it wanted rather than what it really wanted?

6. What, if any, major changes were effected in society through the entertainment media?

7. To what extent did the government and big business manipulate the public's thoughts, values, and style through the electronic entertainment media, especially in entertainment fare that was not overtly propagandistic, such as situation comedies? Is there any way to prove whether they did?

Readings

Developmental School

Andrews, Bart, and Ahrgus Juilliard, Ch. 5, "A Cast of Characters," pp. 60-84, *Holy Mackerel!: The Amos 'n' Andy Story.* New York: Dutton, 1986.

Brode, Douglas, "The Made-For-TV Movie: Emergence of an Art Form," *Television Quarterly* 18 (Fall 1981): 53-78.

Fornatale, Peter, and Joshua E. Mills, Ch. 3, "The Emerging Teen Culture," pp. 35-57, *Radio in the Television Age.* Woodstock, NY: Overlook Press, 1980.

Schultz, Quintin J., "Evangelical Radio and the Rise of the Electronic Church, 1921-1948," *Journal of Broadcasting and Electronic Media* 32 (1986): 289-306.

Cultural School

Anderson, Kent, "Conclusion," pp. 175-183, *Television Fraud: The History and Implications of the Quiz Show Scandals.* Westport, CT: Greenwood Press, 1978.

Austin, Mary, "Petrillo's War," *Journal of Popular Culture* 12 (Summer 1978): 11-18.

Czitrom, Daniel J., Ch. 3, "The Ethereal Hearth: American Radio from Wireless Through Broadcasting, 1892-1940," pp. 60-88, *Media and the American Mind: From Morse to McLuhan.* Chapel Hill: University of North Carolina Press, 1982.

Wertheim, Arthur Frank, Ch. 15, "Allen's Alley," pp. 335-352, *Radio Comedy.* New York: Oxford University Press, 1979.

Progressive School

Gitlin, Todd, "Epilogue," pp. 325-335, *Inside Prime Time.* New York: Pantheon Books, 1983.

Lewis, Peter M., and Corinne Pearlman, Ch. 2, "Tales from Television," pp. 85-108, *Media and Power: From Marconi to Murdoch.* London: Camden Press, 1986.

MacDonald, J. Fred, "Government Propaganda in Commercial Radio: The Case of Treasury Star Parade, 1942-1943," *Journal of Popular Culture* 12 (Fall 1979): 285-304.

Economic School

Hugunin, Marc, "ASCAP, BMI and the Democratization of American Popular Music," *Popular Music and Society* 7 (1979): 8-17.

Sanjek, Russell, Ch. 1, "Building the Marvelous Hit-Making Machine," pp. 1-26, *From Print to Plastic: Publishing and Promoting America's Popular Music,1900-1980*. Brooklyn, NY: Institute for Studies in American Popular Music, 1983.

Nelson, George, Ch. 5, "Production Line," pp. 50-147, *Where Did Our Love Go? The Rise and Fall of the Motown Sound*. New York: St. Martin's Press, 1985.

Index